Contents

Contents

Introduction

With Internet technology developing rapidly, Internet gaming has become ever more popular, while documentation on how to actually make Internet games remains inadequate. *Developer's Guide to Multiplayer Games* provides in-depth coverage of all the major topics associated with online game programming, as well as giving you easy-to-follow, step-by-step tutorials on how to create your own fully functional network library, back-end MySQL database, and complete, working online game!

The book contains two main areas. The first is dedicated to explaining practical theory on how to utilize MySQL, Perl, sockets, and basic Windows dialog programming. The second section consists of five extensive tutorials, leading you through the stages of creating a working online game that you can both learn from and expand upon.

After reading this book, you will have a solid knowledge of online game programming and you will also be able to start making your own online games. Also note that the companion CD-ROM contains all the source code from the book and a ready-to-use version of the network library you will create in the tutorial section.

We hope you enjoy reading and learning from this book as much as we have enjoyed writing it!

About the Authors

Andrew Mulholland

Andrew Mulholland is currently working as lead programmer at a software development company in Scotland. He is also an undergraduate at the University of Abertay in Dundee studying computer games technology. His e-mail address is andrew@dreamcircle.co.uk.

Teijo Hakala is currently studying software engineering at Jyväskylä Polytechnic in Finland and specializes in network design, programming, and optimization. He also has a wide variety of work experience with computer technology. His e-mail address is teijo@dreamcircle.co.uk.

Teijo Hakala

Theory Introduction

The theory section of this book is full of practical information that will help you understand how to make functional online games. We recommend that you read this section thoroughly before attempting the tutorial section, as there is a lot of knowledge that will benefit you here.

This section first covers the basics of dialog-based Windows programming, which we will utilize in the tutorial section to create our login and lobby system for the sample online game. Then we cover how to use MySQL and Perl to create a back-end database for your game, allowing you to interact with game data directly from a web browser. Then we give an introduction to TCP/IP and sockets, followed by how to get started with sockets programming. Finally, we learn about different ways to send data, and how to modify the behavior of our sockets.

First, let's look at how to create dialog-based Windows applications...

#### Chapter 1

Creating Windows Applications in Visual Studio

Introduction

The most essential knowledge anyone can have is the basics. If you already know how to create dialog-based Windows applications, skip past this chapter. If not, this chapter will give you a quick and easy introduction to it so that you will find the rest of this book more accessible.

The reason for learning this is to be able to create our server applications for the Microsoft Windows operating system.

Windows Messaging System

Windows controls everything by the use of its messaging system. This is a fundamental idea to grasp if you wish to create any Windows-based applications. Within this messaging system, tasks to be processed by the operating system are stored in a queue. For example, when a user clicks a button in a window, a message is added to the queue and is then sent to the appropriate window to inform it that the button has been pressed.

When the operating system creates a window, the window continually checks for messages being sent to it. If it receives a relevant message, it will react accordingly; otherwise, it will send it back to the operating system to be reprocessed.

Each window created is assigned a unique handle that is used to control and determine which messages are relevant to that window. In code, this is defined as the HWND, or window handle. The main reason behind this system is to allow for multi-tasking and multithreading. This means that the operating system can run more than one application in one instance, even though a processor can only handle one task at a time.

There is a lot more to windows than this, but this should give you a reasonable overview of how the system works.

Creating a Window

Load Microsoft Visual Studio and select File, New...

The following dialog box should now be visible in the center of the screen.

Figure 1-1

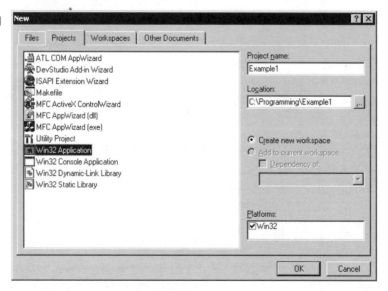

Select the Projects tab at the top of the dialog and then choose the Win32 Application option on the main display. Select the location for your project, enter your project's name, and click OK.

Next, select the type of project you wish to create. Leave it on the default option (An empty project) and click the Finish button. A project information box appears; simply click OK in this box.

Now we are working with the Visual Studio main interface. Currently, ClassView is active, but we are interested in FileView so select this tab.

Figure 1-2

FileView lists all of the C and C++ source and header files that are active in your project. Currently we do not have any files in our project so we need to add our main C++ source file.

Select File, New... as you did before, but this time select the Files tab instead of Projects. The following dialog will be visible.

Figure 1-3

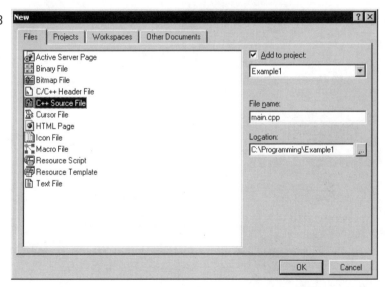

Select C++ Source File as shown in Figure 1-3 and type in the filename as main.cpp. Click the OK button to add this empty file to your project.

You now have your main source file in your project, and it is visible in the Visual Studio editor.

There are two main items required in a standard Windows program: the entry point to your program, which is named WinMain, and the Windows callback procedure (commonly named WndProc), which is used to keep your Windows application up to date.

For what we require though, it is best to take the dialog approach, making it even simpler to design and code. First, we need to add our dialog. Click File,

New... again, but this time select Resource Script. Type in the filename as resource and click OK.

Once this is done, you will notice another tab has appeared between the ClassView and FileView tabs. This tab is called ResourceView and allows you to visually create and edit dialogs for use within your program.

Figure 1-4

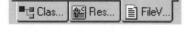

Once you select the ResourceView tab, you will be presented with the resource editor. Right-click on resource.rc in the main view and then left-click on the Insert option. You will then be presented with the Insert Resource dialog box.

Figure 1-5

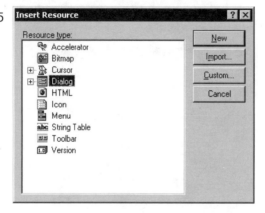

Select Dialog and click New. Now you will see a sample dialog box in front of you. For now, we will not do much to it except change the name of the title bar and its identifier that I will explain after the code below.

Double-click on the sample dialog box that Visual Studio created. Now a dialog properties box can be seen. All we are interested in here is the ID, which will probably be set to Idd_Dialog1, and the Caption, which should be Dialog. Let's change the ID to Idd_Client and the Caption to Window Example.

OK, now it's time to go back and do some code. We have our dialog template that we can call from our code so let's use it. Here is the code required to make your dialog appear on the screen:

```
// Simple Windows Code
#include <windows.h>
#include "resource.h"

LRESULT CALLBACK
ClientDlgProc(HWND DialogWindow, UINT Message, WPARAM wParam, LPARAM lParam)
{
    // Process Messages
```

```
    switch(Message)
    {
    case WM_INITDIALOG:
        return FALSE;

    case WM_COMMAND:
        switch(wParam)
        {
        case IDCANCEL:
            EndDialog(DialogWindow, FALSE);
            return FALSE;
        default:
            break;
        }
        break;

    default:
        break;
    }
    return FALSE;
}

int APIENTRY
WinMain(HINSTANCE hInstance, HINSTANCE hPrevInstance, LPSTR lpCmdLine, int nCmdShow)
{
    DialogBox((HINSTANCE) hInstance, MAKEINTRESOURCE(IDD_CLIENT), NULL,
        (DLGPROC) ClientDlgProc);
    return 0;
}
```

The OK button on the dialog can be pressed but will have no action, whereas the Cancel button will close the dialog.

NOTE   If you get an error and it tells you it can't find afxres.h, you need to install MFC support for Visual Studio, which comes with the Visual Studio package.

If you have never seen Windows code before, the code above may look complex and a little confusing. Welcome to the world of Windows! It's not that bad, honest.

Let's start with the WinMain function. This is simply the point at which Windows starts executing your code. Do not worry about the variables that are passed in; they are controlled by Windows and are beyond the scope of this book.

The main issue here is the DialogBox function and callback procedure (ClientDlgProc) that creates our dialog window on the screen. The first parameter is the instance of the application that you simply take from the first parameter of the WinMain function. Next is the identifier that we set when we created the template for our dialog. The third parameter is of no interest to us so we set it to NULL, but the final one is. This is a pointer to the update function for the dialog. Each dialog you create requires this update function (basically the same idea as a Windows procedure). In this update function is where you set the actions for buttons and other useful tools. So we set this update function to our callback function for the dialog (ClientDlgProc). For example, the identifier for the Cancel button is Idcancel. As you can see in the code, there is a Case statement for the Cancel button so when it is clicked, it will close the dialog window. Other buttons can be easily added to the template using the toolbox on the template editor. Just remember that each button must contain a unique ID so you can reference it from within your code.

Sending Information to Your Window

As well as being useful for debugging, being able to update information to a window is essential knowledge that can be used in many situations, such as displaying how many players are connected to the game server.

First you have to add a static text string to the dialog window. To do this you need to go back to the template editor by selecting the ResourceView tab as before. Then you simply double-click on the Idd_Client text as seen below to bring up your dialog in the main area.

Next, select the *Aa* button from the Controls toolbox and place it somewhere on your dialog as shown in Figure 1-6. Now double-click on the text you added to the dialog box to display its properties.

Figure 1-6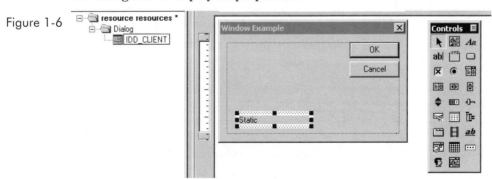

The dialog box shown in Figure 1-7 will now be visible on the screen. All we need to change here is the ID. Change the text Idc_Static to Idc_Serverstatus. This will give it more meaning when it comes to adding it into the code.

Figure 1-7

Now we have some text, and we want to be able to set it to a value from within our code. For example, if we want the text to read "Server Online," add the following lines of code after the line that contains "case WM_INITDIALOG":

```
SendDlgItemMessage(DialogWindow,IDC_SERVERSTATUS, WM_SETTEXT,NULL,(long)"Server
Online");
```

Therefore, when the dialog box is initialized, Windows will send a message to the dialog box to tell it to update the Idc_Serverstatus text with the string you supplied in the function. In this case, it would update the text from "Static" to "Server Online."

The first parameter is the handle to the dialog, which is the first variable that is passed into the dialog update procedure. The second is the identifier for what you want to change or update. Next comes the command that you wish to send. There are many commands and the best way to figure out how they work is just to experiment with them. For now we are using WM_SETTEXT, which tells Windows to change a static text string in a dialog box. The fourth parameter is not used for the WM_SETTEXT command so we simply set it to NULL. The final parameter is used to declare the string with which we want to update the static text, in this case "Server Online." Also, note that the string must be typecast to a long.

TIP   Also try experimenting with editable text. It works on the same principles discussed above, and you simply send a WM_GETTEXT message to retrieve what the user entered.

Introduction to Static Link Libraries

Later, when we create our online tutorial game, we will be using static link libraries to encapsulate all our network and graphics code, which will make it easier to reuse the code for future projects. In addition to the reusability factor, static link libraries also protect your source code, but allow others to use the functionality of your code.

When creating a static link library, you do not require a WinMain function or a Windows update function (WndProc). This is because we are not actually creating a program, rather just a collection of functions that we can use from within our programs. The library is created using standard C/C++ source and header files, but the output is a library rather than a Windows executable.

When you compile your library, the compiler will generate a library file with the extension .lib. To use the functions in your library, you are required to include it in your project and include the header file that was used to create the library (which contains all the external variables, types, and function prototypes).

The easiest way to use your library is to create Lib and Include folders for your library and include those directories in the Visual Studio directory settings that are explained in the tutorial to follow.

Creating a Static Link Library

First, the best thing to do is to create a directory structure on your hard drive for the library to be stored in. From our experience, we recommend the structure shown in Figure 1-8.

Figure 1-8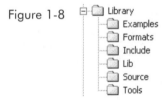

- **Examples**   All example programs that display how to use your library are stored in this folder. This is probably one of the most useful things that can accompany your library since the source code is not visible to any other programmer using it.
- **Formats**   This is where you store any file formats specific to your static link library (i.e., your own 3D model format).
- **Include**   This stores the entire collection of C/C++ header files that are needed to use your library. This is one of the directories that you must set up in Visual Studio to make your library work.
- **Lib**   This is where you actually store your complete library file and the other directory required by Visual Studio. It is a good idea to include both the release and debug versions of your library here so that it is possible to debug and create final release applications with the libraries.
- **Source**   All source code related to your library must be kept in this folder.
- **Tools**   Any programming tools that are used alongside your library are stored here (such as file format converters).

Now that we have our structure, we need to create a static link library project. This is done by selecting File, New… in Visual Studio. The dialog box in Figure 1-9 should now be visible.

Figure 1-9

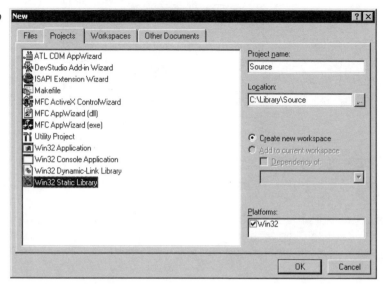

Select the Win32 Static Library option and enter a name for your library. Next, select the location and press the OK button.

In the dialog box that appears, leave both the Pre-Compiled header and MFC support options unchecked as we will not be using either in this book, and click Finish. A project information box is now visible, but simply click OK here.

Next, we need to add our source and header files to the project as you did when creating the window. Remember that this time we do not require the WinMain or Update procedure, just functions that we wish to reuse. Let's call the source file library.cpp and the header file library.h for this example.

If you now press F7, it will build your library and put it in the Release or Debug folder depending on your project configuration. The library will have the same name as your project. For example, if your project is named gamephysics, your library will be named gamephysics.lib.

It is a good idea to make Visual Studio automatically copy your header file and library to the correct directories in your structure to assure that you are always using the latest version. Selecting Project, Settings from the main menu makes the dialog box in Figure 1-10 (shown on the following page) visible.

Set the Output file name for your library to whatever you wish to call your library and choose where you want it to go relative to the directory your source files are in. This must be done for both release and debug configurations. In the previous dialog the debug settings are currently active.

Figure 1-10

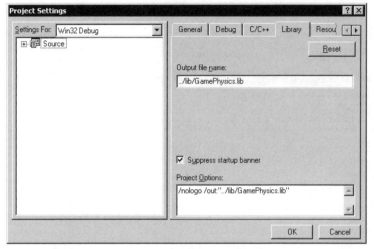

TIP   It is a good idea to have both debug and release versions of your library. Call your release version the correct name (i.e., GamePhysics.lib) and add a suffix to the debug version (i.e., GamePhysicsDebug.lib) to distinguish them easily.

Now the library file is created in the correct directory in our structure when the project is built. We also want to copy our header file to the Include directory of our structure.

As can be seen in Figure 1-11, you simply add a Post-build command that tells the compiler to copy the header file(s) to the Include directory.

Figure 1-11

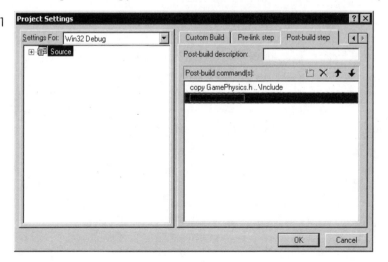

We have now covered the basics on how to create a static link library. The most important thing to remember is to prototype all functions and make all the global variables external that you wish to be accessible outside of your library. In the next section, we will discuss how to set up Visual Studio to find your library.

Using a Static Link Library

Once you have built your library and it is in the correct directories, you need to tell Visual Studio where to look for it. Select Tools, Options… from the main Visual Studio menu to open the Options dialog box.

If the Directories tab is unselected, select it now to display a list of directories like the one in Figure 1-12. Only the top three should be visible unless you have previously added other static libraries.

Figure 1-12
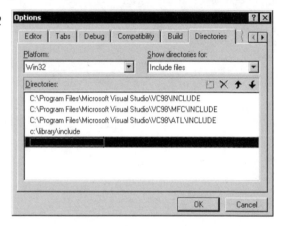

You must now add the Include directory of your library for the Include files and the Lib directory for the Library files. You select which one you wish to add by changing the top-right pull-down box.

Now Visual Studio is able to find and recognize your static link library. To use it in a program you have written, you must first load your project into Visual Studio, then select Project, Settings...

Next, select the Link tab and add your library name before kernel32.lib. Also, remember to include the header file for your library in your main code.

Final Notes

Here we have provided the basics of creating dialog-based applications in Visual Studio. The best thing to do is experiment by creating dialogs, adding buttons, and making the buttons set strings to different values when you press them. Also, learn to use editable text as this is highly useful and allows the user to put feedback into your program.

If you are interested in learning more, there are entire books written on Windows programming and there is also an excellent resource available on the Internet (http://msdn.microsoft.com), but the quick introduction provided here will give you enough knowledge to understand the concepts used in this book.

TIP   *Windows 98 Programming from the Ground Up* by Herbert Schildt provides an excellent way of understanding Windows programming.

Chapter 2

Internet-Based Database Systems

Introduction

This chapter covers how to create a stable and fast database system for your game server. In later chapters you will find out about ways to access it from sockets and the Internet.

Although it is possible to store player information on the player's local machine, in reality it makes much more sense to store the data on the server for many reasons. The first and most important reason is to avoid players running "hacks" on their computer to change their character data in the game or even backing the data up to another file. If the data is stored on the server, it makes it impossible for the player to run a local game hack that will modify the character data. Another reason for this is to allow players to play from different locations and machines without having to copy their character data to another computer.

First, we will cover the installation of MySQL, an excellent, stable, and free database system, on both the Linux and Windows operating systems.

Installing MySQL

Linux Specific

First, you need to install a version of the Linux operating system and set up the Apache web server as well as Perl 5. If you do not already have a copy of Linux, we would recommend Red Hat version 6.2 or greater (http://www.redhat.com/). Next, you need to download the file mysql-3.23.36-pc-linux-gnu-i686.tar.gz (a newer version may be available but this chapter is based on this version) from http://www.mysql.com/Downloads/MySQL-3.23/mysql-3.23.36-pc-linux-gnu-i686.tar.gz or simply copy it off the CD-ROM supplied with the book.

Once you have this file, if it is not already on your Linux machine/server, you need to upload it. When working with Linux, ensure that you are logged in as the root user or some of the topics covered in this chapter may not work correctly. It does not matter where you place this file on your Linux machine as long as you keep a note of where it is.

Go to Linux and change to the directory to which you copied or uploaded the file. Next, you need to enter the following list of commands to unpack and install MySQL:

```
shell> groupadd mysql
shell> useradd -g mysql mysql
shell> cd /usr/local
shell> gunzip < /path/to/mysql-VERSION-OS.tar.gz | tar xvf -
shell> ln -s mysql-VERSION-OS mysql
shell> cd mysql
shell> scripts/mysql_install_db
shell> chown -R mysql /usr/local/mysql
shell> chgrp -R mysql /usr/local/mysql
shell> bin/safe_mysqld --user=mysql &
```

That's all there is to installing MySQL on Linux. The last command you entered started the MySQL daemon that controls all the connections to your database and all the operations you are going to perform on it.

For the next part, you want to be able to access the MySQL console. To do this, type the following from the /usr/local/mysql directory:

```
shell> ./bin/mysql
```

Windows Specific

Assuming you have a working version of Microsoft Windows 9x/NT on your computer, you first need to download from http://www.mysql.com/Downloads/MySQL-3.23/mysql-3.23.36-win.zip or copy from the companion CD the mysql-3.23.36-win.zip file.

Unzip the file to a temporary folder (i.e., C:\temp\mySQL) using a program such as WinZip (http://www.winzip.com). (There is an evaluation version of WinZip on the CD-ROM.)

Next, go to the temporary directory where you extracted the files and double-click on setup.exe to begin the MySQL setup program.

Follow the simple installation through; select the directory you wish to install to, then just select the typical installation option and MySQL will be installed to your computer.

Finally, you need to be able to access the MySQL console. To do this, go to the directory in which you installed MySQL and then go into the bin directory. The MySQL daemon will automatically be running so simply double-click on MySQL.exe to bring up the console window.

The console window should appear as shown in Figure 2-1.

Figure 2-1

NOTE   If for some reason the MySQL daemon is not running, you will want to be able to start it manually. To do this go to the directory which you installed MySQL into, and then go into the bin directory. Here you will find a file called mysqld.exe. Double-click this file to start the MySQL daemon running. If you are running Windows NT, use the mysqld-nt.exe file instead. Also, if you wish the daemon to start every time you load Windows, simply add it to your start up folder in your Start menu.

Overview of MySQL

SQL is an acronym for structured query language. This means it accepts commands in an easy to understand and structured format. We will be using the console mode on MySQL to create our databases and tables that are contained within it. Later in this chapter we are going to cover how to access them from outside the console.

A database is structured as shown in Figure 2-2. You have several records of data per table and several tables per database.

Figure 2-2

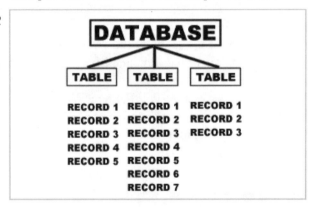

The first thing we need to do is create the database, as it is the foundation of the complete system.

Creating a Database in MySQL

This is the easy part. You need to give your database a name; in this example, we are going to use the name gamedata, as this database is going to store some basic information about an online game.

So to create our gamedata database we would enter the following command at the prompt in the MySQL console:

```
mysql> CREATE DATABASE gamedata;
```

If everything has gone according to plan, it will inform you that the query was OK and that one row was affected.

We now have our database in the system. We can view all the databases that have been created in MySQL by typing the following command:

```
mysql> SHOW DATABASES;
```

The console should now display a list of database names that are on the system; you should also see your gamedata database there. Figure 2-3 shows what the console should be displaying.

Figure 2-3

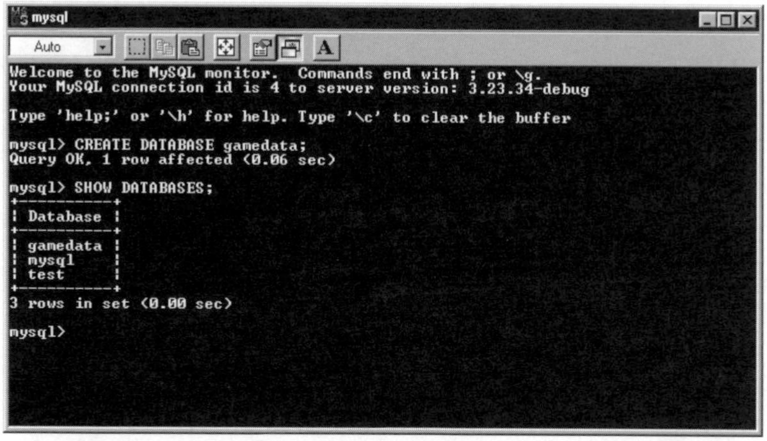

The final thing we must do is select which database we wish to work with. This is done with the following command:

```
mysql> USE gamedata;
```

Now we will move on to how to add your tables into the database.

Adding Tables to a Database

Before adding tables to your database, it is a good idea to decide what data you wish to contain within your tables. The most common types of data used in tables are integers (int), strings (varchar), and time stamps (timestamp). Each table should have a unique identifier, or an integer that is automatically incremented by MySQL every time a record of data is added to the table.

We will start with a simple example. Let's say we have to store several players' character data in a database. For this we must store the following information about the character for each player:

- Character Name
- X Position on the Map
- Y Position on the Map
- Current Experience Level

The character's name will have a maximum length of 30 characters and the other three variables will be integer values. Therefore, we need to create a table that can hold this information and a unique identifier so we have an easy way of identifying the data from other tables without duplicating information (see the section on relational databases). First we must make sure we are using the gamedata database that we created previously. To make sure of this, type the following command:

```
mysql> USE gamedata;
```

Now that is done, we can enter the following command to create our database that we will call playerinfo. Note that it is fine to use the Return key to make it clearer as the statement will only end when you add the semicolon.

```
mysql> CREATE TABLE playerinfo (
mysql> id INT AUTO_INCREMENT,
mysql> name VARCHAR(30),
mysql> xpos INT,
mysql> ypos INT,
mysql> exp INT,
mysql> PRIMARY KEY(id));
```

When you enter this, the console should look as follows.

Figure 2-4

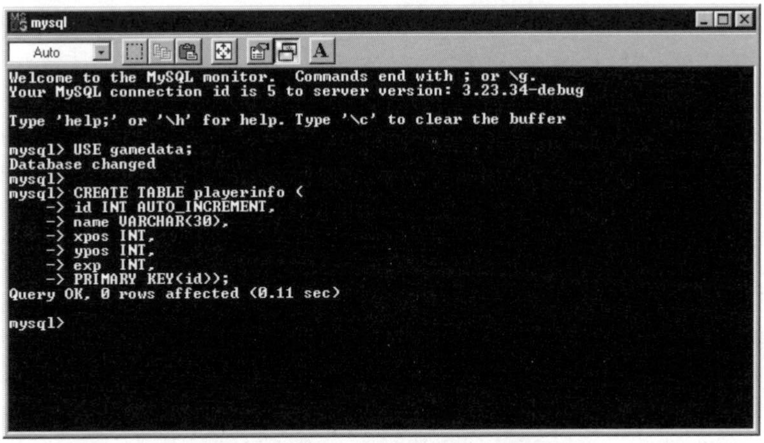

This command will create the playerinfo table that can hold our information and give it a unique identifier that will automatically increment every time a new record of data is added into the table.

The Primary_Key() command is used to optimize the database for searching for a particular variable in a table. Since we will be looking for the ID of a player most, it makes sense to set this to the primary key for the table.

Next, it is a good idea to check that your table has been created correctly. It is easy to correct a mistake at this stage, but becomes much more difficult once you start adding data and using the system.

To check that our table now exists in the database, we want to use the following command:

```
mysql> SHOW TABLES;
```

When you press Return, the following console screen should now be visible.

Figure 2-5

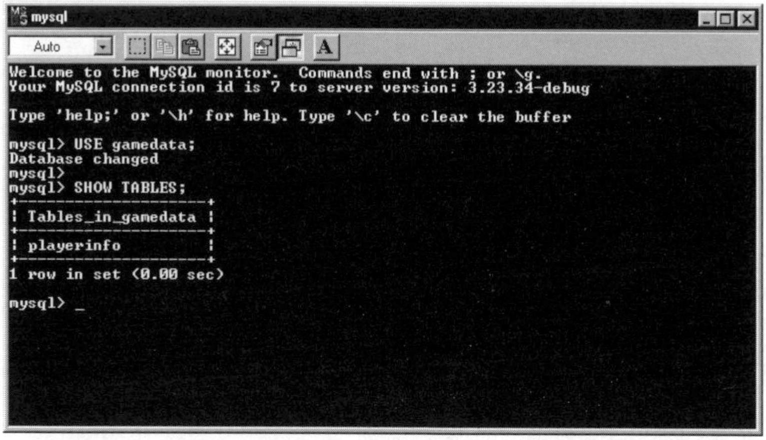

As you can see from the preceding figure, MySQL tells us that there is only one table in the gamedata database now, which is our playerinfo table. More tables can be added to the database, as we will see later in the relational databases section.

Another useful command is the Describe command, which allows us to see all the data in a table. This command can be used to check that our table was created the way we wanted it to be. The command is called as follows:

```
mysql> DESCRIBE playerinfo;
```

Once you press Return, the following will be displayed on the MySQL console.

Figure 2-6

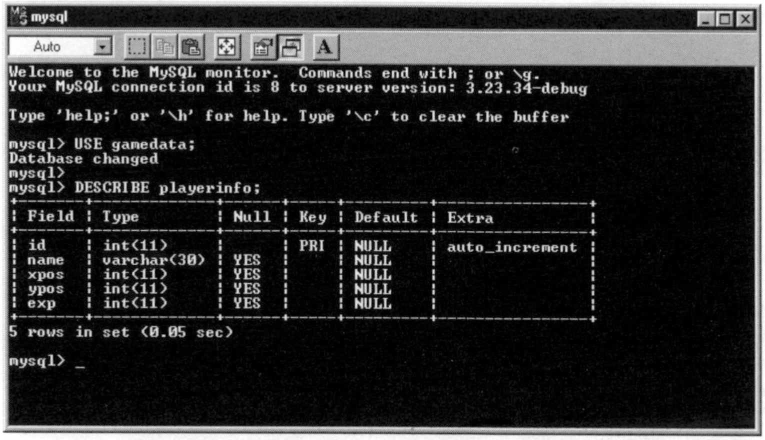

As you can see from this screen, the first column denotes the names of the fields we entered — id, name, xpos, ypos, and exp. The next column tells us the type. This is the one we should check carefully as the database will obviously not work as you would hope if you try to place a string into integer storage. Take note also that the id field is never NULL as it will always be automatically assigned a unique integer value by MySQL every time data is added to the table. The final column specifies any special cases you have assigned to the fields; in this case, we have asked the id field to be assigned a unique number so auto_increment appears in this column.

That's all there is to adding standalone tables that do not interact with each other. We will find out later in this chapter how to add tables that interact with each other using the unique ID system. Next, however, we will cover how to add data into the table we have created from the MySQL console and also from different types of files.

Adding Data to Tables

Data can be added directly into tables from the MySQL console, although there are many other ways to add in data, which we will cover later in this chapter.

To add data to a table directly from the console, we use the MySQL Insert command. Let's say we want to add the following information into the table we created in the last section, playerinfo.

```
Name: Jeff Henderson
X Position: 14
Y Position: 35
Experience: 1431
```

To insert this into our table we would use the following syntax:

```
mysql> INSERT INTO playerinfo VALUES
mysql> (NULL,'Jeff Henderson',14,35,1431);
```

This would be displayed on the MySQL console as follows.

Figure 2-7

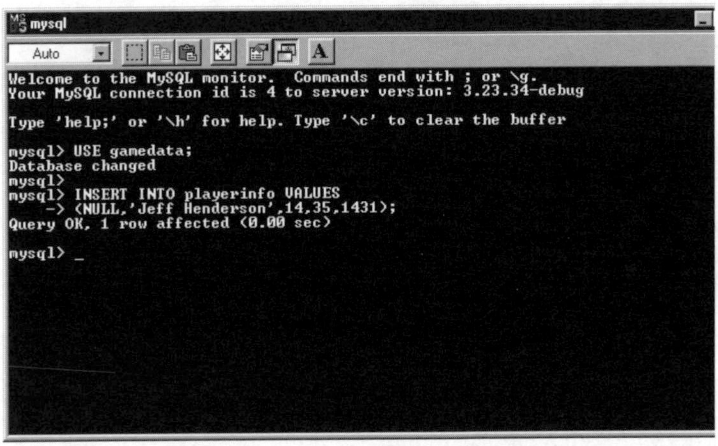

Notice that the first data we enter into the table is a NULL. This is to tell MySQL to automatically assign that data. Since we also have an Auto_Increment setup for the first column of data, it will automatically change that NULL into a unique integer for the data we are entering. The rest is straightforward; first, we tell MySQL what table we wish to insert data into (in this case, playerinfo), followed by the values we wish to insert into the table. We can also add more than one segment of information at once by simply placing a comma after each complete set of data. Let's assume we want to add another three players into the database and their information is as follows:

```
Name: Sandra Smith
X Position: 21
Y Position: 86
Experience: 4563


Name: John Brooke
X Position: 10
Y Position: 5
Experience: 231


Name: Jennifer West
X Position: 13
Y Position: 73
Experience: 5400
```

The console command and screenshot should look as follows:

```
mysql> INSERT INTO playerinfo VALUES
mysql> (NULL,'Sandra Smith',21,86,4563),
mysql> (NULL,'John Brooke',10,5,231),
mysql> (NULL,'Jennifer West',13,73,5400);
```

Figure 2-8

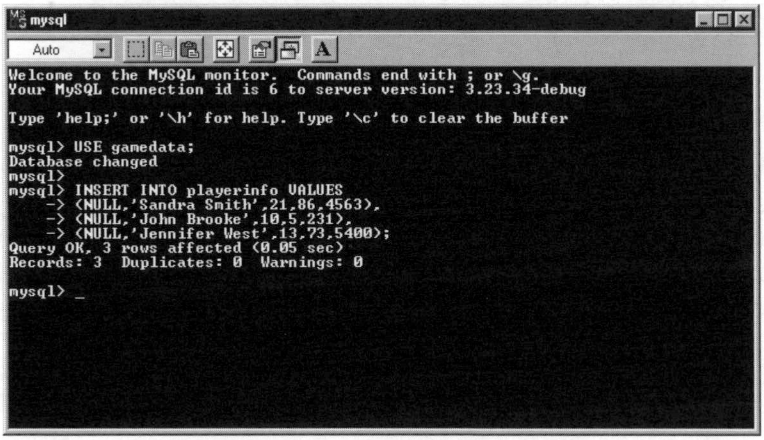

CHAPTER 2

If everything has gone according to plan, we should now have four records of data in our playerinfo table in the gamedata database.

Viewing Data in a Table

We can easily view all the information within a table by using the Select command. You can select any data you want from a table and even specify conditions (for example, only select entries that have more than 1,000 experience points). This is one of the most useful commands to us, and we will be using it extensively in Chapter 3 and in our tutorial game.

To select all the data from our table, we would use the following Select command:

```
mysql> SELECT * FROM playerinfo;
```

This selects all the fields and records from our playerinfo table. Therefore, the output from the console should contain four records of information and display all the data from each of the records. Figure 2-9 shows the expected output.

Figure 2-9

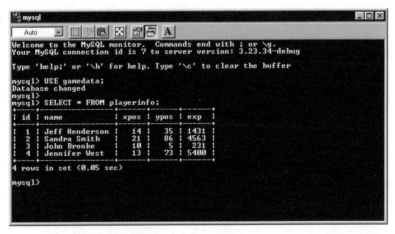

As you can see from the figure, all the data has been entered into the table correctly. Also, note how the id field has been incremented automatically for each record as we intended.

Let's now say we only want to display the name and experience data. Again, we want all the records, but we only want to select the correct fields, which in this case are name and exp. To do this we would again use the Select command, but instead of using the "*" wildcard, we specify the fields we wish to display.

```
mysql> SELECT name,exp FROM playerinfo;
```

The preceding command will select all the name and experience fields from the playerinfo table. Therefore, our expected output will be a four-row list of names and experience levels. This should look as follows.

Figure 2-10

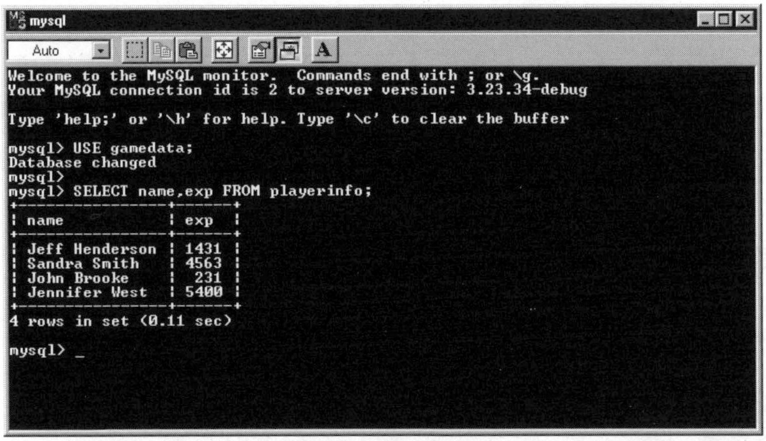

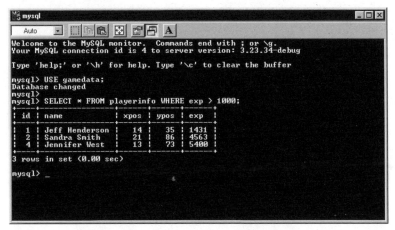

As we mentioned before, we can also use a Where command after Select, to add conditions the data must satisfy before it is selected. Let's say for example, we only wanted to see the players that had more that 1,000 experience points. We would use the following statement to retrieve this information from the table:

```
mysql> SELECT * FROM playerinfo WHERE exp > 1000;
```

When we execute this command by pressing Enter, MySQL will attempt to select all the data for the players that have an experience level greater than 1,000. This means that only Jeff, Sandra and Jennifer should be visible. Figure 2-11 shows the expected output.

Figure 2-11

CHAPTER 2

As well as comparing if a value is greater than a given number, we can also check if it is less than or simply equal to it. Let's get the player's ID and name from the table if his or her y position is equal to 86. We would use the following command to do this:

```
mysql> SELECT id,name FROM playerinfo WHERE ypos = 86;
```

As Sandra Smith is the only player with a y position of 86, she is the only person who should now be displayed in the console. We should only be able to see her ID and name as that is all we asked to select from the table. Figure 2-12 shows the expected output.

Figure 2-12

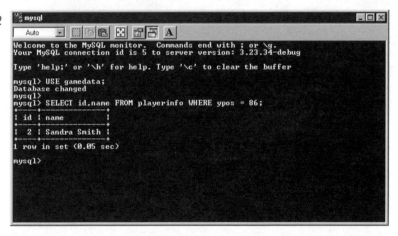

In addition to numeric comparisons, we can also compare strings of text. There are two useful methods for doing this. The first is a straight comparison, to check if one string of text is exactly equal to another. Let's say we want to see the ID, x position, and y position for John Brooke. We would use the following command to select this information from the table.

```
mysql> SELECT id,xpos,ypos FROM playerinfo WHERE name = "John Brooke";
```

Figure 2-13 shows what will happen when we execute the command. As you can see, the id and coordinates for John Brooke are now visible.

Figure 2-13

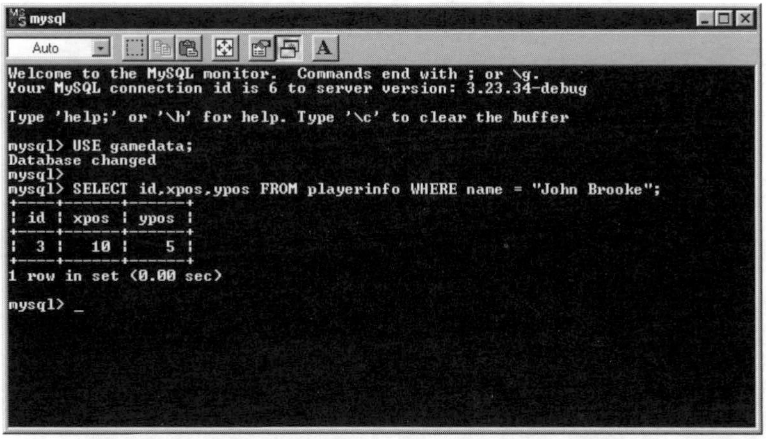

The other method is to use the MySQL Like command that allows you, for example, to select all names starting with a specific letter. If we wanted to select all the players from the table whose names started with the letter "J," we would use the following syntax:

```
mysql> SELECT * FROM playerinfo WHERE name LIKE "J%";
```

When executed, this command would produce the following output on the console.

Figure 2-14

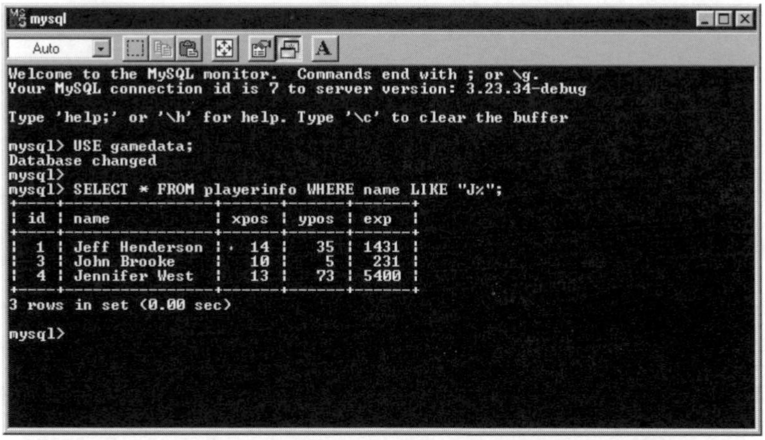

As you can see from the command, the "J%" tells MySQL to select all the names starting with "J." The percentage sign in this case is used as a wildcard and can be used in many combinations to produce useful results. Another example of the Like command would be to select any name (string) that contains a certain letter or phrase.

Let's try to select any name that contains the letter "S" anywhere, not just the start. To do this we would simply place the wildcard (%) at either side of the letter, making the location where it finds the letter irrelevant. We would therefore use the following command to accomplish this:

```
mysql> SELECT * FROM playerinfo WHERE name LIKE "%S%";
```

The only name which does not contain the letter "S" is John Brooke, so the other three names should be visible as shown here.

Figure 2-15

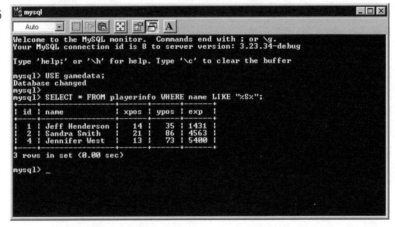

Adding Extra Fields to Tables

Let's say now that we want to add an extra field into our table that will store the date and time the player last logged in to the game. For this data, we use the timestamp storage type in the database. To add a field we use the Alter command. With this command we can add fields and also modify existing fields if we wish, for example, to change the data type. We use the syntax below to add a field to hold the time and date of the players last login:

```
mysql> ALTER TABLE playerinfo ADD lastlogin TIMESTAMP;
```

Here is how it would look when we execute it from the MySQL console.

Figure 2-16

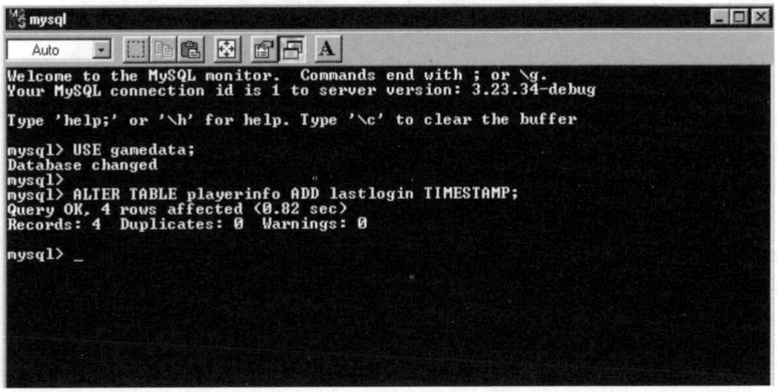

Now, if we use the Describe command on the playerinfo table, we notice that the lastlogin field has been added to the end of the table. To describe the table we use the following command:

```
mysql> DESCRIBE playerinfo;
```

When we execute this, we should see the output from the console as shown in Figure 2-17. Note the new row at the end, which is our new timestamp field.

Figure 2-17

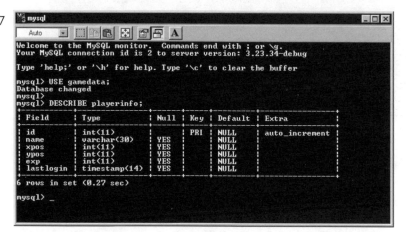

We can also use the Alter command to change the data type of a field. Let's say we have decided to allow the players to have 50 characters in their name instead of the 30 we allocated when we first created the table. To accomplish this we again use the Alter command, but instead of Add we use the Modify command as shown here:

```
mysql> ALTER TABLE playerinfo MODIFY name VARCHAR(50);
```

When we execute the command in the console, we should see that our four rows of data have been affected. The data has not actually changed, although the storage space for the field has. Figure 2-18 shows the expected console output.

Figure 2-18

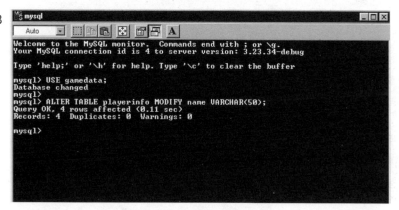

We can again describe the table to check that our changes have gone as planned. Figure 2-19 shows the expected console output from the Describe command.

Figure 2-19

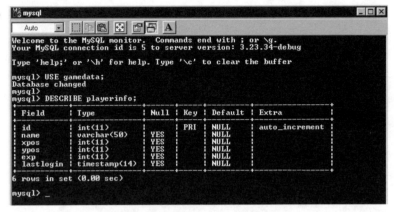

As you can see from the console output, the type for the name field is varchar(50) instead of our original varchar(30).

Updating Data in a Field

Now that we have a timestamp in our table, we wish to set it to the time and date the player last logged in. This value will change each time they login. Up to this point we have had no control of the data after it has been added into a table. Now we are going to learn how to update the data from the console without affecting the rest of the data in the record. In later chapters, we will also learn how to update information remotely both from the Internet (Perl) and from applications (sockets).

In the last section, when we added the timestamp to the table, the four records we previously added to the table's timestamps will be set to the time we added the timestamp field to the table. This can be seen in Figure 2-20.

Figure 2-20

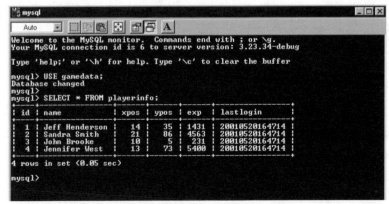

A timestamp is a single large integer that represents the date and time. The first four digits represent the year. The next two represent the month and the two after that represent the day of the month. The next four digits are for the time in 24-hour format. The final two digits represent the seconds. Figure 2-21 shows a summary.

Figure 2-21

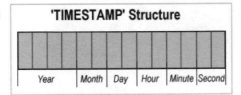

The reasoning for this structure is to allow for easy comparison with other timestamps and easy storage in the database. With this method of storage, it is simple to use basic integer comparisons, such as greater than or less than, to find out if a timestamp is before or after another timestamp or a specific date and/or time. Another feature of the timestamps is if you specify the data in MySQL as NULL for a timestamp, MySQL automatically places the system date and time in the database, which can be very useful to us, as you will see in the example to follow.

Now that we have our timestamp field in our table, let's try updating the values in our four existing entries. To update information in a table, we use the MySQL Update command. Now we will update Jeff Henderson's timestamp to be the current system time. Simply updating the timestamp field with NULL does this. The syntax for this function is:

```
mysql> UPDATE playerinfo SET lastlogin = NULL WHERE name = "Jeff Henderson";
```

First we will tell MySQL that we wish to update a table. Then we specify the table name, which in this case is our playerinfo table. Then we must tell it what to update. Here we tell it to set the lastlogin field to NULL (which means set it to the current date and time). If we excluded the Where from the end of the command, it would simply update all the lastlogin fields for all the entries (records) in the table. So we want to specify which record we wish to update, which in this case is Jeff Henderson's record. When we execute the command, we should see that one row was found and one row was changed. You can see the expected output in Figure 2-22.

Figure 2-22

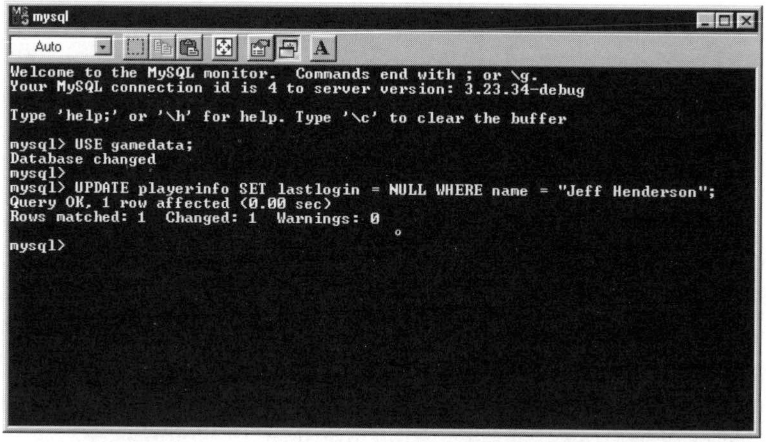

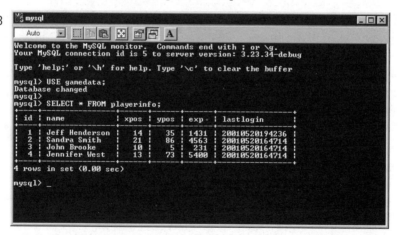

Now, when we select all the data from the table, we notice that Jeff Henderson's lastlogin date and time has been set to the time when we executed the command. See Figure 2-23 for the expected output.

Figure 2-23

In addition to automatically setting the date and time with MySQL, we can manually set it simply by inputting the correct integer, as long as we ensure it is in the correct format. Let's manually set Sandra Smith's lastlogin date to the following:

```
14th March 1999 at 3:35pm (and no seconds)
```

To do this, we again use the Update command, but we do not set the timestamp to NULL. The integers we require for this are as follows:

```
Year: 2001
Month: 03
Day: 14
Hour: 15
Minutes: 35
```

Seconds: 00

Therefore, our integer is: 20010314153500. We then put this into the command as follows:

```
mysql> UPDATE playerinfo SET lastlogin = "20010314153500"
       WHERE name = "Sandra Smith";
```

Our expected output from the execution of this command can be seen in Figure 2-24. Notice that one row (record) was matched and changed.

Figure 2-24

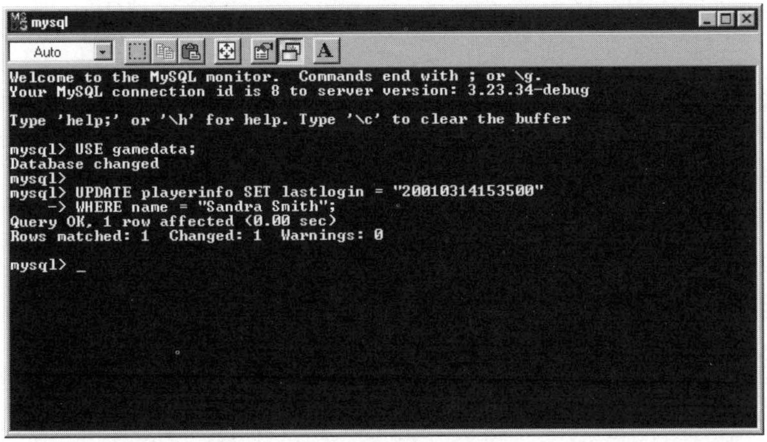

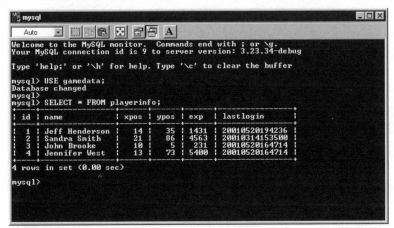

This time when we select all the records from the table, we can see that Sandra's information has been updated to the date and time we specified. See the expected output in Figure 2-25.

Figure 2-25

Note that when you are updating information in a table, you can use any of the Where cases that we have discussed before in the chapter, so we could, for

CHAPTER 2

example, set all the experience levels to 1,000 for people whose names start with "J" like this:

```
mysql> UPDATE playerinfo SET exp = 1000 WHERE name LIKE "J%";
```

When executed, this command will update all the players with a name starting with "J" and set their experience levels to 1,000. In our table, we have three players whose names start with "J," so you can see from Figure 2-26 that there are three matching rows (records) and that three were changed (updated).

Figure 2-26

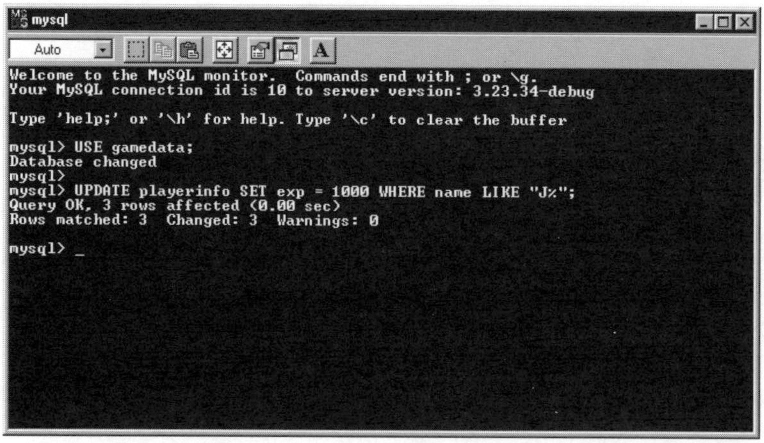

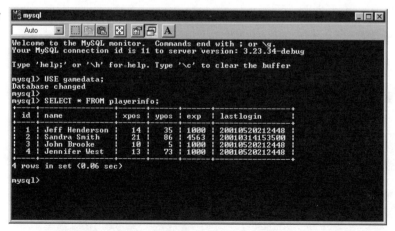

Now, if we select the data, you will see in Figure 2-27 that Jeff, John, and Jennifer all have an experience level of 1,000.

Figure 2-27

It is also possible to check more than one field when updating or selecting information from a table. For example, if you wanted to display the information of all the players whose x coordinate lies between the values of 10 and 20, you would use the following command:

```
mysql> SELECT * FROM playerinfo WHERE xpos > 10 AND xpos < 20;
```

We can also use this method with the Update command. If we wanted to set the experience level to 500 for all the players with an x coordinate greater than 10 and less than 20, we would use the following command:

```
mysql> UPDATE playerinfo SET exp =  500 WHERE xpos > 10 AND xpos < 20;
```

When we execute this command, we will see that two rows (records) have been updated. This can be seen in Figure 2-28.

Figure 2-28

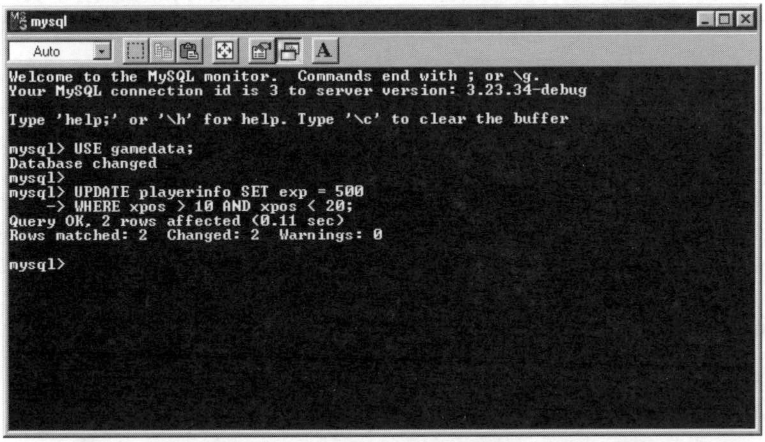

The two records that were updated were Jeff's and Jennifer's. Their x coordinates lie between the parameters we specified, hence they were updated with the new information. The expected output can be seen in Figure 2-29. Notice Jeff's and Jennifer's experience levels are now both set to 500.

Figure 2-29

CHAPTER 2

As you can see, there are many different ways you can update segements of data within the table. You will see many more examples of this in the tutorial game that we develop.

Ordering Output

Another useful service MySQL provides is the ability to easily sort outputted data. It is possible to sort data both in ascending and descending order — the default is ascending. To sort data we use the Order By command. This is used in conjunction with the Select command to produce ordered output. Let's look at a simple example. We want to view all the data in the table, but we wish to sort the names in alphabetical order. We use the following command to do this:

```
mysql> SELECT * FROM playerinfo ORDER BY name;
```

This command will retrieve all the data from the playerinfo table and display it in ascending order (alphabetical). Figure 2-30 shows the expected output from the MySQL console.

Figure 2-30

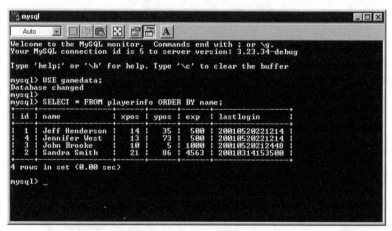

Let's now do the same again but display the names in reverse alphabetical order, that is, in descending order. This is done with the following command:

```
mysql> SELECT * FROM playerinfo ORDER BY name DESC;
```

The command is the same as before, except we add DESC onto the end to tell MySQL that we wish to use descending ordering instead of ascending. If everything has gone according to plan, the names should be in exactly the opposite order from ascending ordering. Figure 2-31 shows the expected output from the console.

Figure 2-31

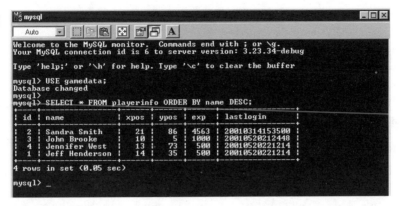

The final part to ordering is ordering multiple fields at once. For example, if we were to order the experience field, we can see that two of the experience values are 500; therefore, the order will be based on the order they are stored in the table. Let's say now that we want to order the table by the player's experience level, but if the experience level is the same as another, we wish to order the table by the player's x position. To do this is relatively simple; all we do is add another parameter onto the Order By command as follows:

```
mysql> SELECT * FROM playerinfo ORDER BY exp,xpos;
```

You can order by as many fields as you wish; just add them in order and follow each field name by a comma. We can see the expected output from the command in Figure 2-32.

Figure 2-32

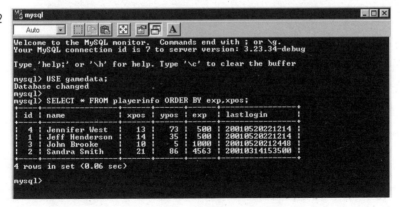

The Order By command is also particularly useful when used with timestamp fields; it allows you to easily see, for example, the people who login to the game the most or least. Another example of its use would be to find out which ten people have the most experience.

Retrieving the Last Data Entered

This is where our id field becomes useful. To retrieve the last data entered, we will first select the maximum id value from the table and store it in a temporary variable within MySQL. (Later, when using Perl and sockets, we will discover other ways to get around this.) To select the maximum ID and store it in a variable (in this case, maxid) from the table, we use the following command:

```
mysql> SELECT @maxid:=MAX(id) FROM playerinfo;
```

This will utilize MySQL's Max function to get the value from the id field with the largest value. The last record we added to the field will have the largest id value. Also notice that we assign the value to a local variable. We declare variables using the @ symbol. Figure 2-33 shows what we expect from the MySQL console.

Figure 2-33

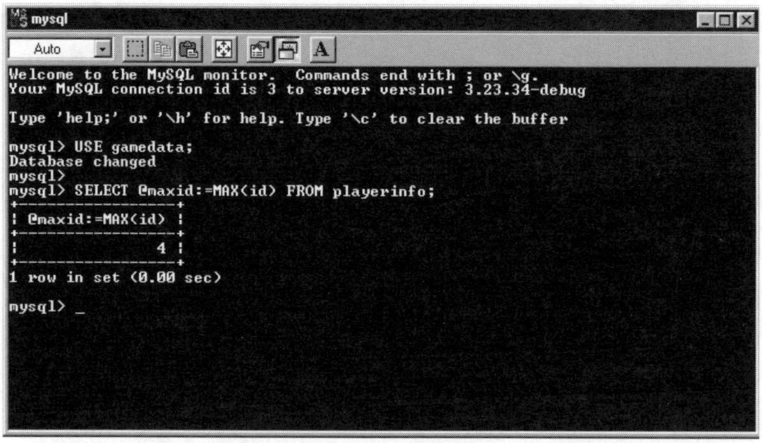

Now, we have the value of the maximum ID in our local variable maxid. We can now use this local variable to retrieve the rest of the data for that player as follows:

```
mysql> SELECT * FROM playerinfo WHERE id = @maxid;
```

Notice that instead of specifying a number for the ID, we are using our local variable maxid to represent the number. Now, when we execute this command, the console will display the final entry that was added to the table, which in this case is "Jennifer." Figure 2-34 on the following page shows our expected console output.

This Max command in association with the timestamp field lastlogin can be used to easily find which player was the last to login. Here is the command we would use to retrieve the player's timestamp who was the last to login:

```
mysql> SELECT @lastlogin:=MAX(lastlogin) FROM playerinfo;
```

Figure 2-34

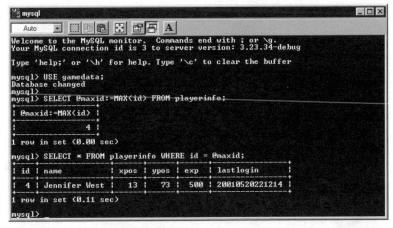

Note that if two players have the same timestamp, MySQL will select both of the players, but it is unlikely that two players will login at exactly the same second in time. If this does occur, we can simply select one or the other.

Now we have the timestamp for the player who logged in last stored in the lastlogin local variable. We can now retrieve the rest of the player's data by carrying out a search based on the timestamp we have in our local variable as follows:

```
mysql> SELECT * FROM playerinfo WHERE lastlogin = @lastlogin;
```

This will retrieve all the information for the player who logged in last. In our database, both Jeff and Jennifer logged in last at exactly the same date, time, and second as you can see in Figure 2-35. Thus, MySQL has selected both of these players.

Figure 2-35

```
Your MySQL connection id is 4 to server version: 3.23.34-debug

Type 'help;' or '\h' for help. Type '\c' to clear the buffer

mysql> USE gamedata;
Database changed
mysql>
mysql> SELECT @lastlogin:=MAX(lastlogin) FROM playerinfo;
+----------------------------+
| @lastlogin:=MAX(lastlogin) |
+----------------------------+
|             20010520221214 |
+----------------------------+
1 row in set (0.05 sec)

mysql> SELECT * FROM playerinfo WHERE lastlogin = @lastlogin;
+----+----------------+------+------+------+----------------+
| id | name           | xpos | ypos | exp  | lastlogin      |
+----+----------------+------+------+------+----------------+
|  1 | Jeff Henderson |   14 |   35 |  500 | 20010520221214 |
|  4 | Jennifer West  |   13 |   73 |  500 | 20010520221214 |
+----+----------------+------+------+------+----------------+
2 rows in set (0.06 sec)

mysql>
```

Limiting Output Data

There is a useful parameter you can include when using the Select command to limit the amount of records MySQL selects from the parameters you specify. For example, you could select all the names that begin with the letter "J," but then limit the output to two records. This is done as follows by using the Limit parameter:

```
mysql> SELECT * FROM playerinfo WHERE name LIKE "J%" LIMIT 2;
```

As you can see, the Select command is used the same as before, but this time we simply add the Limit parameter to the end to limit the output from MySQL to a specified amount of records, which in this case is two. Figure 2-36 shows our expected output from the MySQL console.

Figure 2-36

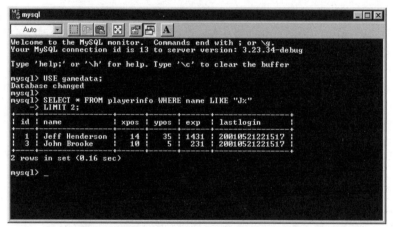

Deleting Data from a Table

Deleting data from a table in MySQL is a simple process, but it is easy to delete more information than you intended if you make a mistake in the command you enter.

First, we will look at how to delete a single item of data. For this we use the same idea as searching, except MySQL will delete all the entries it finds instead of displaying them. We will first delete by the users name. Let's try to delete Jeff Henderson from our table, but leave all the other entries untouched. In MySQL we use the Delete From command, and specify parameters to avoid deleting all the data from the table. We can use the following syntax to delete Jeff from our table:

```
mysql> DELETE FROM playerinfo WHERE name = "Jeff Henderson";
```

When we execute this command, MySQL informs us that one row (record) was affected by the command. In this case, the record has been deleted. This can be seen in Figure 2-37.

Figure 2-37

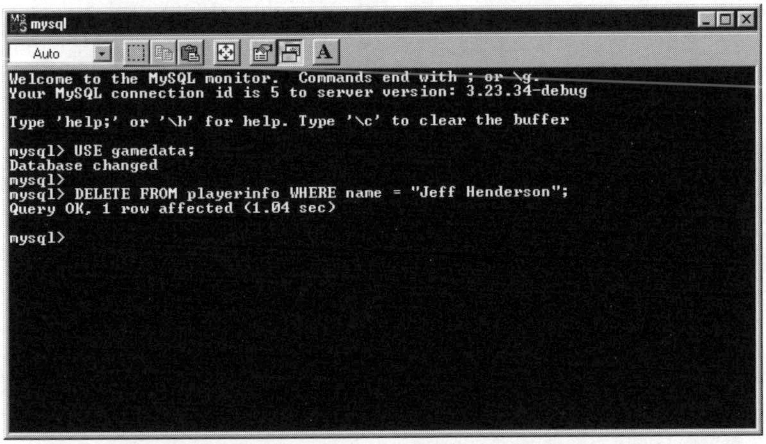

If we now select all the data from the table, you will notice the absence of Jeff's record in the following figure.

Figure 2-38

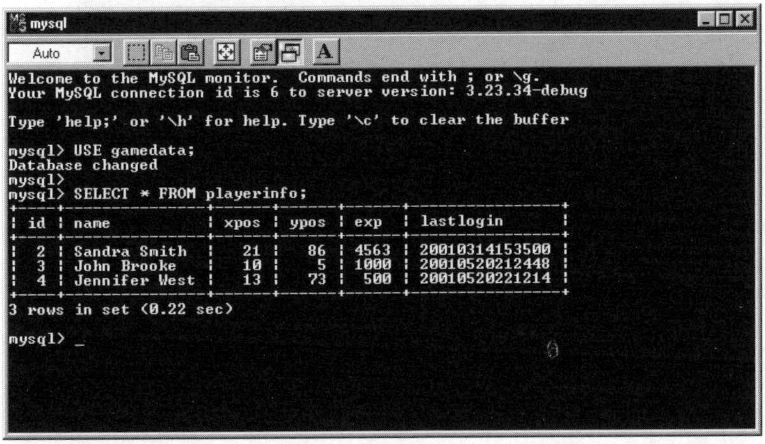

We can also delete from any other field, such as id. This is very useful when we are working with the Internet; you will see why in the following chapter about Perl and the Internet. However, to delete by the id field, we use exactly the same syntax as before, using the Delete From command. We use the following syntax to delete John Brooke from the database, who has an ID number of 3:

```
mysql> DELETE FROM playerinfo WHERE id = 3;
```

When we execute this command, again we will see on the MySQL console that one row has been affected.

Figure 2-39

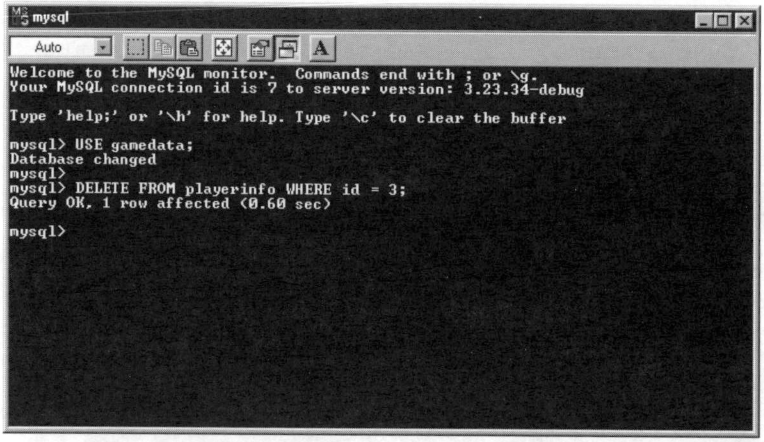

Again, when we now select all the data from the table, we can see we only have two entries remaining. Here is our expected output from the Select command.

Figure 2-40

Finally, we will cover how to delete all the information from a table. Use this command carefully as it is not possible to restore your data once it is deleted. Note that when you delete all the information from a table, the table itself still exists; therefore, it is possible to add new information to it.

To delete all the information from a table, you again use the Delete From command, but this time we do not specify any parameters. As you can see, it could be easy to unintentionally execute this command, which is why we must be careful with our use of it. The command to delete all the information from the playerinfo table is as follows:

```
mysql> DELETE FROM playerinfo;
```

Notice the command is the same as before, but without the parameters. When we execute the command this time, it will say that zero rows were affected; however, it will have deleted all of the data. Figure 2-41 shows the expected output from the console when we execute the command.

Figure 2-41

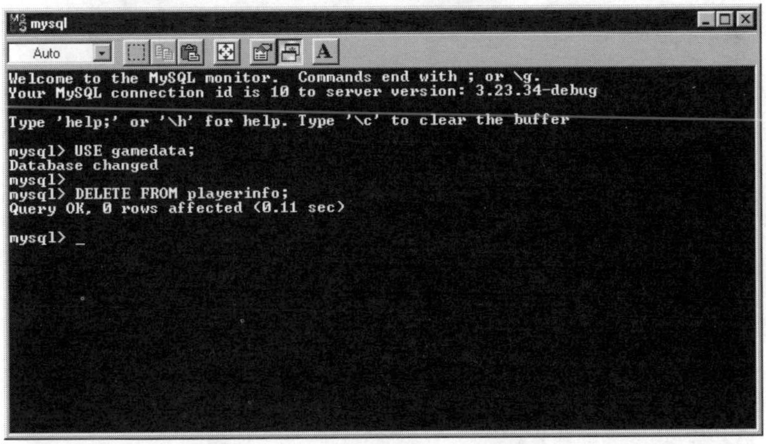

We can check that all the data has been deleted successfully by selecting all the information from the table. If everything has gone according to plan, when we select the data, MySQL will report that the table is an empty set, meaning that the table contains no records. This can be seen in the following figure.

Figure 2-42

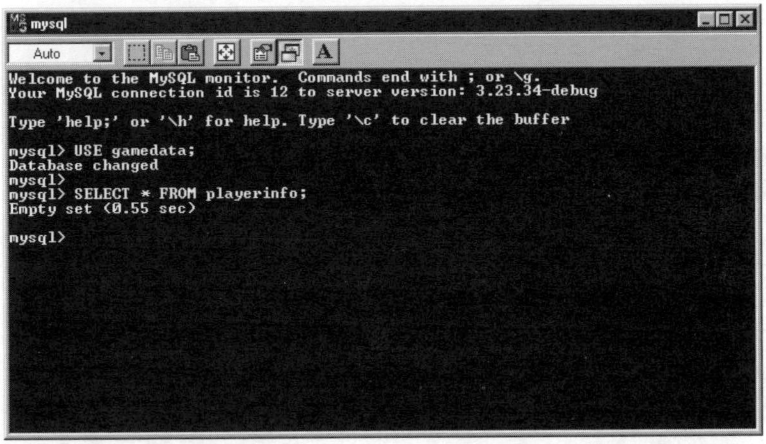

Deleting Tables and Databases

To delete a table from MySQL, we utilize the Drop command. Therefore, to delete our playerinfo table we simply use the following command:

```
mysql> DROP TABLE playerinfo;
```

When we execute this command, we should expect the following output from the MySQL console.

Figure 2-43

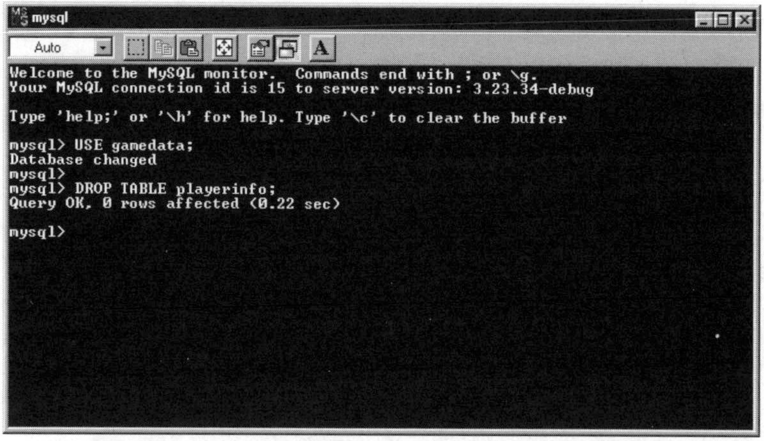

We can now check that the table has been deleted correctly by using the Show Tables command, which we discovered earlier in this chapter. Here is the command to do this again:

```
mysql> SHOW TABLES;
```

When we execute this command, we will see that MySQL informs us we have an empty set. This means that our database no longer contains any tables. If we did have more tables, they would still be visible here. Figure 2-44 shows expected output from the console.

Figure 2-44

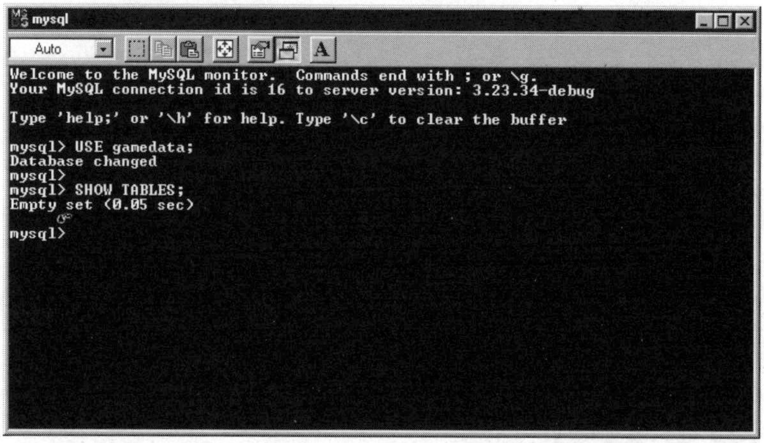

If we then want to delete our entire database from the MySQL system, we would again use the Drop command, but this time tell it we wish to drop a database as follows:

```
mysql> DROP DATABASE gamedata;
```

When executed, this command removes everything associated with the gamedata database, including all data and tables from within the database. Figure 2-45 shows what we expect the console output to be.

Figure 2-45

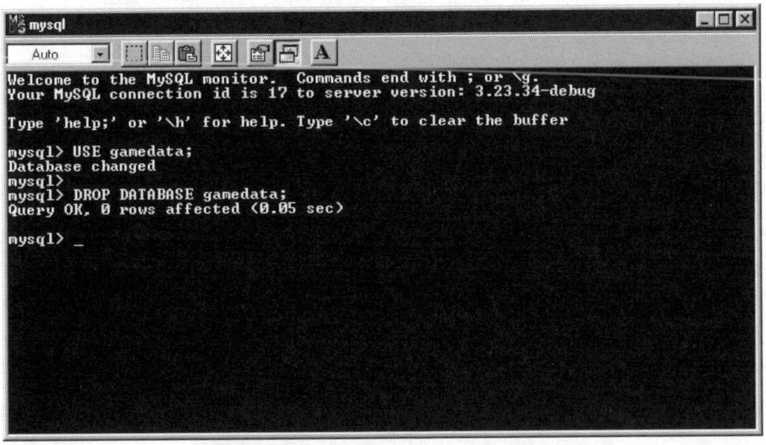

Now we can check that our database was deleted correctly by viewing all the databases in the MySQL system. To view the databases, we use the Show Databases command as we did earlier in this chapter. This is done as follows:

```
mysql> SHOW DATABASES;
```

When we execute this, MySQL will display what databases are currently active in the system. If our database has been deleted correctly, it simply should not be shown here. In the following figure, we can see the expected output from the console.

Figure 2-46

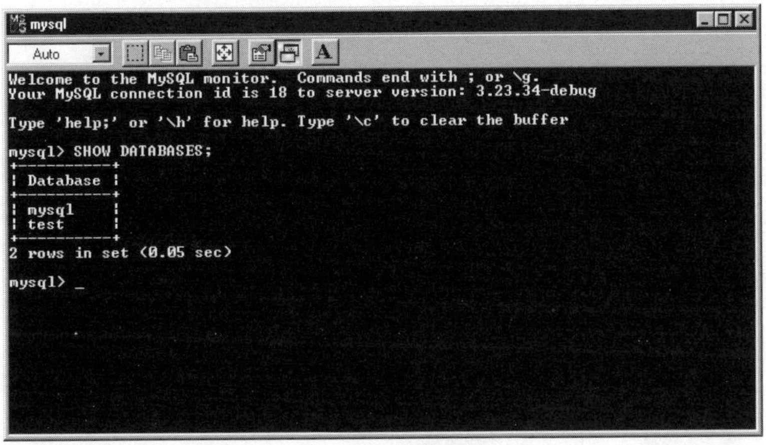

As you can see, only the mysql and test databases remain on the system.

This completes our basic knowledge of creating, using, and deleting a simple database. In the next section, we will go into depth on how to create relational databases, which are very useful, especially for game development. In addition, we will learn how to input information into the database from files and find out how to back up and restore databases to and from files.

Relational Databases

A relational database is a way of storing data that relates to other data without actually duplicating the data. Earlier in this chapter, we added an id field which assigned a unique integer value to each new record of data that was added to a table. This is the key part to using relational databases. Rather than copy the data, we simply place the two IDs in a special relation table for the data we wish to relate.

Now we will plan and create a relational database. We will also be using this technique in the second section of the book, when we create our tutorial online game.

Let's say we wish to create a database to hold the data for players in an online game for which a monthly fee must be paid. As well as holding the player's game data, we also wish to store information as to when he made payments to his account. In addition, we wish to be able to keep a list of friends and enemies that the player makes in the online game. The user can modify whom his friends and enemies are, so the lists will be dynamic. Finally, we also wish to be able to store an unlimited amount of notes about the player. Here is our plan for the tables we would like to include in the database to hold this data in an efficient manner.

Figure 2-47

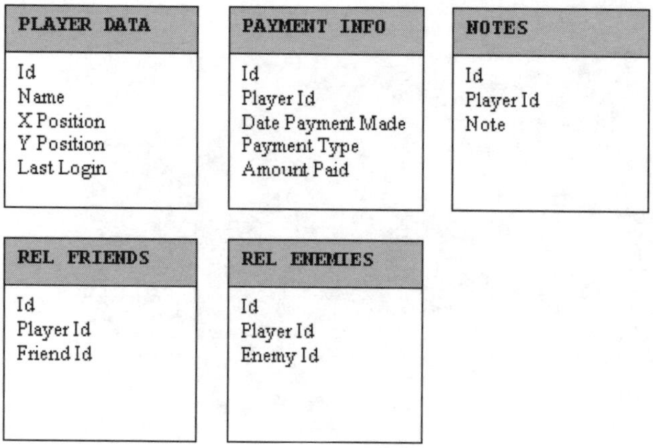

PLAYER DATA	PAYMENT INFO	NOTES
Id	Id	Id
Name	Player Id	Player Id
X Position	Date Payment Made	Note
Y Position	Payment Type	
Last Login	Amount Paid	

REL FRIENDS	REL ENEMIES
Id	Id
Player Id	Player Id
Friend Id	Enemy Id

- **Player Data**   This table is used to hold the player's actual game data. Here we store the player's name, the coordinates in the game, and the date and time when he last logged into the game. In addition, when a player is added, he is assigned a unique ID by MySQL.

- **Payment Info**   Each time a player makes a payment into his online account it is recorded in this table. Each entry is again assigned a unique ID so it can be easily manipulated from the Internet. Next, we enter the ID of the player who is making the payment, followed by the date the payment was made, how it was paid (i.e., Visa, Switch, check, etc.), and the amount that was paid.

- **Notes**   Each note is assigned a unique ID. Next, we add the player's ID to denote to whom the note is relevant. Finally, we have the actual note itself, which will be a simple string of text.

- **Rel Friends**   This is the first of our dedicated relation tables. This table relates a player's ID to a friend's ID. This way, it is easy for us to make a player have an unlimited amount of friends.

- **Rel Enemies**   This final table works in the same way as the Rel Friends table. It simply relates the player's ID to an enemy's ID.

Creating Our Relational Database

When it comes to creating our relational database, we do it in the same manner as earlier in the chapter. First, we must create a database to store our tables of information. Let's call the database onlinegame. As before, we create the database as follows from the MySQL console:

```
mysql> CREATE DATABASE onlinegame;
```

When we execute this command, MySQL will inform us that the query was OK. Now we can check that it was created by using the Show Databases command as follows:

```
mysql> SHOW DATABASES;
```

We should now see that our database has been added to the list. Figure 2-48 shows the expected output from the console.

Figure 2-48

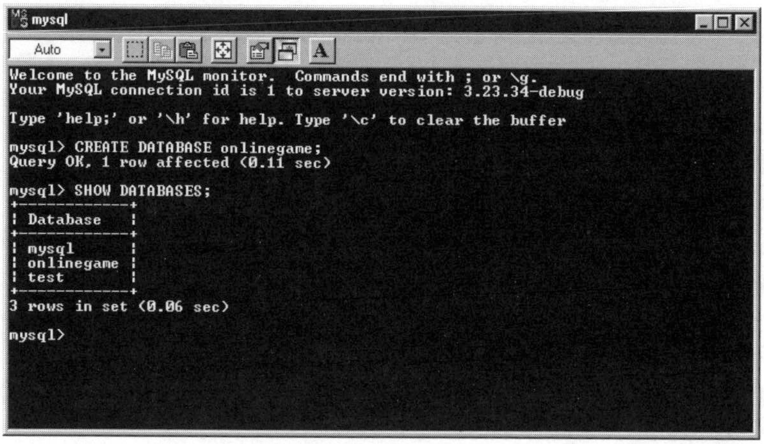

Now that our database has been created, we can start adding tables to hold our data. It does not make any difference in what order we add the tables into the database, so we will just add them in the same order as we explained them earlier. First though, we must tell MySQL that we wish to use the onlinegame database as follows:

```
mysql> USE onlinegame;
```

Now we can move on to adding in our tables.

Player Data

Adding our table information is done in the same way we discussed earlier in the chapter. The player's name will be a 50-character string, the coordinates will be integers, and the lastlogin time will be a timestamp so we can store the date and time in it. We can create this table using the following command:

```
mysql> CREATE TABLE playerdata (
mysql> id INT auto_increment,
mysql> name VARCHAR(50),
mysql> xpos INT,
mysql> ypos INT,
mysql> lastlogin TIMESTAMP,
mysql> PRIMARY KEY(id));
```

Figure 2-49 shows how this would look when we enter it into the MySQL console.

Figure 2-49

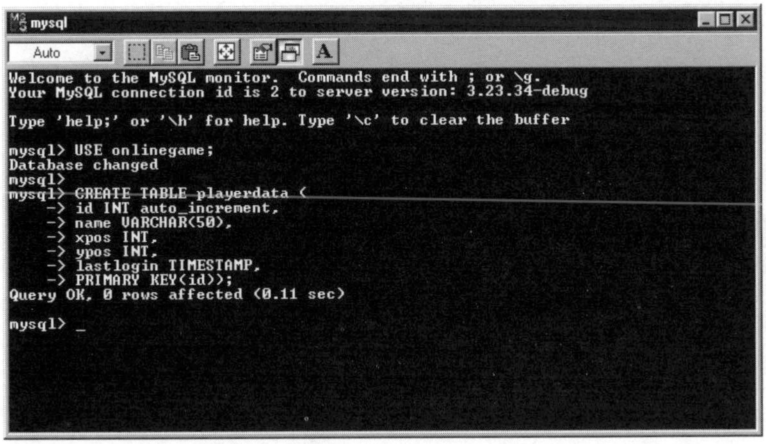

Now is a good time to use the Describe command so we can check that our table has been created as we intended. We use the following syntax to do this:

```
mysql> DESCRIBE playerdata;
```

When we execute the command, the following can be seen displayed on the MySQL console.

Figure 2-50

Be sure to check on this screen that the Type column is correct; a mistake at this stage can be corrected, but if left unnoticed it can be fatal to your game.

The final check we will do for our first table is to make sure it has been added to the database. This is done by using the Show Tables command as follows:

```
mysql> SHOW TABLES;
```

We should now see that our first table is part of our database. Figure 2-51 shows the expected output.

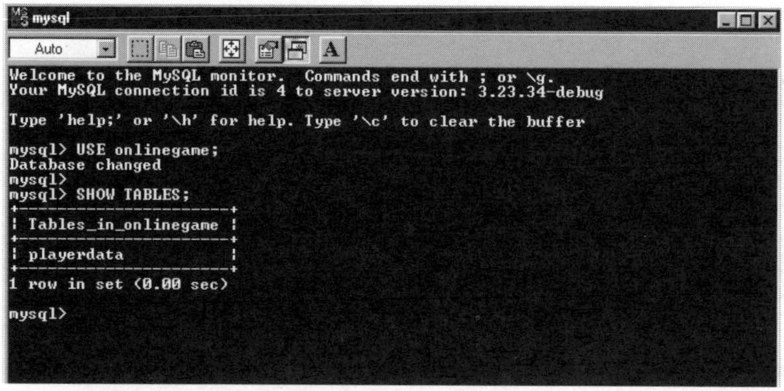

Figure 2-51

Payment Info

The id field for this table will be a standard unique id field. The playerid field, on the other hand, will be a reference to a player's ID that can be used to find the appropriate player in the playerdata table. Next, we wish to store the payment date as a timestamp. The payment type will be a string, whereas the amount paid will be a simple integer value.

```
mysql> CREATE TABLE paymentinfo (
mysql> id INT auto_increment,
mysql> playerid INT,
mysql> datepaid TIMESTAMP,
mysql> type VARCHAR(100),
mysql> amount INT,
mysql> PRIMARY KEY(id));
```

When we enter this table description and execute it in the MySQL console, we expect the following output.

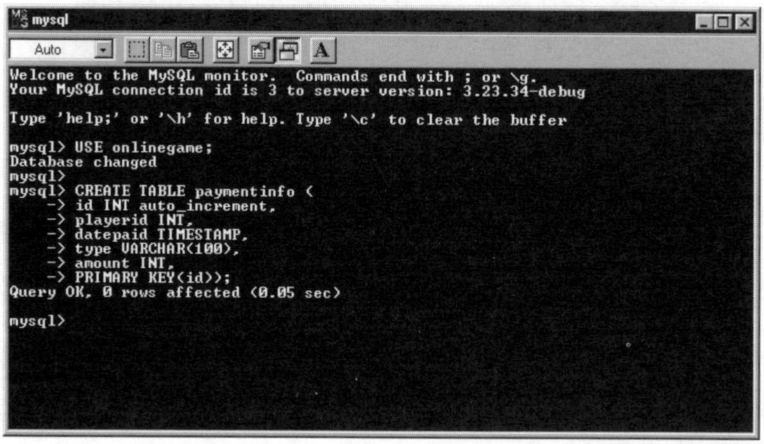

Figure 2-52

Now is the time to check our table for correctness. When we use the Describe command as before, we can check that the fields in our table have been created accurately. Here is the command we use to describe this new table:

```
mysql> DESCRIBE paymentinfo;
```

When we execute this command, we expect to see the following output in the MySQL console.

Figure 2-53

Finally, if we use the Show Tables command again, we can check that we now have two tables in our database as can be seen in the following figure.

Figure 2-54

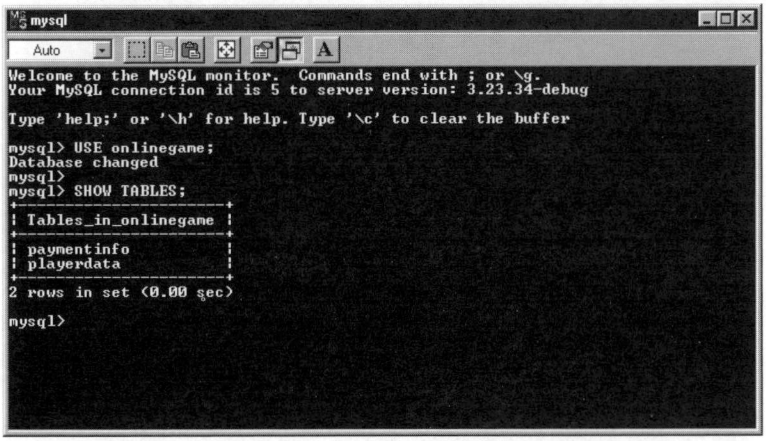

Now we have both the playerdata table and the paymentinfo table in our database. Next, we shall add the notes table, so we can attach several notes to each player in the database.

Notes

This table is very simple and only contains three fields. The first is our unique id, which is standard to all our tables in a relational database. The second holds the player's ID number, so we know which player the note is for. The final field is the note itself, which is a 255-character string. The command to create the notes table is as follows:

```
mysql> CREATE TABLE notes (
mysql> id INT auto_increment,
mysql> playerid INT,
mysql> note VARCHAR(255),
mysql> PRIMARY KEY(id));
```

Here is how this will look once we enter it into the console.

Figure 2-55

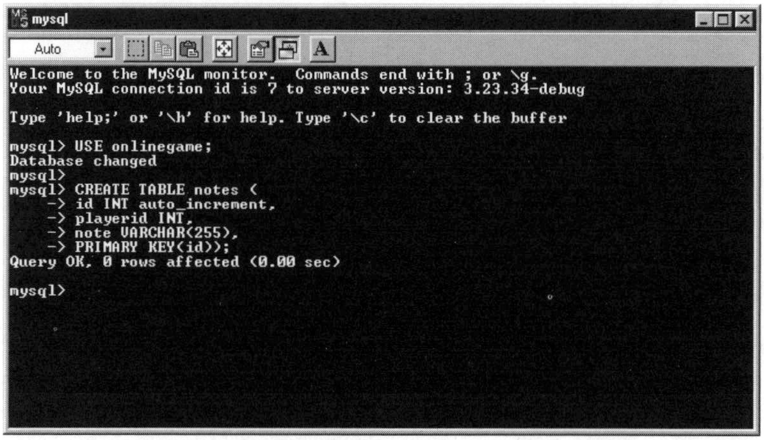

After our table is created, again we must check it for any mistakes. For this we must describe our notes table as follows:

```
mysql> DESCRIBE notes;
```

When we execute this, we should see in the console that our table has been created correctly. Figure 2-56 on the following page shows the expected output from the MySQL console.

Our final check is to show the tables in the database to confirm that we now have three tables. We use the Show Tables command again as follows:

```
mysql> SHOW TABLES;
```

Figure 2-56

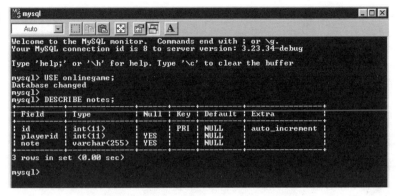

When we then execute this command, we should see that the console now displays the three tables we created as part of the onlinegame database. Our expected output can be seen in the following figure.

Figure 2-57

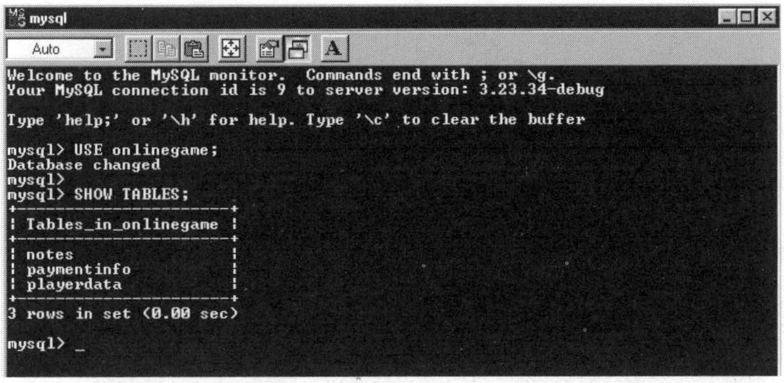

Next we will add our two relational tables so we can assign friends and enemies to players in the database.

Rel Friends

All this table must do is keep note of who each player is friends with. Therefore, we simply match up IDs of who is friends with whom. As is standard, this table must first have the unique id field, followed by an ID for a player, and then an ID for the person with whom that player is friends. This allows us to make a single player friends with many people in the database and also keep track of them easily. To create our relfriends table, we use the following command:

```
mysql> CREATE TABLE relfriends (
mysql> id INT auto_increment,
mysql> playerid INT,
mysql> friendid INT,
mysql> PRIMARY KEY(id));
```

When we enter this into the console, it should look as follows.

Figure 2-58

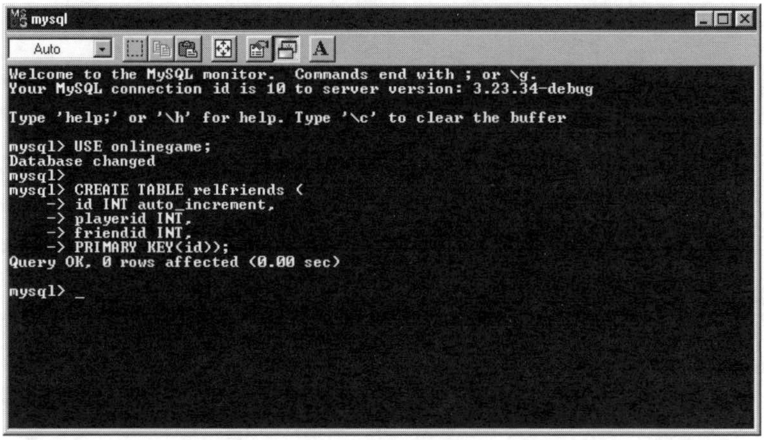

Our next check is to ensure that our table has been created with the correct fields. As before, we use the Describe command to do this:

```
mysql> DESCRIBE relfriends;
```

Figure 2-59 shows the expected output from the console when we execute this command.

Figure 2-59

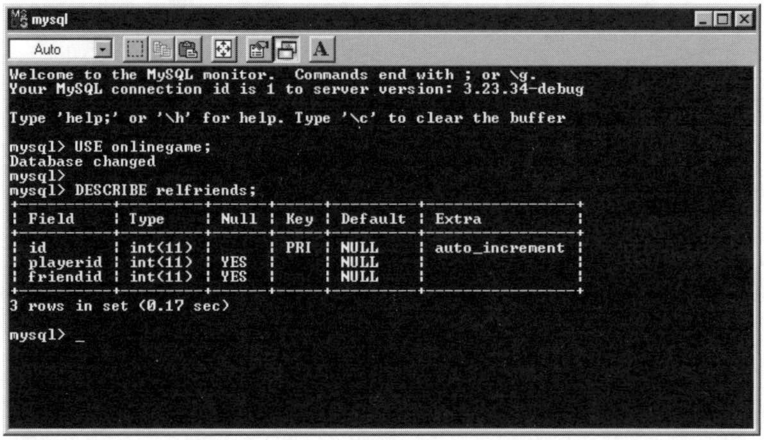

Again, our final check is to make certain that our table has been added correctly to our onlinegame database. For this we use the Show Tables command again:

```
mysql> SHOW TABLES;
```

When we execute this command, the console should display all the tables our database now contains, including our relfriends table. Our expected output can be seen in the following figure.

Figure 2-60

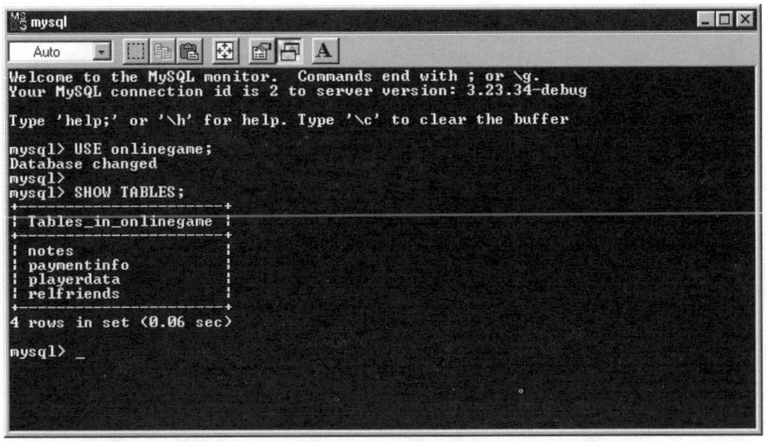

Rel Enemies

The final table we must add to our database is similar to the relfriends table. This table simply keeps track of who a player is enemies with in the database. We create this table in the same way as the relfriends table. Here is the command we use to create this table:

```
mysql> CREATE TABLE relenemies (
mysql> id INT auto_increment,
mysql> playerid INT,
mysql> enemyid INT,
mysql> PRIMARY KEY(id));
```

Figure 2-61 shows how the information will look when we enter it in the MySQL console.

Figure 2-61

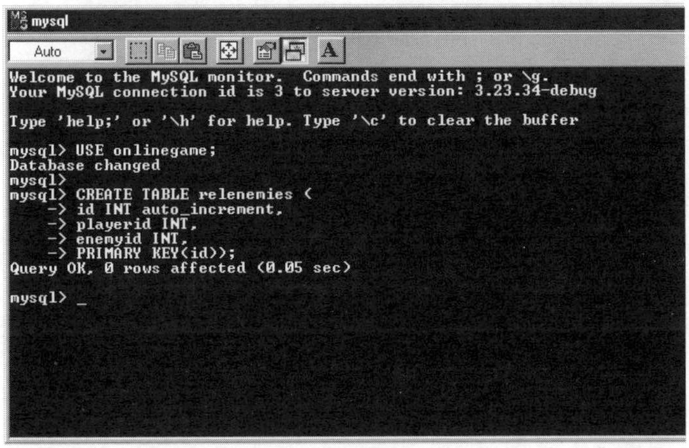

Our first check is again to see that all the fields were created as we intended them to be. Again, we utilize the Describe command to accomplish this:

```
mysql> DESCRIBE relenemies;
```

When we execute this command, we expect to see the following information in the MySQL console.

Figure 2-62

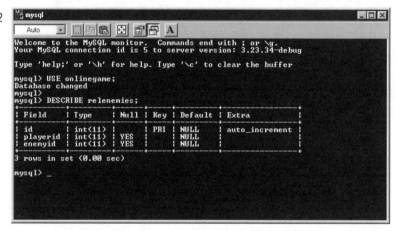

Our final check for our database is to see that all our tables are now in the database. To check this, we again use the Show Tables command:

```
mysql> SHOW TABLES;
```

When we execute this, we can now see that all the tables in our original database plan are part of the onlinegame database in MySQL. Figure 2-63 shows the expected output from the MySQL console.

Figure 2-63

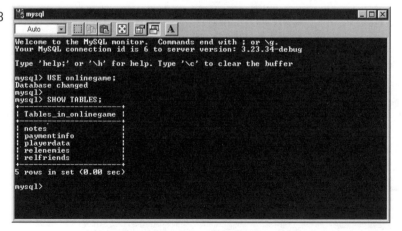

Adding Relational Data

The first thing we must do is add some players into our playerdata table. For now, we will use the console to input the data, although later in this chapter you will find out how to use other programs and files to input the data. Let's start by adding data for five imaginary players for this online game. Here is the data for the players we wish to add:

```
Name:          Andrew Smith
X-pos:         12
Y-pos:         23
Last Login:    23rd May 2001

Name:          Sally Rannor
X-pos:         17
Y-pos:         9
Last Login:    14th June 2001

Name:          Pete Dakkar
X-pos:         5
Y-pos:         31
Last Login:    1st December 2000

Name:          Louise Jennings
X-pos:         17
Y-pos:         14
Last Login:    19th January 2001

Name:          Fred Warran
X-pos:         9
Y-pos:         5
Last Login:    12th July 2001
```

To add this data, we must use the Insert command to enter the data into our playerdata table. Here is the command we use to add the correct data:

```
mysql> INSERT INTO playerdata VALUES
mysql> (NULL,"Andrew Smith",12,23,"20010523000000"),
mysql> (NULL,"Sally Rannor",17,9,"20010614000000"),
mysql> (NULL,"Pete Dakkar",5,31,"20001201000000"),
mysql> (NULL,"Louise Jennings",17,14,"20010119000000"),
mysql> (NULL,"Fred Warran",9,5,"20010712000000");
```

When we execute this Insert command, MySQL should inform us that five rows have been modified. The following figure shows the expected output from the console.

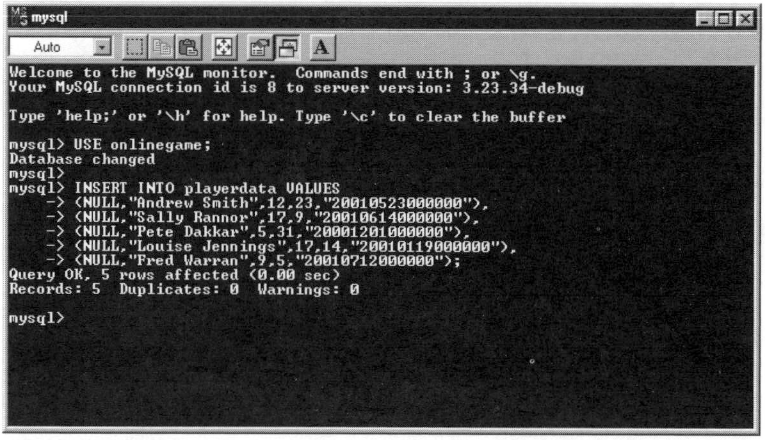

Figure 2-64

If we now select all the data from the playerdata table we will be able to see the data we entered previously as records in the table. To select the data, we use the Select command as before:

```
mysql> SELECT * FROM playerdata;
```

Here is our expected output from the console when we execute the Select command.

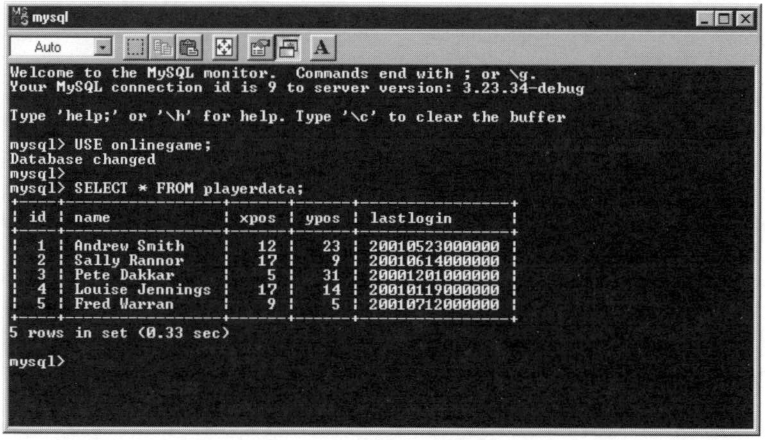

Figure 2-65

Notice now that each of the five players we entered into the table has a unique ID number. We can now add other information into the database based on this unique number. Then, whenever we wish to find data related to a player, we simply search on the playerid field in the other tables.

Let's now add some account information for the players. The account information keeps track of what payments each player on the system has made and how he or she paid it. First let's add three monthly payments made by Sally Rannor. The details for these payments are as follows:

```
1st Payment on the 1st January 2001 by Cheque for $300
2nd Payment on the 1st February 2001 by Visa for $150
3rd Payment on the 1st March 2001 by Visa for $150
```

Since Sally Rannor has an ID number of 2, we wish to include this when we add information regarding the payments into the paymentinfo table. Here is how we add the payment info for Sally Rannor:

```
mysql> INSERT INTO paymentinfo VALUES
mysql> (NULL,2,"20010101000000","Cheque",300),
mysql> (NULL,2,"20010201000000","Visa",150),
mysql> (NULL,2,"20010301000000","Visa",150);
```

This will look as follows when we enter it into the MySQL console.

Figure 2-66

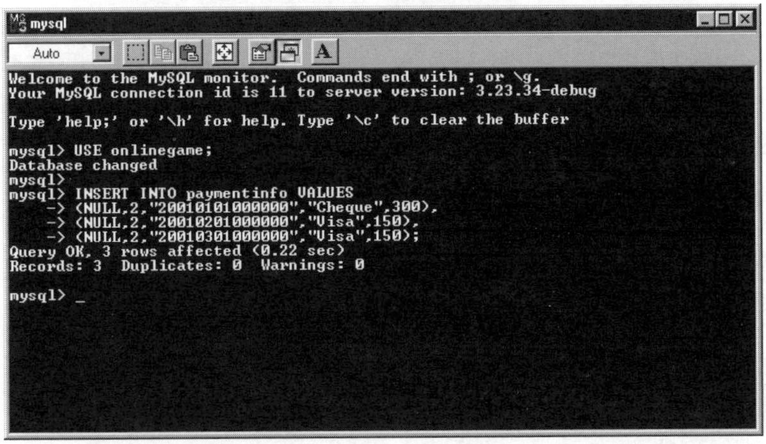

Before we look at the data in the table, let's also add account information for another player in the game, Louise Jennings. Louise's ID number is 4 in the playerdata table, so we use this in the playerid field in the paymentinfo table to determine that the account information is intended for Louise. Let's now add the following two payments to Louise's account:

```
1st Payment on the 1st January 2001 by MasterCard for $300
2nd Payment on the 1st February 2001 by MasterCard for $450
```

To add these payments, we do it in the same way we added Sally's payment, but this time we use Louise's ID number of 4 instead of Sally's, which is 2. Here is the command to add the new account data into the paymentinfo table:

```
mysql> INSERT INTO paymentinfo VALUES
mysql> (NULL,4,"20010101000000","MasterCard",300),
mysql> (NULL,4,"20010201000000","MasterCard",450);
```

Figure 2-67 shows how this will look when we enter this new data into the MySQL console.

CHAPTER 2

Figure 2-67

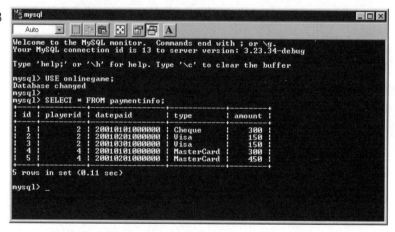

Now that we have entered data for two players' accounts, let's have a look at how it is stored in our relational table.

Figure 2-68

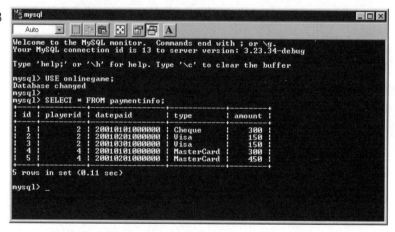

As you can see from the preceding figure, each payment record has its own unique ID as well as an ID to reference which player the data is relevant to. Without the playerdata table, we cannot find out which player has which payment information. Let's say all we know is the name Sally Rannor and we wish to list all the payments she has made into her account. First, we would find out her unique id and store it in a local variable (either in MySQL or the language you are using to access MySQL). This is done as follows:

```
mysql> SELECT @tempid:=id FROM playerdata WHERE name = "Sally Rannor";
```

When this command is executed, it will assign the ID number for Sally Rannor (which is 2 in this case) to the local variable tempid. Figure 2-69 shows our expected output from the MySQL console.

Figure 2-69

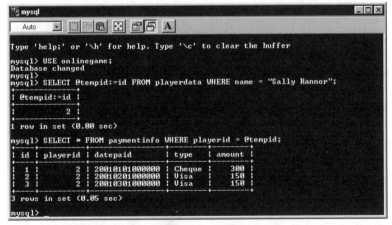

Now that we have the ID for Sally stored in a local variable, we can use this variable as a search parameter on the playerid field in the paymentinfo table. This can be done with the following command:

```
mysql> SELECT * FROM paymentinfo WHERE playerid = @tempid;
```

When we execute this, we should expect the following output from MySQL.

Figure 2-70

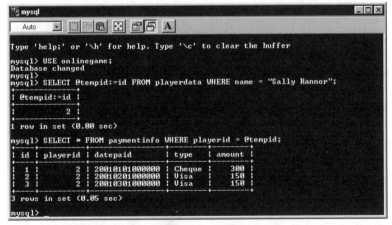

As you can see from the preceding figure, we now have a list of all of Sally Rannor's payments.

We can do this exactly the same way for another player in the database. For example, let's now try and list the payment information for Louise Jennings. First, we retrieve her unique ID number from the playerdata table as follows:

```
mysql> SELECT @tempid:=id FROM playerdata WHERE name = "Louise Jennings";
```

As you can see from the following figure, this selects the value 4 and places it in the tempid variable, which we can use as a search parameter on the paymentinfo table, the same way we did for Sally's information.

Figure 2-71

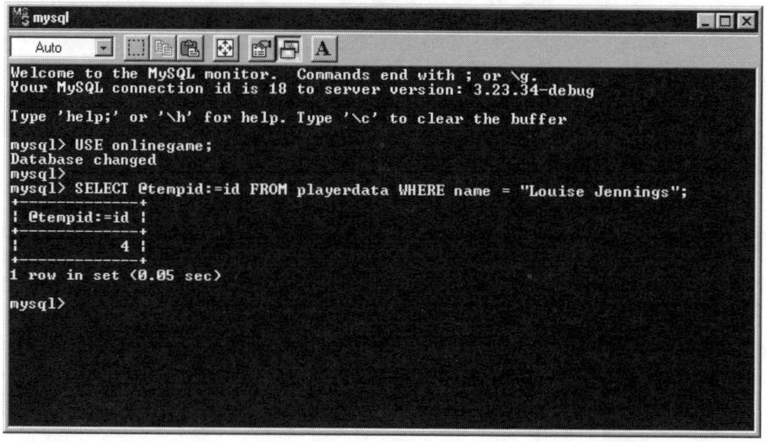

We use exactly the same command as before to search for the payment information because the variable name is the same as before:

```
mysql> SELECT * FROM paymentinfo WHERE playerid = @tempid;
```

Here you can see our expected output, which shows the two payments that Louise has made to her account.

Figure 2-72

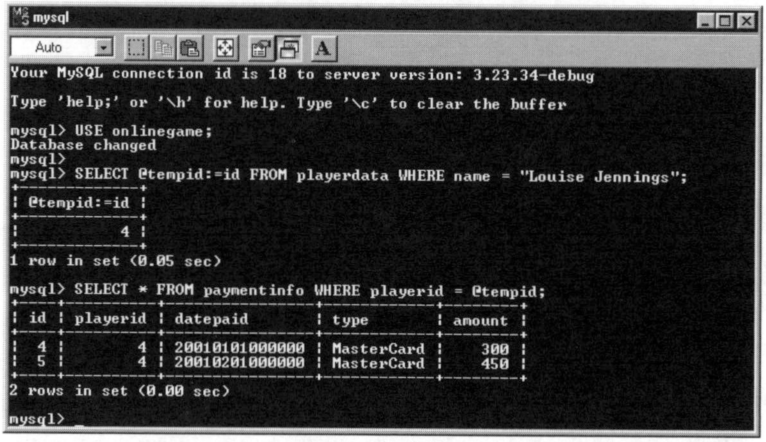

Next, we will add some notes to players in the database. We do this in the same way as we add payment information, using each player's unique identification number. Let's now add the following notes for each of the players.

Notes regarding Andrew Smith

- Requested new password on the 5th May 2001

Notes regarding Sally Rannor

- Account details modified manually on 14th June 2001
- Contacted by email on 16th June 2001 regarding new account details
- No reply received by 18th June 2001
- Contacted again about account details on the 20th June 2001

Notes regarding Pete Dakkar

[None]

Notes regarding Louise Jennings

- Question sent regarding password change on the 9th December 2001
- User replied and confirmed change on the 17th December 2001

Notes regarding Fred Warran

- Sent inactive account letter on the 29th July 2001
- User replied on the 4th August 2001 and wishes to delete account

Now that we know the note data we wish to enter into the database, we simply use the Insert command to place all the data into the notes table, using the correct player's ID number for each note we enter. Here is the command we need to use to add all the notes into the table:

```
mysql> INSERT INTO notes VALUES
mysql> (NULL,1,"Requested new password on the 5th May 2001"),
mysql> (NULL,2," Account Details modified manually on 14th June 2001"),
mysql> (NULL,2,"Contacted by e-mail on 16th June 2001 regarding new
        account details"),
mysql> (NULL,2,"No reply received by 18th June 2001"),
mysql> (NULL,2,"Contacted again about account details on the 20th June 2001"),
mysql> (NULL,4,"Question sent regarding password change on the 9th
        December 2001"),
mysql> (NULL,4,"User replied and confirmed change on the 17th December 2001"),
mysql> (NULL,5,"Sent inactive account letter on the 29th July 2001"),
mysql> (NULL,5,"User replied on the 4th August 2001 and wishes to
        delete account");
```

After we enter all this information on the console, we expect it to look as follows.

Figure 2-73

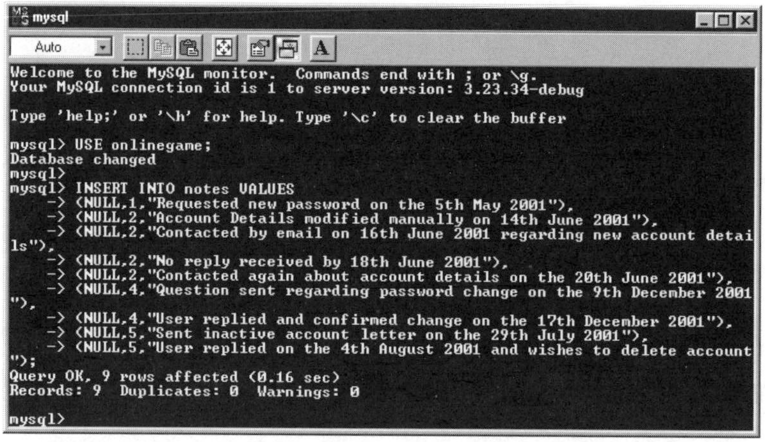

Now that we have the data entered, let's select all the information from the table and look at how it is organized. To select all the data we use the following command as before:

```
mysql> SELECT * FROM notes;
```

When we execute this command, the following will be visible on the MySQL console.

Figure 2-74

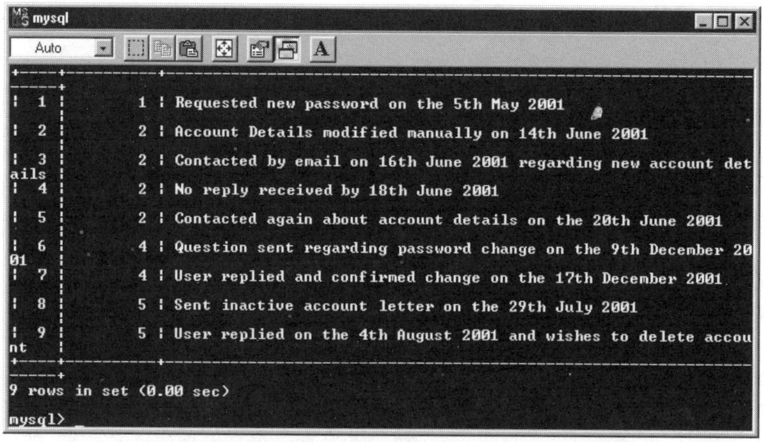

Because there is now more information, not everything is visible on the screen (i.e., the field headings are not visible), but all the information is still in our table. As you can see from the console output, every note has been assigned a unique ID that we can use at a later date to make modifications and also delete the note from a web browser and/or sockets (you will learn more about this in Chapter 5).

Now we will select a set of notes for a single player, as we did earlier with the payment information. Let's try to view all the notes related to Sally Rannor. First we must retrieve her unique ID number from the playerdata table and store it in a local variable. We do this with the following command:

```
mysql> SELECT @tempid:=id FROM playerdata WHERE name = "Sally Rannor";
```

When we execute this command, MySQL will return the value of Sally's ID number and also assign it to our local variable which we have specified here as tempid. Our expected output can be seen in the following figure.

Figure 2-75

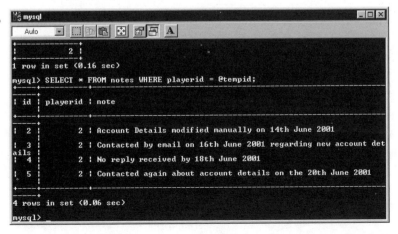

Now we know that Sally has a unique identification number of 2 and that this is stored in our tempid variable. Next, we use this as a parameter for a search on the playerid field in the notes table to retrieve all of the notes relating to player 2, which is Sally. Here is the command we use to acquire all the notes for Sally:

```
mysql> SELECT * FROM notes WHERE playerid = @tempid;
```

Now the console will display the four notes that relate to Sally. This can be seen in the following figure.

Figure 2-76

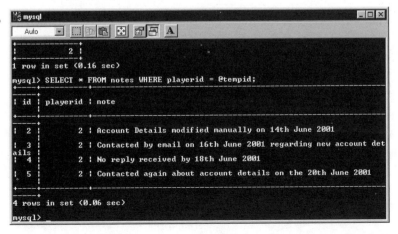

If, for example, you only wanted to get the note descriptions without the id and playerid information, you would use a slightly modified version of the command we used before. This time we specify the exact field, rather than the "*" wildcard we used before:

```
mysql> SELECT note FROM notes WHERE playerid = @tempid;
```

When we execute this command we should now only see the actual notes, without the extra information we selected before. Figure 2-77 shows the expected output from the MySQL console.

Figure 2-77

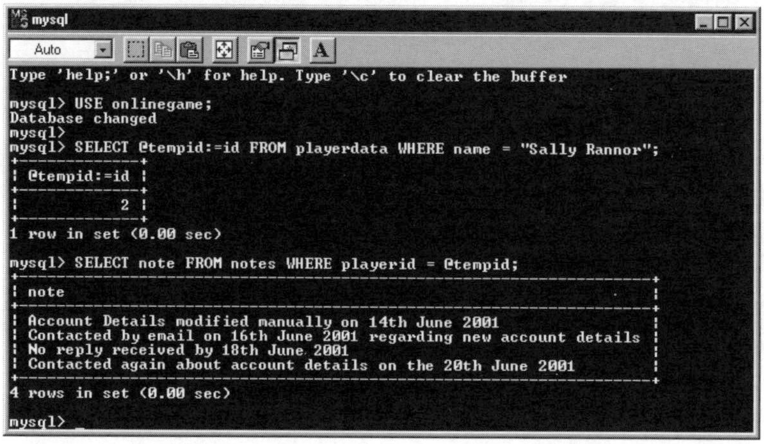

Finally, we will now use the relfriends and relenemies tables to relate players to their friends and enemies within the online game. Let's assume the players have friends and enemies as follows. (Note that the number after each player's name is his or her unique ID from the playerdata table.)

Andrew Smith (1)
    Friends
       Sally Rannor (2)
       Louise Jennings (4)
    Enemies
       Pete Dakkar (3)

Sally Rannor (2)
    Friends
       Andrew Smith (1)
       Louise Jennings (4)
       Fred Warran (5)
    Enemies
       [none]

Pete Dakkar (3)
   Friends
      Fred Warran (5)
   Enemies
      Andrew Smith (1)

Louise Jennings (4)
   Friends
      Andrew Smith (1)
      Sally Rannor (2)
   Enemies
      Fred Warran (5)

Fred Warran (5)
   Friends
      Sally Rannor (2)
      Pete Dakkar (3)
   Enemies
      Louise Jennings (4)

Now that we have our sample relations between the players, we can add them into our two relational tables. We use the Insert command twice, once for each of the relational tables. First, we will add the information into the relfriends table. Here is the command we use to accomplish this:

```
mysql> INSERT INTO relfriends VALUES
mysql> (NULL,1,2),
mysql> (NULL,1,4),
mysql> (NULL,2,1),
mysql> (NULL,2,4),
mysql> (NULL,2,5),
mysql> (NULL,3,5),
mysql> (NULL,4,1),
mysql> (NULL,4,2),
mysql> (NULL,5,2),
mysql> (NULL,5,3);
```

The first value is NULL so MySQL assigns the record a unique ID number (making it easier to modify at a later date), next we have the player's identification number, and finally, the ID number of the person with whom the player is friends. This looks as follows when we enter it into the MySQL console.

Figure 2-78

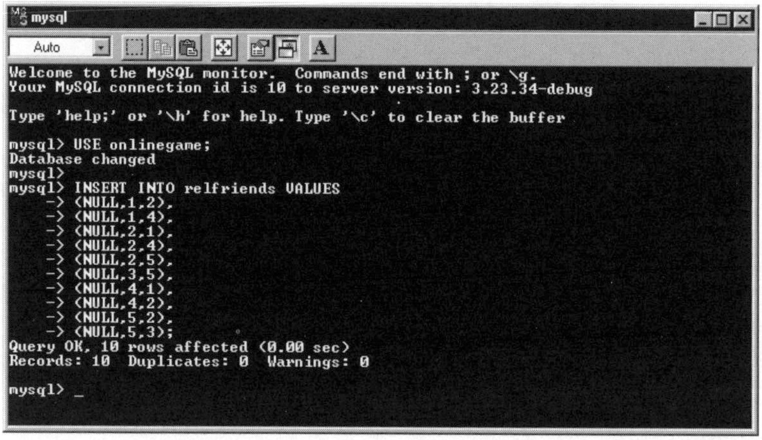

We can now view this information in the friends relational table using the Select command as we have done previously:

```
mysql> SELECT * FROM relfriends;
```

When we execute this command, we can now see a list of relations between the players and their friends' ID numbers. Figure 2-79 shows how this looks on the MySQL console.

Figure 2-79

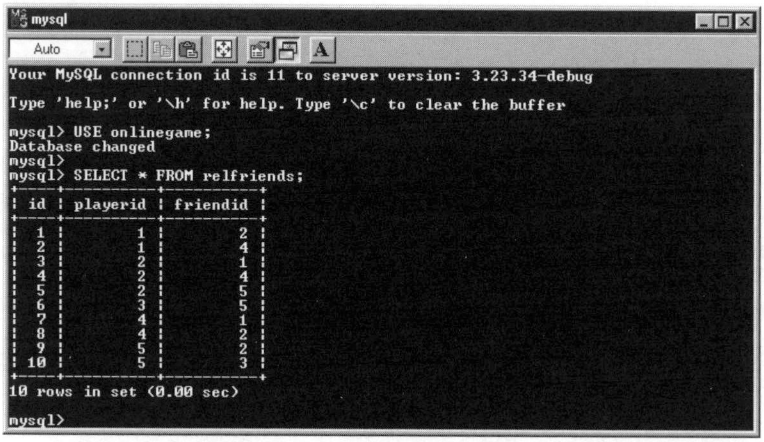

Before we try to manipulate this data, let's first add the data for the player's enemies into the enemies relational table, relenemies. Here is the command we use to add all the enemy relations into the database:

```
mysql> INSERT INTO relenemies VALUES
mysql> (NULL,1,3),
mysql> (NULL,3,1),
mysql> (NULL,4,5),
mysql> (NULL,5,4);
```

This data is very similar to the friends data. The only difference is the final number represents the enemy's unique ID rather than a friend's unique ID. When we enter and execute this data in the MySQL console, we should expect the following output.

Figure 2-80

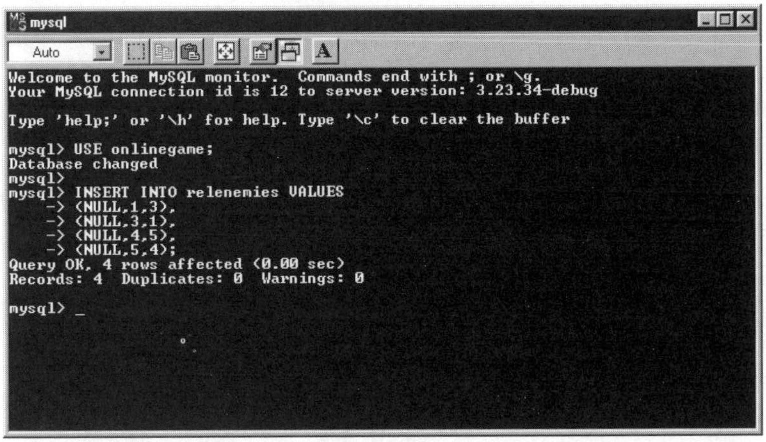

We can view the data we just added to the enemies relational table in the same way we viewed the friends information using the following command:

```
mysql> SELECT * FROM relenemies;
```

When we execute this command, the following output should be visible on the MySQL console.

Figure 2-81

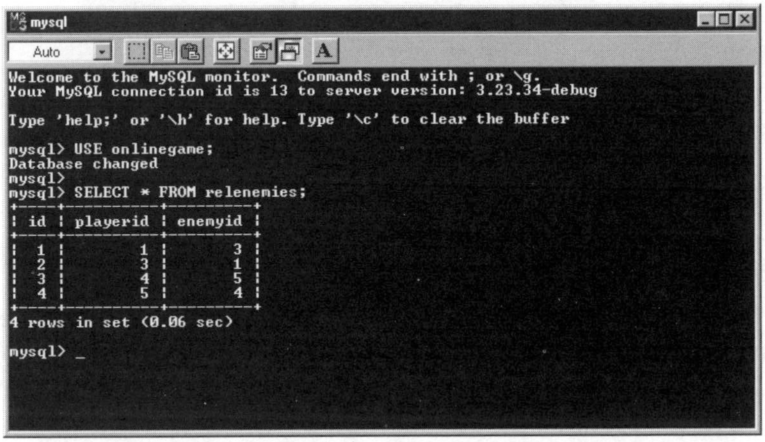

Manipulating the Friend and Enemy Relational Tables

Now that we have data in both our friend and enemy relational tables, we can now manipulate the data with ease, allowing fast and easy access to the information we require. Let's first try to find out all the names of Fred Warran's friends.

Our first task is to find out the unique ID number for Fred Warran. This is done by simply searching for his name in the playerdata table. We will also store the ID number in a local variable called tempid so we can use it in later searches. Here is the command we must use to retrieve his ID number:

```
mysql> SELECT @tempid:=id FROM playerdata WHERE name = "Fred Warran";
```

As you can see in Figure 2-82, MySQL has returned the ID number 5 and also assigned it to our local variable tempid. We now have the correct ID number for the player.

Figure 2-82

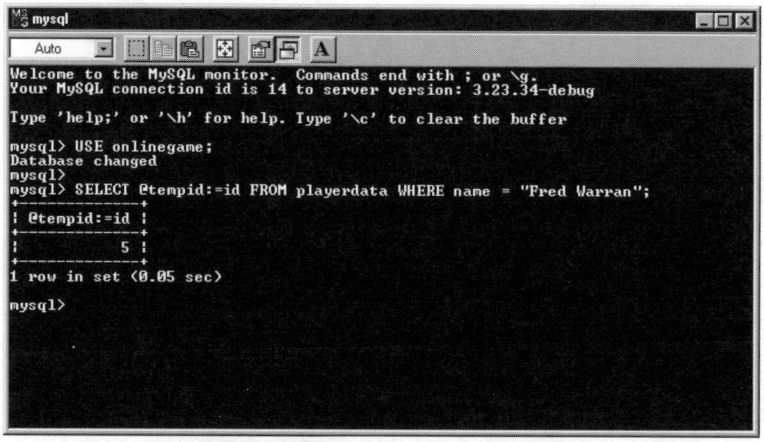

Next, we use the ID number we obtained from the previous search and use it as a parameter for the playerid field when we search in the relfriends table. Here is our command to find the unique identification numbers of Fred Warran's friends:

```
mysql> SELECT friendid FROM relfriends WHERE playerid = @tempid;
```

When we execute this command, MySQL will give us the ID numbers of all of Fred's friends. Figure 2-83 shows the expected output from the console.

Figure 2-83

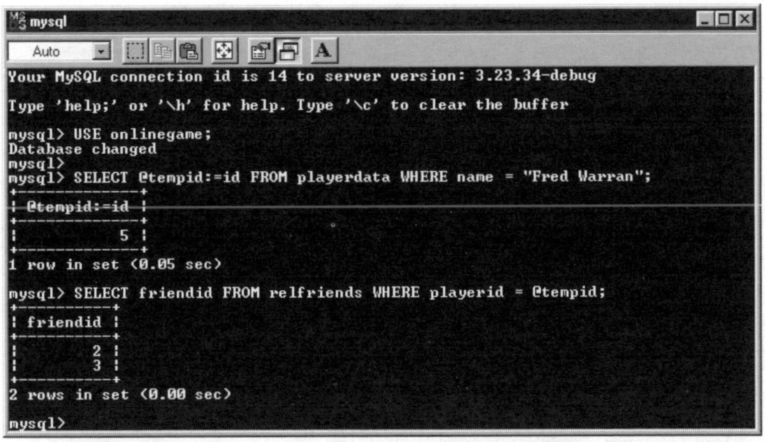

Now we know that Fred has two friends and their unique ID numbers are 2 and 3. We can now use this information to retrieve the names of his two friends from the playerdata table. We simply enter the friendids into parameters of our search (this can be simplified when using Perl and sockets to access MySQL). Here is the command we use to get the names of Fred's friends:

```
mysql> SELECT name FROM playerdata WHERE id = 2 OR id = 3;
```

When we execute this command, MySQL will return the names of the two friends. This can be seen in Figure 2-84.

Figure 2-84

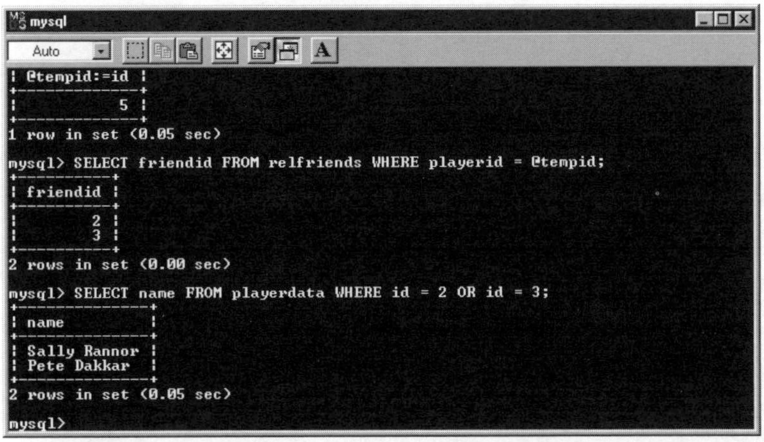

Finding out the enemies of a player can be done in exactly the same way as finding the friends for a player. Let's now try and get a list of the names of Pete Dakkar's enemies.

First we must find out Pete's unique ID number from the playerdata table and store it in a local variable. We do this with the following command:

```
mysql> SELECT @tempid:=id FROM playerdata WHERE name = "Pete Dakkar";
```

When we execute this command, the unique identification number will be stored in the local variable tempid as we specified in the command. The expected output is shown in the following figure.

Figure 2-85

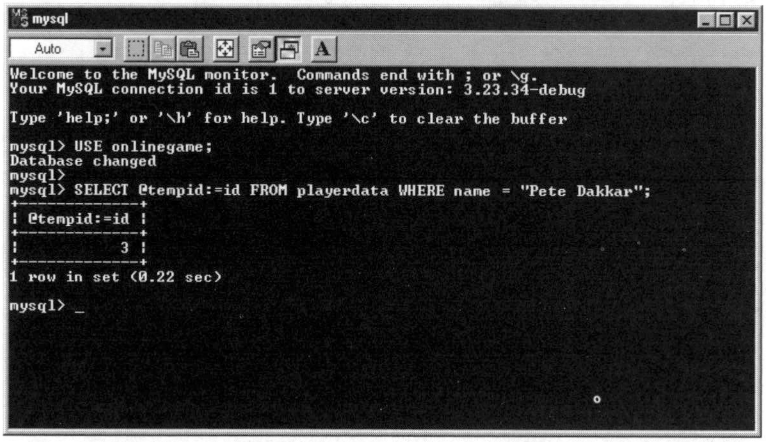

From this, we now know that Pete's identification number is 3; therefore, we can do a search on the playerid field in the relenemies table and retrieve all the ID numbers for the players that Pete is enemies with. Since Pete's ID number is stored in our local variable tempid, we use this instead of the number 3 directly. Here is our command to get the ID numbers of the enemies:

```
mysql> SELECT enemyid FROM relenemies WHERE playerid = @tempid;
```

Here is our expected output from the MySQL console when we execute this command.

Figure 2-86

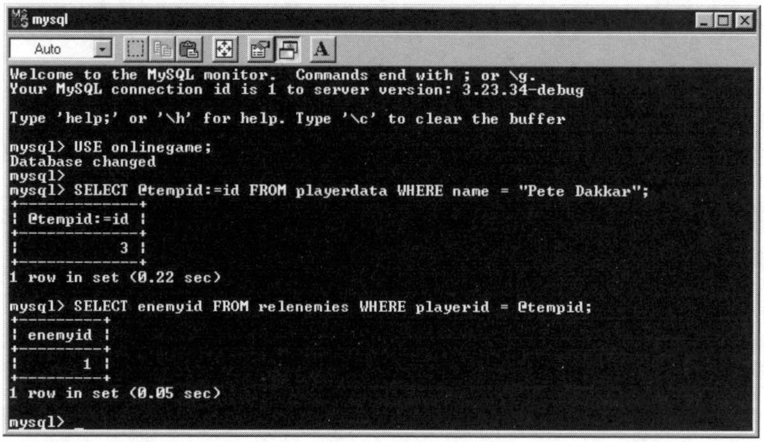

From this output, we can deduce that Pete Dakkar has a single enemy and that enemy's unique identification number is 1. We can now find the name of this enemy by doing a final search on the playerdata table using the enemy's ID number as our parameter. Here is the command we use to retrieve the name:

```
mysql> SELECT name FROM playerdata WHERE id = 1;
```

When we execute this command, we expect the following output from MySQL.

Figure 2-87

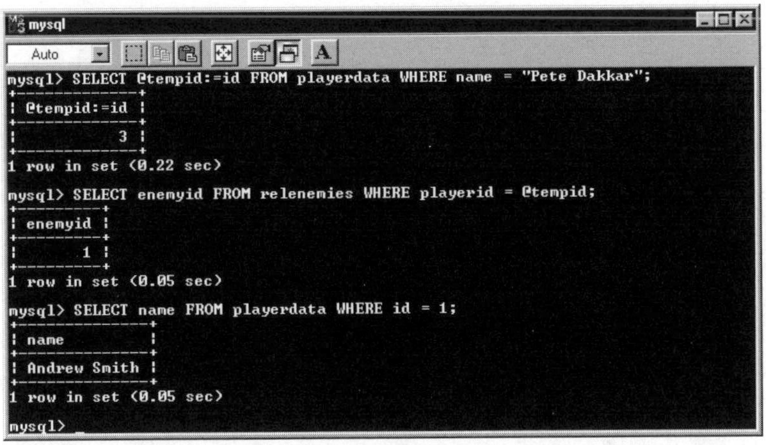

As you can see from the preceding figure, MySQL has returned the name Andrew Smith, which is what we originally entered into the database as an enemy for Pete Dakkar.

This concludes this section on relational databases. We will be using this method to create and use databases in the next chapter on Perl and in our tutorial game later in the book.

Other Methods of Data Input

Here we will discuss other ways to enter data into your MySQL database. This can be very useful if you have a database in another system, and wish to transfer it over to MySQL without having to type in all the data manually.

Text File Input

The easiest way to enter data from a simple text file is to just place a tab after each field of data, with a return at the end of a record. For example, let's create a file called players.txt in Windows Notepad (or another basic text editor) to add a few more players into our playerdata table in the relational database. Note that if you wish to place a NULL value in a column, you must type "\N", without the quotes. Here is how our text file would look for five new entries.

Figure 2-88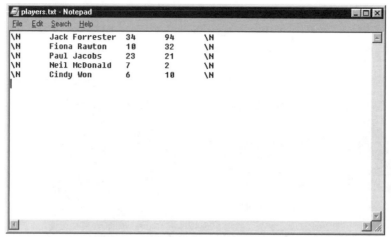

Note that the white space between each entry in the file is a single tab space and you also need an extra tab space at the end of each record (before the return).

Now save the file in the MySQL bin directory to make the file easy to find when we attempt to add the data into our playerdata table. The command we now use to add the records from the file into our playerdata table is as follows:

```
mysql> LOAD DATA LOCAL INFILE "players.txt" INTO TABLE playerdata;
```

When we enter and execute this in the MySQL console, we expect to see the following output.

Figure 2-89

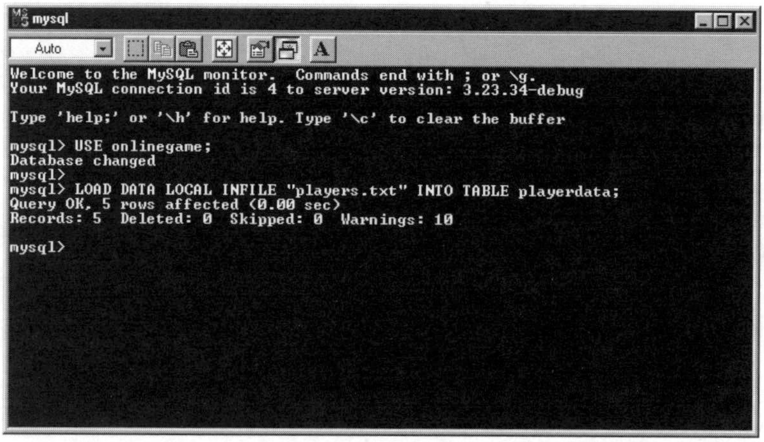

From this, we can see that five records have been added to our database. We can now view these new records by selecting all the information, ordered by the ID number, from the playerdata table using the following command:

```
mysql> SELECT * FROM playerdata ORDER BY id;
```

Here is our expected output from the MySQL console after we execute the preceding command.

Figure 2-90

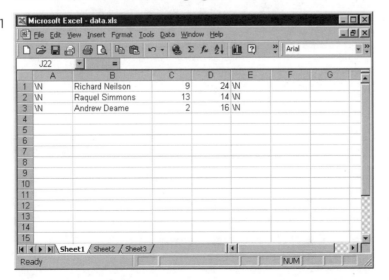

```
Your MySQL connection id is 10 to server version: 3.23.34-debug

Type 'help;' or '\h' for help. Type '\c' to clear the buffer

mysql> USE onlinegame;
Database changed
mysql>
mysql> SELECT * FROM playerdata ORDER BY id;
+----+----------------+------+------+----------------+
| id | name           | xpos | ypos | lastlogin      |
+----+----------------+------+------+----------------+
|  1 | Andrew Smith   |   12 |   23 | 20010523000000 |
|  2 | Sally Rannor   |   17 |    9 | 20010614000000 |
|  3 | Pete Dakkar    |    5 |   31 | 20001201000000 |
|  4 | Louise Jennings|   17 |   14 | 20010119000000 |
|  5 | Fred Warran    |    9 |    5 | 20010712000000 |
|  6 | Jack Forrester |   34 |   94 | 20010530233623 |
|  7 | Fiona Rawton   |   10 |   32 | 20010530233639 |
|  8 | Paul Jacobs    |   23 |   21 | 20010530233653 |
|  9 | Neil McDonald  |    7 |    2 | 20010530233710 |
| 10 | Cindy Won      |    6 |   10 | 20010530233723 |
+----+----------------+------+------+----------------+
10 rows in set (0.06 sec)

mysql>
```

As you can see, the data from our players.txt text file has been added into our database correctly.

Native Database Input

A good way of entering data is to use a program such as Microsoft Excel to enter all your data. You then export the file as a tab-delimited text file and you can load it in the same way we did in the previous example. Let's now try to add another three names into the playerdata table from a Microsoft Excel spreadsheet.

First we create a blank spreadsheet and enter values into the fields so the sheet looks like the following figure.

Figure 2-91

Once our data is entered into the spreadsheet, we then wish to save the file as a tab-delimited text file. To do this, go to File, Save As... from the main menu in Excel. When the save dialog appears, type in the filename as data and set it to save in the MySQL bin directory.

Figure 2-92

If we now examine this file, we will see that it is in the same format as the basic text file we created in the first example. Here is how the text file Excel saved looks in Notepad.

Figure 2-93

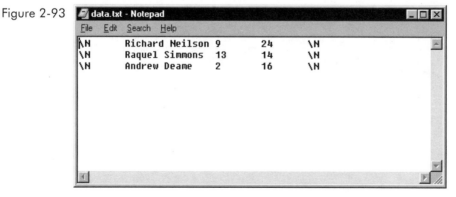

We can then input this data using exactly the same function we did in the first example; the only difference is the filename. Here is the command we use to enter this new data into our playerdata table:

```
mysql> LOAD DATA LOCAL INFILE "data.txt" INTO TABLE playerdata;
```

When we execute this command, the three new entries will be added to the table the same way as in the previous example.

There are also other methods of loading in different formatted data, such as comma-separated values, although this is beyond the scope of this book. If you need more information on this, see the MySQL manual, which comes with the MySQL package and is also available at http://www.mysql.com.

Backup and Restoration of Databases

Now we will learn how to back up and restore our database. As with all data, it is important to make regular backups since data can easily be lost or corrupted. Backing up and restoring data is not difficult and can be accomplished with just a few simple commands.

Backup

Backing up your database is an important task in case of hardware or software failure. It is relatively easy to back up your entire database to a single file and store it on a floppy disk or CD-ROM (depending on the size of the database). To back up a database in MySQL, we use a utility called mysqldump. This utility writes all the information on how to re-create the database and also all the information that is stored in the database to a single text file, which can be used to restore the database with ease.

Let's now try to back up our onlinegame database, which we created in the last section.

If you are using Windows, you need to open the MS-DOS prompt. To do this, click the Start button and select the Run... option. Then type command into the text box and click OK. You will now see an MS-DOS window on the screen. From there, you need to switch to the MySQL bin directory. To do this type the following (or change it depending on where you installed MySQL):

```
cd c:\mysql\bin
```

If you are using Linux, simply change to the bin directory of the MySQL directory.

Next, we need to execute the mysqldump command, specifying what we want to back up and also the filename we want to back up the database to. Here is the command we use to back up our onlinegame database to a file called backup.sql:

```
prompt> mysqldump onlinegame > backup.sql
```

After the utility name, we first specify the name of the database, which in this case is onlinegame. We then add the greater than symbol to tell it to output the data to the following file, which in this example is backup.sql.

Here is how our backup.sql file looks once it has been created.

```
#---------------------------------------------------------
# Server version       3.23.34-debug

#
# Table structure for table 'notes'
#

CREATE TABLE notes (
  id int(11) NOT NULL auto_increment,
  playerid int(11) default NULL,
  note varchar(255) default NULL,
  PRIMARY KEY  (id)
) TYPE=MyISAM;

#
# Dumping data for table 'notes'
#

INSERT INTO notes VALUES (1,1,'Requested new password on the 5th May 2001');
INSERT INTO notes VALUES (2,2,'Account Details modified manually on 14th June
2001');
INSERT INTO notes VALUES (3,2,'Contacted by email on 16th June 2001 regarding new
account details');
INSERT INTO notes VALUES (4,2,'No reply received by 18th June 2001');
INSERT INTO notes VALUES (5,2,'Contacted again about account details on the 20th
June 2001');
INSERT INTO notes VALUES (6,4,'Question sent regarding password change on the 9th
December 2001');
INSERT INTO notes VALUES (7,4,'User replied and confirmed change on the 17th
December 2001');
INSERT INTO notes VALUES (8,5,'Sent inactive account letter on the 29th July 2001');
INSERT INTO notes VALUES (9,5,'User replied on the 4th August 2001 and wishes to
delete account');

#
# Table structure for table 'paymentinfo'
#

CREATE TABLE paymentinfo (
  id int(11) NOT NULL auto_increment,
  playerid int(11) default NULL,
  datepaid timestamp(14) NOT NULL,
  type varchar(100) default NULL,
  amount int(11) default NULL,
  PRIMARY KEY  (id)
```

```
) TYPE=MyISAM;

#
# Dumping data for table 'paymentinfo'
#

INSERT INTO paymentinfo VALUES (1,2,20010101000000,'Cheque',300);
INSERT INTO paymentinfo VALUES (2,2,20010201000000,'Visa',150);
INSERT INTO paymentinfo VALUES (3,2,20010301000000,'Visa',150);
INSERT INTO paymentinfo VALUES (4,4,20010101000000,'MasterCard',300);
INSERT INTO paymentinfo VALUES (5,4,20010201000000,'MasterCard',450);

#
# Table structure for table 'playerdata'
#

CREATE TABLE playerdata (
  id int(11) NOT NULL auto_increment,
  name varchar(50) default NULL,
  xpos int(11) default NULL,
  ypos int(11) default NULL,
  lastlogin timestamp(14) NOT NULL,
  PRIMARY KEY  (id)
) TYPE=MyISAM;

#
# Dumping data for table 'playerdata'
#

INSERT INTO playerdata VALUES (1,'Andrew Smith',12,23,20010523000000);
INSERT INTO playerdata VALUES (2,'Sally Rannor',17,9,20010614000000);
INSERT INTO playerdata VALUES (3,'Pete Dakkar',5,31,20001201000000);
INSERT INTO playerdata VALUES (4,'Louise Jennings',17,14,20010119000000);
INSERT INTO playerdata VALUES (11,'Fred Warran',9,5,20010531000516);
INSERT INTO playerdata VALUES (14,'Andrew Deame',2,16,00000000000000);
INSERT INTO playerdata VALUES (13,'Raquel Simmons',13,14,00000000000000);
INSERT INTO playerdata VALUES (12,'Richard Neilson',9,24,00000000000000);
INSERT INTO playerdata VALUES (10,'Cindy Won',6,10,20010530233723);
INSERT INTO playerdata VALUES (9,'Neil McDonald',7,2,20010530233710);
INSERT INTO playerdata VALUES (8,'Paul Jacobs',23,21,20010530233653);
INSERT INTO playerdata VALUES (7,'Fiona Rawton',10,32,20010530233639);
INSERT INTO playerdata VALUES (6,'Jack Forrester',34,94,20010530233623);

#
# Table structure for table 'relenemies'
#
```

CHAPTER 2

```
CREATE TABLE relenemies (
  id int(11) NOT NULL auto_increment,
  playerid int(11) default NULL,
  enemyid int(11) default NULL,
  PRIMARY KEY  (id)
) TYPE=MyISAM;

#
# Dumping data for table 'relenemies'
#

INSERT INTO relenemies VALUES (1,1,3);
INSERT INTO relenemies VALUES (2,3,1);
INSERT INTO relenemies VALUES (3,4,5);
INSERT INTO relenemies VALUES (4,5,4);

#
# Table structure for table 'relfriends'
#

CREATE TABLE relfriends (
  id int(11) NOT NULL auto_increment,
  playerid int(11) default NULL,
  friendid int(11) default NULL,
  PRIMARY KEY  (id)
) TYPE=MyISAM;

#
# Dumping data for table 'relfriends'
#

INSERT INTO relfriends VALUES (1,1,2);
INSERT INTO relfriends VALUES (2,1,4);
INSERT INTO relfriends VALUES (3,2,1);
INSERT INTO relfriends VALUES (4,2,4);
INSERT INTO relfriends VALUES (5,2,5);
INSERT INTO relfriends VALUES (6,3,5);
INSERT INTO relfriends VALUES (7,4,1);
INSERT INTO relfriends VALUES (8,4,2);
INSERT INTO relfriends VALUES (9,5,2);
INSERT INTO relfriends VALUES (10,5,3);
```

Basically, the file is a batch of commands that MySQL must follow to re-create the database exactly how it was before. The backup file first tells MySQL how to create the table to store the data, then it tells it what data to insert into the table. It then repeats this process for the entire database.

This backup.sql file can then be transferred to another MySQL system, or simply backed up in a safe place.

Restoration

To restore a database, we must first have a single file that was created using the mysqldump utility, which was explained in the previous section. To explain the retoration process, we will use the backup.sql file that we created in the preceding section.

First, we will delete the onlinegame database so we can attempt to restore it from our backup file. To delete the database we use the following command:

```
mysql> DROP DATABASE onlinegame;
```

When this command is executed, the database will be completely removed from the MySQL system. We can ensure that it is gone by executing the following command:

```
mysql> SHOW DATABASES;
```

When we execute this command, notice that only the mysql and test databases are on the system, meaning that the onlinegame database was deleted correctly. Here is our expected output from the console.

Figure 2-94

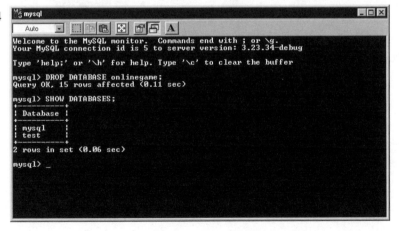

Next, we must create an empty database to restore our backup into. Let's call this new database gamedata. To create this empty, new database we use the following command:

```
mysql> CREATE DATABASE gamedata;
```

This creates our empty database so that when we run the Show Databases command again, this new database will also be listed.

Now we need to exit out of mysql and go to the MySQL bin directory in MS-DOS or Linux, whichever system we are using. To import the data, we simply use the mysql executable, but we add a couple of parameters onto the end so it knows that it must import data into the specified database.

Here is how we restore the onlinegame database from the backup.sql file into our new gamedata database:

```
prompt> mysql gamedata < backup.sql
```

Here is how this command looks in the MS-DOS window.

Figure 2-95

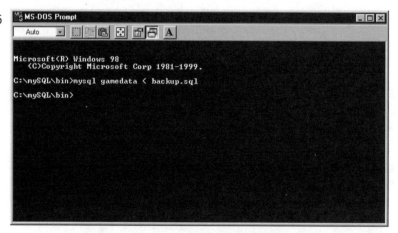

Now our database is fully restored into the gamedata database. Let's check this by attempting to select all the data from the playerdata table. Here is the command we use in the MySQL console to select all the information in the paymentinfo table. (Remember, we must also use the gamedata database.)

```
mysql> SELECT * FROM paymentinfo;
```

When we execute this in the console, notice that all of our original data is now back in the table, in the new database. You can see the expected output in the following figure.

From this we can deduce that the database was restored successfully. If you try selecting the information in the other tables, you will find that all the data is back in place.

Figure 2-96

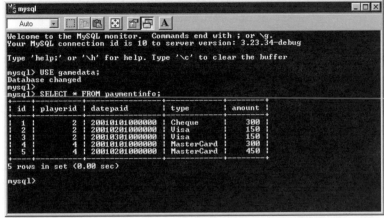

MySQL C++ Interface

The C++ interface for MySQL, MySQL++, gives the database system a practical use from a game developer's point of view. It allows access to a MySQL database via the IP address in which the database is stored. This means data can be easily retrieved and updated from our database within our server applications.

First, you need to either download the zip file mysql++-1.7.1-win32-vc++.zip from http://www.mysql.com/Downloads/mysql++/ or copy the MySQL++ Libraries from the companion CD.

When you extract the libraries with a utility such as Winzip (a trial version is available on the companion CD and also at http://www.winzip.com), you will notice that the library is structured as follows.

Figure 2-97

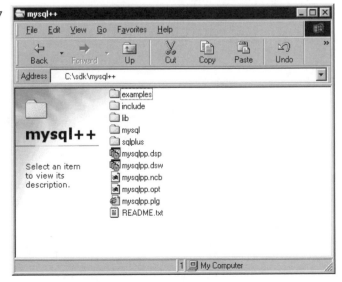

Once extracted, you must then include the lib and include directories in Visual Studio 6.

In addition, you must include the lib and include directories from the MySQL directory. Setting up and using static libraries (such as MySQL++) is explained in detail in Chapter 1. Once the library has been set up, we can then use it to write an application to retrieve data from a database that is stored in mysql.

Let's create a simple console application so we can understand the basics of how to access, retrieve, and update information in a database from a C++ application.

Remember to include the mysql++.lib in your project settings (see Chapter 1 for more details on how to do this). You must also copy the libmySQL.dll from the mySQL++ libraries example directory into your applications directory (or the Windows/system directory) in order for your application to execute correctly.

Example 1 — Connecting and Retrieving Data from MySQL

Here is the C++ code we need to connect to our gamedata database and list all the information from our paymentinfo table. After the code listing we will explain each segment of the code.

```cpp
#include <iostream>
#include <iomanip>
#include <mysql++>

int main(void)
{
    // -> Create a connection to the database
    Connection con("gamedata","127.0.0.1");

    // -> Create a query object that is bound to our connection
    Query query = con.query();

    // -> Assign the query to that object
    query << "SELECT * FROM paymentinfo";

    // -> Store the results from then query
    Result res = query.store();

    // -> Display the results to the console


    // -> Show the Field Headings
    cout.setf(ios::left);
    cout << setw(6) << "id"
         << setw(10)  << "playerid"
```

```
                    << setw(20)  << "datepaid"
                    << setw(20)  << "type"
                    << setw(20)  << "amount"   << endl;

        Result::iterator i;
        Row row;
        // The Result class has a read-only Random Access Iterator
        for (i = res.begin(); i != res.end(); i++)
        {
            row = *i;
            cout << setw(6) << row["id"]
          << setw(10)  << row["playerid"]
          << setw(20)  << row["datepaid"]
          << setw(20)  << row["type"]
          << setw(20)  << row["amount"]   << endl;
        }

        return 1;
    }
```

In the code, we first create a connection to the server the database is stored on. We use the following code segment to achieve this:

```
Connection con("gamedata","127.0.0.1");
```

Connection is simply a class whose constructor takes in the parameters to establish a connection to a MySQL database. The first parameter is the name of the database to which you wish to connect. The second is the IP address of the server on which the database is located. Notice here that the IP address is 127.0.0.1; this is a special IP address that represents the local machine, i.e., the machine on which the C++ application is running.

Next, we create a query object to allow us to pass queries into the connection we have established with the database. This is done with the following code segment:

```
Query query = con.query();
```

We can now use any standard MySQL query that we have used in the MySQL console with this query variable. We process a query using the following code:

```
query << "SELECT * FROM paymentinfo";
```

This code does the same as selecting all the information in the paymentinfo table in the MySQL console.

Next, we store the results from the query in a Result class, which contains a random access iterator for cycling through all the records of data that the query returned. Here is how we assign the query results into the Result class:

```
Result res = query.store();
```

Next, we print the field headings to the screen; this is not essential, but it makes the output data easier to understand.

Now that we have the results in the Result class, we can use the iterator to cycle through all the records that the query returned. We declare the iterator as i in the following code:

```
Result::iterator i;
```

Then we also want to create a Row class, which will hold each record of data as we cycle through the records with the iterator. We create the Row class as follows:

```
Row row;
```

Finally, we cycle through the data, outputting each record to the screen on a new line. We declare which field we wish to print from the current result by accessing the correct part of the row class as follows:

```
row["fieldname"];
```

Following is the code we use to cycle through each record contained in the Result class:

```
for (i = res.begin(); i != res.end(); i++)
{
    row = *i;
}
```

Each time through the loop, the current record is assigned to the Row class so we can access individual fields from each record.

Therefore, we can print each record using the following code within the For loop:

```
cout << setw(6)      << row["id"]
     << setw(10)     << row["playerid"]
     << setw(20)     << row["datepaid"]
     << setw(20)     << row["type"]
     << setw(20)     << row["amount"]   << endl;
```

Figure 2-98 shows the expected output from our C++ application.

Figure 2-98

Example 2 — Updating Data in MySQL from an Application

In this example, we will modify a field of data from our paymentinfo table in the gamedata database. First, we will display the field, then change the value, and then display the field again so we can check that the data has been updated.

We are going to change the payment with an ID number of 4. Instead of the payment type being MasterCard, we now wish it to be American Express. Here is the code for the C++ console application we require to do this. After the code, we explain how it works.

```cpp
#include <iostream>
#include <iomanip>
#include <mysql++>

int main(void)
{
    // -> Create a connection to the database
    Connection con("gamedata","127.0.0.1");

    // -> Create a query object that is bound to our connection
    Query query = con.query();

//// DISPLAY BEFORE UPDATE

    // -> Assign the query to that object
    query << "SELECT * FROM paymentinfo WHERE id = 4";

    // -> Store the results from then query
    Result res = query.store();

    // -> Display the results to the console
```

```
cout << "Before Update" << endl;
cout << "---------------" << endl;
// -> Show the Field Headings
cout.setf(ios::left);
cout << setw(6)  << "id"
     << setw(10) << "playerid"
     << setw(20) << "datepaid"
     << setw(20) << "type"
     << setw(20) << "amount"   << endl;

Result::iterator i;
Row row;
// The Result class has a read-only Random Access Iterator
for (i = res.begin(); i != res.end(); i++)
{
    row = *i;
    cout << setw(6)  << row["id"]
         << setw(10) << row["playerid"]
         << setw(20) << row["datepaid"]
         << setw(20) << row["type"]
         << setw(20) << row["amount"]   << endl;
}


//// UPDATE THE INFORMATION

    // Send an execute an update query in MySQL
    query << "UPDATE paymentinfo SET type = \'American Express\'
        WHERE id = 4";
    query.execute();

//// DISPLAY AFTER UPDATE

    // -> Assign the query to that object
    query << "SELECT * FROM paymentinfo WHERE id = 4";

    // -> Store the results from then query
    res = query.store();

    // -> Display the results to the console
    cout << endl << endl;
    cout << "After Update" << endl;
    cout << "------------" << endl;

    // -> Show the Field Headings
    cout.setf(ios::left);
    cout << setw(6) << "id"
```

```
                    << setw(10)   << "playerid"
                    << setw(20)   << "datepaid"
                    << setw(20)   << "type"
                    << setw(20)   << "amount"    << endl;

        // The Result class has a read-only Random Access Iterator
        for (i = res.begin(); i != res.end(); i++)
        {
            row = *i;
            cout << setw(6) << row["id"]
                 << setw(10)   << row["playerid"]
                 << setw(20)   << row["datepaid"]
                 << setw(20)   << row["type"]
                 << setw(20)   << row["amount"]    << endl;
        }

        return 1;
    }
```

The only major difference in this code is the small segment of code in the middle that updates the field in the paymentinfo table. The code before and after that simply displays the record from the table that we are modifying (in the same way as the last example).

Let's look at the middle segment to see how it works.

First, we set the query to what we want it to be, just as we would enter it in the MySQL console. Notice that we require escape characters (\) before and after the string in the query.

```
query << "UPDATE paymentinfo SET type = \'American Express\' WHERE id = 4";
```

Once we have our query set, we then need to execute the query using the following command.

```
query.execute();
```

We did not require this command before because the Store command that we used to store the results in the Result class automatically executed the query.

When we then execute the application, you will see the values of the record before and after we update the data. Figure 2-99 on the following page shows the output from our application.

As you can see, the type field has been changed successfully from MasterCard to American Express as we intended.

Figure 2-99

Summary

In this chapter, you learned how to create and use a MySQL database from both the MySQL console and a C++ application. In the next chapter, we move on to using the Perl language and integrating a MySQL database with a web site, so that we can display statistics for an online game and manage a game server remotely via the Internet.

Chapter 3

Communicating with the Internet

Introduction

In this chapter, you learn how to use the programming language Perl to access your game data from the Internet so it can be viewed and managed directly from your web browser. First, we will cover the basics of the Perl language. Then, after we have mastered the basics we will look at how to utilize MySQL effectively from within Perl using the Perl Database Interface (DBI) module.

Perl comes as part of the standard install on most Linux packages. To use Perl, you must ensure that you have a cgi-bin set up on your web server. If you do not have this, contact your Internet service provider and ask them to set one up for you. Alternatively, if you are running your own web server, take a look at http://www.perl.com/pub for more information.

Getting Started

First, we are going to look at how to get simple text output to your web browser. For all our programs, we are going to use a helpful Perl library called cgi-lib. In addition to making output a little easier, this library is great for processing information from forms on web pages.

We now need to download this library from http://cgi-lib.stanford.edu/cgi-lib/ or simply copy it off the CD-ROM supplied with this book and upload it (in ASCII mode) to our web server, into the cgi-bin. Once uploaded, we then need to set the permissions for the cgi-lib.pl file to 755.

NOTE File permissions on Linux are assigned for owners, groups, and others. For each of the three, we can specify whether they can read, write, or execute the file. Each number of the triplet represents what permission is granted to each of the three groups of users (owners, groups, others). The following numbers represent the permissions that can be assigned to files.

    READ – 1
    WRITE – 2
    EXECUTE – 4

Therefore, by adding the numbers, we can generate a permission based on the three options in a single number. For example, if we wish to have a write and execute permission but no read, we would use the number 6 (i.e., 2+4). So when we use 755 as the permission, it means the owner of the file has full read, write, and execute access, but groups and other users can only read and execute the file (i.e., 1+4 = 5).

TIP You can find an evaluation version of a Windows-based FTP program on the companion CD-ROM that will allow you to upload your Perl scripts to your web server.

A good editor for Perl scripts is Windows Notepad, as they must be saved with no formatting, i.e., in plaintext format.

Our first script will simply display the words Hello World in our browser window. Let's now have a look at the Perl script we require to do this:

```
#!/usr/bin/perl
require "cgi-lib.pl";

print &PrintHeader;
print "Hello World!";
```

That is all there is to it — four lines of code. Let's look at them individually.

The first line allows the server to find Perl. This location is quite standard, although some Perl installations can be in other locations. If you are unsure, either ask your Internet service provider where it is located, or if you have access to Telnet, use the following command to determine its location:

```
Prompt> whereis perl
```

This will show all locations on the web server in which Perl is located.

Next, we Require the cgi-lib library. This works in a similar way to including files in C/C++, except all the code is contained in a single script (not a header and source file).

Then we call a function from the cgi-lib library that outputs information to the browser so that it accepts HTML.

Finally, we have a simple print statement to output the text we require to the browser.

We will save this file as hello.pl. When we now access this script from a web browser we will be able to see the following output.

Figure 3-1

Debugging Perl

As everyone makes mistakes, it is a good idea to know how to find your mistakes easily. If there is a problem with your Perl script and you try to execute it, the following screen will be visible in the web browser.

Figure 3-2

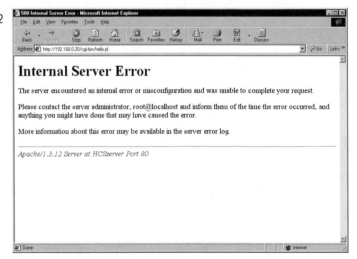

Indeed, this screen is of no help to us. It just notifies us that a problem occurred when trying to execute the Perl script. The first thing to check is that the script was uploaded to the server in ASCII format. If the script was uploaded as a binary, this error will occur. If that was not the problem, try to browse over the script for obvious mistakes such as semicolons missing from the end of lines and other such mistakes.

If that fails, then you can execute the script manually from the server. First, change to the directory you uploaded the script to and type the following command on the server, replacing "script.pl" with the script you are trying to correct:

```
Prompt> perl script.pl
```

Note that this is not always helpful, but it is better than an internal server error message!

More Text Output Routines

Let's now make a small modification to this first script so that it will print the text ten times, instead of just once. To do this, all we have to do is add a simple For loop around the text as can be seen in the following updated code:

```perl
#!/usr/bin/perl
require "cgi-lib.pl";

print &PrintHeader;

for($i=0;$i<10;$i++)
{
    print "Hello World!<BR>";
}
```

As you can see in the preceding code, we have added two new items. The first is the For loop, which loops ten times before it terminates. The second is the <BR> after the "Hello World!" text. When we print information to the browser, we are actually printing HTML; therefore, we can use any HTML tags within the print statement. In the next script, we will cover how to print chunks of HTML with ease. We will save this updated script as hello2.pl. Once we upload and call the script from our web browser, we can expect the following output.

Figure 3-3

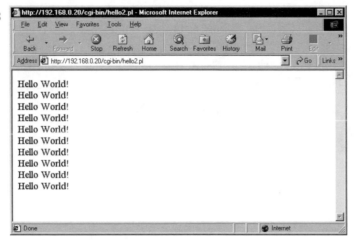

Now let's look at a useful way of printing segments of HTML to the browser. To print a segment of HTML, we tell the print statement to output everything after it until it reaches a statement that marks the end of the printing. Let's look at the following code that shows this in action:

```perl
#!/usr/bin/perl
require "cgi-lib.pl";

print &PrintHeader;

print<<ENDOFCHUNK;

<HTML>
 <TITLE>Perl Generated Page
 </TITLE>

 <BODY>
  <CENTER>This is a chunk of HTML that we want to print from a perl script.</CENTER>
  <BR>
  <CENTER>
   <FONT color="red">
    By using this variation of the 'print' command, we can easily print areas of
    HTML to the web browser from our Perl Script.
   </FONT>
  </CENTER>
 </BODY>
</HTML>

ENDOFCHUNK
```

In this code, the print<<ENDOFCHUNK; statement tells Perl to output everything to the browser after that point until it reaches the keyword EndOfChunk. We do not have to use EndOfChunk; this keyword can be anything we desire.

We will call this Perl script chunk.pl. Here is our expected output when we access it from the web browser.

Figure 3-4

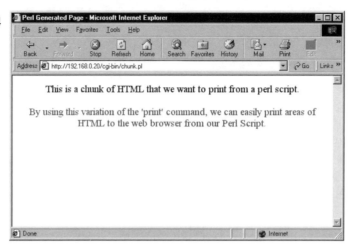

Using Files and Templates

Using files makes it easy for us to store and retrieve data from the web server. We can simply write information we wish to record to files on the server via a Perl script, then retrieve the data at a later date from the same or another Perl script. Also by utilizing templates, we can easily customize the way we output our data by editing simple HTML header and footer pages which are added above and below, respectively, to all our outputted data from our Perl script.

Reading in a Text File

In Perl, it is possible to write and read files from the server. First, we'll discover how to load a simple text file that is stored on the server and display the contents to the web browser. Let's now create a text file in Notepad called myfile.txt that contains the following text:

"This is a short paragraph stored in a file. By using the file operations in Perl, it is easy to load in this file and display it in a web browser."

Save this file and upload it to the cgi-bin on the web server (in the same location as your Perl scripts). Now that our file is on the server, let's make the script that will load it and display it to the web browser. Here is the script we require to do this:

```perl
#!/usr/bin/perl
require "cgi-lib.pl";

print &PrintHeader;

open(FILE_HANDLE, "<myfile.txt");
@FileData = <FILE_HANDLE>;
close(FILE_HANDLE);

foreach $line (@FileData)
{
    print $line
}
```

First, we open the file with the following command:

```perl
open(FILE_HANDLE, "<myfile.txt");
```

This command opens the file myfile.txt for reading (this is what the less than (<) sign signifies; if we wanted to write to the file, we would use the greater than (>) sign instead) and assigns it to the identifier FILE_HANDLE. Note that we can change FILE_HANDLE to anything we desire.

Once our file is open, we then assign the whole file to an array called FileData with the following command:

```perl
@FileData = <FILE_HANDLE>;
```

Now that we have the contents of the file in an array, we no longer require the file so we can close it with the following command:

```perl
close(FILE_HANDLE);
```

Notice here that we specify the identifier FILE_HANDLE so it knows which file we wish to close.

With all the data in our array, we can cycle through each line of the array and then print each line to the browser with the final segment of the code:

```perl
foreach $line (@FileData)
{
    print $line
}
```

Each line from the array is temporarily stored in the line variable, which is then printed to the browser.

We will name this script file.pl. Figure 3-5 shows what we expect from the browser when we run the script.

CHAPTER 3

Figure 3-5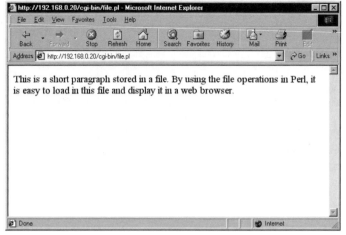

Writing to a Text File

Writing to a file on the server is just as easy as reading one. Let's try to create a new file and save a string of text into it. The string of text we are going to attempt to save is "Qwerty" and we are going to save it to a file called saved.txt.

Following is the script that we need to do this:

```perl
#!/usr/bin/perl
require "cgi-lib.pl";

print &PrintHeader;

open(FILE_HANDLE, ">saved.txt");
print FILE_HANDLE "Qwerty";
close(FILE_HANDLE);

print "Saving Completed!";
```

Again, we open the file with the Open command and assign it to the FILE_ HANDLE identifier. This time, however, we use the greater than sign instead of the less than sign to specify that we want to write a new file, rather than simply read as we did before. Notice that we also set the name of the file to be created here.

Next, we use the following line to output our string to the file:

```perl
print FILE_HANDLE "Qwerty";
```

We use the print statement, but instead of outputting the text to the web browser, we specify that we wish it to be written to the file represented by the FILE_ HANDLE identifier. Next, we close the file and print "Saving Completed!" to the browser so we know when the file has been written to. We will save this script as file2.pl. Figure 3-6 shows the expected output from the web browser when we execute the script.

Figure 3-6

Now if we look at the file we saved on the server, we can see that it contains the string "Qwerty" as we intended. Here is how the file looks in Notepad.

Figure 3-7

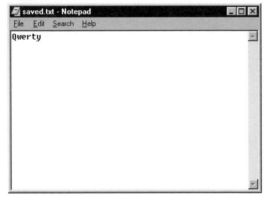

Using Templates

By utilizing templates, we can make all information we output from Perl look professional. The idea behind templates is to have a header and footer HTML file stored on the server that will act as the design for our page. Following is the HTML code we need for our header and footer files, which we will save as header.html and footer.html respectively.

header.html

```
<HTML>
```

```
<TITLE>
 Template Header
</TITLE>
<BODY>
 <CENTER>
  <TABLE CELLPADDING=0 CELLSPACING=0 WIDTH=600>
   <TR BGCOLOR=#9894E4>
    <TD> 
    </TD>
   </TR>
   <TR BGCOLOR=#9894E4>
    <TD>
     <CENTER>
      THIS IS THE HEADER
     </CENTER>
    </TD>
   </TR>
   <TR BGCOLOR=#9894E4>
    <TD> 
    </TD>
   </TR>
   <TR BGCOLOR=#ffffff>
    <TD>
```

footer.html

```
    </TD>
   </TR>
   <TR BGCOLOR=#9894E4>
    <TD>
      
    </TD>
   </TR>
   <TR BGCOLOR=#9894E4>
    <TD>
     <CENTER>
      THIS IS THE FOOTER
     </CENTER>
    </TD>
   </TR>
   <TR BGCOLOR=#9894E4>
    <TD>
      
    </TD>
   </TR>
  </TABLE>
```

```
    </CENTER>
   </BODY>
  </HTML>
```

Notice that we start a table data field in the header and then close it in the footer. This is so that all the information we output in Perl will appear between the header and footer.

To make using the header and footer files easy, we will create two functions that we can reuse to load and display the header and footer file.

Here is the function that we need to create to display our header file:

```
sub print_header()
{
    print &PrintHeader;
    open(FILE_HANDLE, "<header.html");
    @FileData = <FILE_HANDLE>;
    close(FILE_HANDLE);

    foreach $line (@FileData)
    {
        print $line;
    }
}
```

Notice here that we have moved the print &PrintHeader statement into this function to make our code even simpler. This code is the same as what we created before when we loaded a file and displayed it from the server. Notice also that the file loaded in is header.html, which is the header file we created previously. Next, we need to create the function to display the footer file. Here is how our footer display function looks:

```
sub print_footer()
{
    open(FILE_HANDLE, "<footer.html");
    @FileData = <FILE_HANDLE>;
    close(FILE_HANDLE);

    foreach $line (@FileData)
    {
        print $line;
    }
}
```

This is virtually identical to the header display function, with the exception of the print &PrintHeader statement, which is not required in this function. Also note that the file loaded in this time is footer.html and not header.html.

Now that we have coded functions to load and display our template files, we need to upload the template files to the cgi-bin, the same place the Perl scripts go. Here is a script that utilizes these new functions and displays a line of text between the header and footer:

```perl
#!/usr/bin/perl
require "cgi-lib.pl";

sub print_header()
{
    print &PrintHeader;
    open(FILE_HANDLE, "<header.html");
    @FileData = <FILE_HANDLE>;
    close(FILE_HANDLE);

    foreach $line (@FileData)
    {
        print $line;
    }
}

sub print_footer()
{
    open(FILE_HANDLE, "<footer.html");
    @FileData = <FILE_HANDLE>;
    close(FILE_HANDLE);

    foreach $line (@FileData)
    {
        print $line;
    }
}

&print_header;
print "<center>This text will appear in the middle, between the header and
footer.</center>";
&print_footer;
```

Notice that we have included the functions in the code. Later in this chapter we discover how to create a library of useful reusable functions, making our code cleaner and easier to read. For now, let's ignore the functions we created previously and focus on the actual code. The code below does the work in this script.

```perl
&print_header;
print "<center>This text will appear in the middle, between the header and
footer.</center>";
&print_footer;
```

First, we call the Print_Header function that loads our header file from the server and displays it to the browser. Next, we display a string of text in the usual manner with the Print command. Then finally, we call the Print_Footer function that loads and displays the footer file we have stored on the server.

We will save this script as template.pl. Figure 3-8 shows the expected output from the web browser.

Figure 3-8

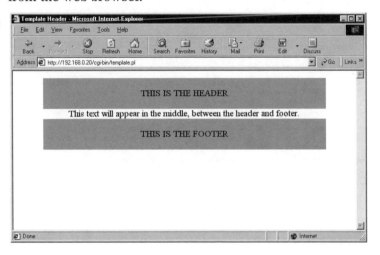

Using Forms

Forms are a valuable tool, especially when we want to add or modify information in a database. They allow input in various formats directly from the web browser that can be taken as variables into Perl scripts via either tagging the data onto the end of the web address or writing it to the HTML header.

A form can be stored on a standard HTML document, but then reference a Perl script in the Action parameter, so the script is able to process the information the user entered. Let's now look at the following HTML document that contains a form that references the Perl script we are going to create next:

form.html

```
<HTML>
 <TITLE>
  Form Page
 </TITLE>
 <BODY>
  <CENTER>
   Please enter the following details:
  </CENTER>
  <P>
```

```
<FORM METHOD="GET" ACTION="http://192.168.0.20/cgi-bin/form.pl">
 <TABLE WIDTH=400>
  <TR>
   <TD>Title:</TD>
   <TD>
    <SELECT NAME="Title" size="1">
     <OPTION VALUE="Mr" selected>Mr
     <OPTION VALUE="Mrs">Mrs
     <OPTION VALUE="Miss">Miss
     <OPTION VALUE="Ms">Ms
     <OPTION VALUE="Dr">Dr
    </SELECT>
   </TD>
  </TR>
  <TR>
   <TD>First Name:</TD>
   <TD><INPUT TYPE="text" NAME="Firstname"></TD>
  </TR>
  <TR>
   <TD>Surname:</TD>
   <TD><INPUT TYPE="text" NAME="Surname"></TD>
  </TR>
  <TR>
   <TD>Email:</TD>
   <TD><INPUT TYPE="text" NAME="Email"></TD>
  </TR>
  <TR>
   <TD COLSPAN=2>
     
   </TD>
  </TR>
  <TR>
   <TD COLSPAN=2>
    <CENTER>
     <INPUT TYPE="SUBMIT" VALUE="SEND INFORMATION">
    </CENTER>
   </TD>
  </TR>
 </TABLE>
</FORM>
</BODY>
</HTML>
```

This is standard HTML code for a form, but notice the Action part of the
<FORM> declaration:

```
ACTION="http://192.168.0.20/cgi-bin/form.pl">
```

This is an exact URL to where the script is located; in this case it is located at the IP address 192.168.0.20 and the file is named form.pl.

Therefore, when the user clicks the Submit button on the form, this script will be called and executed so that it can process the information obtained by the form. Note also that we have given each file a meaningful name. For example, the final field takes the user's e-mail address; therefore we have named this field Email. This is very important when we are taking in a lot of information as it can easily get out of hand. Remember also that the naming of the fields is case sensitive.

Figure 3-9 shows the output from our form when displayed on the browser. Note that it is not important where the form is stored (i.e., it does not need to be located in the cgi-bin) as it references the script with a direct URL.

Figure 3-9

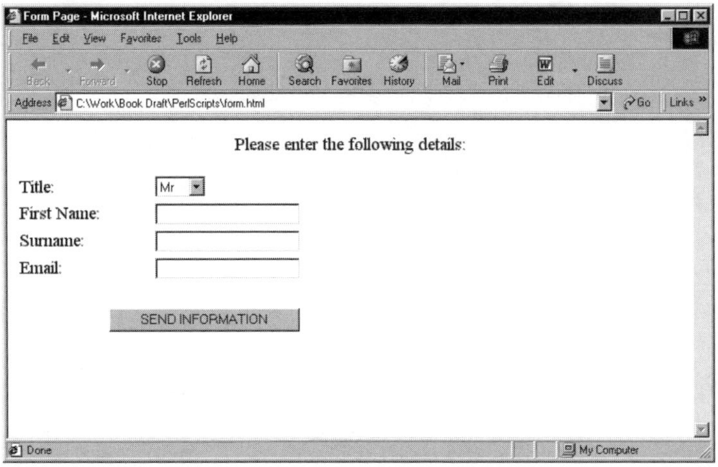

Now that we have our form page, we need to create the script to process the information. For this example, we put the information that was obtained by the form into variables, then simply output the information back to the web browser. Obviously, once we have the information stored within variables in Perl, we can easily manipulate the information in any way we require.

Here is the script we require for retrieving and displaying the information the user enters into the form:

form.pl

```perl
#!/usr/bin/perl
require "cgi-lib.pl";

# Retrieve the data from the form

(%input,    # The CGI data
 $text,     # Munged version of the text field entered by the user
 $field);   # Each of the fields (used for testing)
```

```
&ReadParse(\%input);

($Title    = $input{'Title'})    =~ s/\n/\n<BR>/g;
($Firstname = $input{'Firstname'}) =~ s/\n/\n<BR>/g;
($Surname  = $input{'Surname'})  =~ s/\n/\n<BR>/g;
($Email    = $input{'Email'})    =~ s/\n/\n<BR>/g;


# Display the data to the browser

print &PrintHeader;

print<<ENDOFCHUNK;

<P>
Here is the data we collected from the form
<P>
The fullname of the user was: $Title $Firstname $Surname
<P>
And their email address was: $Email
<P>

ENDOFCHUNK
```

First, we utilize a function called ReadParse which is part of the cgi-lib library. This gets all the information from the URL or HTML header (depending on the form method) and places it neatly into the associative Input array. This is done with the following code segment:

```
(%input,    # The CGI data
 $text,     # Munged version of the text field entered by the user
 $field);   # Each of the fields (used for testing)

&ReadParse(\%input);
```

Once we have the data in our Input array, we then need to slightly modify it and place it in a variable so it is more accessible to us. This is done with the following command:

```
($Title    = $input{'Title'})    =~ s/\n/\n<BR>/g;
```

Note that this is standard for any data we wish to retrieve from the form. In this case, we are retrieving the field called Title and storing it in the variable $Title.

Finally, once we have all the data in accessible variables, we can then use them as normal. The final code segment simply prints them to the browser to prove that they were taken in from the form correctly. Following is the final code segment which prints the data:

```
print<<ENDOFCHUNK;

<P>
Here is the data we collected from the form
<P>
The fullname of the user was: $Title $Firstname $Surname
<P>
And their email address was: $Email
<P>

ENDOFCHUNK
```

Let's now look at the output from the form/script. First, we fill in the details of the form as shown in the following figure.

Figure 3-10

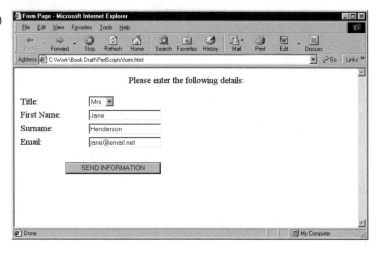

Then, once the details are complete, we expect to see the following output from the script when the Send Information button is pressed.

Figure 3-11

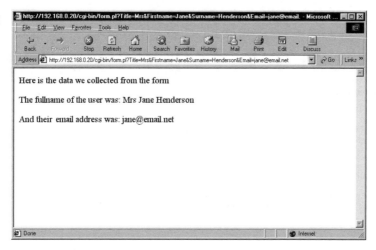

As you can see from this figure, the information was correctly retrieved from the form. Also, notice the URL in the address bar:

```
http://192.168.0.20/cgi-bin/form.pl?Title=Mrs&Firstname=Jane&Surname=Henderson&Email
=jane@email.net
```

As you can see, it contains all the information that was sent by the form. This is because we used the Get method for sending information. By using this method, all the information is simply written to the URL. The other method that can be used is the Post method, which writes the information to the HTML header, making it invisible to the user. In general terms, it makes more sense to use the Get method for debugging as you can easily see what information is being sent by forms into your scripts. For a release version, however, using the Post method makes the script look more professional.

We could make a slight modification to the script so that the information is saved to a file, rather than the browser, using the following code:

```
form2.pl

#!/usr/bin/perl
require "cgi-lib.pl";

# Retrieve the data from the form

(%input,   # The CGI data
 $text,    # Munged version of the text field entered by the user
 $field);  # Each of the fields (used for testing)

&ReadParse(\%input);

($Title     = $input{'Title'})        =~ s/\n/\n<BR>/g;
```

```
($Firstname = $input{'Firstname'})  =~ s/\n/\n<BR>/g;
($Surname   = $input{'Surname'})    =~ s/\n/\n<BR>/g;
($Email     = $input{'Email'})      =~ s/\n/\n<BR>/g;

# Save the form data to file

open(FILE_HANDLE, ">formsave.txt");

print FILE_HANDLE "$Title\n";
print FILE_HANDLE "$Firstname\n";
print FILE_HANDLE "$Surname\n";
print FILE_HANDLE "$Email\n";

close(FILE_HANDLE);

# Tell the user the saving has been completed

print &PrintHeader;
print "Save Completed";
```

Note that we also need to make a small modification to the form HTML page so that it references this new script form2.pl rather than the original form.pl. Here is the modified version of the line we are required to change in the form page:

```
<FORM METHOD="GET" ACTION="http://192.168.0.20/cgi-bin/form2.pl">
```

In this new script, we retrieve the data in the same manner, but this time, we open a file called formsave.txt on the server, then save each field of data to a new line in the file. Let's fill in some details on the form and see how it looks in the file when it is saved. Figure 3-12 shows the new form page with the details completed.

Figure 3-12

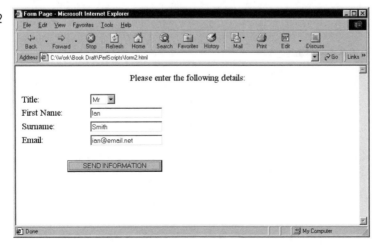

CHAPTER 3

Now when we press the Send Information button, the data will be sent to our new script and the following will be visible on the browser.

Figure 3-13

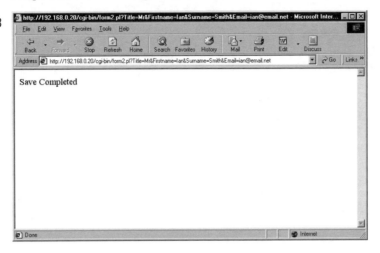

We can see that the data was sent correctly by looking at the URL in the address bar. If we now take a final look at the file we saved, we can see that the information has been saved correctly, with the contents of each field on a new line. Figure 3-14 shows the created file in Notepad.

Figure 3-14

Command Processing

When creating scripts it is a good idea to create them in a modular way so code can be easily reused in later projects without being rewritten from scratch. A good way to achieve this is to have a command system, which internally calls the correct functions or scripts to process the specified command. Let's look at the following HTML form. This form will allow the user to print a string of text either in red, blue, or green.

form3.html

```
<HTML>
 <TITLE>
```

```
    Form Page
  </TITLE>
  <BODY>
   <CENTER>
    Please select the color for the text:
   </CENTER>
   <P>
   <FORM METHOD="GET" ACTION="http://192.168.0.20/cgi-bin/core.pl">
    <TABLE WIDTH=400>
     <TR>
      <TD>Color:</TD>
      <TD>
       <SELECT NAME="Command" size="1">
        <OPTION VALUE="Red" selected>Red
        <OPTION VALUE="Green">Green
        <OPTION VALUE="Blue">Blue
       </SELECT>
      </TD>
     <TR>
      <TD COLSPAN=2>
        
      </TD>
     </TR>
     <TR>
      <TD COLSPAN=2>
       <CENTER>
        <INPUT TYPE="SUBMIT" VALUE="DISPLAY TEXT">
       </CENTER>
      </TD>
     </TR>
    </TABLE>
   </FORM>
  </BODY>
 </HTML>
```

Notice that the action for the form is to call a script called core.pl. This script will contain our command system that will react to the color the user selected. Also, we will store a separate function for each command in its own script file to show how we can make scripts more modular and reusable.

Figure 3-15 shows how the form looks when we load it into a web browser.

Figure 3-15

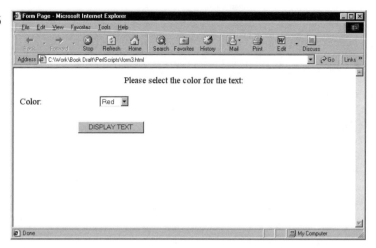

First we must create the individual scripts that we will need to display the text in the three different colors. Here are the listings for the three files we require for this:

red.pl

```perl
#!/usr/bin/perl
require "cgi-lib.pl";

# Function: Display a red string of text
sub DisplayRed()
{
    print &PrintHeader;
    print "<FONT COLOR=RED>THIS IS A RED STRING OF TEXT</FONT>";
}
```

green.pl

```perl
#!/usr/bin/perl
require "cgi-lib.pl";

# Function: Display a green string of text
sub DisplayGreen()
{
    print &PrintHeader;
    print "<FONT COLOR=GREEN>THIS IS A GREEN STRING OF TEXT</FONT>";
}
```

blue.pl

```perl
#!/usr/bin/perl
require "cgi-lib.pl";

# Function: Display a blue string of text
sub DisplayBlue()
{
    print &PrintHeader;
    print "<FONT COLOR=BLUE>THIS IS A BLUE STRING OF TEXT</FONT>";
}
```

Now that we have our three required functions in separate scripts, we need to create our core.pl script that will enable them to work correctly. Here is the complete code listing for our main script, core.pl:

core.pl

```perl
#!/usr/bin/perl
require "cgi-lib.pl";


# Retrieve the data from the form

(%input,    # The CGI data
 $text,     # Munged version of the text field entered by the user
 $field);   # Each of the fields (used for testing)

&ReadParse(\%input);


# Include required modules

require "red.pl";
require "green.pl";
require "blue.pl";


# Process the command and call the correct function to deal with it

($Command    = $input{'Command'})       =~ s/\n/\n<BR>/g;

if     ($Command eq "Red")     { &DisplayRed;   }
elsif ($Command eq "Green")    { &DisplayGreen; }
elsif ($Command eq "Blue")     { &DisplayBlue;  }
else                           { &DisplayError; }
```

```
# Function: No command was found to display an error
sub DisplayError()
{
    print &PrintHeader;
    print "Sorry, no command was found to process your request!";
}
```

First, we start the script as normal, ensuring that we retrieve the data from the form. The first new part we discover is where we include the other modules that are required to allow this script to operate correctly. In this case we need to include the three scripts we created previously, red.pl, green.pl, and blue.pl. Here is the code segment that enables us to do this:

```
require "red.pl";
require "green.pl";
require "blue.pl";
```

Next, we retrieve the command that was sent to the script using the following line of code:

```
($Command    = $input{'Command'})      =~ s/\n/\n<BR>/g;
```

Once we have the command stored in a variable, we can then create an If-Else statement that contains a list of valid commands and also what function should be called if that command is requested. Here is the code that handles each command we have available:

```
if    ($Command eq "Red")     { &DisplayRed;   }
elsif ($Command eq "Green")   { &DisplayGreen; }
elsif ($Command eq "Blue")    { &DisplayBlue;  }
else                          { &DisplayError; }
```

In this case we have three commands — Red, Green, and Blue — which in this statement call DisplayRed, DisplayGreen, and DisplayBlue respectively. Notice also that we have a final function on the final Else statement, DisplayError. This is to ensure that if the command cannot be handled by the script, the user sees a friendly screen rather than an ugly error message.

Finally, we add a simple error handling function to display a message to the user in case the command could not be handled. Here is the final code segment that we need to do this:

```
# Function: No command was found to display an error
sub DisplayError()
{
    print &PrintHeader;
    print "Sorry, no command was found to process your request!";
}
```

Figure 3-16 shows sample output from the script. If the user selects red from the form and clicks the Display Text button, the following screen can be seen.

Figure 3-16

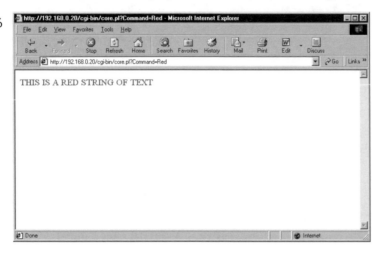

Notice the following URL in the address bar. (Note that the IP address will vary depending on where you are testing the scripts.)

```
http://192.168.0.20/cgi-bin/core.pl?Command=Red
```

Note how the command is set to Red. Let's now give the script a command that it cannot handle by manually editing the URL to the following:

```
http://192.168.0.20/cgi-bin/core.pl?Command=Orange
```

When we attempt to process this unhandled command, the script will fall back to the DisplayError function and therefore display the following screen.

Figure 3-17

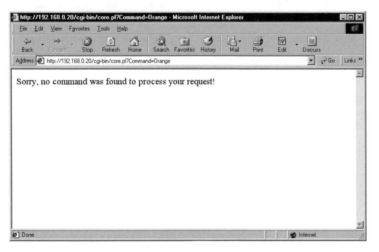

The great advantage to this modularity is the ease of adding new features into the script. Let's now add the ability to display an orange string. All we need to do for this is first create an orange.pl module to handle the orange text display. The code listing for this new script is as follows:

orange.pl

```perl
#!/usr/bin/perl
require "cgi-lib.pl";

# Function: Display a orange string of text
sub DisplayOrange()
{
    print &PrintHeader;
    print "<FONT COLOR=ORANGE>THIS IS AN ORANGE STRING OF TEXT</FONT>";
}
```

Once we have our new module, it is then relatively simple to fit it into our core.pl script. First, we must include this new script with the rest of the modules; therefore, we add the following line after the other Require statements:

```perl
require "orange.pl";
```

Finally, we must also add a handle for the Orange command in our command system; therefore, we need to insert the following line after the line that handles the Blue command:

```perl
elsif ($Command eq "Orange")    { &DisplayOrange;  }
```

Here is our final complete core.pl code listing:

core.pl

```perl
#!/usr/bin/perl
require "cgi-lib.pl";


# Retrieve the data from the form

(%input,    # The CGI data
 $text,     # Munged version of the text field entered by the user
 $field);   # Each of the fields (used for testing)

&ReadParse(\%input);


# Include required modules

require "red.pl";
```

```perl
require "green.pl";
require "blue.pl";
require "orange.pl";


# Process the command and call the correct function to deal with it

($Command    = $input{'Command'})      =~ s/\n/\n<BR>/g;

if    ($Command eq "Red")        { &DisplayRed;    }
elsif ($Command eq "Green")      { &DisplayGreen;  }
elsif ($Command eq "Blue")       { &DisplayBlue;   }
elsif ($Command eq "Orange")     { &DisplayOrange; }
else                             { &DisplayError;  }

# Function: No command was found to display an error
sub DisplayError()
{
    print &PrintHeader;
    print "Sorry, no command was found to process your request!";
}
```

Now re-enter the URL that the script previously failed to process:

```
http://192.168.0.20/cgi-bin/core.pl?Command=Orange
```

The script now has the ability to handle the Orange command, so we can expect the following output to the web browser.

Figure 3-18

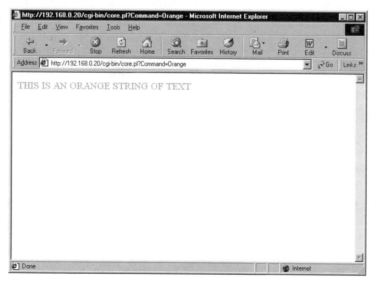

Retrieving the Date and Time

It is useful to know how to retrieve the system date and time as it can be used for many different applications.

There is a highly useful function built into Perl that can retrieve all the information we could possibly desire relating to the current date and time from the operating system. This function is called localtime.

Following is a script called time.pl, which utilizes the localtime function and displays certain information to the browser in an organized format.

time.pl

```perl
#!/usr/bin/perl
require "cgi-lib.pl";

($sec, $min, $hour, $mday, $mon, $year, $wday, $ydat, $isdst) = localtime();

@Day   = ('Sunday','Monday','Tuesday','Wednesday','Thursday','Friday','Saturday',);
@Month = ('January','February','March','April','May','June','July','August',
          'September','October','November','December');

# Required Year Adjustment
$year += 1900;

print &PrintHeader;

print "Today is a $Day[$wday] and is day $mday of the month $Month[$mon]
      of the year $year";
print "<BR><BR>";
print "When this script was executed the time was $hour:$min and $sec second(s)";
```

First, we retrieve all the data we can from the localtime function and store it all in variables using the following line of code:

```perl
($sec, $min, $hour, $mday, $mon, $year, $wday, $ydat, $isdst) = localtime();
```

Below is a description of what each variable represents:

$sec — Current second
$min — Current minute
$hour — Current hour
$mday — Current day of the month
$mon — Current month (0 to 11)
$year — The number of years that have passed since 1900
$wday — The day of the week (0 to 6 where Sunday is 0)
$yday — The day of the year (1 to 366)

$isdst — This is true if the specified time occurs during daylight savings time and is false otherwise.

Now that we know what each of the variables are for, it is also a good idea to create arrays so we can reference the names of the weekdays and months with ease. We do this with the following two arrays that we define after we have obtained the date and time:

```
@Day = ('Sunday','Monday','Tuesday','Wednesday','Thursday','Friday','Saturday',);
@Month = ('January','February','March','April','May','June','July','August',
          'September','October','November','December');
```

Next, we need to make an adjustment to the $year variable as it currently holds the number of years that have passed since 1900, not the current year. We can correct this simply by adding 1900 to the current value of the $year variable with the following line of code:

```
# Required Year Adjustment
$year += 1900;
```

Finally, we output the information to the browser with the following code segment:

```
print &PrintHeader;

print "Today is a $Day[$wday] and is day $mday of the month $Month[$mon]
       of the year $year";
print "<BR><BR>";
print "When this script was executed the time was $hour:$min and $sec second(s)";
```

Notice here how we simply reference the arrays containing the names with the variables we obtained from the localtime function to display the correct day of the week and also the month.

Figure 3-19 shows the expected output from the web browser when we execute this script.

Figure 3-19
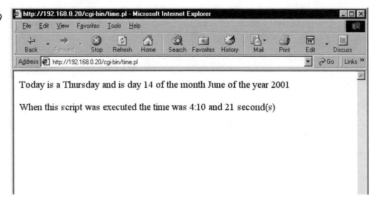

Installing the Perl Database Interface (DBI)

Before we can gain access to MySQL from Perl, it is essential that we install the Database Interface module. Once this module is installed, it allows us relatively easy access to MySQL, which lets us create some very powerful scripts since we have such a stable data store.

First, though, let's get the Database Interface module installed and configured. You now need the DBI-1.18.tar.gz ZIP file that contains the DBI module; this can be found on the companion CD-ROM or can be downloaded from http://www.mysql.com/Downloads/Contrib/.

Once you have this file on your Linux web server, you then need to extract it to a directory using the following command"

```
prompt> gunzip < DBI-1.18.tar.gz | tar xvf -
```

Now you need to change to the directory to which you just extracted the files with the following command:

```
prompt> cd DBI-1.18
```

Next, type the following command and press Return. This generates the makefile so that we are able to set up the interface module correctly.

```
prompt> perl Makefile.PL
```

Now that we have the makefile, enter the following command to compile the interface module:

```
prompt> make
```

Once this is complete, we can then install it with the following command:

```
prompt> make install
```

Now that we have the DBI module installed, we need to add MySQL support by installing the MySQL module for DBI. You now require the Msql-Mysql-modules-1.2216.tar.gz ZIP file that contains this module; it can either be copied from the CD-ROM supplied with this book or downloaded from http://www.mysql.com/Downloads/Contrib/.

Again, we need to first extract this ZIP file to its own directory using the following command:

```
prompt> gunzip < Msql-Mysql-modules-1.2216.tar.gz | tar xvf —
```

Once all the files are extracted, we then need to change to the directory by using the following command:

```
prompt> cd Msql-Mysql-modules-1.2216
```

Now, we need to install this in a similar way to the DBI module. First, we need to create the makefile with the following command:

```
prompt> perl Makefile.PL
```

This time you will be presented with options. Since we will only be working with MySQL, you can select the MySQL only option when you are asked which drivers you wish to install. Next, you will be asked if you require MysqlPerl emulation; simply answer "n" to this question as we do not require it. You can then leave the MySQL directory to the default setting by pressing Enter when asked (unless you have manually installed it to a different directory). Finally, simply press Enter to the next four options as they are only required for testing purposes.

Now that we have our makefile created, we then need to execute the following command:

```
prompt> make
```

Once this has finished compiling the MySQL interface module, we then need to execute the following command to install the module into the Perl Database Interface module.

```
prompt> make install
```

Now we are ready to use the MySQL database interface from within our Perl scripts.

Connecting and Disconnecting

First, we will look at how we connect and disconnect to a MySQL database from within a Perl script. Let's create a simple database in MySQL with which we can test our scripts. We will create a database called perltest. This is done with the following MySQL console command:

```
mysql> CREATE DATABASE perltest;
```

Now that we have a database, we can attempt to connect and disconnect from it. Here is a simple script that allows us to connect and disconnect from the perltest database we created:

```
#!/usr/bin/perl
require "cgi-lib.pl";

# Use the Database Interface Module
use DBI();

print &PrintHeader;
print "Attempting to Connect to database \'perltest\'...<p>";
```

```
# Connect to the database.
$dbh = DBI->connect("DBI:mysql:database=perltest;host=localhost",
                    "root", "",
                    {'RaiseError' => 1});

print "Connected to database \'perltest\'<p>";

print "Attempting to disconnect from database \'perltest\'...<p>";

# Disconnect from the database
$dbh->disconnect();

print "Disconnected successfully from database \'perltest\'<p>";
```

First we tell Perl we wish to use the Database Interface (DBI) module using the following line of code:

```
use DBI();
```

Next, we use the DBI to connect to the database using the following code segment:

```
$dbh = DBI->connect("DBI:mysql:database=perltest;host=localhost",
                    "root", "",
                    {'RaiseError' => 1});
```

Here, we first specify the database, which is perltest in this example. Next, we state where the database is stored. Since we are running the database on the same machine as the scripts, we simply enter localhost. The next two parameters are to specify the username and password required to connect to the database. Currently, our database does not require a password so we simply specify the root user and an empty string for the password. Finally, we state that an error is to be raised if a problem occurs; therefore we will get an internal server error if anything goes wrong while attempting to connect. Notice also that the Connect function returns a handle to the database so we can easily manipulate it once we are connected. In this example we store the database handle in a variable called dbh.

Now that we have connected to our database, in this example, we then wish to disconnect from the database using the following line of code:

```
$dbh->disconnect();
```

Notice here that we use the database handle we obtained from the Connect function to disconnect from the database.

If we then execute the script, we will expect the following output on the web browser.

Figure 3-20

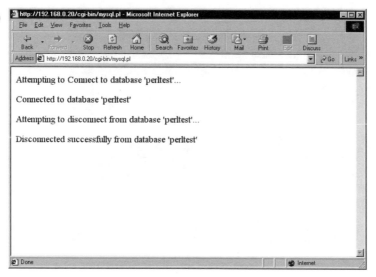

Retrieving and Displaying Data

Now that we know how to connect and disconnect from a database, we will cover how to retrieve information from the database and then display it in a readable format on the web browser.

Let's first create a table in the perltest database and add some values into it via the MySQL console. We are able to do this from Perl, but that will be covered in a later section in this chapter. First, we select the perltest database, then create a table called playerdata with the following MySQL command:

```
mysql> USE perltest;
mysql> CREATE TABLE playerdata (
mysql> id INT auto_increment,
mysql> title VARCHAR(10),
mysql> firstname VARCHAR(100),
mysql> surname VARCHAR(100),
mysql> email VARCHAR(255),
mysql> PRIMARY KEY(id));
```

This is a simple table that will hold the player's title, first name, surname, and e-mail address. Here is how this table should look in the MySQL console when we use the following Describe command:

```
mysql> DESCRIBE playerdata;
```

Figure 3-21

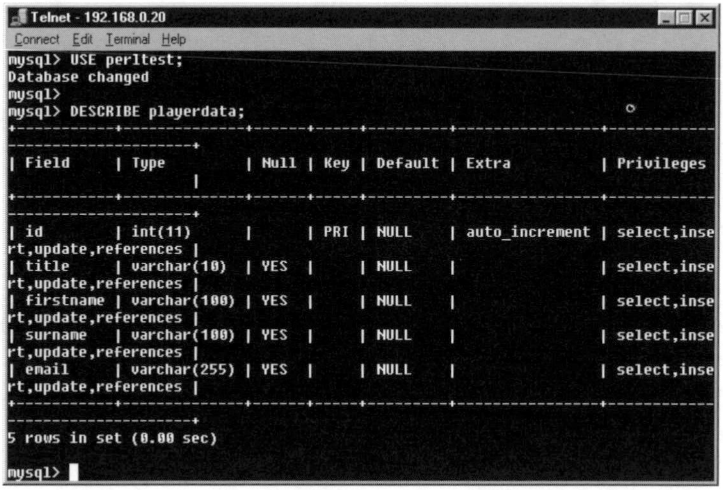

Let's now add some sample data into this table via the console so we can retrieve it later from a Perl script. We use the following command to add some sample data to this table:

```
mysql> INSERT INTO playerdata VALUES
mysql> (NULL,"Mr","John","Smith","j.smith@email.net"),
mysql> (NULL,"Ms","Sandra","Hay","sandra@email.net"),
mysql> (NULL,"Miss","Jenny","Indar","j.indar@email.net");
```

Once we have added the sample data, we can test that it was correctly added to the database using the following command (this selects all the data from the table):

```
mysql> SELECT * FROM playerdata;
```

Figure 3-22 shows the expected output from the MySQL console when we execute this command.

Figure 3-22

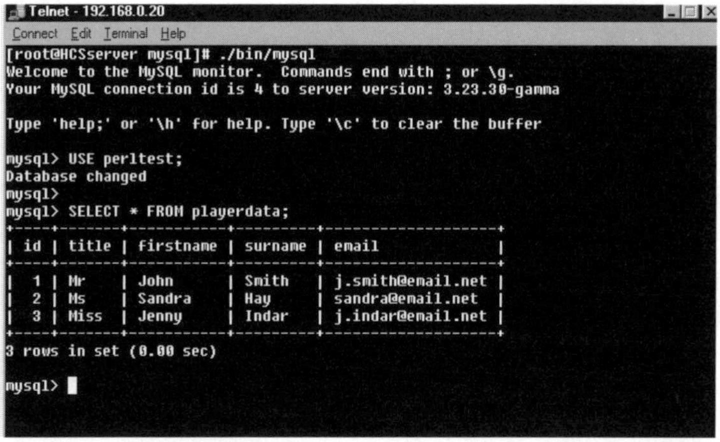

Now that we have a database, table, and sample data, we can create a Perl script to retrieve this sample data from the table and output it to the web browser. Here is the script we require to do this:

mysql2.pl

```perl
#!/usr/bin/perl
require "cgi-lib.pl";

# Use the Database Interface Module
use DBI();

# Print the HTML header and table headings
print &PrintHeader;

print<<HTML;

<HTML>
 <BODY>
  <CENTER>
   <TABLE BORDER=1 WIDTH=600>
    <TR>
     <TD><B><CENTER>Title</TD>
     <TD><B><CENTER>Firstname</TD>
     <TD><B><CENTER>Surname</TD>
     <TD><B><CENTER>Email Address</TD>
    </TR>

HTML

# Connect to the database.
$dbh = DBI->connect("DBI:mysql:database=perltest;host=localhost",
                    "root", "",
                    {'RaiseError' => 1});

# Prepare the Required Query
$sth = $dbh->prepare("SELECT * FROM playerdata");

# Check the Query was created okay
if (!$sth)
{
    die "Error:" . $dbh->errstr . "\n";
}

# Execute the Query and check it was successful
if (!$sth->execute)
{
```

```
        die "Error:" . $sth->errstr . "\n";
}

# Cycle through all the records obtained by the Query
while($ref = $sth->fetchrow_arrayref)
{
    $Title       = $$ref[1];
    $Firstname   = $$ref[2];
    $Surname     = $$ref[3];
    $Email       = $$ref[4];

# Display current record as part of a table
print<<HTML;

<tr>
 <td>$Title</td>
 <td>$Firstname</td>
 <td>$Surname</td>
 <td>$Email</td>
</tr>

HTML

}

# End the Query
$sth->finish();

# Disconnect from the database
$dbh->disconnect();

# End the Table and HTML Document
print "</TABLE></BODY></HTML>";
```

First, we print the HTML header to the browser. We retrieve the start of the table we need to hold the data from MySQL. Here is the code segment we require to accomplish this:

```
print &PrintHeader;

print<<HTML;

<HTML>
 <BODY>
  <CENTER>
   <TABLE BORDER=1 WIDTH=600>
    <TR>
```

```
<TD><B><CENTER>Title</TD>
<TD><B><CENTER>Firstname</TD>
<TD><B><CENTER>Surname</TD>
<TD><B><CENTER>Email Address</TD>
</TR>
```

HTML

Once we have our table and headings, we can then attempt to connect to the database using the code we discovered in the previous section. Here is the code we require to connect:

```
# Connect to the database.
$dbh = DBI->connect("DBI:mysql:database=perltest;host=localhost",
                    "root", "",
                    {'RaiseError' => 1});
```

Once we have established a connection, we have a handle to our database stored in the variable dbh (the Connect function returns the handle). We can then use this to generate a query using the following code segment:

```
# Prepare the Required Query
$sth = $dbh->prepare("SELECT * FROM playerdata");
```

For this, we utilize the Prepare function from the database handle dbh, which sets up the query for execution. A handle to the query is then stored in the variable sth. Note here that the Prepare function returns the handle to the query. In this case we have chosen to Select all the fields and records from the playerdata table.

Once we have prepared the query, we then need to check that it exists, then execute it with the following code:

```
# Check the Query was created okay
if (!$sth)
{
    die "Error:" . $dbh->errstr . "\n";
}

# Execute the Query and check it was successful
if (!$sth->execute)
{
    die "Error:" . $sth->errstr . "\n";
}
```

Once our query has been executed, we can then access the data that was retrieved by the execution. To do this, we can obtain each record of data in order using the following line of code:

```
$ref = $sth->fetchrow_arrayref;
```

CHAPTER 3

This stores the data in a variable called ref from which we can access the individual fields from a record. Note that in this example we have placed this statement in a While loop as follows:

```
while($ref = $sth->fetchrow_arrayref)
{
}
```

This While loop will get each record one at a time until there are no more records remaining.

Let's now look at how we access the individual fields from the ref variable. To access the fields from our database, we use the following code segment:

```
$Title        = $$ref[1];
$Firstname    = $$ref[2];
$Surname      = $$ref[3];
$Email        = $$ref[4];
```

We access the fields in a similar way to accessing an array. Note that our data starts at $$ref[0], but this field only holds the unique ID number; therefore we are not interested in it here. Note also that the numbers represent the order in which the fields are stored in the table in the MySQL database.

Once we have our fields stored in variables, it is then simply a case of displaying HTML to the browser, using the values to fill in required information. This is accomplished in the next code segment:

```
# Display current record as part of a table
print<<HTML;

<tr>
 <td>$Title</td>
 <td>$Firstname</td>
 <td>$Surname</td>
 <td>$Email</td>
</tr>

HTML
```

After the While loop has cycled through all the records that were retrieved from the database, we are finished with the query. To end the query we use the following line of code:

```
# End the Query
$sth->finish();
```

All that we have left to do now is close our connection to the database and finish off the HTML code for the end of the table. This is done in the following code segment:

```
# Disconnect from the database
$dbh->disconnect();


# End the Table and HTML Document
print "</TABLE></BODY></HTML>";
```

If we then execute the script from the web browser, we can expect to see the following output on the browser.

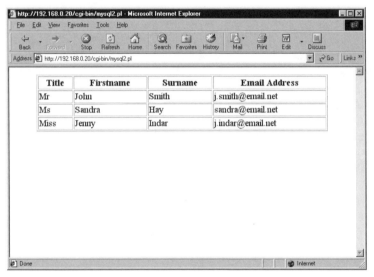

Title	Firstname	Surname	Email Address
Mr	John	Smith	j.smith@email.net
Ms	Sandra	Hay	sandra@email.net
Miss	Jenny	Indar	j.indar@email.net

Adding New Data

As well as retrieving data in Perl scripts, we can also add new records of information into a table with the use of forms. For this example, we will first remove all the sample data from the playerdata table we created in the previous section with the following MySQL console command:

```
mysql> DELETE FROM playerdata;
```

Next, we need to create a form that will allow the user to add a new record of data into the database. We require the following HTML to create this form page:

input.html

```
<HTML>
 <TITLE>
  Form Page
 </TITLE>
 <BODY>
  <CENTER>
   Please enter the following details and then click the button to add a new
   record into MySQL:
  </CENTER>
  <P>
  <FORM METHOD="GET" ACTION="http://192.168.0.20/cgi-bin/mysql3.pl">
   <TABLE WIDTH=400>
    <TR>
     <TD>Title:</TD>
     <TD>
      <SELECT NAME="Title" size="1">
       <OPTION VALUE="Mr" selected>Mr
       <OPTION VALUE="Mrs">Mrs
       <OPTION VALUE="Miss">Miss
       <OPTION VALUE="Ms">Ms
       <OPTION VALUE="Dr">Dr
      </SELECT>
     </TD>
    </TR>
    <TR>
     <TD>First Name:</TD>
     <TD><INPUT TYPE="text" NAME="Firstname"></TD>
    </TR>
    <TR>
     <TD>Surname:</TD>
     <TD><INPUT TYPE="text" NAME="Surname"></TD>
    </TR>
    <TR>
     <TD>Email:</TD>
     <TD><INPUT TYPE="text" NAME="Email"></TD>
    </TR>
    <TR>
     <TD COLSPAN=2>
       
     </TD>
    </TR>
    <TR>
     <TD COLSPAN=2>
      <CENTER>
       <INPUT TYPE="SUBMIT" VALUE="ADD RECORD TO DATABASE">
```

```
          </CENTER>
        </TD>
      </TR>
    </TABLE>
  </FORM>
  </BODY>
</HTML>
```

When we load this page into the web browser it will look as follows. Note that it will not actually be able to do anything yet as we have not yet created the script it requires to operate correctly.

Figure 3-24

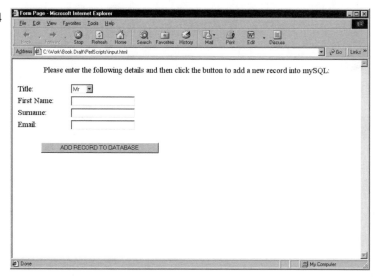

Here is the code listing for the script we need to create for this form to allow it to input the data in our playerdata table in the perltest database. Note that the script will also display the current records in the database.

mysql3.pl

```perl
#!/usr/bin/perl
require "cgi-lib.pl";

# Use the Database Interface Module
use DBI();

# Retrieve the data from the form

(%input,   # The CGI data
 $text,    # Munged version of the text field entered by the user
 $field);  # Each of the fields (used for testing)
```

```perl
&ReadParse(\%input);

# Process the form data
($Title    = $input{'Title'})      =~ s/\n/\n<BR>/g;
($Firstname = $input{'Firstname'}) =~ s/\n/\n<BR>/g;
($Surname   = $input{'Surname'})   =~ s/\n/\n<BR>/g;
($Email     = $input{'Email'})     =~ s/\n/\n<BR>/g;

# Connect to the database.
$dbh = DBI->connect("DBI:mysql:database=perltest;host=localhost",
                    "root", "",
                    {'RaiseError' => 1});

# Add the new record
$dbh->do("INSERT INTO playerdata VALUES
(NULL,\"$Title\",\"$Firstname\",\"$Surname\",\"$Email\")");

# Disconnect from the database
$dbh->disconnect();

# Print the HTML header and table headings
print &PrintHeader;

print<<HTML;

<HTML>
 <BODY>
  <CENTER>
   <TABLE BORDER=1 WIDTH=600>
    <TR>
     <TD><B><CENTER>Title</TD>
     <TD><B><CENTER>Firstname</TD>
     <TD><B><CENTER>Surname</TD>
     <TD><B><CENTER>Email Address</TD>
    </TR>

HTML

# Connect to the database.
$dbh = DBI->connect("DBI:mysql:database=perltest;host=localhost",
                    "root", "",
                    {'RaiseError' => 1});

# Prepare the Required Query
$sth = $dbh->prepare("SELECT * FROM playerdata");
```

```perl
# Check the Query was created okay
if (!$sth)
{
    die "Error:" . $dbh->errstr . "\n";
}

# Execute the Query and check it was successful
if (!$sth->execute)
{
    die "Error:" . $sth->errstr . "\n";
}

# Cycle through all the records obtained by the Query
while ($ref = $sth->fetchrow_arrayref)
{
    $Title      = $$ref[1];
    $Firstname  = $$ref[2];
    $Surname    = $$ref[3];
    $Email      = $$ref[4];

# Display current record as part of a table
print<<HTML;

<tr>
 <td>$Title</td>
 <td>$Firstname</td>
 <td>$Surname</td>
 <td>$Email</td>
</tr>

HTML

}

# End the Query
$sth->finish();

# Disconnect from the database
$dbh->disconnect();

# End the Table and HTML Document
print "</TABLE></BODY></HTML>";
```

Only the top area of the script is new; the rest is taken directly from the mysql2.pl script. Let's look at how we process the form data and add it as a new record into the MySQL database.

First, we retrieve the form data from the URL using the following code segment:

```
# Retrieve the data from the form

(%input,    # The CGI data
 $text,     # Munged version of the text field entered by the user
 $field);   # Each of the fields (used for testing)

&ReadParse(\%input);
```

Once we have the data stored in an array, we then need to process the data into a usable format. This is done with the following code segment:

```
# Process the form data
($Title    = $input{'Title'})     =~ s/\n/\n<BR>/g;
($Firstname = $input{'Firstname'}) =~ s/\n/\n<BR>/g;
($Surname   = $input{'Surname'})   =~ s/\n/\n<BR>/g;
($Email    = $input{'Email'})     =~ s/\n/\n<BR>/g;
```

Notice here that we are taking in the information from the four input boxes we have in the form. Once we have the data into Perl, we then need to establish a connection to the database in the usual manner. This is done with the following code segment:

```
# Connect to the database.
$dbh = DBI->connect("DBI:mysql:database=perltest;host=localhost",
                    "root", "",
                    {'RaiseError' => 1});
```

Now that we have our connection, we simply call the Do function from the database handle and enter the query we wish to perform. In this case we need to use the Insert command to add a new record of information into the table. This is accomplished with the following line of code:

```
# Add the new record
$dbh->do("INSERT INTO playerdata VALUES
(NULL,\"$Title\",\"$Firstname\",\"$Surname\",\"$Email\")");
```

Notice here how we just replace the parameters of the Insert command, where we would normally enter a string, with the correct variable we obtained from our HTML form.

After this command, the information has been added into the database; therefore, we no longer require the connection and disconnect with the following line of code:

```
# Disconnect from the database
$dbh->disconnect();
```

The rest of this script is then identical to the mysql2.pl script that we created previously in this chapter.

Let's look at what happens now when we attempt to add a new record via the HTML form we created. In the following figure, you can see some data that we have entered into the form.

Figure 3-25

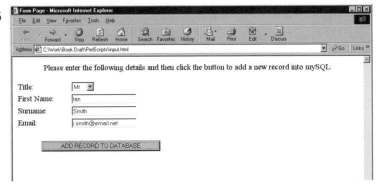

If we then click the Add Record to Database button, we can see that the record has been added to the database as it is visible in the table. This can be seen in the following screen shot of the web browser.

Figure 3-26

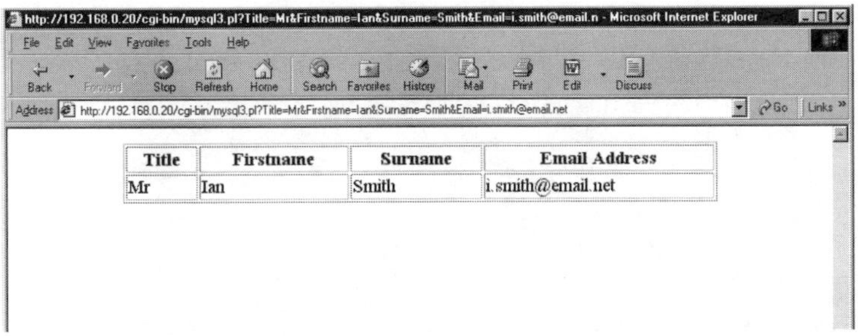

We can then repeat this process with a new set of details. Figure 3-27 shows the form with different details we also wish to add into our database via the form.

Figure 3-27

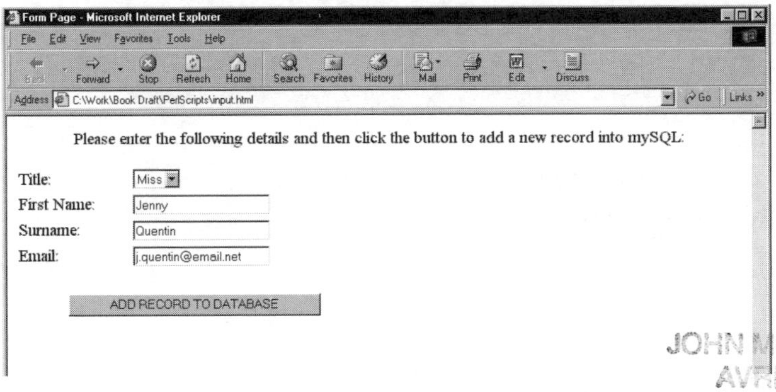

LIVERPOOL
JOHN MOORES UNIVERSITY
AVRIL ROBARTS LRC
TEL. 0151 231 4022

This time, when the Add Record to Database button is clicked, both the first record we added and also this new record have been retrieved from the database. This can be seen in the following figure.

Figure 3-28

Finally, we can then view the details that have been added in the MySQL console to confirm that the data has been added correctly. This is accomplished by using the following MySQL console commands:

```
mysql> USE perltest;
mysql> SELECT * FROM playerdata;
```

When we execute these commands, the following screen will be visible in the MySQL console.

Figure 3-29

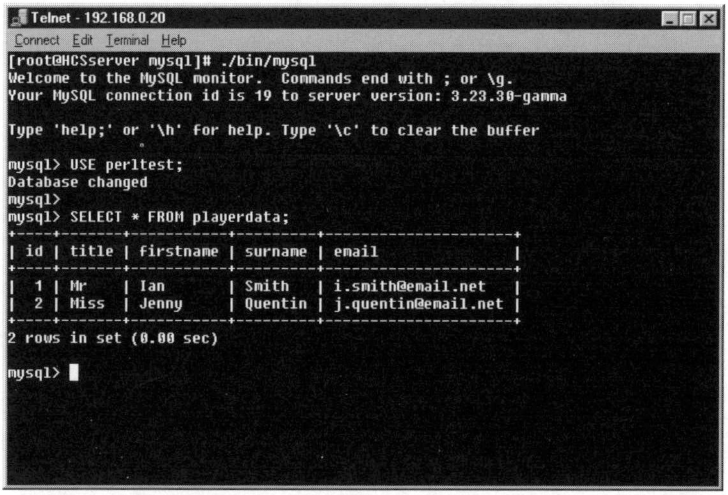

As you can see from the figure, the data has been successfully entered into the database by the Perl script.

Using the Unique ID Field

We will now discover how to effectively use the unique ID field we include in all our tables. To demonstrate how we can use this, we are going to modify our previous script mysql3.pl to allow the modification and deletion of records directly from the web browser. In addition, we will be giving the script more structure by implementing a command system. Here is the complete script that we will name mysql4.pl. Note that this time we will not require the HTML form; this will be integrated into the Perl script.

mysql4.pl

```perl
#!/usr/bin/perl
require "cgi-lib.pl";

# Use the Database Interface Module
use DBI();

# Retrieve the data from the form

(%input,    # The CGI data
 $text,     # Munged version of the text field entered by the user
 $field);   # Each of the fields (used for testing)

&ReadParse(\%input);

# Process the command and call the correct function to deal with it

($Command     = $input{'Command'})      =~ s/\n/\n<BR>/g;

if    ($Command eq "AddData")        { &AddData;    }
elsif ($Command eq "DoAddData")      { &DoAddData; }
elsif ($Command eq "ModifyData")     { &ModifyData;   }
elsif ($Command eq "DoModifyData")   { &DoModifyData; }
elsif ($Command eq "DeleteData")     { &DeleteData; }
else                                 { &DisplayData; }


# DisplayData: This function is used to access all the available functionality of
the system
sub DisplayData()
{

# Print the HTML header and table headings
print &PrintHeader;
```

```perl
print<<HTML;

<HTML>
 <BODY>
  <CENTER>
   <TABLE BORDER=1 CELLSPACING=0 CELLPADDING=5 WIDTH=600>
    <TR>
     <TD><B><CENTER>Title</TD>
     <TD><B><CENTER>Firstname</TD>
     <TD><B><CENTER>Surname</TD>
     <TD><B><CENTER>Email Address</TD>
     <TD COLSPAN=2><B><CENTER>Action</TD>
    </TR>

HTML

# Connect to the database.
$dbh = DBI->connect("DBI:mysql:database=perltest;host=localhost",
                    "root", "",
                    {'RaiseError' => 1});

# Prepare the Required Query
$sth = $dbh->prepare("SELECT * FROM playerdata");

# Check the Query was created okay
if (!$sth)
{
    die "Error:" . $dbh->errstr . "\n";
}

# Execute the Query and check it was successful
if (!$sth->execute)
{
    die "Error:" . $sth->errstr . "\n";
}

# Cycle through all the records obtained by the Query
while ($ref = $sth->fetchrow_arrayref)
{
    $Id          = $$ref[0];
    $Title       = $$ref[1];
    $Firstname   = $$ref[2];
    $Surname     = $$ref[3];
    $Email       = $$ref[4];

# Display current record as part of a table
print<<HTML;
```

```
<tr>
 <td>$Title</td>
 <td>$Firstname</td>
 <td>$Surname</td>
 <td>$Email</td>
 <td><CENTER> [ <A HREF="http://192.168.0.20/cgi-bin/mysql4.pl?Command=ModifyData&
     Selection=$Id">MODIFY</A> ] </td>
 <td><CENTER> [ <A HREF="http://192.168.0.20/cgi-bin/mysql4.pl?Command=DeleteData&
     Selection=$Id">DELETE</A> ] </td>
</tr>

HTML

}

# End the Query
$sth->finish();

# Disconnect from the database
$dbh->disconnect();

# End the Table and HTML Document
print "</TABLE>";
print "<CENTER><BR><A
HREF=\"http://192.168.0.20/cgi-bin/mysql4.pl?Command=AddData\">Add New
Record...</A>";
print "</BODY></HTML>";

}

# AddData: Function to allow new records to be added to the system
sub AddData()
{
print &PrintHeader;
print<<HTML;

<HTML>
 <TITLE>
  Form Page
 </TITLE>
 <BODY>
  <CENTER>
   Please enter the following details and then click the button to add a new
   record into MySQL:
  </CENTER>
  <P>
```

```
<FORM METHOD="GET" ACTION="http://192.168.0.20/cgi-bin/mysql4.pl">
 <CENTER>
 <TABLE WIDTH=400>
  <TR>
   <TD>Title:</TD>
   <TD>
    <SELECT NAME="Title" size="1">
     <OPTION VALUE="Mr" selected>Mr
     <OPTION VALUE="Mrs">Mrs
     <OPTION VALUE="Miss">Miss
     <OPTION VALUE="Ms">Ms
     <OPTION VALUE="Dr">Dr
    </SELECT>
   </TD>
  </TR>
  <TR>
   <TD>First Name:</TD>
   <TD><INPUT TYPE="text" NAME="Firstname"></TD>
  </TR>
  <TR>
   <TD>Surname:</TD>
   <TD><INPUT TYPE="text" NAME="Surname"></TD>
  </TR>
  <TR>
   <TD>Email:</TD>
   <TD><INPUT TYPE="text" NAME="Email"></TD>
  </TR>
  <TR>
   <TD COLSPAN=2>
     
   </TD>
  </TR>
  <TR>
   <TD COLSPAN=2>
    <CENTER>
     <INPUT TYPE="HIDDEN" NAME="Command" VALUE="DoAddData">
     <INPUT TYPE="SUBMIT" VALUE="ADD RECORD TO DATABASE">
    </CENTER>
   </TD>
  </TR>
 </TABLE>
</FORM>
<FORM METHOD="GET" ACTION="http://192.168.0.20/cgi-bin/mysql4.pl">
 <TABLE WIDTH=400>
  <TR>
   <TD COLSPAN=2>
    <CENTER>
```

```
          <INPUT TYPE="SUBMIT" VALUE="CANCEL">
        </CENTER>
      </TD>
    </TR>
  </TABLE>
 </CENTER>
 </FORM>
</BODY>
</HTML>

HTML
}

# DoAddData: Used to input the new record into the MySQL Database
sub DoAddData()
{
# Process the form data
($Title    = $input{'Title'})      =~ s/\n/\n<BR>/g;
($Firstname = $input{'Firstname'}) =~ s/\n/\n<BR>/g;
($Surname  = $input{'Surname'})    =~ s/\n/\n<BR>/g;
($Email    = $input{'Email'})      =~ s/\n/\n<BR>/g;

# Connect to the database.
$dbh = DBI->connect("DBI:mysql:database=perltest;host=localhost",
                    "root", "",
                    {'RaiseError' => 1});

# Add the new record
$dbh->do("INSERT INTO playerdata VALUES
(NULL,\"$Title\",\"$Firstname\",\"$Surname\",\"$Email\")");

# Disconnect from the database
$dbh->disconnect();

print &PrintHeader;
print<<HTML
<HTML><BODY><CENTER><P>
New Record has been successfully added!
<P>
<FORM METHOD="GET" ACTION="http://192.168.0.20/cgi-bin/mysql4.pl">
 <CENTER>
  <INPUT TYPE="SUBMIT" VALUE="OK">
 </CENTER>
</FORM>
</CENTER></BODY></HTML>

HTML
```

```perl
}

# ModifyData: Function to allow the user to make changes to existing data
sub ModifyData()
{
# First retrieve the current data from MySQL

# Get the unique id from the URL
($Selection     = $input{'Selection'})        =~ s/\n/\n<BR>/g;

# Now get the data using the unique id...

# Connect to the database.
$dbh = DBI->connect("DBI:mysql:database=perltest;host=localhost",
                    "root", "",
                    {'RaiseError' => 1});

# Prepare the Required Query
$sth = $dbh->prepare("SELECT * FROM playerdata WHERE id = $Selection");

# Check the Query was created okay
if (!$sth)
{
    die "Error:" . $dbh->errstr . "\n";
}

# Execute the Query and check it was successful
if (!$sth->execute)
{
    die "Error:" . $sth->errstr . "\n";
}

# Copy the record data to variables
$ref = $sth->fetchrow_arrayref;

$Title          = $$ref[1];
$Firstname      = $$ref[2];
$Surname        = $$ref[3];
$Email          = $$ref[4];

# End the Query
$sth->finish();

# Disconnect from the database
$dbh->disconnect();
```

```
# Print the Form (with the current values as the default)
print &PrintHeader;
print<<HTML;

<HTML>
 <TITLE>
  Form Page
 </TITLE>
 <BODY>
  <CENTER>
   Please change the required details:
  </CENTER>
  <P>
  <FORM METHOD="GET" ACTION="http://192.168.0.20/cgi-bin/mysql4.pl">
   <CENTER>
   <TABLE WIDTH=400>
    <TR>
     <TD>Title:</TD>
     <TD>
      <SELECT NAME="Title" size="1">

HTML

if($Title eq "Mr")
{
print<<HTML;
      <OPTION VALUE="Mr" selected>Mr
      <OPTION VALUE="Mrs">Mrs
      <OPTION VALUE="Miss">Miss
      <OPTION VALUE="Ms">Ms
      <OPTION VALUE="Dr">Dr
HTML
}
if($Title eq "Mrs")
{
print<<HTML;
      <OPTION VALUE="Mr">Mr
      <OPTION VALUE="Mrs" selected>Mrs
      <OPTION VALUE="Miss">Miss
      <OPTION VALUE="Ms">Ms
      <OPTION VALUE="Dr">Dr
HTML
}
if($Title eq "Miss")
{
print<<HTML;
      <OPTION VALUE="Mr">Mr
```

```
                <OPTION VALUE="Mrs">Mrs
                <OPTION VALUE="Miss" selected>Miss
                <OPTION VALUE="Ms">Ms
                <OPTION VALUE="Dr">Dr
HTML
}
if($Title eq "Ms")
{
print<<HTML;
        <OPTION VALUE="Mr">Mr
        <OPTION VALUE="Mrs">Mrs
        <OPTION VALUE="Miss">Miss
        <OPTION VALUE="Ms" selected>Ms
        <OPTION VALUE="Dr">Dr
HTML
}
if($Title eq "Dr")
{
print<<HTML;
        <OPTION VALUE="Mr">Mr
        <OPTION VALUE="Mrs">Mrs
        <OPTION VALUE="Miss">Miss
        <OPTION VALUE="Ms">Ms
        <OPTION VALUE="Dr" selected>Dr
HTML
}

print<<HTML;

      </SELECT>
     </TD>
    </TR>
    <TR>
     <TD>First Name:</TD>
     <TD><INPUT TYPE="text" NAME="Firstname" VALUE="$Firstname"></TD>
    </TR>
    <TR>
     <TD>Surname:</TD>
     <TD><INPUT TYPE="text" NAME="Surname" VALUE="$Surname"></TD>
    </TR>
    <TR>
     <TD>Email:</TD>
     <TD><INPUT TYPE="text" NAME="Email" VALUE="$Email"></TD>
    </TR>
    <TR>
     <TD COLSPAN=2>
       
```

```
        </TD>
      </TR>
      <TR>
       <TD COLSPAN=2>
        <CENTER>
         <INPUT TYPE="HIDDEN" NAME="Command" VALUE="DoModifyData">
         <INPUT TYPE="HIDDEN" NAME="Selection" VALUE="$Selection">
         <INPUT TYPE="SUBMIT" VALUE="MAKE CHANGES TO DATABASE">
        </CENTER>
       </TD>
      </TR>
     </TABLE>
   </FORM>
   <FORM METHOD="GET" ACTION="http://192.168.0.20/cgi-bin/mysql4.pl">
    <TABLE WIDTH=400>
     <TR>
      <TD COLSPAN=2>
       <CENTER>
        <INPUT TYPE="SUBMIT" VALUE="CANCEL">
       </CENTER>
      </TD>
     </TR>
    </TABLE>
   </CENTER>
   </FORM>
 </BODY>
</HTML>

HTML
}


# DoModifyData: Used to make changes to the record within MySQL
sub DoModifyData()
{
# Process the form data
($Title     = $input{'Title'})      =~ s/\n/\n<BR>/g;
($Firstname = $input{'Firstname'})  =~ s/\n/\n<BR>/g;
($Surname   = $input{'Surname'})    =~ s/\n/\n<BR>/g;
($Email     = $input{'Email'})      =~ s/\n/\n<BR>/g;
($Selection = $input{'Selection'})  =~ s/\n/\n<BR>/g;


# Connect to the database.
$dbh = DBI->connect("DBI:mysql:database=perltest;host=localhost",
                    "root", "",
                    {'RaiseError' => 1});
```

```perl
# Update the record
$dbh->do("UPDATE playerdata SET title     = \"$Title\"     WHERE id = $Selection");
$dbh->do("UPDATE playerdata SET firstname = \"$Firstname\" WHERE id = $Selection");
$dbh->do("UPDATE playerdata SET surname   = \"$Surname\"   WHERE id = $Selection");
$dbh->do("UPDATE playerdata SET email     = \"$Email\"     WHERE id = $Selection");

# Disconnect from the database
$dbh->disconnect();

print &PrintHeader;
print<<HTML
<HTML><BODY><CENTER><P>
Record has been updated successfully!
<P>
<FORM METHOD="GET" ACTION="http://192.168.0.20/cgi-bin/mysql4.pl">
 <CENTER>
  <INPUT TYPE="SUBMIT" VALUE="OK">
 </CENTER>
</FORM>
</CENTER></BODY></HTML>

HTML
}


# DeleteData: Used to remove a record from the MySQL database
sub DeleteData()
{
# Retrieve the unique id of the record to delete
($Selection    = $input{'Selection'})      =~ s/\n/\n<BR>/g;

# Connect to the database.
$dbh = DBI->connect("DBI:mysql:database=perltest;host=localhost",
                    "root", "",
                    {'RaiseError' => 1});

# Delete the record
$dbh->do("DELETE FROM playerdata WHERE id = $Selection");

# Disconnect from the database
$dbh->disconnect();

print &PrintHeader;
print<<HTML
<HTML><BODY><CENTER><P>
Record has been deleted!
<P>
<FORM METHOD="GET" ACTION="http://192.168.0.20/cgi-bin/mysql4.pl">
```

```
<CENTER>
 <INPUT TYPE="SUBMIT" VALUE="OK">
</CENTER>
</FORM>
</CENTER></BODY></HTML>

HTML
}
```

Let's now look in detail at how this script operates and utilizes the unique ID system.

First, we have our command system that processes all the different features our script contains. Here is the code segment for the command system:

```
# Process the command and call the correct function to deal with it

($Command     = $input{'Command'})      =~ s/\n/\n<BR>/g;

if    ($Command eq "AddData")      { &AddData;    }
elsif ($Command eq "DoAddData")    { &DoAddData;  }
elsif ($Command eq "ModifyData")   { &ModifyData;    }
elsif ($Command eq "DoModifyData") { &DoModifyData; }
elsif ($Command eq "DeleteData")   { &DeleteData; }
else                               { &DisplayData; }
```

Notice here that the default command is DisplayData, which simply displays the data currently in our playerdata table in MySQL and gives the users options to utilize the other commands. Also note that in addition to functions for adding and modifying the data, AddData and ModifyData, we also have DoAddData and DoModifyData. The first functions are used to get the required input from the user, such as new record data or changes to be made to a current record. The DoAddData and DoModifyData actually update the database and give the user notification that the task has been carried out successfully. Let's now look at each individual function in detail, starting with the default function, DisplayData.

DisplayData Function

The DisplayData function is very similar to the mysql3.pl script that we created previously. First, we print the headings for the table in which we are going to display the database information using the following code segment:

```
print<<HTML;

<HTML>
 <BODY>
  <CENTER>
```

```
<TABLE BORDER=1 CELLSPACING=0 CELLPADDING=5 WIDTH=600>
 <TR>
  <TD><B><CENTER>Title</TD>
  <TD><B><CENTER>Firstname</TD>
  <TD><B><CENTER>Surname</TD>
  <TD><B><CENTER>Email Address</TD>
  <TD COLSPAN=2><B><CENTER>Action</TD>
 </TR>
```

HTML

Notice here how we have added an extra heading called Action. This new column will be where the commands the users can use for each record, such as Modify and Delete, will be located.

Next, we connect to the database and process our query, which is simply to select all the data from our playerdata table. Here is the code segment we require to do this:

```
# Connect to the database.
$dbh = DBI->connect("DBI:mysql:database=perltest;host=localhost",
                    "root", "",
                    {'RaiseError' => 1});


# Prepare the required query
$sth = $dbh->prepare("SELECT * FROM playerdata");


# Check the query was created okay
if (!$sth)
{
    die "Error:" . $dbh->errstr . "\n";
}


# Execute the query and check it was successful
if (!$sth->execute)
{
    die "Error:" . $sth->errstr . "\n";
}
```

The next code for displaying each record is where we utilize the unique IDs. When we retrieve the data from the record, this time we also note the unique ID for the player in a variable called ID. This can be seen in the following code:

```
while ($ref = $sth->fetchrow_arrayref)
{
    $Id             = $$ref[0];
    $Title          = $$ref[1];
    $Firstname      = $$ref[2];
```

```
$Surname        = $$ref[3];
$Email          = $$ref[4];
```

Now that we have the unique ID, we can send it to the Modify and Delete functions when required so we know exactly which record we are referring to. Let's look at the next code segment to get a clearer view of this:

```
print<<HTML;

<tr>
 <td>$Title</td>
 <td>$Firstname</td>
 <td>$Surname</td>
 <td>$Email</td>
 <td><CENTER> [ <A HREF="http://192.168.0.20/cgi-bin/mysql4.pl?Command=ModifyData&
     Selection=$Id">MODIFY</A> ] </td>
 <td><CENTER> [ <A HREF="http://192.168.0.20/cgi-bin/mysql4.pl?Command=DeleteData&
     Selection=$Id">DELETE</A> ] </td>
</tr>

HTML

}
```

Here, we specify links to the script and manually add the command and selection to the end of the URL. Let's take a look at the URL we use to modify the player's information:

```
http://192.168.0.20/cgi-bin/mysql4.pl?Command=ModifyData&Selection=$Id
```

As you can see, we specify the command as ModifyData so when the URL is called, it will process the ModifyData command from the command system. Also notice that we set the value of a Selection variable to the ID of the player. This value is taken from the URL in the ModifyData function and used to modify the correct record, as we will see in the function's description.

After we have finished outputting the table we retrieved from the database, we can then end the query and close the connection to the database with the following code segment:

```
# End the Query
$sth->finish();

# Disconnect from the database
$dbh->disconnect();
```

The final feature we require in this function is the ability for the user to add new data into the table. This is accomplished by finishing off the table and adding the following hyperlink:

```
# End the Table and HTML Document
print "</TABLE>";
print "<CENTER><BR><A
HREF=\"http://192.168.0.20/cgi-bin/mysql4.pl?Command=AddData\">Add New
Record...</A>";
print "</BODY></HTML>";

}
```

Notice here that we are again manually specifying the command AddData directly into the URL.

AddData Function

All we are really doing in this function is displaying the HTML form that the user can use to input the correct data. Notice though that before we add the Submit button for the form, we have added this new line of code:

```
<INPUT TYPE="HIDDEN" NAME="Command" VALUE="DoAddData">
```

What this line does is send an extra field of data in the same manner as if it had been entered by the user. The difference is that it is not visible to the user on the HTML page and the value is not changeable. As you can see, the Type is set to Hidden. Notice that we set the Name to Command and the Value to DoAddData. What this means is that when the script is called, the command will be DoAddData so the command system will call the DoAddData function.

The other new addition is the Cancel button. This button allows us to return to the main screen without adding any data into the database. We have implemented the button with this following code segment:

```
<FORM METHOD="GET" ACTION="http://192.168.0.20/cgi-bin/mysql4.pl">
  <TABLE WIDTH=400>
   <TR>
    <TD COLSPAN=2>
     <CENTER>
      <INPUT TYPE="SUBMIT" VALUE="CANCEL">
     </CENTER>
    </TD>
   </TR>
  </TABLE>
 </CENTER>
</FORM>
```

All this button does is call the script with no command variable set; therefore, it calls the DisplayData function, which is what we desire in this case.

DoAddData Function

This function is used to actually add the data the user entered into a new record in our MySQL database. In addition, once this has been completed, it will give the user confirmation and allow them to return to the main screen.

First, we input the data from the URL with the following code segment:

```
# Process the form data
($Title     = $input{'Title'})     =~ s/\n/\n<BR>/g;
($Firstname = $input{'Firstname'}) =~ s/\n/\n<BR>/g;
($Surname   = $input{'Surname'})   =~ s/\n/\n<BR>/g;
($Email     = $input{'Email'})     =~ s/\n/\n<BR>/g;
```

Next, we make a connection to the database with the following code segment:

```
# Connect to the database.
$dbh = DBI->connect("DBI:mysql:database=perltest;host=localhost",
                    "root", "",
                    {'RaiseError' => 1});
```

Then we insert the new record of data into the playerdata table with the following line of code:

```
# Add the new record
$dbh->do("INSERT INTO playerdata VALUES
(NULL,\"$Title\",\"$Firstname\",\"$Surname\",\"$Email\")");
```

We now no longer require our connection to the database so we disconnect using the standard method as can be seen in the next line of code:

```
# Disconnect from the database
$dbh->disconnect();
```

Finally, we display a string of text to inform the user the information was added to the database successfully. We also give them an OK button to allow them to return to the main screen of the system. This OK button is a simple form, using the same technique we used to create our Cancel button in the AddData function. Here is the final code segment for displaying the confirmation:

```
print &PrintHeader;
print<<HTML
<HTML><BODY><CENTER><P>
New Record has been successfully added!
<P>
<FORM METHOD="GET" ACTION="http://192.168.0.20/cgi-bin/mysql4.pl">
 <CENTER>
  <INPUT TYPE="SUBMIT" VALUE="OK">
 </CENTER>
</FORM>
```

```
</CENTER></BODY></HTML>

HTML
}
```

Modify Function

This function allows the user to modify data that has been previously added into the database. What we must first do is begin the function and retrieve the unique ID of the record we wish to modify from the URL. This is done with the following segment of code:

```
sub ModifyData()
{

# First retrieve the current data from MySQL

# Get the unique id from the URL
($Selection      = $input{'Selection'})      =~ s/\n/\n<BR>/g;
```

Now that we have the selection, we need to establish a connection to the database in the standard way with the following code:

```
# Connect to the database.
$dbh = DBI->connect("DBI:mysql:database=perltest;host=localhost",
                    "root", "",
                    {'RaiseError' => 1});
```

Once our connection is established, we need to prepare the query to obtain the correct data from the database, based upon the unique ID number stored in our Selection variable. We can accomplish this with the following line of code:

```
# Prepare the Required Query
$sth = $dbh->prepare("SELECT * FROM playerdata WHERE id = $Selection");
```

Now that the query is prepared, we need to execute it with the following code:

```
# Check the Query was created okay
if (!$sth)
{
    die "Error:" . $dbh->errstr . "\n";
}

# Execute the Query and check it was successful
if (!$sth->execute)
{
    die "Error:" . $sth->errstr . "\n";
}
```

Next, we can transfer the data we obtained from the database into variables in Perl. This is done with the next segment of code:

```
# Copy the record data to variables
$ref = $sth->fetchrow_arrayref;

$Title       = $$ref[1];
$Firstname   = $$ref[2];
$Surname     = $$ref[3];
$Email       = $$ref[4];
```

We are now finished with our query and database connection, so we can end them both with the following code segment:

```
# End the Query
$sth->finish();

# Disconnect from the database
$dbh->disconnect();
```

Now we can print the start of our form, so the user is able to modify the data. This is done with the following code:

```
# Print the Form (with the current values as the default)
print &PrintHeader;
print<<HTML;

<HTML>
 <TITLE>
  Form Page
 </TITLE>
 <BODY>
  <CENTER>
   Please change the required details:
  </CENTER>
  <P>
  <FORM METHOD="GET" ACTION="http://192.168.0.20/cgi-bin/mysql4.pl">
   <CENTER>
   <TABLE WIDTH=400>
    <TR>
     <TD>Title:</TD>
     <TD>
      <SELECT NAME="Title" size="1">
```

CHAPTER 3

Note that we have stopped at the start of the Title pull-down box. Because we wish to set the default values to the values stored in the database, we need to select the correct title in the pull-down box. This is done with several If statements as can be seen in the following code segment:

```
HTML

if($Title eq "Mr")
{
print<<HTML;
        <OPTION VALUE="Mr" selected>Mr
        <OPTION VALUE="Mrs">Mrs
        <OPTION VALUE="Miss">Miss
        <OPTION VALUE="Ms">Ms
        <OPTION VALUE="Dr">Dr
HTML
}
if($Title eq "Mrs")
{
print<<HTML;
        <OPTION VALUE="Mr">Mr
        <OPTION VALUE="Mrs" selected>Mrs
        <OPTION VALUE="Miss">Miss
        <OPTION VALUE="Ms">Ms
        <OPTION VALUE="Dr">Dr
HTML
}
if($Title eq "Miss")
{
print<<HTML;
        <OPTION VALUE="Mr">Mr
        <OPTION VALUE="Mrs">Mrs
        <OPTION VALUE="Miss" selected>Miss
        <OPTION VALUE="Ms">Ms
        <OPTION VALUE="Dr">Dr
HTML
}
if($Title eq "Ms")
{
print<<HTML;
        <OPTION VALUE="Mr">Mr
        <OPTION VALUE="Mrs">Mrs
        <OPTION VALUE="Miss">Miss
        <OPTION VALUE="Ms" selected>Ms
        <OPTION VALUE="Dr">Dr
HTML
}
if($Title eq "Dr")
{
print<<HTML;
        <OPTION VALUE="Mr">Mr
        <OPTION VALUE="Mrs">Mrs
```

```
        <OPTION VALUE="Miss">Miss
        <OPTION VALUE="Ms">Ms
        <OPTION VALUE="Dr" selected>Dr
HTML
}

print<<HTML;
```

Now we can end the pull-down box and continue until we reach the Firstname input box. Here is the code up to this point:

```
    </SELECT>
   </TD>
  </TR>
  <TR>
   <TD>First Name:</TD>
```

For the next line, we would normally add the following line of code:

```
<TD><INPUT TYPE="text" NAME="Firstname"></TD>
```

This would add an empty input box that accepted text information. However, because we wish to set the initial value to that of Firstname from the database, we use this next line of code instead:

```
<TD><INPUT TYPE="text" NAME="Firstname" VALUE="$Firstname"></TD>
```

As you can see, all we have done is add a new Value parameter and set its value to the variable Firstname.

Notice that this technique is repeated for the Surname and Email fields in this final segment of code:

```
   </TR>
   <TR>
    <TD>Surname:</TD>
    <TD><INPUT TYPE="text" NAME="Surname" VALUE="$Surname"></TD>
   </TR>
   <TR>
    <TD>Email:</TD>
    <TD><INPUT TYPE="text" NAME="Email" VALUE="$Email"></TD>
   </TR>
   <TR>
    <TD COLSPAN=2>
      
    </TD>
   </TR>
   <TR>
    <TD COLSPAN=2>
     <CENTER>
```

```
          <INPUT TYPE="HIDDEN" NAME="Command" VALUE="DoModifyData">
          <INPUT TYPE="HIDDEN" NAME="Selection" VALUE="$Selection">
          <INPUT TYPE="SUBMIT" VALUE="MAKE CHANGES TO DATABASE">
        </CENTER>
      </TD>
    </TR>
   </TABLE>
  </FORM>
  <FORM METHOD="GET" ACTION="http://192.168.0.20/cgi-bin/mysql4.pl">
   <TABLE WIDTH=400>
    <TR>
     <TD COLSPAN=2>
      <CENTER>
       <INPUT TYPE="SUBMIT" VALUE="CANCEL">
      </CENTER>
     </TD>
    </TR>
   </TABLE>
  </CENTER>
  </FORM>
 </BODY>
</HTML>

HTML
}
```

As you can see, the rest of the ModifyData function is very similar to the AddData function.

DoModifyData Function

This function processes the changes the user made in the ModifyData function and makes the appropriate updates to the MySQL database.

First, we start the function and then store the data obtained from the ModifyData function into variables in Perl, including the Selection value which contains our required unique ID. This is done with the following code:

```
sub DoModifyData()
{
# Process the form data
($Title        = $input{'Title'})     =~ s/\n/\n<BR>/g;
($Firstname    = $input{'Firstname'}) =~ s/\n/\n<BR>/g;
($Surname      = $input{'Surname'})   =~ s/\n/\n<BR>/g;
($Email        = $input{'Email'})     =~ s/\n/\n<BR>/g;
($Selection    = $input{'Selection'}) =~ s/\n/\n<BR>/g;
```

Once we have our required data stored in variables, we can then establish the connection to the database with the following code:

```
# Connect to the database.
$dbh = DBI->connect("DBI:mysql:database=perltest;host=localhost",
                    "root", "",
                    {'RaiseError' => 1});
```

Now that we have our connection, we can update all the information relative to the record that has the same unique ID as is stored in our Selection variable. Here is the code segment we use to modify the information in the database:

```
# Update the records
$dbh->do("UPDATE playerdata SET title     = \"$Title\"     WHERE id = $Selection");
$dbh->do("UPDATE playerdata SET firstname = \"$Firstname\" WHERE id = $Selection");
$dbh->do("UPDATE playerdata SET surname   = \"$Surname\"   WHERE id = $Selection");
$dbh->do("UPDATE playerdata SET email     = \"$Email\"     WHERE id = $Selection");
```

Notice here how we utilize the ID variable with the Where statement. This is the key idea behind using unique IDs.

After our data is updated, we no longer require our database connection, so we can disconnect using the standard method:

```
# Disconnect from the database
$dbh->disconnect();
```

Finally, we display notification to the user to inform him or her that the requested modifications were successful. Also, we provide an OK button to allow the user to return to the DisplayData function. This is accomplished in the following final code segment:

```
print &PrintHeader;
print<<HTML
<HTML><BODY><CENTER><P>
Record has been updated successfully!
<P>
<FORM METHOD="GET" ACTION="http://192.168.0.20/cgi-bin/mysql4.pl">
 <CENTER>
  <INPUT TYPE="SUBMIT" VALUE="OK">
 </CENTER>
</FORM>
</CENTER></BODY></HTML>

HTML
}
```

CHAPTER 3

DeleteData Function

The final function in this script is the DeleteData function, which allows the user to completely remove a record from the database.

First, the function needs to get the unique ID of the record to be deleted. This is sent from the DisplayData function when the user clicks on the appropriate Delete link. Here is the code to start the function and retrieve the unique ID into a variable called Selection:

```
sub DeleteData()
{

# Retrieve the unique id of the record to delete
($Selection     = $input{'Selection'})       =~ s/\n/\n<BR>/g;
```

Once we have the unique ID, we then establish a connection to the database using the following code:

```
# Connect to the database.
$dbh = DBI->connect("DBI:mysql:database=perltest;host=localhost",
                    "root", "",
                    {'RaiseError' => 1});
```

Now that we have a connection, we want to delete the record with an ID number that is the same as our unique ID, which is stored in our Selection variable. This can be accomplished with the following line of code:

```
# Delete the record
$dbh->do("DELETE FROM playerdata WHERE id = $Selection");
```

Notice here how we compare the Selection variable to ID in the Where statement. This means that it will only delete the record with the matching ID, which is what we require in this case.

After our record has been deleted, we can close the connection to the MySQL database:

```
# Disconnect from the database
$dbh->disconnect();
```

All that remains for this function is to display notification to the user that the record has been successfully deleted and provide an OK button with which to return to the DisplayData function. This is accomplished with the following code segment:

```
print &PrintHeader;
print<<HTML
<HTML><BODY><CENTER><P>
Record has been deleted!
```

```
<P>
<FORM METHOD="GET" ACTION="http://192.168.0.20/cgi-bin/mysql4.pl">
 <CENTER>
  <INPUT TYPE="SUBMIT" VALUE="OK">
 </CENTER>
</FORM>
</CENTER></BODY></HTML>

HTML
}
```

We have covered all the functions in our mysql4.pl script, so let's look at how it operates on the web browser. When we run the script we will be presented with the following screen. (Note that data that has been previously entered into the table may vary.)

Figure 3-30

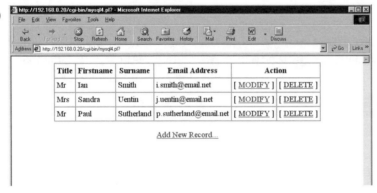

This is the output from the DisplayData function. As you can see, the user has the option to modify or delete each record. First, though, we will look at what happens when we click the Add New Record… link. When this is clicked, the following screen should be visible to the user.

Figure 3-31

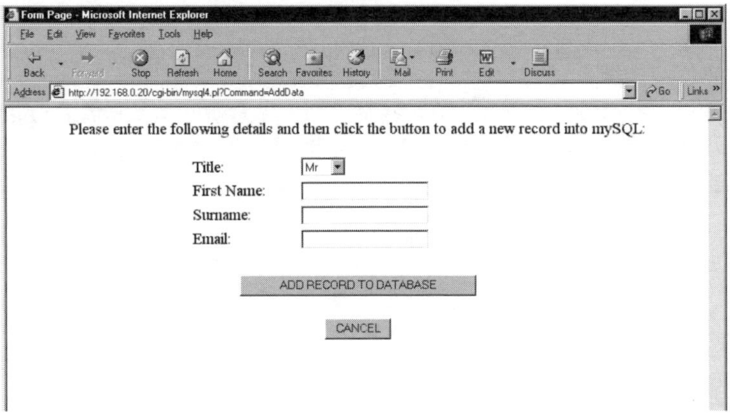

Now we will add details for a player named Miss Jenny Hay, who has the e-mail address j.hay@email.net. Here is how the screen looks when this data is entered.

Figure 3-32

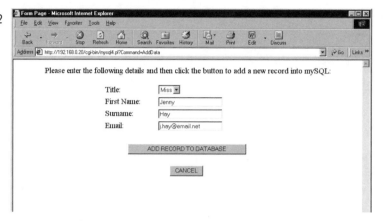

Now that we have the information filled in on the form, we can click the Add Record to Database button to input the data into the MySQL database. When we click this button, the following notification screen is visible.

Figure 3-33

When we click the OK button, we are returned to the main screen again, where we can see that the new record has been added to the database. Also notice that the options have also been added automatically for this new record.

Figure 3-34

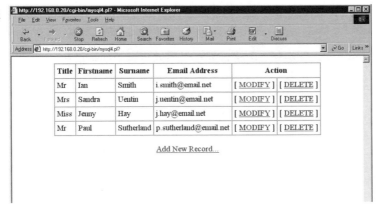

Click on the Modify link for our new Jenny Hay record. When we do this, the script will call the ModifyData function and display a form with the current data for Jenny filled in, allowing us to easily make modifications to her record. Figure 3-35 shows the ModifyData screen.

Figure 3-35

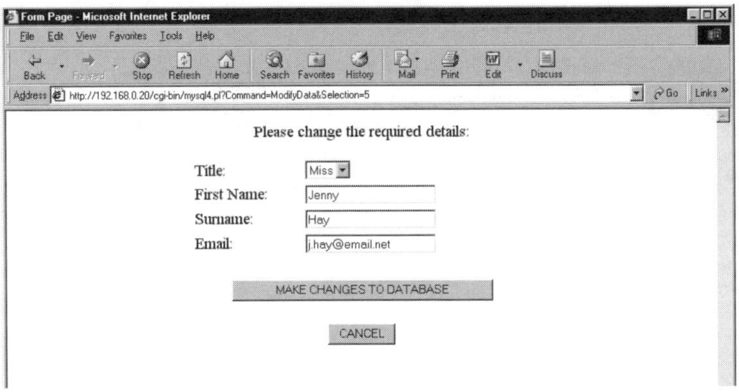

Change the name on this screen from Miss Jenny Hay to Mr John Hay. Here is how the form should look when we make this modification.

Figure 3-36

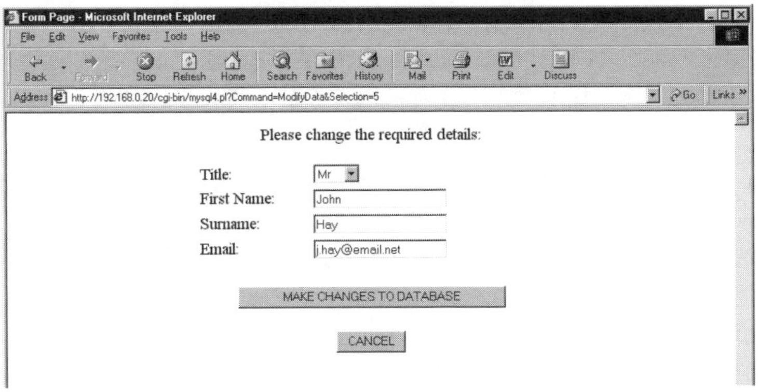

When we then click the Make Changes to Database button, the database is updated and the following notification screen is visible in the web browser.

Figure 3-37

When we click the OK button, we are returned to the main screen. We can now see that the record has been updated successfully on this screen. Figure 3-38 shows the updated record on the main screen.

Figure 3-38

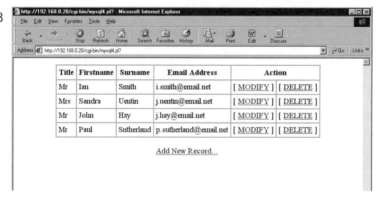

The final option the script has is to delete the records. Let's now attempt to delete the record we just modified, John Hay's record. To do this we simply click on the Delete link to the right of the record. When we click this link, the record is removed from the database and the following notification screen is then visible.

Figure 3-39

When we click the OK button to return to the main screen, we can see that the record has been removed from the database successfully as it is no longer visible in the table. Figure 3-40 shows the main screen after the deletion of the record.

Figure 3-40

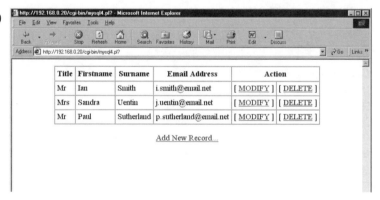

Adding a Search Facility

Now that we have covered the use of unique ID values, let's look at how to implement a search facility into our scripts. As we are using a database for our data storage, it is very easy and fast to search through data.

Let's make a modification to the previous script we created, mysql4.pl, so that there is a search box on the main screen. This search box will allow the user to search both the firstname and surname fields for a value. When the user performs the search, a new screen will be displayed with the search results and an option to return to the main screen. Following is the complete code listing, including the new search facility. We have called this modified script mysql5.pl. Note how we have added an extra command into the command system to accommodate the new search functions.

mysql5.pl

```perl
#!/usr/bin/perl
require "cgi-lib.pl";

# Use the Database Interface Module
use DBI();

# Retrieve the data from the form

(%input,    # The CGI data
 $text,     # Munged version of the text field entered by the user
 $field);   # Each of the fields (used for testing)

&ReadParse(\%input);

# Process the command and call the correct function to deal with it

($Command      = $input{'Command'})      =~ s/\n/\n<BR>/g;

if     ($Command eq "AddData")        { &AddData;  }
elsif ($Command eq "DoAddData")       { &DoAddData; }
elsif ($Command eq "ModifyData")      { &ModifyData;  }
elsif ($Command eq "DoModifyData")    { &DoModifyData; }
elsif ($Command eq "DeleteData")      { &DeleteData; }
elsif ($Command eq "SearchData")      { &SearchData; }
else                                  { &DisplayData; }

# DisplayData: This function is used to access all the available functionality
of the system
sub DisplayData()
{

# Print the HTML header and table headings
print &PrintHeader;

print<<HTML;

<HTML>
 <BODY>
  <CENTER>

HTML
# New Search Feature
print<<HTML;

<FORM METHOD="GET" ACTION="http://192.168.0.20/cgi-bin/mysql5.pl">
```

```html
<B>Search for:</B>
<INPUT TYPE="TEXT" NAME="SearchString">
<INPUT TYPE="HIDDEN" NAME="Command" VALUE="SearchData">
<INPUT TYPE="SUBMIT" VALUE="Search...">
</FORM>

<BR>
   <TABLE BORDER=1 CELLSPACING=0 CELLPADDING=5 WIDTH=600>
    <TR>
     <TD><B><CENTER>Title</TD>
     <TD><B><CENTER>Firstname</TD>
     <TD><B><CENTER>Surname</TD>
     <TD><B><CENTER>Email Address</TD>
     <TD COLSPAN=2><B><CENTER>Action</TD>
    </TR>
```

HTML

```perl
# Connect to the database.
$dbh = DBI->connect("DBI:mysql:database=perltest;host=localhost",
                    "root", "",
                    {'RaiseError' => 1});

# Prepare the Required Query
$sth = $dbh->prepare("SELECT * FROM playerdata");

# Check the Query was created okay
if (!$sth)
{
    die "Error:" . $dbh->errstr . "\n";
}

# Execute the Query and check it was successful
if (!$sth->execute)
{
    die "Error:" . $sth->errstr . "\n";
}

# Cycle through all the records obtained by the Query
while ($ref = $sth->fetchrow_arrayref)
{
    $Id        = $$ref[0];
    $Title     = $$ref[1];
    $Firstname = $$ref[2];
    $Surname   = $$ref[3];
    $Email     = $$ref[4];
```

```
# Display current record as part of a table
print<<HTML;

<tr>
 <td>$Title</td>
 <td>$Firstname</td>
 <td>$Surname</td>
 <td>$Email</td>
 <td><CENTER> [ <A HREF="http://192.168.0.20/cgi-bin/mysql5.pl?Command=ModifyData&
      Selection=$Id">MODIFY</A> ] </td>
 <td><CENTER> [ <A HREF="http://192.168.0.20/cgi-bin/mysql5.pl?Command=DeleteData&
      Selection=$Id">DELETE</A> ] </td>
</tr>

HTML

}

# End the Query
$sth->finish();

# Disconnect from the database
$dbh->disconnect();

# End the Table and HTML Document
print "</TABLE>";
print "<CENTER><BR><A
HREF=\"http://192.168.0.20/cgi-bin/mysql5.pl?Command=AddData\">Add New
Record...</A>";
print "</BODY></HTML>";

}

# AddData: Function to allow new records to be added to the system
sub AddData()
{
print &PrintHeader;
print<<HTML;

<HTML>
 <TITLE>
  Form Page
 </TITLE>
 <BODY>
  <CENTER>
    Please enter the following details and then click the button to add
    a new record into MySQL:
```

```
</CENTER>
<P>
<FORM METHOD="GET" ACTION="http://192.168.0.20/cgi-bin/mysql5.pl">
 <CENTER>
 <TABLE WIDTH=400>
  <TR>
   <TD>Title:</TD>
   <TD>
    <SELECT NAME="Title" size="1">
     <OPTION VALUE="Mr" selected>Mr
     <OPTION VALUE="Mrs">Mrs
     <OPTION VALUE="Miss">Miss
     <OPTION VALUE="Ms">Ms
     <OPTION VALUE="Dr">Dr
    </SELECT>
   </TD>
  </TR>
  <TR>
   <TD>First Name:</TD>
   <TD><INPUT TYPE="text" NAME="Firstname"></TD>
  </TR>
  <TR>
   <TD>Surname:</TD>
   <TD><INPUT TYPE="text" NAME="Surname"></TD>
  </TR>
  <TR>
   <TD>Email:</TD>
   <TD><INPUT TYPE="text" NAME="Email"></TD>
  </TR>
  <TR>
   <TD COLSPAN=2>
     
   </TD>
  </TR>
  <TR>
   <TD COLSPAN=2>
    <CENTER>
     <INPUT TYPE="HIDDEN" NAME="Command" VALUE="DoAddData">
     <INPUT TYPE="SUBMIT" VALUE="ADD RECORD TO DATABASE">
    </CENTER>
   </TD>
  </TR>
 </TABLE>
</FORM>
<FORM METHOD="GET" ACTION="http://192.168.0.20/cgi-bin/mysql5.pl">
 <TABLE WIDTH=400>
  <TR>
```

```
        <TD COLSPAN=2>
         <CENTER>
          <INPUT TYPE="SUBMIT" VALUE="CANCEL">
         </CENTER>
        </TD>
      </TR>
    </TABLE>
   </CENTER>
   </FORM>
 </BODY>
</HTML>

HTML
}

# DoAddData: Used to input the new record into the MySQL Database
sub DoAddData()
{
# Process the form data
($Title     = $input{'Title'})      =~ s/\n/\n<BR>/g;
($Firstname = $input{'Firstname'})  =~ s/\n/\n<BR>/g;
($Surname   = $input{'Surname'})    =~ s/\n/\n<BR>/g;
($Email     = $input{'Email'})      =~ s/\n/\n<BR>/g;

# Connect to the database.
$dbh = DBI->connect("DBI:mysql:database=perltest;host=localhost",
                    "root", "",
                    {'RaiseError' => 1});

# Add the new record
$dbh->do("INSERT INTO playerdata VALUES
(NULL,\"$Title\",\"$Firstname\",\"$Surname\",\"$Email\")");

# Disconnect from the database
$dbh->disconnect();

print &PrintHeader;
print<<HTML
<HTML><BODY><CENTER><P>
New Record has been successfully added!
<P>
<FORM METHOD="GET" ACTION="http://192.168.0.20/cgi-bin/mysql5.pl">
 <CENTER>
  <INPUT TYPE="SUBMIT" VALUE="OK">
 </CENTER>
</FORM>
</CENTER></BODY></HTML>
```

```
HTML
}

# ModifyData: Function to allow the user to make changes to existing data
sub ModifyData()
{

# First retrieve the current data from MySQL

# Get the unique id from the URL
($Selection      = $input{'Selection'})        =~ s/\n/\n<BR>/g;

# Now get the data using the unique id...

# Connect to the database.
$dbh = DBI->connect("DBI:mysql:database=perltest;host=localhost",
                    "root", "",
                    {'RaiseError' => 1});

# Prepare the Required Query
$sth = $dbh->prepare("SELECT * FROM playerdata WHERE id = $Selection");

# Check the Query was created okay
if (!$sth)
{
    die "Error:" . $dbh->errstr . "\n";
}

# Execute the Query and check it was successful
if (!$sth->execute)
{
    die "Error:" . $sth->errstr . "\n";
}

# Copy the record data to variables
$ref = $sth->fetchrow_arrayref;

$Title        = $$ref[1];
$Firstname    = $$ref[2];
$Surname      = $$ref[3];
$Email        = $$ref[4];

# End the Query
$sth->finish();

# Disconnect from the database
```

```
$dbh->disconnect();

# Print the Form (with the current values as the default)
print &PrintHeader;
print<<HTML;

<HTML>
 <TITLE>
  Form Page
 </TITLE>
 <BODY>
  <CENTER>
   Please change the required details:
  </CENTER>
  <P>
  <FORM METHOD="GET" ACTION="http://192.168.0.20/cgi-bin/mysql5.pl">
   <CENTER>
   <TABLE WIDTH=400>
    <TR>
     <TD>Title:</TD>
     <TD>
      <SELECT NAME="Title" size="1">

HTML

if($Title eq "Mr")
{
print<<HTML;
      <OPTION VALUE="Mr" selected>Mr
      <OPTION VALUE="Mrs">Mrs
      <OPTION VALUE="Miss">Miss
      <OPTION VALUE="Ms">Ms
      <OPTION VALUE="Dr">Dr
HTML
}
if($Title eq "Mrs")
{
print<<HTML;
      <OPTION VALUE="Mr">Mr
      <OPTION VALUE="Mrs" selected>Mrs
      <OPTION VALUE="Miss">Miss
      <OPTION VALUE="Ms">Ms
      <OPTION VALUE="Dr">Dr
HTML
}
if($Title eq "Miss")
{
```

```
print<<HTML;
      <OPTION VALUE="Mr">Mr
      <OPTION VALUE="Mrs">Mrs
      <OPTION VALUE="Miss" selected>Miss
      <OPTION VALUE="Ms">Ms
      <OPTION VALUE="Dr">Dr
HTML
}
if($Title eq "Ms")
{
print<<HTML;
      <OPTION VALUE="Mr">Mr
      <OPTION VALUE="Mrs">Mrs
      <OPTION VALUE="Miss">Miss
      <OPTION VALUE="Ms" selected>Ms
      <OPTION VALUE="Dr">Dr
HTML
}
if($Title eq "Dr")
{
print<<HTML;
      <OPTION VALUE="Mr">Mr
      <OPTION VALUE="Mrs">Mrs
      <OPTION VALUE="Miss">Miss
      <OPTION VALUE="Ms">Ms
      <OPTION VALUE="Dr" selected>Dr
HTML
}

print<<HTML;

    </SELECT>
   </TD>
  </TR>
  <TR>
   <TD>First Name:</TD>
   <TD><INPUT TYPE="text" NAME="Firstname" VALUE="$Firstname"></TD>
  </TR>
  <TR>
   <TD>Surname:</TD>
   <TD><INPUT TYPE="text" NAME="Surname" VALUE="$Surname"></TD>
  </TR>
  <TR>
   <TD>Email:</TD>
   <TD><INPUT TYPE="text" NAME="Email" VALUE="$Email"></TD>
  </TR>
  <TR>
```

```
        <TD COLSPAN=2>
          
        </TD>
       </TR>
       <TR>
        <TD COLSPAN=2>
         <CENTER>
          <INPUT TYPE="HIDDEN" NAME="Command" VALUE="DoModifyData">
          <INPUT TYPE="HIDDEN" NAME="Selection" VALUE="$Selection">
          <INPUT TYPE="SUBMIT" VALUE="MAKE CHANGES TO DATABASE">
         </CENTER>
        </TD>
       </TR>
      </TABLE>
     </FORM>
     <FORM METHOD="GET" ACTION="http://192.168.0.20/cgi-bin/mysql5.pl">
      <TABLE WIDTH=400>
       <TR>
        <TD COLSPAN=2>
         <CENTER>
          <INPUT TYPE="SUBMIT" VALUE="CANCEL">
         </CENTER>
        </TD>
       </TR>
      </TABLE>
     </CENTER>
     </FORM>
    </BODY>
   </HTML>

HTML
}

# DoModifyData: Used to make changes to the record within MySQL
sub DoModifyData()
{
# Process the form data
($Title     = $input{'Title'})     =~ s/\n/\n<BR>/g;
($Firstname = $input{'Firstname'}) =~ s/\n/\n<BR>/g;
($Surname   = $input{'Surname'})   =~ s/\n/\n<BR>/g;
($Email     = $input{'Email'})     =~ s/\n/\n<BR>/g;
($Selection = $input{'Selection'}) =~ s/\n/\n<BR>/g;


# Connect to the database.
$dbh = DBI->connect("DBI:mysql:database=perltest;host=localhost",
                    "root", "",
                    {'RaiseError' => 1});
```

```perl
# Update the records
$dbh->do("UPDATE playerdata SET title     = \"$Title\"     WHERE id = $Selection");
$dbh->do("UPDATE playerdata SET firstname = \"$Firstname\" WHERE id = $Selection");
$dbh->do("UPDATE playerdata SET surname   = \"$Surname\"   WHERE id = $Selection");
$dbh->do("UPDATE playerdata SET email     = \"$Email\"     WHERE id = $Selection");

# Disconnect from the database
$dbh->disconnect();

print &PrintHeader;
print<<HTML
<HTML><BODY><CENTER><P>
Record has been updated successfully!
<P>
<FORM METHOD="GET" ACTION="http://192.168.0.20/cgi-bin/mysql5.pl">
 <CENTER>
  <INPUT TYPE="SUBMIT" VALUE="OK">
 </CENTER>
</FORM>
</CENTER></BODY></HTML>

HTML
}

# DeleteData: Used to remove a record from the MySQL database
sub DeleteData()
{

# Retrieve the unique id of the record to delete
($Selection     = $input{'Selection'})        =~ s/\n/\n<BR>/g;

# Connect to the database.
$dbh = DBI->connect("DBI:mysql:database=perltest;host=localhost",
                    "root", "",
                    {'RaiseError' => 1});

# Delete the record
$dbh->do("DELETE FROM playerdata WHERE id = $Selection");

# Disconnect from the database
$dbh->disconnect();

print &PrintHeader;
print<<HTML
<HTML><BODY><CENTER><P>
Record has been deleted!
```

```
<P>
<FORM METHOD="GET" ACTION="http://192.168.0.20/cgi-bin/mysql5.pl">
 <CENTER>
  <INPUT TYPE="SUBMIT" VALUE="OK">
 </CENTER>
</FORM>
</CENTER></BODY></HTML>

HTML
}

# SearchData: Searches the database and outputs the results in a formatted manner.
sub SearchData()
{

# Get the Search String from the URL
($SearchString     = $input{'SearchString'})        =~ s/\n/\n<BR>/g;

print<<HTML;

<HTML>
 <BODY>
  <CENTER>

<B>-= Search Results =-
<P>
   <TABLE BORDER=1 CELLSPACING=0 CELLPADDING=5 WIDTH=600>
    <TR>
     <TD><B><CENTER>Title</TD>
     <TD><B><CENTER>Firstname</TD>
     <TD><B><CENTER>Surname</TD>
     <TD><B><CENTER>Email Address</TD>
    </TR>

HTML

# Connect to the database.
$dbh = DBI->connect("DBI:mysql:database=perltest;host=localhost",
                    "root", "",
                    {'RaiseError' => 1});

# Prepare the Required Query
$sth = $dbh->prepare("SELECT * FROM playerdata WHERE firstname LIKE
\"\%$SearchString\%\" OR surname LIKE \"\%$SearchString\%\"");

# Check the Query was created okay
if (!$sth)
```

```
{
    die "Error:" . $dbh->errstr . "\n";
}

# Execute the Query and check it was successful
if (!$sth->execute)
{
    die "Error:" . $sth->errstr . "\n";
}

# Cycle through all the records obtained by the Query
while ($ref = $sth->fetchrow_arrayref)
{
    $Id         = $$ref[0];
    $Title      = $$ref[1];
    $Firstname  = $$ref[2];
    $Surname    = $$ref[3];
    $Email      = $$ref[4];

# Display current record as part of a table
print<<HTML;

<tr>
 <td>$Title</td>
 <td>$Firstname</td>
 <td>$Surname</td>
 <td>$Email</td>
</tr>

HTML

}

# End the Query
$sth->finish();

# Disconnect from the database
$dbh->disconnect();

# Print the rest of the table and return button

print<<HTML;

</TABLE>
<P>
<FORM METHOD="GET" ACTION="http://192.168.0.20/cgi-bin/mysql5.pl">
 <CENTER>
```

```
  <INPUT TYPE="SUBMIT" VALUE="OK">
 </CENTER>
</FORM>
</CENTER></BODY></HTML>

HTML

}
```

Let's now look at how we have implemented the search feature. First, we have added the following line of code into our command system:

```
elsif ($Command eq "SearchData")    { &SearchData; }
```

Now if the script is passed the command SearchData, the SearchData function will be called.

Next, we have added the following code segment to the DisplayData function to make a search input box appear above the table:

```
HTML
# New Search Feature
print<<HTML;

<FORM METHOD="GET" ACTION="http://192.168.0.20/cgi-bin/mysql5.pl">
 <B>Search for:</B>
 <INPUT TYPE="TEXT" NAME="SearchString">
 <INPUT TYPE="HIDDEN" NAME="Command" VALUE="SearchData">
 <INPUT TYPE="SUBMIT" VALUE="Search...">
</FORM>
```

This simple form calls our mysql5.pl script with the SearchData command. Notice that we have used a Hidden field to specify the SearchData command. Also notice that we have set the value of the Submit button to "Search..." to indicate that this button initiates a search.

Finally, we have our SearchData functions. Let's take a step-by-step look at how these functions work. First, we start the function and retrieve the SearchString variable from the URL (i.e., what the user is searching for). This is done with the following code segment:

```
sub SearchData()
{

# Get the Search String from the URL
($SearchString    = $input{'SearchString'})     =~ s/\n/\n<BR>/g;
```

Next, we need to print the heading "Search Results" and the table header. This is done with the following code:

```
print<<HTML;

<HTML>
 <BODY>
  <CENTER>

<B>-= Search Results =-
<P>
   <TABLE BORDER=1 CELLSPACING=0 CELLPADDING=5 WIDTH=600>
    <TR>
     <TD><B><CENTER>Title</TD>
     <TD><B><CENTER>Firstname</TD>
     <TD><B><CENTER>Surname</TD>
     <TD><B><CENTER>Email Address</TD>
    </TR>

HTML
```

Now that we have our table ready for the search results, we can open the connection to the database with the following code:

```
# Connect to the database.
$dbh = DBI->connect("DBI:mysql:database=perltest;host=localhost",
                    "root", "",
                    {'RaiseError' => 1});
```

Once our connection is established, we use the following code segment to query the database, using the SearchString variable to compare the firstname and surname fields:

```
# Prepare the Required Query
$sth = $dbh->prepare("SELECT * FROM playerdata WHERE firstname LIKE
\"\%$SearchString\%\" OR surname LIKE \"\%$SearchString\%\"");
```

Notice here that we use the Like statement and also the % symbol to allow for partial matches.

Once our query is prepared, we can then execute it with the following code segment:

```
# Check the Query was created okay
if (!$sth)
{
    die "Error:" . $dbh->errstr . "\n";
}

# Execute the Query and check it was successful
if (!$sth->execute)
{
```

LIVERPOOL JOHN MOORES UNIVERSITY
LEARNING & INFORMATION SERVICES

```
        die "Error:" . $sth->errstr . "\n";
}
```

Now that we have our results, we can cycle through them and display them as separate entries in the table. Note that this code is very similar to how we display the entries in the DisplayData function.

```
# Cycle through all the records obtained by the Query
while ($ref = $sth->fetchrow_arrayref)
{
    $Id              = $$ref[0];
    $Title           = $$ref[1];
    $Firstname       = $$ref[2];
    $Surname         = $$ref[3];
    $Email           = $$ref[4];

# Display current record as part of a table
print<<HTML;

<tr>
 <td>$Title</td>
 <td>$Firstname</td>
 <td>$Surname</td>
 <td>$Email</td>
</tr>

HTML

}
```

After all the data has been displayed, we can end the query and disconnect from the database with the following code:

```
# End the Query
$sth->finish();

# Disconnect from the database
$dbh->disconnect();
```

Finally, all we need to do now is end the table and display a button to allow the user to return to the main screen. This is accomplished with the following code segment:

```
# Print the rest of the table and return button

print<<HTML;

</TABLE>
<P>
```

```
<FORM METHOD="GET" ACTION="http://192.168.0.20/cgi-bin/mysql5.pl">
 <CENTER>
  <INPUT TYPE="SUBMIT" VALUE="OK">
 </CENTER>
</FORM>
</CENTER></BODY></HTML>

HTML

}
```

When we now execute the mysql5.pl script, the following screen will be visible to the user.

Figure 3-41

As you can see from the preceding figure, the script is the same, but now there is a search box above the table.

In this example, we will now type "ian" into the search box and click the Search button. When this is done, the following screen will be visible.

Figure 3-42

Summary

In this chapter, you learned the basics of Perl and how to interface with a MySQL database from the Internet using Perl. With this knowledge, it is easy to create interactive web-based tools for your game to allow easy management of players and features in the game. For example, you could allow players to login to a web site using their game account and allow them to modify or delete their player profile for the game, using the same MySQL database the game utilizes.

Introduction to TCP/IP

Introduction

Modern computer games take advantage of the Internet, the world's largest network, more and more each day. If we want to use the full potential of it in a game, we must understand how the Internet works. It doesn't help much if we can write flawless code but the theory isn't right. This chapter introduces you to TCP/IP, and teaches you how to write TCP/IP applications, or more accurately games, using the sockets application program interface (API).

What is a Protocol?

To fully understand what TCP/IP is, we must understand what a network protocol is. Basically, a network protocol is the language that two or more computers use when they share information with each other. Naturally, all the computers must speak the same language to make the information flow between them. Imagine yourself speaking to a foreigner who speaks a different language than you. You probably will not understand anything this person says. This would be the same as two computers using different protocols to communicate with each other. Each computer simply will not understand what the other is trying to send to it. Hence, no information is shared between them.

A protocol defines the rules of communication and the format of the data. Protocols are standards that work on different kinds of computers. This means that if two computers can be physically connected into a network, they can share information no matter what operating system they are running or even what type of computers they are as long as they use the same protocol.

OSI Model

The International Organization for Standardization (ISO) developed a model for data communications in the late 1970s, called the Open Systems Interconnection (OSI) model. This model is the standard for all data communications, and it also defines the basics of other standards. The model is based on seven layers, all of which have their own unique area of the data communication process. These layers are connected to each other one by one. In between each pair of layers is an interface that these layers use to work with each other. OSI defines these layers' functions and interfaces. It does not define how the layers are created. This makes it easy to create new data communication solutions based on the OSI model. But more importantly, it makes it easy to modify the existing ones. Because of this, we have the ability to choose from many different options to act on one layer. A good example is TCP and UDP, which are described later in this chapter. These two protocols belong to the transport layer, and we can choose which one to use in our application. We don't have to worry about anything extra, because the interface between the transport layer and the two other layers connected to it makes sure that the data flows correctly. Figure 4-1 shows the OSI model layers and their order.

Figure 4-1

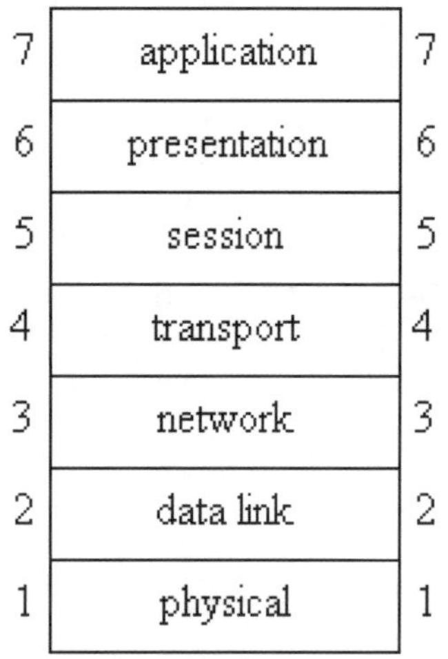

7	application	7
6	presentation	6
5	session	5
4	transport	4
3	network	3
2	data link	2
1	physical	1

OSI Model Layers

- **Layer 1: Physical**   The first layer takes care of all the physical data transfers. It includes all the physical electronic devices such as circuits, cables, and connectors. Basically, it defines the medium to be used in the data transfer.

- **Layer 2: Data link**   The second layer consists of our computer's network interface card and the device driver. The data is put into frames. The frames are checked for errors and they are fixed if any errors exist. As game developers we should not worry much about this layer, because if the hardware can do normal networking, we have no problems.

- **Layer 3: Network**   The third layer is taken care of by the Internet Protocol (IP). It addresses the packets and frames, and routes them to the correct address over subnets. We'll discuss IP in more detail in the following section.

- **Layer 4: Transport**   Layer 4 defines the method of data transfer. Depending on the method, the data is checked for errors, big packets are repackaged into smaller packets, and care is taken that the data is sent and received correctly. These features vary from method to method. This layer is the most interesting layer for the network programmer, as TCP and UDP, which are described later in this chapter, belong to this layer.

- **Layer 5: Session**   The fifth layer is fairly simple. It defines how two computers establish and end a session. It also takes care of the synchronization of the session. It defines when a computer can transfer data and when it can receive data.

- **Layer 6: Presentation**   The sixth layer takes care of possibly compressing and/or encrypting data. It defines how the data looks when it is being transferred.

- **Layer 7: Application**   The seventh layer defines the network application, such as file transfers or e-mail.

A good example of the usage of the OSI model is a normal phone conversation. The telecommunication companies provide us layer 1 — the cables and connectors in which the conversation is transferred from one place to another. Other companies take care of layer 2 — they build phones for us. The telephone companies' switches belong to layer 3. They direct the call to the correct place. Our phones use the method of transfer used by the switches and other phones to make our voice move from one place to another; this is layer 4. We are on layer 5 when we dial the number to call and the phone on the other end rings. Modern phones modulate our speech using a method called pulse code modulation (PCM); that belongs to layer 6. Now we have a complete phone conversation (layer 7).

Internet Protocol

The protocol used in Internet communications is a protocol called TCP/IP. As the name tells us, it is divided into two layers. These layers are part of the Open Systems Interconnection (OSI) model. See the section titled "OSI Model" for a description of this model. Transmission Control Protocol (TCP) is part of the transport layer of the OSI model, and Internet Protocol (IP) is part of the network layer. TCP/IP is a protocol suite that has more members than the name tells us. One important member is another protocol from the transport layer — User Datagram Protocol (UDP). Both TCP and UDP are connected to the IP protocol.

Because the OSI model is based on layers, it is easy to develop better and better network solutions by just replacing one layer with a new, better one. We can change our network interface card (NIC), drivers, or network connection type, or we can develop a better protocol. All of these possibilities are happening all the time all around the world. Companies develop new NICs and people buy them. The same companies develop new drivers for their cards and people install them on their computers. For some people this is not enough — they want better Internet connections. Also, the Internet Protocol is improving. The current version is IPv4, but the next public version is IPv6.

Requirements of the modern computer culture grow every day. As computers get faster and faster, people are buying more and more computers. But the reason people buy computers is not just because they are fast. The reason is the Internet. Imagine what an average computer user did with his or her computer in the 1970s or 1980s. Most likely, word processing was one of the most common reasons for buying a computer then. Back then, an average user had not even heard of such a thing as the Internet. Or even if they had, they didn't dream of ever using it at home. Back to the present. Now people need computers for everything. Or at least they think they need them. Getting an Internet connection is very easy now and even fairly cheap, so there really is no point in not getting it. And this is leading to problems. The number of free IP addresses is running out quickly as companies reserve many addresses for themselves and individuals reserve their own IPs — not necessarily for all the time, but at least for the time they are online.

Demand for a good network system for universities was increasing in the U.S. in the 1960s. This led to the development of IPv4 during the 1970s. Its addresses consist of four decimal dotted bytes, such as 192.168.0.1. But because the human mind is better with names than numbers, some IP addresses are given names (for example, www.huntedcow.co.uk). A Domain Name System (DNS) then looks up the name and the corresponding IP address number.

The addresses are divided into subnets — class A, class B, and class C. Class A means that the first byte of the address is used to define the subnet. The very first bit is set to 0, to identify that it is a class A address. This bit is taken from the network byte, so only the remaining seven bits are used for identifying the network. The last three bytes are used to define the address itself. In class B, the first two bytes define the subnet and the other two the address. The first two bits of a class B address are 1 and 0, leaving 14 bits for the network part. Naturally in class C the first three bytes define the subnet and the last byte the address. The first three bits of class C addresses are 1, 1, and 0, and the next 21 bits are used for the network part. There are about 16,000,000 class A IP addresses, and they are all in use. Class B consists of about 65,000 addresses and class C of 254 addresses. The whole address space of IPv4 is about 4 billion addresses. Four billion is a big number, but it will not be big enough for IP addresses in the future.

Class D addresses are multicast addresses. The first four bits are the identifier bits. On a class D address they are 1, 1, 1, and 0. Multicast defines a group of IP addresses. So when you send something to a multicast address, you are not sending to a single computer but a group of computers. Class E addresses are reserved for future use. Figure 4-2 shows the different address classes and how their data space is divided.

Figure 4-2

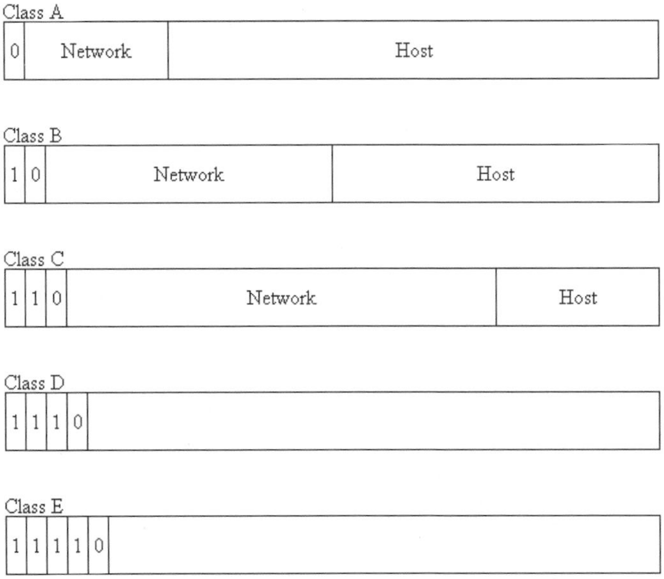

Class A

| 0 | Network | Host |

Class B

| 1 | 0 | Network | Host |

Class C

| 1 | 1 | 0 | Network | Host |

Class D

| 1 | 1 | 1 | 0 | |

Class E

| 1 | 1 | 1 | 1 | 0 | |

The solution for the problem is IPv6. Among other improvements, it provides a new 128-bit addressing system that increases the address space so much that we would need to colonize new worlds to use them all. Well, at least that's the way it looks right now. Only the future will tell if it is true.

IPv6 was developed in the 1990s and it is most likely going to be put into wide-spread use during the next decade. Because of this, it is a good idea to prepare for it now. There's no point in making a network application that may not work tomorrow. Of course, IPv6 is compatible with IPv4 to a certain point, but to be absolutely sure we should develop our applications to be protocol independent from the beginning. This text teaches you how to do this, so keep reading.

Introduction to the Transport Layer

As we have learned already, the TCP/IP protocol suite consists of two layers of the OSI model — network and transport. The transport layer is as important a part of TCP/IP as the network layer. For the network programmer, it is the most interesting part of it. When we write network applications, we write commands for the transport layer.

In Internet communications using TCP/IP, the transport layer is either Transmission Control Protocol (TCP) or User Datagram Protocol (UDP).

> **NOTE** We can also use raw sockets to get a direct connection in our code to the Internet Protocol, bypassing TCP and UDP. This is beyond the scope of this book though.

Transmission Control Protocol

Transmission Control Protocol is a connection-oriented protocol. This means that every time we want to communicate with a remote host, we must first establish a connection. Once we have established a connection, we do not have to worry about directing the messages we sent to the correct place. When we are done with the connection, we must close it. TCP is also a reliable protocol. It makes sure the other end receives the messages we send, and it handles such things as duplicated packets.

Sometimes when a packet is sent to the network, it may get lost for a while. This may happen, for example, if a router is experiencing some problems. The packet gets stuck on the router so the receiving host never sends a confirmation that the packet has reached its destination. The sending host assumes that the packet is lost forever and retransmits it after a certain time. This new packet may find another route to the receiving host while the original packet is still stuck on the router. If the router starts working normally again, it routes the packet to the correct place and the receiving host may receive the same packet again. This packet is a duplicate; TCP notices it and destroys it, as it is not needed anymore.

User Datagram Protocol

User Datagram Protocol is, unlike TCP, a connectionless protocol. No connection is established between the two communicating hosts. The sending host must define the target address every time it sends something. When a host receives a message, it knows where the message came from, and it can transmit something back to the remote host. UDP is not reliable, as it does not ensure that the transmission is received. It also does not take care of duplicates, but with UDP duplicates are not that common because the sending host won't retransmit anything if the message is not received — simply because it does not care. UDP can be used in applications that need the best possible efficiency but very little reliability. Computer games fall into this category, and that is why UDP is very important to us.

UDP can be made reliable too, but it requires that we write the needed checking algorithms ourselves. Some checking is always good, but no one forces us to make any.

Ports

Taking into account that most network application servers today are very simple, it would be foolish to make one network server run only one service. A game server may require all of the server's resources, so there are exceptions too. But how can we identify the service we want to use if the server is running dozens of services? We cannot connect every service one by one and check if it is the one we want, as this may take a long period of time, and some services may seem like the one we are looking for but are not. Therefore, we need to allocate each service a number, which we need to define when we are connecting to it. These numbers are called port numbers.

A port number is a 16-bit value, so there are 65,535 possible ports available (no such thing as port 0). Actually, available ports are not that straightforward. Ports from 1 to 1,023 are so-called well-known ports, and we cannot use these ports for our servers. These ports are reserved for common network services such as FTP (port 21) and daytime server (port 13), etc. Ports from 1,024 to 65,535 basically are free to be used, but it is a good idea to check that the port you are about to pick is not used by any other known service. The Internet Assigned Numbers Authority (IANA) records the used ports if they are well known enough.

TCP and UDP ports are unique. For example, TCP port 1,024 is not the same as UDP port 1,024. Usually, if a port number is registered by the IANA, it is registered for both protocols at the same time, even if the application does not use both protocols at that time.

We need to define the port number only for the server. Clients use so-called ephemeral ports, which we have no control over. The kernel of the operating system chooses them for us. The range of the ephemeral ports varies from platform to platform. We can see this in Figure 4-3. We can also assign an ephemeral port for a server, but only in a special case, which is beyond the scope of this book.

Figure 4-3

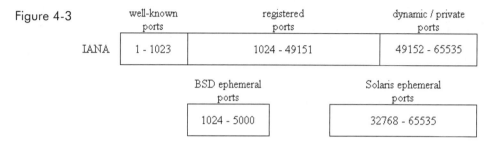

well-known ports	registered ports	dynamic / private ports
1 - 1023	1024 - 49151	49152 - 65535

IANA

BSD ephemeral ports	Solaris ephemeral ports
1024 - 5000	32768 - 65535

Introduction to Sockets

Sockets API is a programming interface that we use to write network applications. It is a multi-platform API, so we can make different operating systems communicate with each other using sockets. This text teaches you how to make your network code function on multiple platforms without making any changes to the code.

There is no clear definition of what a socket is. Different people have different opinions about them, but the basic idea is clear. Basically, a socket is a pipe between two computers on a network in which the data flows. It is not the physical cable or anything concrete like that. A socket exists only in the world of bits and bytes. The two computers have their own unique socket, and these sockets can be identified as the two ends of the pipe. Request for Comment number 147 (RFC147) defines what a socket is for the ARPA network. As the ARPA network is the predecessor of the Internet, this documentation applies to Internet sockets as well.

Figure 4-4

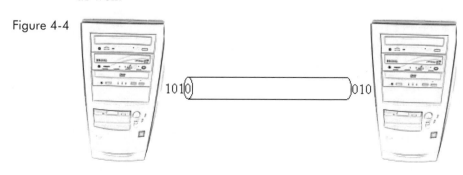

In the computer memory, sockets are 32-bit numbers. So when a new socket is created, it is given a unique number that defines the socket on the local computer.

Socket Types

There are two kinds of sockets available: stream sockets and datagram sockets. A stream socket is a connection-oriented socket, so a connection has to be established before it can send or receive data. Stream sockets use the TCP transport protocol. A datagram socket is a connectionless socket. Datagram sockets use the UDP transport protocol.

You may think now that a connection must be established before usage. However, it is not as straightforward as it sounds. We can think of this in terms of multiple levels of connections. The last level is when we have established the connection between two stream sockets. Before that there is a level where there is no real connection, but the two hosts know of each other and their addresses. Now they can sort of throw things at each other and hope that they reach their destination. With an established connection the two hosts could throw the things into a pipe (the connection between the two hosts), and the probablity of receiving the data would be much higher than without a connection.

In a stream socket, the data flows constantly in the socket, as the name suggests. It works like a stream of water, except that it moves in both ways. Stream sockets are reliable in many ways. Both sides know if the other side disconnects or crashes and cannot receive anything anymore. Every packet is monitored to see that it reaches its destination. If a packet has not reached its destination in a certain amount of time, it will be retransmitted.

In a datagram socket the data is transmitted in datagrams. This means that whenever there is something to send, the data is sent to the address defined. When there is nothing to send, no data flows between the two hosts. If one side crashes, the other side will not notice this if there has not been a system built that checks to see if the other side is alive. Datagram sockets are not reliable. The packets are not monitored by TCP/IP to make sure they reach their destination. If we want, we can create our own monitoring system, but if we use UDP for the monitoring system, the monitoring system will not be reliable. This can get very confusing, so some people use only stream sockets.

Address

Each socket has its own address information. We can create a socket on any port as long as the port is free and available for use. We can also define the IP address to connect to for every socket. Usually, on a server application, a single socket is not enough. We need one socket to listen to the incoming clients and another socket to handle the client/server communication. At the same time, the listening socket is still listening for clients, and it creates a new socket for all other clients as well. This type of server is called a concurrent server. If the server uses only one socket to do all the communication, it can communicate with only one client at once. This type of server is called an iterative server. When creating computer games, we need to process multiple clients at once, so a concurrent server is the only way to do it. Chapter 5 covers both iterative and concurrent servers.

Platforms

The sockets API works on many platforms, and because it does, we should know how to take advantage of it. This book covers Unix (Linux) and Windows versions of the API; once we are done, we will know how to write code that works on both platforms.

Originally the sockets API was developed for the Unix operating system. 4.2BSD (Berkeley Software Distribution) system had the first version of sockets in 1983. At the same time, TCP/IP was released widely to the public for the first time. From that, the API has developed. Many Unix platforms use the same networking code as BSD does, but Linux does not. Linux's network code has been written from scratch, but this does not mean that these different implementations would not be compatible. Linux is a free and very popular Unix-based operating system. All Unix code in this book has been developed and tested on a Linux system.

Many non-Unix operating systems have the sockets API as well. For example, Windows has its own sockets library called WinSock (Windows Sockets). WinSock is compatible with BSD sockets, but it also has many new features that the BSD version does not have. Because of operating system differences there are some noticeable differences in the APIs, but they do not interfere with the compatibility when connecting two computers. The latest version of WinSock is WinSock2. WinSock2 software development kit (SDK) is available from the Internet on various FTP servers. This SDK is required for writing applications that use WinSock.

History of WinSock

The Windows Socket API was born October 10, 1991, at Interop '91 in San Jose, California. A committee was established to design a specification for a sockets library for the Windows operating system. The proposal for this idea came from Martin Hall of JSB Corporation. There have been over 40 companies involved in the design of WinSock. WinSock is not the property of Microsoft, although it is an important part of Windows nowadays. It was developed by independent sources who were interested in taking part in this project. In January 20, 1993, the specification for WinSock 1.1 was published. This version had support for TCP/IP only.

WinSock2 was published in 1996. It provided support for multiple transport protocols, such as Novell IPX/SPX and Digital's DECNet. Also, the OSI model is now officially supported. Version 2 also includes features like multicasting and Quality of Service (QoS). Both of these features are explained later in this book.

WinSock is currently consistent with version 4.3 of the Berkeley Software Distribution sockets.

Choosing the Platform

Because we are writing games, we consider WinSock essential for us. The fact is that Windows is the operating system most games are written for, so you may be wondering why we need Unix code too. Well, of course we could write the game for Unix platforms, but the main reason is the server. Most network games use Unix as the platform for their servers. There are many reasons for this, but the two most important reasons are the great stability of all Unix systems and easy remote controlling. Every Unix system can be controlled remotely, so we do not actually have to sit down in front of the server machine every time we want to control the server somehow. Using Windows 9x as the server platform is out of the question because of some certain restrictions. Windows NT and Windows 2000 are good options for the server platform. These systems do not have the same restrictions as Windows 9x systems have, because they have been designed for different kinds of usage. In the end, it is up to you which operating system you wish to use. But remember, the client and the server can be run on different platforms.

Summary

In this chapter we learned the basics of TCP/IP networks and sockets. We learned what a socket is and how it originated. We also learned some history of the TCP/IP protocol. More importantly, we learned the structure of TCP/IP and the basic idea of how it works. We need this knowledge to understand network programming. Now that we know what the Sockets API is, we are ready to learn how to write network applications using it.

CHAPTER 4

Chapter 5

Basic Sockets Programming

Introduction

The Unix sockets API does not require any extra initialization before we can actually use the sockets. However, this is not the case for Windows Sockets. What we need to initialize is the WinSock 2 Dynamic Linking Library (DLL) and then enumerate the available protocols. As this book focuses only on the TCP/IP protocol, we only look for TCP and UDP protocols. Next, we learn the basic initialization functions of WinSock. Then we see how to actually use them by creating an initialization function that does all the necessary initialization.

WinSock Initialization

Before we are able to use the WinSock API, we need to go through some basic initialization, which is explained here.

WSAStartup Function (Win32)

```
int WSAStartup(WORD wVersionRequested, LPWSADATA lpWSAData);
```

The WSAStartup function is used to initialize the WinSock API. As the first parameter, we must provide the version number we request. It is a Word value, and so we must fill the variable using the Makeword macro. Makeword creates an unsigned 16-bit integer from the two unsigned characters we give it. The second parameter is a pointer used to get the data out of the WinSock DLL. The data is stored in WSAData data type.

The function returns zero if everything went fine. If not, it returns one of the non-zero values listed in Table 5-1.

Table 5-1: WSAStartup function return values

WSASYSNOTREADY	The network subsystem is not ready.
WSAVERNOTSUPPORTED	The version we requested is not supported.
WSAEINPROGRESS	A blocking WinSock 1.1 operation is in progress, or the service provider's callback function is in progress.
WSADPROCLIM	The limit of WinSock tasks has been reached.
WSAEFAULT	lpWSAData is not a valid pointer.

WSACleanup Function (Win32)

```
int WSACleanup(void);
```

We use WSACleanup to uninitialize the WinSock API. This function will unregister the WinSock DLL used by our application. Windows keeps a record of all the DLLs used by applications. It updates the reference count of each DLL, and if it is higher than zero, Windows knows that this DLL is used by an application and therefore it is kept open in the system memory. If the reference count is zero, the DLL is not open.

It is our responsibility as programmers to keep Windows aware of all the registered DLLs. In other words, we must call WSACleanup at the end of every WinSock application if the WinSock API has been initialized.

The return value is zero if the operation was successful. On error, the return value is SOCKET_ERROR, but we can get a more accurate error value by using WSAGetLastError. Table 5-2 lists the return values of WSACleanup function.

Table 5-2: WSACleanup function return values

WSANOTINITIALISED	WinSock API is not initialized.
WSAENETDOWN	A network subsystem error occurred.
WSAEINPROGRESS	A blocking WinSock 1.1 operation is in progress, or the service provider's callback function is in progress.

WSAEnumProtocols Function (Win32)

```
int WSAEnumProtocols(LPINT lpiProtocols, LPWSAPROTOCOL_INFO lpProtocolBuffer,
                     LPDWORD lpdwBufferLength);
```

This function is used to enumerate the available protocols on the local computer. The first parameter is a pointer to a list of protocols we wish to look for. We must create an integer list of the protocols. In this text we use only TCP and UDP, so we put only these two in the list:

■ IPPROTO_TCP — Transmission Control Protocol

■ IPPROTO_UDP — User Datagram Protocol

The second parameter is a pointer to a WSAProtocol_Info buffer that is filled when the function is run.

The third parameter is a value-result parameter. It is used to tell the function how big a buffer we need for the protocols, but the function may also change it if it is not big enough. This is important, because when we start enumerating the protocols, we actually run this function twice. The first time we do not fill the first two parameters at all, because all we need to do is get the buffer size. We provide a pointer to a zero-size buffer, so the function will increase the size for us. The next time we run the function, we give it all the needed parameter info, and we also give it the buffer size we got from the first call to WSAEnumProtocols.

WinSock Initialization Function

```
int NET_InitializeWinSock(void)
{
    WORD versionRequested;
    WSADATA wsaData;
    DWORD bufferSize = 0;
    LPWSAPROTOCOL_INFO ProtocolInfo;
    int NumProtocols;

    // Start WinSock2
    versionRequested = MAKEWORD(2, 0);
    int error = WSAStartup(versionRequested, &wsaData);

    if(error)
    {
        return 1;
    }
    else
    {
        // Make sure that the WinSock2 DLL supports the version we want
        if(LOBYTE(wsaData.wVersion) != 2 || HIBYTE(wsaData.wVersion) != 0)
```

```
        {
            WSACleanup();
            return 1;
        }
    }

    // Call WSAEnumProtocols to figure out how big of a buffer we need
    error = WSAEnumProtocols(NULL, NULL, &bufferSize);

    if( (error != SOCKET_ERROR) && (WSAGetLastError() != WSAENOBUFS) )
    {
        WSACleanup();
        return 1;
    }

    // Allocate a buffer, call WSAEnumProtocols to get an array
    // of WSAPROTOCOL_INFO structs
    ProtocolInfo = (LPWSAPROTOCOL_INFO) malloc(bufferSize);

    if(ProtocolInfo == NULL)
    {
        WSACleanup();
        return 1;
    }

    // Allocate memory for protocol list and define what
    // protocols to look for
    int *protos = (int *) calloc(2, sizeof(int));
    protos[0] = IPPROTO_TCP;
    protos[1] = IPPROTO_UDP;

    NumProtocols = WSAEnumProtocols(protos, ProtocolInfo, &bufferSize);
    free(protos);
    protos = NULL;

    free(ProtocolInfo);
    ProtocolInfo = NULL;

    if(NumProtocols == SOCKET_ERROR)
    {
        WSACleanup();
        return 1;
    }

    return 0;
}
```

The preceding code shows us how to initialize WinSock API. It is a function from the network library we will create later. But as this function is essential for getting WinSock ready to be used, we introduce it now. Next, we will go through all the important parts to see what is really happening.

First, we use the Makeword macro to fill the word versionRequested with the information we want. In this case, we want to check that the version number of WinSock DLL is 2.0, so we fill the word with bytes representing 2 and 0. Then we run WSAStartup to start initializing the WinSock API.

```
versionRequested = MAKEWORD(2, 0);
int error = WSAStartup(versionRequested, &wsaData);
```

The function fills wsaData for us. We check the wsaData's wVersion member (word) to see what version the DLL supports. Now we use LOBYTE and HIBYTE macros to check the two bytes of the word. If the bytes do not match the version number we want, we clean up WinSock and return 1 to tell that there was an error:

```
if(LOBYTE(wsaData.wVersion) != 2 || HIBYTE(wsaData.wVersion) != 0)
{
    WSACleanup();
    return 1;
}
```

Next, we need to find out how big a buffer we need for the protocols. We use WSAEnumProtocols for this. During the initialization process, we run this function twice. The first time we run it, we do not provide any parameters for it other than the last one. That is the buffer size parameter. The function will increase the buffer size for us if it is too small. We start with a zero-size buffer, so the first time we run the function, it will fail for sure. We want this function to fail for now. This means that if the function does not return SOCKET_ERROR, something is wrong. We can assume that since the buffer size is set to zero, the error is telling us the buffer size is too small.

Then we check that the last error occurred because the buffer was too small. We do this by using WSAGetLastError function. If the buffer was too small, the last error message was WSAENOBUFS. If it was something else, there is something else wrong and we should quit the initialization process.

```
error = WSAEnumProtocols(NULL, NULL, &bufferSize);
if( (error != SOCKET_ERROR) && (WSAGetLastError() != WSAENOBUFS) )
{
    WSACleanup();
    return 1;
}
```

This is how we define the protocols we are looking for:

```
int *protos = (int *) calloc(2, sizeof(int));
protos[0] = IPPROTO_TCP;
protos[1] = IPPROTO_UDP;
```

First, we allocate memory for the protocol list quite normally, and then simply fill the list with protocols we want. Because we only want the two TCP/IP protocols, that is what we put in the list. The order of the list members doesn't matter; it does not affect anything.

Finally, we get to enumerate the actual protocols. We now have all the information we need for the second call to WSAEnumProtocols. For the first parameter we provide the protocol list; for the second, the protocol information structure pointer; and for the last, the buffer size. The return value is the number of protocols it found. The return value is SOCKET_ERROR if something is wrong. We do not need to check what actually is wrong. It is enough to know that something did go wrong, and we stop initializing if this happens.

```
NumProtocols = WSAEnumProtocols(protos, ProtocolInfo, &bufferSize);
```

NOTE WSAEnumProtocols looks for protocols installed on your Windows operating system. If you do not have TCP/IP protocols installed on your operating system, WSAEnumProtocols will not find them.

Error Handling

The previous code listing contains one WinSock function we have not discussed yet. This is the WSAGetLastError function. It is a WinSock-only function.

WSAGetLastError Function (Win32)

```
int WSAGetLastError(void);
```

This function retrieves the last error value that occurred in the last Windows sockets operation function. Some functions only inform you that an error occurred but do not give the actual error value. This function is then used to get the error value. The return value is the last error value.

Unix does not have a function to receive the last error occurred, but it does have the global variable Errno that works just like the return value of WSAGetLastError, but you do not have to fetch it by running a function. The error values on different platforms may have equal integer values (they also may differ), but their constant names usually are not the same. For example, WinSock error values also have the prefix "WSA."

Sockets Data Types

Sockets have more than one address data type. This is because different protocols require unique information. We can still write protocol-independent code thanks to the generic address data type. All these data types are explained here.

Platform Specific Data Types

As we will be writing our code for multiple platforms, we must be aware of data types that mean the same thing on different platforms. We can easily define new data types and rename the required data types to match the other platform's types. This can be done because usually only the data type name is different; the actual data is the same. Table 5-3 shows two data types that have different names on Unix and Win32, but are really the same thing.

Table 5-3

	Unix	Win32
Address length data type	socklen_t	int
Socket descriptor data type	int	SOCKET

From now on we use the more informative data type name in the text and all source code examples. For socket address length, we use socklen_t instead of int, and for socket descriptors, we use SOCKET instead of int.

We learn how to create these new definitions for our data types in Tutorial 2, "Creating Your Network Library."

Address Structures

The address information of the sockets are stored in structures. Naturally, IPv4 and IPv6 have their own structures.

IPv4 Address Structure

The following code shows the structure for IPv4:

```
struct in_addr
{
    in_addr_t s_addr;          // 32-bit IP address
};

struct sockaddr_in
{
```

```
        uint8_t sin_len;                // structure length: 16 bytes
        sa_family_t sin_family;         // protocol family: AF_INET
        in_port_t sin_port;             // 16-bit port number
        struct in_addr sin_addr;        // 32-bit IP address
        char sin_zero[8];               // Not used
};
```

Let's take a look at the structure members. The structure length variable is handled by kernel, so we do not need to worry about it. The protocol family for IPv4 addresses is always AF_INET. The port number is stored in a 16-bit unsigned integer. The value is stored in network byte order. The IP address is stored in a 32-bit unsigned integer, and it is also stored in network byte order, rather than the normal decimal dotted format. We discuss how to get the decimal dotted format out of the 32-bit unsigned integer later.

IPv6 Address Structure

The following code listing shows us the IPv6 address structure:

```
struct in6_addr
{
    uint8_t s6_addr[16];            // 128-bit IP address
};


#define SIN6_LEN                    // required for the compiler

struct sockaddr_in6
{
    uint8_t sin6_len;               // structure length: 24 bytes
    sa_family_t sin6_family;        // protocol family: AF_INET6
    in_port_t sin6_port;            // 16-bit port number
    uint32_t sin6_flowinfo;         // 32-bit flow label and priority
    struct in6_addr sin6_addr;      // 128-bit IP address
};
```

Sin6_Len must be defined if the length member is supported by the system. The structure length of an IPv6 address is 24 bytes, but the kernel takes care of this. The protocol family for IPv6 addresses is AF_INET6. The port number is a 16-bit unsigned integer, just like the IPv4 ports. The IPv6 address structure has a new member that is not included in the IPv4 address structure. This stores the flow label and priority values. The first 24 bits are used for the flow label, and the next 4 bits are used for the priority. The remaining 4 bits are reserved for future use. The IP address is stored in 16 8-bit unsigned integers.

Generic Address Structure

Having more than one protocol family to be used creates a small problem. Because IPv4 and IPv6 have their own address structures, we cannot pass either of the structures as a pointer to any socket functions that use the address structure as a parameter, and still remain protocol independent. That is why we have a generic address structure. The following code listing shows us the generic address structure:

```
struct sockaddr
{
    uint8_t sa_len;            // structure length
    sa_family_t sa_family;     // protocol family
    char sa_data[14];          // the address (either IPv4 or IPv6)
};
```

Now, by typecasting the protocol-specific address structures into this generic structure, we can use any version of address structures in any of the socket functions. Of course, the functions must have this generic structure as the parameter instead of the protocol-specific ones.

Typecasting means that you are providing a mask for your pointer in the memory. This mask is used to divide the block of memory into the variables that are stored there. There is no need to typecast a pointer if the data type we want to use is the original data type. The beginning of the data types must match the generic one. But as we see in the protocol-specific address structures and the generic address structure, only the first two members of the structures match perfectly. The third member in the generic structure is chars only, and these chars are used to store the actual address information. The function itself must understand this. Figure 5-1 shows an example of how the typecast "mask" works. In this example, the first two members of the casted structure are 8-bit integers, or shorts (an X in the memory block means 8 bits), and after that there are only characters, which hold the data in a format that can be transformed into any data type.

Figure 5-1: Typecasting

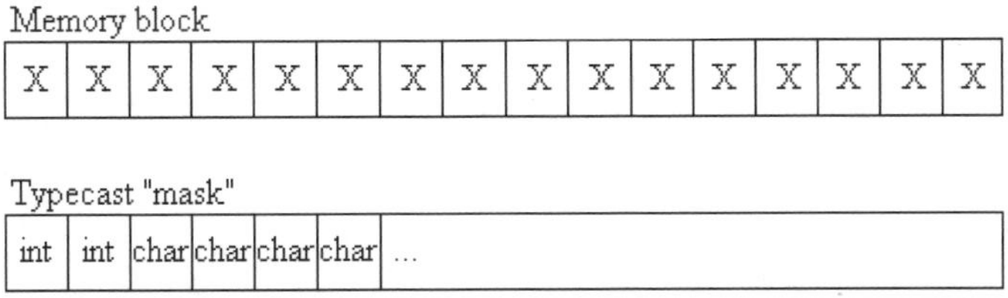

Memory block

| X | X | X | X | X | X | X | X | X | X | X | X | X | X | X | X |

Typecast "mask"

| int | int | char | char | char | char | ... |

TIP As you have probably already noticed, typecasting is a useful way to make one code work with various data types. It is a good idea to take advantage of it whenever possible.

Basic Sockets Functions

There are some functions in the sockets API that almost all sockets applications use at some point. These functions are explained in this section.

Socket Function (Unix, Win32)

```
SOCKET socket(int family, int type, int protocol);
```

This function creates a socket with the provided information. This function only creates the descriptor of the socket; it does not really start using any port or any IP address yet. If you are familiar with Unix programming, you may notice that the socket descriptors are just like file descriptors on Unix.

The first parameter (int family) specifies the protocol family. It can be one of these:

- AF_INET — IPv4 protocols
- AF_INET6 — IPv6 protocols
- AF_ROUTE — Routing sockets

There are more options for this parameter on different platforms. We cover only the first two, AF_INET and AF_INET6, in this text.

The second parameter (int type) defines the socket type, which can be one of the following:

- SOCK_STREAM — Stream socket
- SOCK_DGRAM — Datagram socket
- SOCK_RAW — Raw socket

This book covers only SOCK_STREAM and SOCK_DGRAM. SOCK_STREAM is used for TCP sockets, and SOCK_DGRAM is used for UDP sockets.

The third parameter (int protocol) is set to zero when using either stream or datagram sockets.

Win32 return values:

- Success: A nonnegative descriptor (integer)
- Failure: INVALID_SOCKET

Unix return values:

- Success: A nonnegative descriptor (integer)
- Failure: –1

Bind Function (Unix, Win32)

```
int bind(SOCKET s, const struct sockaddr *addr, socklen_t addrlen);
```

The Bind function is the function that makes your socket have its own address information, i.e., the IP address and port number. This function binds the local address information to each socket. You cannot define a non-local IP address when calling Bind, but you can define any port number (keeping in mind that not all ports are available ports). This function is usually used right after the call to the Socket function.

You cannot listen to incoming events if you have not bound the socket to the port to be listened to.

Both stream and datagram sockets must be bound to an address before they can be used. You do not have to bind a client's local sockets, but it is OK to do so.

The first parameter (SOCKET s) defines the unbound socket to be bound. The socket must have been created with the Socket function.

The second parameter (const struct sockaddr *addr) is a pointer to a sockaddr address information structure.

The third parameter (socklen_t addrlen) is the size of the address information structure.

The address you are about to bind may already be in use by another application or by your own application. If this is the case, bind returns (the value must be retrieved by using the WSAGetLastError function in Windows or the errno variable in Unix) the error value EADDRINUSE (Unix) or WSEADDRINUSE (Windows). With certain socket options we can still bind the address, even if it is already in use.

If you set the port number to zero, the operating system's kernel will choose an ephemeral port for you. Usually this is the first free ephemeral port. Client applications use ephemeral ports because there really is no need for us to know the port the client uses. The remote host the client is sending data to can figure out the port itself.

If we have multiple network interface cards on our local host, we can either choose the IP address for the socket ourself, or we can make the kernel choose it for us. To do this, we use the the constant INADDR_ANY.

NOTE A single host can have multiple IP addresses if it has multiple network interface cards. Usually only server machines have this kind of arrangement.

If an error is encountered with the Bind function, we must use the WSAGetLast-Error function in Windows or the errno variable in Unix to get the actual error value.

Win32 return values:

■ Success: 0

■ Failure: SOCKET_ERROR

Unix return values:

■ Success: 0

■ Failure: –1

Connect Function (Unix, Win32)

```
int connect(SOCKET s, const struct sockaddr *addr, socklen_t addrlen);
```

This function is used to connect a TCP client and server. We do not need to know the client's address information, hence there is no need to call the Bind function on the client before we call Connect. The kernel will do all the dirty work for us in this case. It chooses the ephemeral port and retrieves the IP address information.

The first parameter (SOCKET s) defines the socket to connect.

The second parameter (const struct sockaddr *addr) must provide the information about the server's address: IP address and port number. If we fail to give the correct address of the server, the connection will fail.

The third parameter (socklen_t addrlen) is used to define the length of the address structure in bytes.

This function does not return before the TCP's three-way handshake is complete. If an error occurs before that, the function will return. So when this function returns, we know that either the connection is established or it could not be established.

The client will wait a total of 75 seconds for the remote server to respond to its SYN segment of the three-way handshake. If no response is received during this time, the function returns an error. If the client does receive a response to the SYN segment, but it is an RST (reset), it means that the server machine is running but is not waiting for connections at the TCP port we specified. The function will return an error value.

These and any other specific error values must be retrieved by using the WSAGetLastError function in Windows or the errno variable in Unix.

Win32 return values:

■ Success: 0

■ Failure: SOCKET_ERROR

Unix return values:

■ Success: 0

■ Failure: –1

Listen Function (Unix, Win32)

```
int listen(SOCKET s, int backlog);
```

The Listen function is used for connection-oriented sockets to set the socket to listen for incoming connections. This means that it is not used for UDP sockets. This function is called after the calls to the Socket and Bind functions. This function must be called before the Accept function is called. This is a server-side function.

The first parameter (SOCKET s) must be a bound, unconnected socket. The socket must have been created with the Socket function, and it must be bound with the Bind function.

The second and last parameter (int backlog) defines the maximum amount of connections allowed. This sounds very simple, but in fact it is not. First of all, all operating systems have their own maximum for this. For example, Windows NT 4.0 Server has a maximum backlog value of 100. Normally, on operating systems that are not designed for server usage, the backlog value is about 4 or 5.

The kernel keeps track of two connection queues: incomplete and complete connections. The latter is clear; these are the connections that have been established all the way. This means that the TCP three-way handshake is complete with them. The incomplete connections are connections that have the first part of the TCP three-way handshake complete. On the packet level it means that the first SYN packet from the client has been received by the server. The sum of these two queues cannot exceed the backlog value. After this function successfully returns, the used socket is called a listening socket.

If the backlog value is set to be larger than the operating system's maximum, the value is silently set to the nearest valid value. Silently means that there is no way to know about it; no error value is returned. If the queue is full and there is an incoming connection, Listen will return EConnRefused on Unix or WSAE-ConnRefused on Windows. These error values must be retrieved by the WSAGetLastError function in Windows or the errno variable in Unix.

Win32 return values:

- Success: 0
- Failure: SOCKET_ERROR

Unix return values:

- Success: 0
- Failure: –1

Accept Function (Unix, Win32)

```
int accept(SOCKET s, struct sockaddr *addr, socklen_t *addrlen);
```

This function is used to accept an incoming TCP connection. It is run after the Listen function has filled the completed connections queue with at least one connection. When the queue is empty and this function is run, depending on the socket I/O option (blocking or non-blocking) the process is either put to sleep or it moves on to the next command. Like Listen, this is a server-side function.

The first parameter (SOCKET s) defines the socket that holds the connection to be accepted. This must be a listening socket.

The second parameter (struct sockaddr *addr) is used to get the address information of the client whose connection we are just about to accept. This parameter can be set to NULL if we are not interested in this information.

The third parameter (socklen_t *addrlen) is a value-result parameter, which must be set to the size of the address structure before calling Accept. When the function returns, this parameter holds the number of bytes allocated for the address structure by the function. It can be set to NULL if we are not interested in this information. After Accept successfully returns, the used socket is called a connected socket.

The return value is a new descriptor for the socket if everything went fine. The listening socket given to the function as a parameter stays untouched. It is not removed, and its descriptor is not changed. We can still listen for new incoming connections with the very same socket. What we get out of Accept is a brand new connected socket.

If there was an error, Accept returns an error value indicating this, but to get the accurate error values we use the WSAGetLastError function in Windows or the errno variable in Unix.

So if we have a TCP server that will serve multiple clients at once, we create one listening socket and then spawn new connected sockets for each connection.

Win32 return values:

- Success: A nonnegative descriptor (integer)
- Failure: INVALID_SOCKET

Unix return values:

- Success: A nonnegative descriptor (integer)
- Failure: –1

Close Function (Unix)/Closesocket Function (Win32)

```
int close(SOCKET s);
int closesocket(SOCKET s);
```

Unix and Windows versions of this function differ by name, but the use is the same on both operating systems.

This function closes the TCP socket. Before actually terminating the connection, TCP will send all queued data. We cannot send or receive any more data even if the connection has not been terminated for good. When all queued data is sent, TCP's four-packet termination process initiates. We can make this function work differently by adjusting socket options. We discuss these options in Chapter 6, "I/O Operations."

The socket descriptor is returned to be reused. So after closing a socket we may encounter a socket with the same descriptor as the socket we closed. They have nothing do with each other, though. For example, if we close a socket and then immediately create a new one, the new socket must be initialized normally even if the descriptor is the same as the one we just closed.

If an error occurs, we need to use the WSAGetLastError function in Windows or the errno variable in Unix to retrieve the actual error value.

Win32 return values:

- Success: 0
- Failure: SOCKET_ERROR

Unix return values:

- Success: 0
- Failure: –1

Input/Output Functions

There are four basic functions for sending/receiving data in the sockets API — two for each operation. All four are explained here.

Send Function (Unix, Win32)

```
int send(SOCKET s, const void *buf, size_t len, int flags);
```

This function is used to send data to a socket. The socket must be successfully connected before this function can be used. This function is usually used by stream (TCP) sockets only, but it is possible to use this with datagram (UDP) sockets, too. The UDP socket must be connected using the sockets Connect function, but that is beyond the scope of this book.

The first parameter (SOCKET s) is the socket to which we want to send the data (must be a connected socket).

The second parameter (const void *buf) is the data itself. It is a pointer to a buffer containing the data we want to send.

The third parameter (size_t len) defines the number of bytes to send. We do not need to send the whole data buffer (and it is not always even possible).

The fourth and final parameter (int flags) is used to set different flags (options) on with the current send process. These flags are temporary, so they must be set every time they are required by a send process. We can OR various flags together. Table 5-4 lists the possible flags.

HINT OR ing is a bit-wise operation. Bit-wise operations are the most low-level operations available as computers work using bits, ones, and zeroes. Because of this, they are also very fast and take very little memory. I recommend that you learn more about bit-wise operations and to use them wherever possible.

Table 5-4: Send/Sendto flags

Flags	Description	Unix	Win32
MSG_DONTROUTE	Target host is locally connected to the network. Do not look for the target host from a routing table.	Yes	Yes
MSG_DONTWAIT	Set the current output non-blocking. Do not wait for the output of data.	Yes	No
MSG_OOB	Send out-of-band data.	Yes	Yes

When Send returns, it either returns the amount of bytes sent or indicates that an error occurred. We cannot send zero-size data with TCP protocol. If we get a zero return value from Send, it means that the other host has closed the connection or the connection is broken. If there was an error, we need to retrieve the actual error values by using the WSAGetLastError function in Windows or the errno variable in Unix. Even if Send returns successfully, it does not mean that the other end successfully received the data.

Win32 return values:

- Success: Number of bytes sent
- Failure: SOCKET_ERROR

Unix return values:

- Success: Number of bytes sent
- Failure: –1

Recv Function (Unix, Win32)

```
int recv(SOCKET s, void *buf, size_t len, int flags);
```

This function is very similar to the Send function, but naturally this time we are receiving data and not sending it. The parameters are almost the same:

The first parameter (SOCKET s) is the socket where we want to receive the data. It must be a connected socket.

The second parameter (void *buf) is the data buffer. It is a pointer to a buffer where we want to store the data.

The third parameter (size_t len) defines the number of bytes to receive.

The fourth parameter (int flags) works the same way as in the Send function. We can set temporary socket input options on here by ORing various options together, or simply set one on. Table 5-5 lists the input flags.

Table 5-5: Recv/Recvfrom flags

Flag	Description	Unix	Win32
MSG_DONTWAIT	Set the current output non-blocking. Do not wait for the output of data.	Yes	No
MSG_OOB	Receive out-of-band data.	Yes	Yes
MSG_PEEK	Peek at the incoming data. The data is copied to the receive buffer, but it is not removed from the incoming data queue.	Yes	Yes
MSG_WAITALL	Wait for all the data to be received before returning.	Yes	No

The return value of Recv tells us how many bytes it received or in case of an error, an error value. If Recv returns zero, the other side has closed the connection or the connection is broken. If there was an error, we need to retrieve the actual error values by using the WSAGetLastError function in Windows or the errno variable in Unix.

Win32 return values:

- Success: Number of bytes received
- Failure: SOCKET_ERROR

Unix return values:

- Success: Number of bytes received
- Failure: –1

Sendto Function (Unix, Win32)

```
int sendto(SOCKET s, const void *buf, size_t len, int flags, const struct sockaddr
*to, socklen_t addrlen);
```

Like the Send function, this function is also used to send data to a socket. With this function it is not necessary that the socket is connected. This function is normally used for datagram (UDP) socket output, but it can be used for stream (TCP) sockets too.

The first parameter (SOCKET s) is the socket where we want to send the data.

The second parameter (const void *buf) is the data itself. It is a pointer to a buffer containing the data we want to send.

The third parameter (size_t len) defines the number of bytes to send. We do not need to send the whole data buffer (and it is not always even possible).

The fourth parameter (int flags) is used to set different flags (options) on with the current send process. These flags are temporary so they must be set every time they are required by a send process. We can OR various flags together. The flags listed in Table 5-4 work with the Sendto function also.

The fifth parameter (const struct sockaddr *to) is the address structure to which we want to send the data. The address structure must contain the IP address and port.

The sixth and last parameter (socklen_t addrlen) is used to define the size of the address structure.

Similar to the Send function, when Sendto returns, it returns the amount of bytes sent or indicates that an error occurred. It is OK to send zero-size datagrams. When we send zero-size datagrams, only the IP (v4 or v6) header and the UDP header are sent. So Sendto can return zero and still function normally. If there was an error, we need to retrieve the actual error values by using the WSAGetLastError function in Windows or the errno variable in Unix. If Sendto returns successfully, it does not necessarily mean that the other end successfully received the data.

Win32 return values:

- Success: Number of bytes sent
- Failure: SOCKET_ERROR

Unix return values:

- Success: Number of bytes sent
- Failure: –1

Recvfrom Function (Unix, Win32)

```
int recvfrom(SOCKET s, void *buf, size_t len, int flags, struct sockaddr *from,
socklen_t *addrlen);
```

This function is usually used for datagram (UDP) socket input. It is similar to the Recv function, but we define the IP address and port to read from as well as the socket.

The first parameter (SOCKET s) is the socket we want to receive the data.

The second parameter (void *buf) is the data buffer. Again, it is a pointer to a buffer where we want to store the data.

The third parameter (size_t len) defines the number of bytes to receive.

The fourth parameter (int flags) is used to set the temporary input flags. Table 5-5 lists the possible flags.

The fifth parameter (struct sockaddr *from) is a pointer to the address structure that holds the address information of the host from which we want to receive data.

The sixth parameter (socklen_t *addrlen) is a value-result argument. It defines the size of the address structure, and it also returns the updated size when the function returns.

The number of received bytes is returned again if everything went fine. Unlike with Recv function, a zero return value does not mean that the other host has closed the connection; there is no such thing as a connection in UDP. This also means that we can write datagrams of the size zero. If there was an error, we need to retrieve the actual error values by using the WSAGetLastError function in Windows or the errno variable in Unix.

Win32 return values:

- Success: Number of bytes received
- Failure: SOCKET_ERROR

Unix return values:

- Success: Number of bytes received
- Failure: –1

Address Data Conversion Functions

We humans prefer to have our information in written text or numbers instead of just ones and zeroes like computers. An Internet address is one thing that may be displayed in many ways, depending on who, or better yet what, uses it. Humans can remember these addresses best when they are written text, for example "www.huntedcow.co.uk." As computers do not have to worry about forgetting anything, they can be optimized to store the addresses in a format that takes the least amount of memory.

We have three functions for IPv4 addresses and two functions for IPv6 addresses. These two new functions are protocol independent though, so it does not matter which protocol we use with them.

We explain only one of these functions here because we only need that function in our network library, and the others are easy to understand after you understand this one.

Inet_aton Function (Unix, Win32)

```
int inet_aton(const char *string, struct in_addr *address);
```

This function converts the provided string address into a network byte ordered binary value. Note that depending on the DNS server configuration, the string can be an IP address in numeric, decimal dotted format or in written text as most web addresses are.

Client/Server Programming

Now that we have everything set up for the actual network programming, we can move on to writing our server and client code. Servers and clients work very much differently. For most of the time the server is waiting for connections to come in. Once one does come in, it serves the client that is connected.

Server Methods

Servers can be very passive applications. There can be times when they do not do anything at all. This can happen if there are no clients to be served. We must keep this in mind when creating the servers, because if we set our server to loop when there are no connections, it can easily drain all the CPU time just by running an "empty" loop.

If our server is supposed to serve only one client at a time, it is called an iterative server. It does not listen for incoming connections once a connection is already open. When the connection terminates, the server starts to listen for a new connection again. This kind of server is not very useful, because multiple clients may be "on hold" since the server can process only one connection at a time.

Computer games' servers simply cannot work this way, because it is against the principal idea of these servers. The idea is that multiple players connect to a server and then communicate via that server to play the game. That is why this kind of playing is called "multiplay."

Servers that process multiple clients at once are called concurrent servers. When the server is started, it starts listening for incoming connections. When a connection comes in, it creates a child process (a thread) and the main program continues listening for incoming connections. The main program in this case is often also a thread, and not really the actual main program. The reason is simple: If it were the main program, it would not be much of a server. The main program is the very core, the part that initiates the listening functions and so on.

Figure 5-2 shows how a concurrent server works. The listening socket is always there, and depending on the state of the application (i.e., will it allow any more connections), it will accept all the new connections coming in. Clients 1-3 have already established a connection, and are being served normally by the server. Client 4 has just connected to the server, and it is still in the process of the TCP three-way handshake. The listening socket is already free and has started to listen for more connections.

Looking from outside, a concurrent UDP server works the same way as TCP servers. Clients inform that they are there and the server takes care of them. There are lots of technical differences though, and these are discussed in the next section.

Figure 5-2:
A concurrent
server

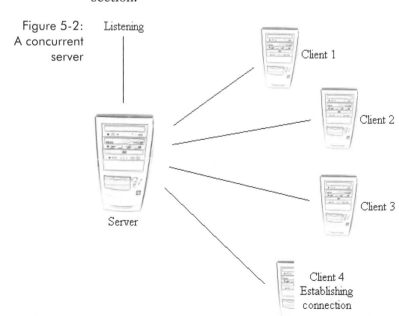

Listening

Client 1

Client 2

Client 3

Server

Client 4
Establishing
connection

Clients

Clients are active applications. They initiate the connection to the server, so they never wait for things to happen (other than wait for data from the server).

The client application is the application that the normal user uses. In the world of gaming, the client is the game itself. The player should not know anything else about the server, except the address and port number. Sometimes even this information is built into the game, so the player does not have to set the IP address or port manually.

When working in a local area network (LAN), we can create a server search system, which is one way to remove the need for manually setting the address information. We discuss this system in Chapter 6, "I/O Operations."

Byte Ordering

There is no standard way of ordering the bytes in computer memory. Nowadays, PCs often use Intel's way of ordering the bytes, which is to store the bytes in little-endian order. That means that if we have a 2-byte variable, the last actual byte is stored first in the memory. Big-endian order means that the bytes are stored in the correct order, first byte first.

Different processors store and access the bytes differently. Like we've already said, Intel's way is to store them in little-endian order. But because we are creating multi-platform applications, we cannot use only this one way. We must have a way to transform the bytes into a format that all computers understand. Therefore, we have to use network byte order. The network byte order is big-endian with the Internet protocols we use. There are functions to convert network byte ordered bytes into host byte ordered. These functions are explained in Appendix A.

Figure 5-3:
Byte
ordering

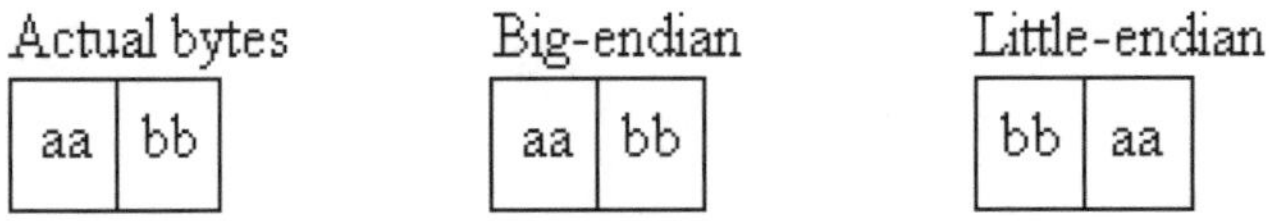

Actual bytes	Big-endian	Little-endian
aa | bb	aa | bb	bb | aa

Creating a Server

Now we are going to learn how to create a server. We learn how to create the server on Unix and Windows, using both TCP and UDP. First, let's go through the most important events when creating a server.

Every sockets application (client, server) must first create the socket. Depending on the protocols we use, the parameters change accordingly:

```
// A stream (TCP) IPv4 socket
SOCKET listeningSocket;

listeningSocket = socket(AF_INET, SOCK_STREAM, 0);
```

Then, when the socket is successfully created, we usually fill in the address information of the server. We do not have to enter the local IP address of the server if we have only one network interface card on the server machine. If we had more than one we would just enter the IP address we want to use. We assume that there is only one card, so we let the kernel automatically fill the IP address. But we do have to enter the port number ourselves. We must remember the restrictions that exist when choosing a port number for our server. Chapter 4, "Introduction to TCP/IP" goes through those things that limit port number availability.

```
struct sockaddr *servAddr;
struct sockaddr_in *inetServAddr;
int portNumber;

// Allocate memory for the address structure and set it to zero.
servAddr = (struct sockaddr *) malloc(sizeof(sockaddr));
memset((char *) servAddr, 0, sizeof(sockaddr));

// Fill the address structure.
servAddr->sa_family      = (u_short) AF_INET;
inetServAddr             = (struct sockaddr_in *) servAddr;
inetServAddr->sin_port   = htons((u_short) portNumber);
```

Of course, if we are developing a server for personal use only (LAN only), we can forget some of the restrictions. But even in this case we cannot freely take just any number, because the operating systems use some ports without having any external application installed. Because we are developing a game server for the public, we must choose a port that has no restrictions at all.

Once we have filled in the required address information, we must bind this information to the socket we created in the beginning:

```
// Bind the address information to the socket.
error = bind(listeningSocket, servAddr, sizeof(sockaddr));
```

> **NOTE** Whatever we are programming, we should never forget to check every possible function for errors. A lot of crashes for which people blame the operating system are actually caused by an application that does not handle errors properly.

We then need to separate the TCP and UDP code from each other, because of their obvious differences.

TCP

As we have learned before, TCP is the easy transport protocol (for the programmer). This is also true when creating servers. All we need to do now is make the server listen for incoming connections and accept them. For every new connection, the server creates a child process and a new socket (if we are talking about a concurrent server).

```
// Listen for incoming connections. Queue max 5 connections.
error = listen(listeningSocket, 5);

...

// Accept the connection. Accept is a blocking function.
connectedSocket = accept(listeningSocket, NULL, NULL);
```

Figure 5-4 shows a normal TCP client/server operation. You can see how much easier and faster it is to use UDP in Figure 5-5.

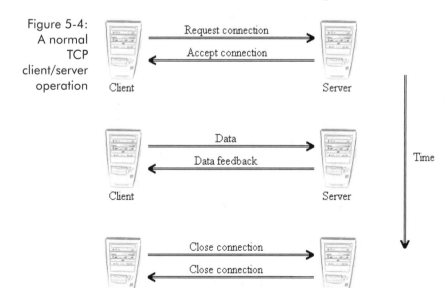

Figure 5-4:
A normal
TCP
client/server
operation

UDP

Because UDP is a connectionless protocol, it does not have a function for listening for incoming connections. The principal idea of UDP is that it simply does not have to listen to them. It just reads the incoming datagrams and acts how the programmer wants it to act.

Figure 5-5:
A normal
UDP
client/server
operation

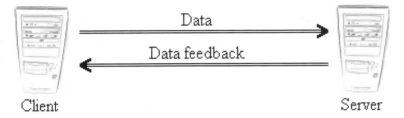

But how do we keep the server organized with all the clients sending data to it? A game server needs to send data to a client pretty much whenever it is required, so we cannot let the client do all the active sending.

The solution for this is a so-called knocking system. When the client wants to tell the server that it exists and wants to interact with the server, the client sends a "knock" datagram to the server. This datagram can be anything; it is up to you what information is stored within it. When the server receives a datagram or message like this, it updates its list of clients and either creates a new child process to serve the client or simply acknowledges that there may be incoming messages from that client. In the latter case the server uses the one and only socket to interact with all the clients. Problems may occur if many clients want to send data to the server at the same time. That is why we stick to the child process method. The knocking system is explained in whole in Tutorial 2, "Creating Your Network Library."

A UDP server that uses only one socket to interact with the clients must always retrieve the address information when it is receiving data (assuming that it wants to send data back also). With UDP we cannot simply send data to a socket without providing the exact address. This kind of server is not necessarily an iterative server. It may process multiple clients at a time, because it responds only when the client sends data to the server.

Simple Echo TCP Server

It is time to actually create our very first sockets application: a simple echo TCP server. This server is an iterative server (serves only one client at a time), and its function is to send back a character in uppercase. The protocol used is TCP, but later we will see how easy it is to make a UDP server out of our existing TCP code. This example program is of no real use and is intended to just show you the basic idea of every server, which is the following: A request from the client is sent to the server, and the server sends feedback to the client. In this example, the request is simply the letter sent to the server, and the feedback is the uppercase letter that is sent back to the client.

The following code listing shows the simple echo TCP server in its entirety. The code is written for the Windows operating system, but it is easy to change it so that it compiles and runs on Unix, too. But this is not the idea of this example, so let's skip it for now.

The functional concept of this server is that the server listens for a connection to come in, and when one does, it accepts it. Then the client is supposed to be sending single letters to the server, and the server will send them back in uppercase. If the user on the client end enters the letter "q" (lowercase), the server stops functioning automatically. The whole application is stopped, so it will not accept any other connections. For this example there is no need to write any extra checking if the user is exiting on the client end, because the Recv function will notice if the connection is closed.

```
#ifndef _WINSOCKAPI_
#define _WINSOCKAPI_
#endif

#include <windows.h>
#include <winsock2.h>

#include <stdio.h>

// Declare the sockets we use.
SOCKET listeningSocket;
SOCKET connectedSocket;

int InitSockets(void)
{
    struct sockaddr *servAddr;
    struct sockaddr_in *inetServAddr;

    int error = 0;
```

```
// Create the socket.
listeningSocket = socket(AF_INET, SOCK_STREAM, 0);

if(listeningSocket == INVALID_SOCKET)
{
    printf("error: socket() failed");
    return -1;
}

// Allocate memory for the address structure and set it to zero.
servAddr = (struct sockaddr *) malloc(sizeof(sockaddr));
memset((char *) servAddr, 0, sizeof(sockaddr));

// Fill the address structure.
servAddr->sa_family      = (u_short) AF_INET;
inetServAddr             = (struct sockaddr_in *) servAddr;
inetServAddr->sin_port   = htons((u_short) 9009);

// Bind the address information to the socket.
error = bind(listeningSocket, servAddr, sizeof(sockaddr));

if(error == SOCKET_ERROR)
{
    printf("error: bind() failed");
    free(servAddr);
    return -1;
}

free(servAddr);
servAddr = NULL;

// Listen for incoming connections. Queue only one connection.
error = listen(listeningSocket, 1);

if(error == SOCKET_ERROR)
{
    printf("error: listen() failed");
    return -1;
}

// Accept the connection. Accept is a blocking function.
connectedSocket = accept(listeningSocket, NULL, NULL);

if(connectedSocket == INVALID_SOCKET)
{
    printf("error: socket() failed");
    return -1;
```

```
        }

        return 0;
}

void ServerProcess(void)
{
    int connectionOpen;

    char buf[2];

    connectionOpen = 1;

    // Loop as long as connection is open.
    while(connectionOpen)
    {
        // Read the incoming data from the connected socket.
        if(recv(connectedSocket, buf, 2, 0))
        {
            // Set the received letter to uppercase and
            // make sure the string ends after that by setting the next
            // byte to NULL.
            buf[0] = toupper(buf[0]);
            buf[1] = '\0';

            printf("Got message from client: %s\n", buf);

            // Send the feedback.
            if(send(connectedSocket, buf, 2, 0) == SOCKET_ERROR)
            {
                connectionOpen = 0;
            }
        }
        else
        {
            closesocket(connectedSocket);
            connectionOpen = 0;
        }
    }
}

int main(void)
{
    if(NET_WinSockInitialize() != 0)
    {
        printf("Critical error, quitting\n");
```

```
        return -1;
    }

    if(InitSockets() != 0)
    {
        printf("Critical error, quitting\n");

        WSACleanup();

        return -1;
    }

    ServerProcess();

    WSACleanup();

    return 0;
}
```

Now let's see what is going on in the program. Let's begin from the main function as that is the place where the application always starts.

Main Function

You may notice that there is not much in the main function; specifically there are no basic socket functions at all. But there are two function calls that are very important (of course, all the function calls are required for the application to work). Let's have a closer look at them:

```
NET_WinSockInitialize();
```

This is the function we introduced at the beginning of this chapter. It belongs to the network library that we will create later on. This function initializes the WinSock API for us. After a successful call, the WinSock API is ready to be used.

NOTE   On Unix, we do not call the function NET_WinSockInitialize because we do not use WinSock under Unix.

```
WSACleanup();
```

This function is a very important function also. It is used to uninitialize WinSock. We are not allowed to exit the application without calling this function, if the WinSock API is initialized. As we have already learned, one of this function's tasks is to unregister the WinSock DLL from our application. Windows' DLL registration system will lose track of all the actually registered DLLs if we do not call this function at the end of each WinSock application.

InitSockets Function

The InitSockets function performs all the initialization of sockets so that they can be used and the server process itself can start. Let's take a look:

```
listeningSocket = socket(AF_INET, SOCK_STREAM, 0);

if(listeningSocket == INVALID_SOCKET)
{
    printf("error: socket() failed");
    return -1;
}
```

Here we create the listening socket and check that it is successfully created. A listening socket is a socket that the server uses to listen for incoming connections. Once a connection comes in and it is accepted, the server will start using a connected socket and leave the listening socket free for other clients.

The socket we create here is an IPv4 stream socket. Because it is a stream socket, it uses the TCP transport protocol. The flag parameter is set to zero as it is currently not used in the sockets API. Then we check whether the socket descriptor is invalid. If it is, we simply exit the program. If the socket is created as it is supposed to be, we move on.

```
servAddr = (struct sockaddr *) malloc(sizeof(sockaddr));
memset((char *) servAddr, 0, sizeof(sockaddr));

// Fill the address structure.
servAddr->sa_family        = (u_short) AF_INET;
inetServAddr               = (struct sockaddr_in *) servAddr;
inetServAddr->sin_port     = htons((u_short) 9009);
```

Now we fill the address information of the server. First, we need to allocate memory for the structure and set it to zero. Then we fill the structure with the required information: protocol family and port number. No need to tell the program the IP address of the computer as it can automatically retrieve it. If there is more than one network interface card installed, we can choose the one we want here. For this example program we have selected the port number 9009.

```
// Bind the address information to the socket.
error = bind(listeningSocket, servAddr, sizeof(sockaddr));

if(error == SOCKET_ERROR)
{
    printf("error: bind() failed");
    free(servAddr);
    return -1;
}
```

```
    free(servAddr);
    servAddr = NULL;
```

Now that we have the address information ready in the structure, let's tell the socket to use that information. We bind the information to the listening socket with the Bind function. Again, we must check that an error occurred in the call to Bind. If so, we need to free the allocated memory before we are allowed to exit. If everything went fine, we free the memory we allocated for the address structure and move on.

```
    // Listen for incoming connections. Queue only one connection.
    error = listen(listeningSocket, 1);

    if(error == SOCKET_ERROR)
    {
        printf("error: listen() failed");
        return -1;
    }
```

Everything is ready for listening for incoming connections. At first glance it may seem weird that it is just one call to a function without a "loop as long as there are no connections coming in" loop. Does the function just run once and then the process moves on to the next one? In this case, no. Some theory is required here to understand this. A socket can be blocking or non-blocking. With a blocking socket, some socket functions will go to sleep while there is no action of any kind that needs to be processed. A non-blocking socket, on the other hand, will not put the functions into sleep. Once the functions are called, they check to see if there is an action to process; if there is not, they return and the next command (function) of the process is run. By default, all sockets are blocking. Blocking and non-blocking I/O is discussed more in Chapter 6, "I/O Operations."

So if we see a fragment of code similar to the preceding code, we cannot say how the application will perform as we do not know if the socket is blocking or not. But as we do know that it is blocking in this example, we know that the application will stop at the Listen function as long as there are no incoming connections.

Now we put the listening socket to the use it is created for by passing it as a parameter to the Listen function. We set the backlog value to one because our server will process only one client at a time and, better yet, one client per instance.

Again, we cannot forget to check for any errors. If Listen fails, we exit the application.

```
    // Accept the connection.
    connectedSocket = accept(listeningSocket, NULL, NULL);
```

```
if(connectedSocket == INVALID_SOCKET)
{
    printf("error: socket() failed");
    return -1;
}
```

Excellent. Now we have reached the Accept function, so we know that someone wants to connect to our server. So we now create a new socket for the soon-to-be-connected client. We pass the listening socket as a parameter to Accept, as the connection we want to accept is on that socket. We have no interest in knowing the address information of the client, so pass NULLs as the two remaining parameters.

Yes, you guessed correctly; next, we check for errors. If the connected socket is invalid after a call to Accept, we exit the application. If it is valid, we are done initializing the server.

ServerProcess Function

Now we get to the server process itself. This function has the main loop that every program has. It is looped as long as the connection is open. Let's have a closer look at the input/output functions we use here:

```
// Read the incoming data from the connected socket.
if(recv(connectedSocket, buf, 2, 0))
{
    // Set the received letter to uppercase and
    // make sure the string ends after that by setting the next
    // byte to NULL.
    buf[0] = toupper(buf[0]);
    buf[1] = '\0';

    printf("Got message from client: %s\n", buf);

    // Send the feedback.
    if(send(connectedSocket, buf, 2, 0) == SOCKET_ERROR)
    {
        connectionOpen = 0;
    }
}
else
{
closesocket(connectedSocket);
    connectionOpen = 0;
}
```

At this point of the program, we can forget about the listening socket. This program is not going to use it anymore. The socket we use from now on is the connected socket that we got from the Accept function.

Let's get the data flowing then! We call the Recv function inside an If statement because we need to know if Recv really read data from the socket, or if it returned zero indicating that the connection has been closed or is lost. This is possible with a blocking socket, as Recv will not return before it has data to read or before it notices that the connection is closed. A non-blocking socket would return zero from a call to Recv if there is no data to read, but the connection is still alive.

We read the data to a very small buffer — in this example, only 2 bytes in size. When we notice that data has arrived, we process it. First, we simply set the received letter to uppercase, and then make sure the next letter is NULL. Therefore, the string ends after the first letter. After this is done, we show the user what we received and send it back to the client. If we could not send the data (if Send returns less than zero) we assume that the connection is broken and exit the program.

We close the socket and exit the program if the Recv function returns zero. Remember that in this example, because the sockets we use are blocking, the socket functions do not return if there is nothing happening (for example, if Recv is not receiving data).

Simple Echo UDP Server

As we want to use UDP as well as TCP in our socket programs, we now modify the simple echo TCP server code to work with UDP. Modifying the TCP code is rather easy. The following code listing shows the complete UDP server code:

```
#ifndef _WINSOCKAPI_
#define _WINSOCKAPI_
#endif

#include <windows.h>
#include <winsock2.h>

#include <stdio.h>

// Declare the sockets we use.
SOCKET Socket;

int InitSockets(void)
{
    struct sockaddr *servAddr;
    struct sockaddr_in *inetServAddr;
```

```
        int error = 0;

        // Create the socket.
        Socket = socket(AF_INET, SOCK_DGRAM, 0);

        if(Socket < 0)
        {
            printf("error: socket() failed");
            return -1;
        }

        // Allocate memory for the address structure and set it to zero.
        servAddr = (struct sockaddr *) malloc(sizeof(sockaddr));
        memset((char *) servAddr, 0, sizeof(sockaddr));

        // Fill the address structure.
        servAddr->sa_family       = (u_short) AF_INET;
        inetServAddr              = (struct sockaddr_in *) servAddr;
        inetServAddr->sin_port    = htons((u_short) 9009);

        // Bind the address information to the socket.
        error = bind(Socket, servAddr, sizeof(sockaddr));

        if(error == SOCKET_ERROR)
        {
            printf("error: bind() failed");
            free(servAddr);
            return -1;
        }

        free(servAddr);
        servAddr = NULL;

        return 0;
}

void ServerProcess(void)
{
        struct sockaddr_in inetClientAddr;
        int clientLen;

        int connectionOpen;

        char buf[2];

        clientLen = sizeof(inetClientAddr);
```

```
            connectionOpen = 1;

            // Loop as long as connection is open.
            while(connectionOpen)
            {
                // Read the incoming data from the connected socket.
                if(recvfrom(Socket, buf, 2, 0, (struct sockaddr *) &inetClientAddr,
                &clientLen))
                {
                    // Set the received letter to uppercase and
                    // make sure the string ends after that by setting the next
                    // byte to NULL.
                    buf[0] = toupper(buf[0]);
                    buf[1] = '\0';

                    printf("Got message from client: %s\n", buf);

                    // Send the feedback.
                    if(sendto(Socket, buf, 2, 0,
                        (struct sockaddr *) &inetClientAddr, clientLen) == SOCKET_ERROR)
                    {
                        connectionOpen = 0;
                    }
                }
                else
                {
                    connectionOpen = 0;
                }
            }
}

int main(void)
{
    if(NET_WinSockInitialize() != 0)
    {
        printf("Critical error, quitting\n");

        return -1;
    }

    if(InitSockets() != 0)
    {
        printf("Critical error, quitting\n");

        WSACleanup();
```

```
            return -1;
    }

    ServerProcess();

    WSACleanup();

    return 0;
}
```

The biggest change in the UDP code in comparison to the TCP code is that we have only one socket. On the TCP server, we had a listening socket and a connected socket. On the UDP server we have only one "generic" socket, because there is no need to listen for incoming connections and connect them. This one UDP socket just reads the incoming data and sends data back.

Let's take a closer look at the changes.

InitSockets Function

First, we change the calls to the Socket and Bind functions to match the two preceding function calls. We have replaced the listening socket with the "generic" socket and we are now creating a datagram socket instead of a stream socket.

```
Socket = socket(AF_INET, SOCK_DGRAM, 0);
...
error = bind(Socket, servAddr, sizeof(sockaddr));
```

After calling Bind, we are done. If we were using TCP, we would start the listening process now. But with UDP there is no need, so we can start the server process function right after we have bound the local address information to the socket.

ServerProcess Function

For the server processing function we declare two new variables that are not used in the TCP version. The first one is the Internet client address structure, and the second one is an integer holding the length of the structure. We need to set the length variable to the size of the structure before we pass it to any function.

```
struct sockaddr_in inetClientAddr;
int clientLen;


...


clientLen = sizeof(inetClientAddr);
```

The next thing we have changed is that we have replaced the Recv and Send functions with Recvfrom and Sendto functions. They work almost like the ones in the TCP version, but there are two new parameters in Recvfrom and Sendto.

```
if(recvfrom(Socket, buf, 2, 0, (struct sockaddr *) &inetClientAddr, &clientLen))

...

if(sendto(Socket, buf, 2, 0, (struct sockaddr *) &inetClientAddr, clientLen) ==
SOCKET_ERROR)
```

We must pass the address information structure and its length as parameters in both functions. In Recvfrom, the address structure is filled by the function. When the function is receiving data, it fills the structure with the corresponding address from which the data is coming. The function also updates the length variable, as it is a value-result argument.

So now that we have the address information of where the data originated, we use it to send data to the correct host. We pass the address structure and the length of the structure to Sendto, updated by Recvfrom. This way we are always sending data to the correct host, because in this example program we only send data when we have first received it. If we had a program that requires sending data even when we have not received anything (we need the address information though, hence at least one datagram must have been received before), we need to store all the addresses of the clients to which we want to send data. That is why it is a good idea to have some kind of a system where there is a dedicated message for informing the server of the client. We discuss this "knocking" system in Tutorial 2, "Creating Your Network Library."

These are all the changes we need to make the server work using the UDP protocol. The UDP version of the server works a little bit differently as it will not exit when the client is shut down. This is because there is no connection that is closed. This feature has its pluses and minuses. One good thing is that the server can be used effectively because only one process is running all the time. One bad thing could be the fact that we do not know if a client crashes or something else like that happens. But, as we have already said many times: UDP is unreliable, but it can be made reliable.

Creating a Client

What would we do with a server if we did not have a client application? Nothing. So let's make one. Remember that in computer games, the game itself is the client, so you must design your game so that sending and receiving data is not interfering with other parts of the game too much. Too much? It is almost impossible to make it work so that the communications library would not have any effect on the game flow. The simple echo client source code is shown in its entirety in the section titled "Simple Echo TCP Client."

First, let's look at the functions we need for all clients.

TCP

We create the client-side socket exactly like the one on the server. We must set it to use the same protocols on both ends (IPv4 and TCP in this case):

```
SOCKET Socket;
Socket = socket(AF_INET, SOCK_STREAM, 0);
```

Next, we convert the Internet address from the server IP number to a form that the computer can use. After that, we fill the address structure, but we do not bind this address to the socket ourselves because the Connect function will do it for us.

```
struct sockaddr_in inetServAddr;
int portNumber;

u_long inetAddr = inet_addr(IPaddress);

memset((char *) &inetServAddr, 0, sizeof(inetServAddr));
inetServAddr.sin_family          = AF_INET;
inetServAddr.sin_port            = htons((u_short) portNumber);
inetServAddr.sin_addr.s_addr     = inetAddr;

error = connect(Socket, (struct sockaddr *) &inetServAddr, sizeof(inetServAddr));
```

That is all the basic initializing there is to do on the client side when using TCP the protocol.

UDP

Creating a UDP socket requires only one modification: Change the second parameter of the Socket function to SOCK_DGRAM.

```
SOCKET Socket;
Socket = socket(AF_INET, SOCK_DGRAM, 0);
```

We fill the address structure in the same way as when using TCP, without any changes.

As UDP protocol is a connectionless protocol, we do not need to run the Connect function at all. This is the biggest difference in initializing client sockets.

When sending data to a UDP server, we need to pass the address information of the server to the sending function every time we run it. Therefore, we must store the address structure globally to be able to access it from all functions.

Simple Echo TCP Client

```
#ifndef _WINSOCKAPI_
#define _WINSOCKAPI_
#endif

#include <windows.h>
#include <winsock2.h>

#include <stdio.h>

// Declare the only socket we need.
SOCKET Socket;

int InitSockets(char *IPaddress)
{
    struct sockaddr_in inetServAddr;
    int error = 0;

    // Create a TCP socket.
    Socket = socket(AF_INET, SOCK_STREAM, 0);

    if(Socket < 0)
    {
        printf("error: socket() failed");
        return -1;
    }

    // Create the Internet address from the IP number
    u_long inetAddr = inet_addr(IPaddress);

    memset((char *) &inetServAddr, 0, sizeof(inetServAddr));
    inetServAddr.sin_family        = AF_INET;
    inetServAddr.sin_port          = htons((u_short) 9009);
    inetServAddr.sin_addr.s_addr   = inetAddr;

    // Try to connect the TCP server.
```

```c
    error = connect(Socket, (struct sockaddr *) &inetServAddr,
    sizeof(inetServAddr));

    if(error != 0)
    {
        printf("error: could not find server.\n");
        return -1;
    }

    return 0;
}

void ClientProcess(void)
{
    int connectionOpen;

    char transmitBuf[3];
    char receiveBuf[3];
    strcpy(transmitBuf, "");
    strcpy(receiveBuf, "");

    connectionOpen = 1;

    // Loop as long as connection is open.
    while(connectionOpen)
    {
        // Get the string to send.
        if(gets(transmitBuf))
        {
            if(strcmp(transmitBuf, "q") == 0)
            {
                closesocket(Socket);
                connectionOpen = 0;
                break;
            }

            // Send the transmit buffer to the socket.
            if(send(Socket, transmitBuf, 2, 0) == SOCKET_ERROR)
            {
                connectionOpen = 0;
            }
        }

        // Read the incoming data from the connected socket.
        if(recv(Socket, receiveBuf, 2, 0))
        {
            printf("Got reply from server: %s\n", receiveBuf);
```

```
            }
            else
            {
                connectionOpen = 0;
            }
        }
    }
}

int main(int argc, char *argv[])
{
    if(argc < 2)
    {
        printf("Usage: SimpleEchoTCPClient.exe <Server IP>\n");
        return -1;
    }

    NET_WinSockInitialize();

    if(InitSockets(argv[1]) != 0)
    {
        printf("Critical error, quitting\n");

        WSACleanup();

        return -1;
    }

    ClientProcess();

    WSACleanup();

    return 0;
}
```

As we can see in the code listing, the client source code is not very different from the server code. Let's see what is different.

Main Function

The only difference between this function and the server code is the following piece of code: the two parameters in the main function, the If statement, and the call to InitSockets function. The If statement checks whether the user provided enough arguments when running the executable. Argument number one is the executable name itself (in the form the user entered it); argument two in this case should be the IP address of the server. If there are not enough arguments, the program displays a "usage" message telling the user what arguments are needed.

The call to the InitSockets function is a little bit different, because now we need to pass the IP address information to it. Other parts of the main function are similar to the server code — just some simple function calls and the cleanup code.

```
int main(int argc, char *argv[])
{
    if(argc < 2)
    {
        printf("Usage: SimpleEchoTCPClient.exe <Server IP>\n");
        return -1;
    }

    ...

    if(InitSockets(argv[1]) != 0)
    ...
```

InitSockets Function

The most obvious change in this function is that we provide the server IP address within a parameter. We need to do this to make it possible to enter any IP address when running the client. We could hardcode an address to the code, but that would not be very wise. Then we should always have the server on the hardcoded IP address (which is not always even possible).

```
int InitSockets(char *IPaddress)

// Create a TCP socket.
Socket = socket(AF_INET, SOCK_STREAM, 0);
```

As we can see in the following code, the socket is created exactly as it is on the server end. There is really no way to make it different, because we must use the very same protocols. Once more we must check for errors.

```
if(Socket < 0)
{
    printf("error: socket() failed");
    return -1;
}
```

Now that we have the server IP address in a string, we need to convert it to a form the computer understands. After that, we reset the address structure memory to zero. Then, we fill the address information structure with this address and the well-known port number, which is 9009 in this example. We must convert the integer value 9009 (host byte ordered value) to network byte ordered format. We also set the protocol family to AF_INET, because we use IPv4.

```
// Create the Internet address from the IP number
u_long inetAddr = inet_addr(IPaddress);

memset((char *) &inetServAddr, 0, sizeof(inetServAddr));
inetServAddr.sin_family            = AF_INET;
inetServAddr.sin_port              = htons((u_short) 9009);
inetServAddr.sin_addr.s_addr       = inetAddr;
```

All there is left to do in this function is to connect the server using the Connect function. Notice that we do not call Bind at all on the client. This is because we do not have to; Connect does the address binding for us. Therefore, we must provide the address structure we just filled for Connect. We typecast the structure to the generic address format, because the Connect function is designed to work on both IPv4 and IPv6, so it accepts only generic-format addresses.

```
// Try to connect the TCP server.
error = connect(Socket, (struct sockaddr *) &inetServAddr, sizeof(inetServAddr));

if(error != 0)
{
    printf("error: could not find server.\n");
    return -1;
}
```

It is very important to check for errors here. If there is an error, it usually means that we could not find the server. Other errors may occur too, but usually it is enough to inform the user that we could not connect to the server.

The Connect function is also a blocking function, but not like the other blocking functions. If we set the socket to non-blocking mode, the Connect function is not affected by this. It will still wait a certain amount of time for the connection to succeed. After that time, it will fail.

ClientProcess Function

This function naturally matches the ServerProcess function on the server. Its function is to wait for the user to enter the letter and send it. After that, it will wait for a response from the server, then the loop starts all over again.

Notice we have separate buffers for transmitting and receiving to prevent mix-ups. The application could work with one buffer only, but it is much better for the programmer that we have two buffers. In bigger programs it is sometimes a must to have different buffers.

```
char transmitBuf[3];
char receiveBuf[3];
strcpy(transmitBuf, "");
strcpy(receiveBuf, "");
```

Here we get the letter to send into the transmit buffer using the Gets function. Some problems arise if the user enters more than one letter, but in this example we do not concentrate on that because it really is beyond the scope of this example. For now it is enough that we take care of this on the server by making sure the string ends after the first letter.

Next, we check if the letter entered was "q" (lowercase). If it was, we close the socket and exit the loop, thus exiting the whole program. The server will notice that we have closed the socket and it will exit, too. If the letter we entered was something other than "q", we send it to the server. Because a string always contains at least 2 bytes, assuming that the string is not empty (one letter plus NULL), and because we want to send only one letter, we send 2 bytes.

If Send returns SOCKET_ERROR, something went wrong, so we exit the program without any extra checking.

```
// Get the string to send.
if(gets(transmitBuf))
{
    if(strcmp(transmitBuf, "q") == 0)
    {
        closesocket(Socket);
        connectionOpen = 0;
        break;
    }

    // Send the transmit buffer to the socket.
    if(send(Socket, transmitBuf, 2, 0) == SOCKET_ERROR)
    {
        connectionOpen = 0;
    }
}
```

After we have sent the data to the server, we immediately start to wait for the response by using the function Recv. If the amount of bytes received is more than zero (the return value of Recv is more than zero), it means that data has successfully arrived. If not, we exit the loop and the whole program.

```
// Read the incoming data from the connected socket.
if(recv(Socket, receiveBuf, 2, 0))
{
    printf("Got reply from server: %s\n", receiveBuf);
}
else
{
    connectionOpen = 0;
}
```

After this the loop starts all over again, assuming that no errors have been encountered or that the user did not enter the letter "q".

Simple Echo UDP Client

```c
#ifndef _WINSOCKAPI_
#define _WINSOCKAPI_
#endif

#include <windows.h>
#include <winsock2.h>

#include <stdio.h>

// Declare the only socket we need.
SOCKET Socket;

struct sockaddr_in inetServAddr;
int servLen = sizeof(inetServAddr);

int InitSockets(char *IPaddress)
{
    int error = 0;

    // Create a TCP socket.
    Socket = socket(AF_INET, SOCK_DGRAM, 0);

    if(Socket < 0)
    {
        printf("error: socket() failed");
        return -1;
    }

    // Create the Internet address from the IP number
    u_long inetAddr = inet_addr(IPaddress);

    memset((char *) &inetServAddr, 0, sizeof(inetServAddr));
    inetServAddr.sin_family        = AF_INET;
    inetServAddr.sin_port          = htons((u_short) 9009);
    inetServAddr.sin_addr.s_addr   = inetAddr;

    return 0;
}

void ClientProcess(void)
{
```

```c
        int connectionOpen;

        char transmitBuf[3];
        char receiveBuf[3];
        strcpy(transmitBuf, "");
        strcpy(receiveBuf, "");

        connectionOpen = 1;

        // Loop as long as connection is open.
        while(connectionOpen)
        {
            // Get the string to send.
            if(gets(transmitBuf))
            {
                // Send the transmit buffer to the socket.
                if(sendto(Socket, transmitBuf, 2, 0,
                    (struct sockaddr *) &inetServAddr, servLen) == SOCKET_ERROR)
                {
                    connectionOpen = 0;
                }
            }

            // If the letter the user entered is "q", stop the application.
            if(strcmp(transmitBuf, "q") == 0)
            {
                connectionOpen = 0;
                break;
            }

            // Read the incoming data from the connected socket.
            if(recvfrom(Socket, receiveBuf, 2, 0, NULL, NULL))
            {
                printf("Got reply from server: %s\n", receiveBuf);
            }
            else
            {
                connectionOpen = 0;
            }
        }
}

int main(int argc, char *argv[])
{
    if(argc < 2)
    {
        printf("Usage: SimpleEchoTCPClient.exe <Server IP>\n");
```

```
        return -1;
    }

    NET_WinSockInitialize();

    if(InitSockets(argv[1]) != 0)
    {
        printf("Critical error, quitting\n");

        WSACleanup();

        return -1;
    }

    ClientProcess();

    WSACleanup();

    return 0;
}
```

This code listing shows the UDP version of the simple echo client. It is not much different from the TCP version. Let's take a look what has changed.

InitSockets Function

We create the socket exactly like in the TCP version, but with one change. Instead of creating a stream socket, we create a datagram socket. To do this, we set the second parameter to SOCK_DGRAM.

```
Socket = socket(AF_INET, SOCK_DGRAM, 0);
```

Then we fill the address information structure that holds the server's address. Again, we do it exactly like in the TCP version, only this time the structure is a global variable as we need it elsewhere in the code. Once the structure is filled completely, we are done. There is no need to call Bind or Connect. We can move on to the client process function.

ClientProcess Function

In this function, we replace the Send and Recv functions with the Sendto and Recvfrom functions and remove the socket closing functions. Unlike in the server-side code, we do not need to receive any data before we know the address of the server. This is obvious, is it not? If we do not know the address of the server, we hit the wall. We cannot do anything without that piece of information. Fortunately, in computer games today, the servers can be found automatically using a built-in or external application that uses a server (we do not need to know the address of this server; it is built-in) to retrieve the IP addresses and ports of the servers. Let's assume that we know the address of the simple echo server, and that we have entered the correct address when running this client. Now we use the address information structure that we filled in the InitSockets function to send the data to the correct host. We assume that the server address does not change and we do not care about checking the address structure returned by Recvfrom.

```
if(sendto(Socket, transmitBuf, 2, 0, (struct sockaddr *) &inetServAddr,
servLen) == SOCKET_ERROR)

...

if(recvfrom(Socket, receiveBuf, 2, 0, NULL, NULL))
```

NOTE It is possible that the server address changes in between a Sendto and Recvfrom. For example, a concurrent UDP server spawns the connections on new ephemeral ports, because it must use the well-known port for listening for the incoming connections. So when a client sends data to the server, the server spawns a child process and a new port for that "connection." Then, when the client receives data from the server next time; it must update its address information of the server because the port has changed.

Running the Simple Echo Application

To try out the simple echo application, we must first start the server program and then start the client program. We must start the programs in this order, because the client application will exit if it cannot find anything on the server port.

So, to run the server, type the following at the prompt:

```
> SimpleEchoTCPServer.exe
```

Then, we run the client passing the server IP address as the first and only argument:

```
> SimpleEchoTCPClient.exe 127.0.0.1
```

In this example, we are running both programs on the same host, and therefore we can use the IP address 127.0.0.1, which is a local host address. Every time you use this address, you are pointing to your own computer.

Now that both of the programs are running, we can start sending data back and forth. On the client side, enter any letter except "q" and press Enter. You will see on the server side how the letter is received, and almost immediately on the client side how the letter is sent back in uppercase.

To stop the application, enter the letter "q" on the client program. The TCP version will end both client and server, but the UDP version ends only the client. Figures 5-6 and 5-7 show a normal run of the simple echo application.

Figure 5-6:
Simple echo
server
running

Image 5-7:
Simple echo
client
running

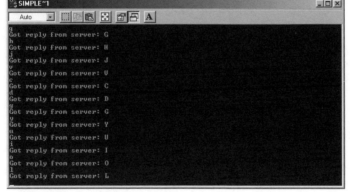

Summary

In this chapter, we saw the basic socket functions for the first time. We learned about the parameters we pass to them and the values they return. We found out some of the technical differences between TCP and UDP. More importantly, we learned how to use the functions in real life, by creating our first sockets application, the simple echo application. We can now move on to more advanced technology.

Chapter 6

I/O Operations

Introduction

A network input/output operation requires more knowledge than just the knowledge of sending and receiving data. We need to know when to start receiving the data and how to set it up. This chapter discusses the input/output operations of socket network events. We will also learn a new way to send data and how to modify the way our sockets act.

Detecting Network Events

To be able to start reading the socket for incoming data at the correct time, we need to know when there is anything to read. Of course, we could poll the read function on the socket all the time, but that is not always a good way to do it. We need to be able to wake up the read function whenever there is any incoming data. The following functions are used to accomplish this:

- Select — Unix, Win32
- WSAAsyncSelect/WSAEventSelect — Win32

Select Function (Unix, Win32)

```
int select(int maxfdp1, fd_set *readset, fd_set *writeset, fd_set *exceptset, const
struct timeval *timeout);
```

The Select function is used to set the kernel to wake up the process when a network event occurs. We can set the function to wake up the process on any type of network event (writing, reading, and exception condition pending) at the same time. Plus, we can set a timeout value to make the process wake up after a certain amount of time.

The first parameter (int maxfdp1) defines the number of socket descriptors to test for network events. Its value is set to the highest socket descriptor to test plus one, because it is the number of descriptors (the descriptor values begin at 0). So if we want to test our socket for network events, we should set this value to (at least) the socket descriptor plus one.

The second, third, and fourth parameters (fd_set *readset, fd_set *writeset, fd_set *exceptset) define the network events for which we want to test. We discuss only the reading and writing events in this book. These parameters are pointers to FD_SET type of data, which are used to store the notification of a possible network event. After the Select function is run, we check if the socket is a member of a set by using the macro FD_SET. The macros are explained later in this chapter.

The fifth and final parameter (const struct timeval *timeout) defines the timeout value for the function. This is a pointer to a TimeVal structure, which holds two members: seconds and microseconds. To make the function wait forever, we set this parameter to NULL. We can set the timeout value to 0 seconds and 0 microseconds. In that case the function returns immediately after first checking for network events.

Win32 return values:
- Success: Positive number of ready descriptors/0 on timeout
- Failure: SOCKET_ERROR

Unix return values:
- Success: Positive number of ready descriptors/0 on timeout
- Failure: –1

Macros

The following four macros are used to modify and check the socket descriptor sets.
- FD_ZERO
- FD_SET
- FD_CLR
- FD_ISSET

FD_ZERO resets a set so that no socket descriptors belong to it. It is a good idea to do this before any other macro is used.

FD_SET adds the socket descriptor to the set.

FD_CLR removes the socket from the set.

FD_ISSET checks to see if the socket descriptor is a member of the set.

WSAAsyncSelect Function (Win32)

```
int WSAAsyncSelect(SOCKET s, HWND hWnd, unsigned int wMsg, long lEvent);
```

This function is used to set the kernel of Windows send a message to notify of a network event on a socket. This system can tell about numerous network events, including the following:

- FD_READ — Ready to read data
- FD_WRITE — Ready to write data
- FD_ACCEPT — Incoming connection
- FD_CLOSE — Socket closing

The first parameter (SOCKET s) defines the socket to monitor. This does not have to be a connected socket because we can also monitor for incoming connections with this function. Note that datagram sockets do not tell about incoming connections — only stream sockets do.

The second parameter (HWND hWnd) defines the window handle to which to send the message.

The third parameter (unsigned int wMsg) defines the message to send when the event defined by the fourth parameter occurs. We can (and should) create our own message for this.

The fourth parameter (long lEvent) defines the network event(s) to monitor. We can define multiple events at once by ORing them together here; for example, FD_READ | FD_WRITE.

Win32 return values:

- Success: 0
- Failure: SOCKET_ERROR

WSAEventSelect Function (Win32)

```
int WSAEventSelect(SOCKET s, WSAEVENT hEventObject, long lNetworkEvents);
```

This function sets an event object to receive a notification of the specified network events. The event object can then be used to see which network event happened, if any. The network events we can specify are exactly the same as in the WSAAsyncSelect function.

This function gives us some more breathing room because we do not have to tie the network events to a window. We can specify any number of event objects and then use them wherever we wish.

The first parameter (SOCKET s) defines the socket to monitor.

The second parameter (WSAEVENT hEventObject) defines the event object handle that will receive the notification of the network events.

The third parameter (long lNetworkEvents) defines the network events to monitor. As in the WSAAsyncSelect function, we can OR multiple events together.

Win32 return values:

■   Success: 0

■   Failure: SOCKET_ERROR

WSAWaitForMultipleEvents Function (Win32)

```
DWORD WSAWaitForMultipleEvents(DWORD cEvents, const WSAEVENT far *lphEvents, BOOL
fWaitAll, DWORD dwTimeOUT, BOOL fAlertable);
```

This function polls for an event to happen and tells us if there is a network event that we should process. This function returns when either there is a network event happening (one we are waiting for) or the timeout value has been reached. We can set this value to infinite so the function returns only when an event occurs.

The first parameter (DWORD cEvents) is the number of events to wait for. This is the amount of members in the lphEvents array (parameter two). At least one must be specified, but we cannot specify more than what WSA_Maximum_Wait_Events specifies.

The second parameter (const WSAEVENT far *lphEvents) is a pointer to the array of network event objects.

The third parameter (BOOL fWaitAll) defines whether the function should wait for all the events to occur before it returns. The possible values are TRUE and FALSE (1 and 0). If set to FALSE, this function returns when at least one event occurs.

The fourth parameter (DWORD dwTimeOUT) defines the timeout value in milliseconds. If this value is reached, the function returns no matter what. This means that even if the fWaitAll flag is set to TRUE and the timeout value is reached, the function returns.

The fifth and final parameter (BOOL fAlertable) defines if the function should return if there is an I/O completion routine queued by the system for execution. The possible values are TRUE and FALSE (1 and 0).

Win32 return values:

■   Success/Failure: The event object that caused the function to return

Event Object

An event object is a normal Windows handle that is used to store the state of a network event (or any other event). For example, if we want to know when there is data to read on a socket, we create an event object, set it to inform us of incoming network events, and check its state.

Let's take a look at a more detailed example. First, we create the event object handle and a socket:

```
HANDLE readEvent;
SOCKET s;
```

We presume the socket is initialized properly somewhere. Then we set the event object to receive notification of incoming data:

```
WSAEventSelect(s, readEvent, FD_READ);
```

And finally, when we are ready to read data off a socket, we check if there is anything to read.

```
WSAEVENT EventArray[1];
EventArray[0] = SocketInputEvent;

int waitStatus = WSAWaitForMultipleEvents(1, EventArray, FALSE, WSA_INFINITE,
FALSE);
```

Multithreading

It is safe to say that multithreading is a must in a non-iterative network application. It is the only way to keep all the clients handled properly by the server, because there can be multiple clients connected to one server at a time. If each client should wait for the server to handle the other clients first, we could call our system "Wait Wait Wait."

NOTE   A UDP server does not need multithreading as much as a TCP server. This is because a UDP client can just "throw in" a message to the server, then wait for a response from the server and we are done. The server could handle all the clients on one socket, thus removing one reason for multithreading. It depends on the design of the UDP network application whether we should use multithreading or not.

What is Multithreading?

Before we tell you how to make our application multithreaded, let's take a moment to think about what multithreading really is. Multithreading means that there is more than one process running in one application. These processes run constantly and at the same time. All the threads and the main application share the same memory. This means that if you have a global variable, it can be accessed and modified by each thread. Each process usually has its own loop to keep it running. A normal single-threaded application has only one main loop, which is the backbone of the application. When this loop breaks, the application terminates. This is the same for every extra thread. When a thread reaches the end of the thread function, it terminates and the thread is destroyed. When the main application ends, so do the threads.

Although the threads seem to be running all at the same time, this is not actually true on a single-processor system. One processor can process only one thing at a time, so the threads are really run one by one, but only a little bit at a time.

A real life example explains this best. Imagine you have three papers to write. You could write one completely and then write the next one and so on. But if you wanted to write all the papers at the same time (for some weird reason), you would have to write, one word at a time for each paper. First, you write one word on the first paper, then write one on the next one, and lastly write one on the third one. Well you are not really writing them at the same time, but if you do it really fast (I mean really fast), it seems like you actually are writing them at the same time, because the words seem to appear on the papers at the same time. This is exactly the same for multithreading. It is all about speed.

CreateThread Function (Win32)

```
HANDLE CreateThread(LPSECURITY_ATTRIBUTES lpThreadAttributes, DWORD dwStackSize,
LPTHREAD_START_ROUTINE lpStartAddress, LPVOID lpParameter, DWORD dwCreationFlags,
LPWORD lpThreadId);
```

The CreateThread function creates a new thread on Windows.

The first parameter (LPSECURITY_ATTRIBUTES lpThreadAttributes) is a pointer to a security attributes structure. In this book we always set this to NULL.

The second parameter (DWORD dwStackSize) defines the stack size for the thread. If this is set to zero, the default value is used. The default value is the size of the calling thread's stack size.

The third parameter (LPTHREAD_START_ROUTINE lpStartAddress) specifies the thread's routine function.

The fourth parameter (LPVOID lpParameter) is a pointer to the parameter that will be passed to the thread's routine function.

The fifth parameter (DWORD dwCreationFlags) defines the flags for how to create the thread. We can only set this to zero or Create_Suspended. If the latter is used, the thread starts in suspended mode and will not start before the ResumeThread function is called.

The sixth parameter (LPWORD lpThreadId) is a pointer to a variable that will receive the thread identifier.

Win32 return values:

- Success: Handle to the thread
- Failure: NULL

Pthread_Create Function (Unix)

```
pthread_create(pthread_t *tid, const pthread_attr_t *attr, void *(*func)(void *),
void *arg);
```

Pthread_Create function creates a new thread on Unix. This is similar to Windows' CreateThread function.

The first parameter (pthread_t *tid) is a pointer to the variable that will receive the thread identifier.

The second parameter (const pthread_attr_t *attr) is a pointer to the thread attributes variable. Usually we set this parameter to NULL to use the defaults.

The third parameter (void *(*func)(void *)) defines the thread routine function. This is similar to the Windows CreateThread function's lpStartAddress parameter.

The fourth and last parameter (void *arg) specifies the parameter to pass to the thread routine function. This is similar to the Windows CreateThread function's lpParameter parameter.

Unix return values:

- Success: 0
- Failure: Non-zero

I/O Strategy

Each network application has its own input/output strategy. Input/output strategy means how the data flow is controlled within the application. For example, will the server open multiple sockets for the clients (UDP), or will it use multithreading? Let's take a look at some of the possible strategies:

- Blocking I/O
- Non-blocking I/O
- Signal-driven I/O
- Multiplexing I/O

Blocking I/O

Blocking I/O is the simplest form of I/O strategies. As we have learned before, a socket can be blocking or non-blocking. A blocking socket means that some of the socket functions we run, such as passing a blocking socket as a parameter, wait for the action to be fulfilled before they return. For example, if we try to read data off a blocking socket, the read function we use will not return before the data is read. If there is no one sending anything to that socket, the function will block until someone sends data to it. Each socket is blocking by default.

Figure 6-1

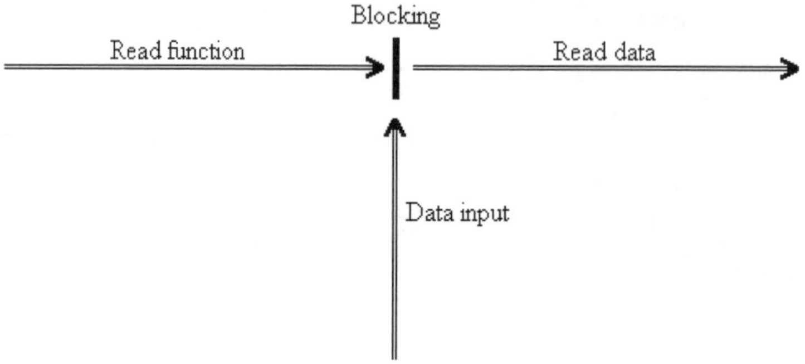

Non-blocking I/O

We can set a socket non-blocking if we want to. Then the socket functions will return even if the action cannot be fulfilled immediately. Usually this means that we need to loop the function to create our own blocking effect. This is called polling. If we were not polling the incoming data, we would most likely miss it because the data must have reached the local host before we call the function to read the data.

Figure 6-2

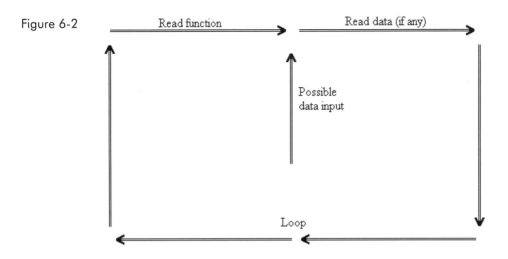

Signal-Driven I/O

We do not always have to use the data reading function to monitor the socket for incoming data. We can set up our operating system to signal us when incoming data is available for us to read. Then all we have to do is call the function to read the data from the socket. The obvious advantage in this strategy compared to the two earlier ones is that we can do other things while we wait for the data to come in. The application that waits for data input can run the rest of the application while there no data is to be read. Then when data input exists, everything else is stopped for the time it takes to read the data and possibly process it.

Figure 6-3

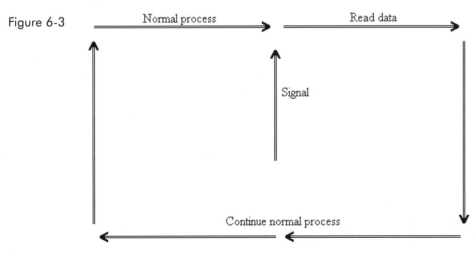

Multiplexing I/O

Another way to avoid using the actual data reading function to tell if there is incoming data is to use the Select function. It is used similarly to a blocking socket read function call, because the Select function will stop and wait for the data to come in. Multiplexing means that we have multiple sources, but we use only one at a time. We need to be able to choose the source that has something to offer us. We use the Select function for that. This is the advantage of multiplexing I/O; we can wait for more than one socket to have data to read with one function call.

Figure 6-4

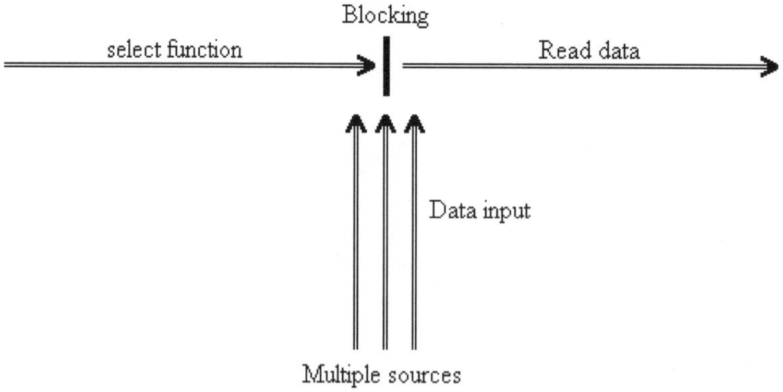

By combining these I/O strategies with multithreading, we can unleash all the power of our network applications.

I/O Control

Now that we know some of the possible I/O strategies, we need to know how to get our sockets to work using the strategy we choose. Some do not need any extra setting up, but some do. Also we can create some nice features for our network application by controlling the I/O mode of our sockets. To control the input/output mode of our sockets, we use the following two functions:

■ Ioctl/IoctlSocket
■ SetSockOpt

Ioctl (Unix)/IoctlSocket Function (Win32)

```
int ioctl(int fd, int request, … /* void *arg */ );

int ioctlsocket(SOCKET s, long cmd, u_long FAR *argp);
```

The preceding two functions work in the same way; Ioctl is for Unix and IoctlSocket is for Windows.

These functions are used to control the I/O mode of the socket. The most common use for these functions is setting the blocking/non-blocking mode of a socket.

The first parameter (int fd/SOCKET s) defines the socket to control.

The second parameter (int request/long cmd) is the command to give the socket. This is used with the third parameter (void *arg/u_long FAR *argp), which tells the function how to give out the command.

The Windows version (IoctlSocket) does not have all the commands that the Unix version (Ioctl) has. The only command we really use within this book is Fionbio, which sets or clears the non-blocking flag of the socket.

Win32 return values:

- Success: 0
- Failure: SOCKET_ERROR

Unix return values:

- Success: 0
- Failure: –1

An example best explains the usage of this function. To set a socket into non-blocking mode, we call the I/O control function like this:

```
u_long on = 1;

ioctl(mysocket, FIONBIO, &on); // UNIX
ioctlsocket(mysocket, FIONBIO, &on); // WINDOWS
```

And similarly, to set the non-blocking mode off:

```
u_long off = 0;

ioctl(mysocket, FIONBIO, &off); // UNIX
ioctlsocket(mysocket, FIONBIO, &off); // WINDOWS
```

SetSockOpt/GetSockOpt Function (Unix, Win32)

```
int setsockopt(int sockfd, int level, int optname, const void *optval, socklen_t
optlen);

int getsockopt(int sockfd, int level, int optname, void *optval, socklen_t *optlen);
```

These functions are used to set and get the socket options. There are numerous socket options available, but we discuss only a few in this book.

The first parameter of both set and get functions (int sockfd) defines the socket for which to set the option.

The second parameter of both functions (int level) specifies the level at which the options are defined. Possible values (for compatibility issues) are SOL_SOCKET and IPPROTO_TCP.

The third parameter is also the same for both functions (int optname); it defines the actual option to set.

The fourth parameter of SetSockOpt (const void *optval) is a pointer to the buffer where the value for the option is stored.

The fourth parameter of GetSockOpt (void *optval) is a pointer to the buffer where the value of the option will be stored.

The fifth parameter of both functions (socklen_t optlen/socklen_t *optlen) defines the size of the buffer used in the fourth parameter.

In this book we use only the SOL_SOCKET level, as the other levels are beyond scope of this book. Here are some options from the SOL_SOCKET level that we should be aware of:

- SO_BROADCAST — Set/get broadcasting on/off
- SO_LINGER — Set/get lingering on/off
- SO_RCVBUF — Set/get receive buffer size
- SO_SNDBUF — Set/get send buffer size
- SO_TYPE — Get socket type

Win32 return values:

- Success: 0
- Failure: SOCKET_ERROR

Unix return values:

- Success: 0
- Failure: –1

Let's take a look at an example of how to make our socket linger on a call to Close/CloseSocket to make sure all the data is sent before the socket is closed:

```
struct linger Ling;

Ling.l_onoff = 1;
Ling.l_linger = 0;

setsockopt(mysocket, SOL_SOCKET, SO_LINGER, (const char *) &Ling, sizeof(struct
linger));
```

Now when we want to close the socket, we should put the Close/CloseSocket function call in a loop that loops as long as the function returns successfully:

```
shutdown(mysocket, SD_BOTH); // WINDOWS

int ret = WSAEWOULDBLOCK;

while(ret == WSAEWOULDBLOCK)
    ret = closesocket(mysocket); // WINDOWS


—

shutdown(mysocket, SD_RDWR); // UNIX

int ret = WSAEWOULDBLOCK;

while(ret == WSAEWOULDBLOCK)
    ret = close(mysocket); // UNIX
```

Shutdown Function (Unix, Win32)

```
int shutdown(int sockfd, int howto);
```

This function is used to disable sending and receiving on a socket. It does not close the socket, but depending on the parameters we pass to it, the socket will not be able to send or receive any more data.

The first parameter (int sockfd) is used to select the socket to shut down.

The second parameter (int howto) specifies how to shut down the socket. The possible values are given in Table 6-1.

Table 6-1: HowTo parameter values for both Unix and Windows

OS	Shut reading	Shut writing	Shut both
Unix	SHUT_RD	SHUT_WR	SHUT_RDWR
WINDOWS	SD_RECEIVE	SD_SEND	SD_BOTH

Win32 return values:

- Success: 0
- Failure: SOCKET_ERROR

Unix return values:

- Success: 0
- Failure: –1

Broadcasting

Broadcasting is a very useful way of sending data. When you broadcast, you send to everybody on the network with only one call to the sending function. There are some restrictions though, which make broadcasting much less interesting than it first sounds. First of all, it can be used only with datagram sockets. This means that we need to use UDP if we want to broadcast. The second, and much more limiting, issue is that it can be used only on a local area network. We cannot broadcast messages through the Internet, because broadcasting works using a unique broadcast IP address that every LAN has. Usually it is of the form subnet.255. For example, if our subnet is 192.168.0, the broadcast address is 192.168.0.255.

> **NOTE** IPv6 does not support broadcasting. IPv6 uses multicasting instead, but that is beyond the scope of this book.

Searching for Servers

One very good use for broadcasting is to search for available servers on a LAN. Everybody who has played a network game on a LAN knows that it is very boring to enter the IP address of a certain server to be able to connect to it each time. And if you do not know what servers there are to join, you have to find that out beforehand. Broadcasting is a solution for this. We assume that all the servers use the same port, and that the client application (the game) knows this port number. Then, all we need to do is broadcast to that port number and wait for the servers to send their info to us. All the servers that are up and running in the LAN will receive the broadcast message. They can find out the client's address from the datagram and send a reply to that address. The client will then build up a list of servers that replied within a certain amount of time.

Broadcast Function

To make our socket broadcast, we need to set the socket option of it as shown in the following code. We also need to create a datagram socket and fill in the address information so that the data is sent to the broadcast address. In this example we use the address 192.168.0.255.

```
void Broadcast(char *buf, size_t count)
{
    // Define on
    const int on = 1;

    // Create a datagram socket
```

```
    SOCKET sock;
    sock = socket(AF_INET, SOCK_DGRAM, 0);

    struct sockaddr_in servaddr;
    socklen_t len;

    // Use the example broadcast address
    u_long inetAddr = inet_addr("192.168.0.255");

    // Fill address information structure
    memset(&servaddr, 0, sizeof(struct sockaddr_in));
    servaddr.sin_family      = AF_INET;
    servaddr.sin_port        = htons(9009);
    servaddr.sin_addr.s_addr = inetAddr;

    len = sizeof(servaddr);

    // Set socket broadcasting option on
    setsockopt(sock, SOL_SOCKET, SO_BROADCAST,
        (const char *) &on, sizeof(on));

    // Broadcast!
    sendto(sock, buf, count, 0,
        (struct sockaddr *) &servaddr, len);
}
```

First, we must define the socket option switch in a variable, because the SetSockOpt function always retrieves the switch from a variable:

```
// Define on
const int on = 1;
```

Then we create a normal datagram socket to be used in the broadcasting operation:

```
// Create a datagram socket
SOCKET sock;
sock = socket(AF_INET, SOCK_DGRAM, 0);
```

Next, the address information structure must be filled in with the correct information. The IP address is set to the example broadcast address 192.168.0.255. The port number is set to 9009, assuming that is the port that all the recipents use:

```
// Use the example broadcast address
u_long inetAddr = inet_addr("192.168.0.255");

// Fill address information structure
memset(&servaddr, 0, sizeof(struct sockaddr_in));
servaddr.sin_family      = AF_INET;
```

```
servaddr.sin_port        = htons(9009);
servaddr.sin_addr.s_addr = inetAddr;
```

And finally, the socket option SO_BROADCAST is set on and we broadcast the message using the normal Sendto function:

```
// Set socket broadcasting option on
setsockopt(sock, SOL_SOCKET, SO_BROADCAST,
    (const char *) &on, sizeof(on));

// Broadcast!
sendto(sock, buf, count, 0,
    (struct sockaddr *) &servaddr, len);
```

Summary

In this chapter we learned what I/O strategies we can use in our network applications and how to implement them. We also learned the concept of multithreading and the reasons to use it. Along with the I/O methods, we discovered a new way to send data efficiently in a LAN — by broadcasting. We are now ready to create our own network library.

Tutorial Introduction

The tutorial section leads you step by step through how to create a working online game. Since we wish to focus on the network programming side, we have supplied you with a simple openGL-based 2D graphics library.

The first tutorial consists of an introduction to our graphics library. It explains the basics of the library and also gives you code examples to experiment with. Then we move on to developing our network library. The network library we create is reusable so it can be used in your own online titles as well as in our sample online game. Once we have the foundations, we then move on to how to implement login and lobby systems, ready for implementing our online game. Then, in the final tutorial, we develop our working online game that you can both learn from and expand upon.

By creating these tutorials, we have aimed to give you a practical hands-on approach to learning how to create an online game. We have found that many books focus on how things work, rather than explaining how to actually get it working so you can experiment with it.

Remember that all the source code for the tutorials can be found on the CD-ROM supplied with this book.

Now, let's look at the first tutorial on how to use our 2D library...

Using Our 2D Library

Introduction

In this first tutorial, we will cover the use of the simple 2D openGL library that we will be using in the following tutorials to create our online network game. The reason we are covering this is to keep confusing graphics code from getting in the way of the core network code, making the network code easier for us to understand. You will be able to quickly understand and use our 2D library, or if you prefer, you can use your own DirectX or openGL routines.

Configuring Visual Studio

The openGL library and our 2D library are located on the CD that accompanies this book. First, you must add the 2D library's API directory into the Visual Studio environment. To do this, select Tools, Options... from the main Visual Studio menu. Now, select the Directories tab on the dialog box that is now visible in the center of the screen.

Figure 1

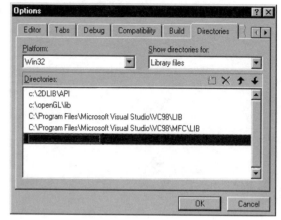

Next, add the library's API directory to both the Include files and Library files directory lists. This will allow Visual Studio to find the 2D library when you try to compile a program that uses it.

Finally, you need to add the openGL library into Visual Studio. You do this in the same way except you need to add the Include folder into the Include directories and the Library folder into the Library directories.

If you would like additional information on the creation and use of static link libraries, see Chapter 1.

Creating a Skeleton Project

It is generally a good idea to create some basic code that never changes so you can reuse it in future programs and projects. Here we create a simple windowed program using the 2D graphics library that will create a window on the screen. This skeleton can be developed further into any Windows application, as you will see throughout this online game tutorial.

First, we must create a workspace for our project. This entails creating a project, adding our 2D library and openGL into the workspace, and finally adding a main source file to code in.

Creating the Workspace

To create our workspace, select File, New... from the main Visual Studio menu. Next, click the Projects tab and select Win32 Application (not a console application). Set where you wish the project to be created (i.e., c:\Projects\) and finally the name for the project (i.e., OnlineGame). Once you click OK, the next window will ask which type of application you would like to create. For now, leave it as an empty project and click Finish. Simply click OK on the next screen, as it is just a summary of what you have done.

Now that we have our workspace created, we need to add the 2D library into the workspace so it is compiled with our code (so the functions are available to us).

Adding the Static Libraries

To do this, select Project then Settings from the main Visual Studio menu. On the dialog that appears, change the drop-down box at the top left from Win32 Debug to All Configurations. This means when we do add in the library it will be included in both debug and release versions of our game code. Next, select the Link tab on the right of the dialog and then add the following line before kernel32.lib:

```
opengl32.lib glu32.lib glaux.lib 2dlib.lib
```

This will add the required openGL libraries and our 2D library into the workspace when we compile the program.

Figure 2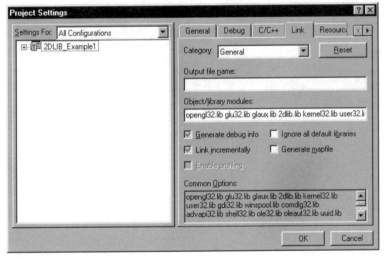

Adding the Source File

Finally, we need to add our main source file into the project. To do this, select File, New... from the main Visual Studio menu and select the Files tab on the dialog that appears. Now select C++ Source File and type "main" in the File name edit box. Click OK and the main source file will be added into our project.

Creating a Basic Windowed Application with 2DLib

Our workspace is now ready to add code into. For the 2D library to function, we need to create a Windows message loop and a callback function for the window, which is passed into the 2D library as a parameter. Now we will cover the main parts of the main program. The complete code can be found at the end of this section.

The WinMain Function

```
int WINAPI WinMain(HINSTANCE hThisInst, HINSTANCE hPrevInst, LPSTR lpszArgs,
int nWinMode)
{

    MSG msg;

    GFX_Init("App Title", 640, 480, 16, 0, WndProc);

    while(msg.message != WM_QUIT)
    {
        if(PeekMessage(&msg, NULL, 0, 0, PM_REMOVE))
        {
            TranslateMessage(&msg);
            DispatchMessage(&msg);
        }
        else
        {
            GFX_Begin();
            {

            }
            GFX_End();
        }
    }

    GFX_Shutdown();
    return msg.wParam;
}
```

The preceding code segment is the main Windows message loop, but it also contains our initialization code and main drawing loop. Let's now break the code up a bit.

```
GFX_Init("App Title", 640, 480, 16, 0, WndProc);
```

This function sets up our window to be ready for use by the 2D graphics library. The first parameter is the title of the window, although this is not relevant if you wish to create a full-screen application. The next two parameters determine the width and height of the window in pixels. The fourth specifies the color depth you wish to use; usually this is set to 16 bits per pixel, but other values such as 24 and 32 can be used too. The next parameter is a flag to determine whether you wish to run the application full screen or not; set this to 0 for windowed or 1 for full-screen mode. The final parameter is a pointer to the Windows procedure function that is explained in the following section.

Next is the message loop for Windows; this controls all the Windows messages that are required to allow the program to run correctly in the Windows environment.

```
while(msg.message != WM_QUIT)
{
    if(PeekMessage(&msg, NULL, 0, 0, PM_REMOVE))
    {
        TranslateMessage(&msg);
        DispatchMessage(&msg);
    }
    else
    {
        GFX_Begin();
        {
        }
        GFX_End();
    }
}
```

As you can see in the preceding code, the Windows messaging loop is a simple While loop that continues until a quit message is received. The PeekMessage function is a faster method of the GetMessage function and is the optimal way to get Windows messages. This is not important for us, but the Else part of the If statement is. This is where we place all our 2D drawing commands; it is, if you like, our game loop.

Once the 2D library is initialized using the GFX_Init() function, you must call GFX_Begin() before you start drawing and GFX_End() once everything is drawn. The first function is used to clear the drawing buffer for your next frame of graphics to be drawn to it. The ending function is used to swap the buffer onto the visible screen so that the user can see it without any shearing or other nasty graphical glitches.

Finally, once the user quits the program, the graphics library must be shut down; to do this, we simply call GFX_Shutdown() after the While loop. This closes the graphics library and frees any memory that was allocated internally by the 2D graphics library.

The Windows Procedure

Every time our window receives a Windows message, such as a key being pressed on the keyboard, this function is called to process the message correctly. The code that follows is the entire Windows procedure.

```
LRESULT CALLBACK WndProc(HWND hWnd, UINT uMsg, WPARAM wParam, LPARAM lParam)
{
    switch (uMsg)
    {
        case WM_CLOSE:
        {
            PostQuitMessage(0);
            return 0;
        }

        case WM_KEYDOWN:
        {
            keys[wParam] = TRUE;
            return 0;
        }

        case WM_KEYUP:
        {
            keys[wParam] = FALSE;
            return 0;
        }

        case WM_SIZE:
        {
            GFX_Resize(LOWORD(lParam),HIWORD(lParam));
            return 0;
        }
    }

    // Pass All Unhandled Messages To DefWindowProc
    return DefWindowProc(hWnd,uMsg,wParam,lParam);
}
```

In basic terms, the function is simply a switch statement that reacts correctly to different events (Cases) in windows. If the function has no handling routine for an event, it simply passes it back to Windows to be dealt with accordingly.

It is possible to add other event handles into this procedure, but the four we have included in this skeleton application are all that are required for now. Let's have a look at the events in a little more detail.

The WM_CLOSE Event

```
case WM_CLOSE:
{
    PostQuitMessage(0);
    return 0;
}
```

This event is triggered when the user clicks on the X button at the top right of a window, or when a close message is manually sent to the window. When a WM_CLOSE message is sent, this routine sends out a WM_QUIT message that, if you remember from earlier, is the condition for our main While loop (i.e., when a WM_QUIT message is received, our program will shut down and exit).

The WM_KEYDOWN Event

```
case WM_KEYDOWN:
{
    keys[wParam] = TRUE;
    return 0;
}
```

In the 2D library, we have defined an array that allows easy use of the keyboard without having to learn DirectInput or another similar input library. When a key has been pressed down on the keyboard, this routine sets the correct key in the array to TRUE, meaning that the key is currently down. Later in this tutorial we will cover how to use the keyboard for input.

The WM_KEYUP Event

```
case WM_KEYUP:
{
    keys[wParam] = FALSE;
    return 0;
}
```

This routine works in the same way as the WM_KEYDOWN routine, except that it handles the event of a key being released on the keyboard. When the key has been released, it sets the correct value in the keys array to FALSE, meaning the key is not being pressed.

The WM_SIZE Event

```
case WM_SIZE:
{
    GFX_Resize(LOWORD(lParam),HIWORD(lParam));
    return 0;
}
```

This event handles the resizing of a windowed mode application. It is not relevant for full-screen applications, but it does not do any harm to leave it in. It tells the 2D library the new width and height of the window so that it can react accordingly. (The width is the low word of the lParam and the height is the high word of the lParam.)

The Complete Code

The final part we require is what files we must include. We need to include the Windows header file (since we are creating a Windows application), the three openGL header files for the 2D library, and finally the 2D library's header files. Therefore, our complete code listing for the skeleton application resembles the following.

```
#include <windows.h>
#include <gl/gl.h>
#include <gl/glu.h>
#include <gl/glaux.h>
#include <2dlib.h>


// WINDOWS PROCEDURE
LRESULT CALLBACK WndProc(HWND hWnd, UINT uMsg, WPARAM wParam, LPARAM lParam)
{
    switch (uMsg)
    {
        case WM_CLOSE:
        {
            PostQuitMessage(0);
            return 0;
        }

        case WM_KEYDOWN:
        {
            keys[wParam] = TRUE;
            return 0;
        }

        case WM_KEYUP:
        {
            keys[wParam] = FALSE;
            return 0;
        }

        case WM_SIZE:
        {
```

```
                        GFX_Resize(LOWORD(lParam),HIWORD(lParam));
                        return 0;
            }
        }

        // Pass All Unhandled Messages To DefWindowProc
        return DefWindowProc(hWnd,uMsg,wParam,lParam);
    }


    // WINDOWS MESSAGE LOOP AND APPLICATION ENTRY POINT
    int WINAPI WinMain(HINSTANCE hThisInst, HINSTANCE hPrevInst, LPSTR lpszArgs, int
    nWinMode)
    {

        MSG msg;

        GFX_Init("Skeleton App", 640, 480, 16, 0, WndProc);

        while(msg.message != WM_QUIT)
        {
            if(PeekMessage(&msg, NULL, 0, 0, PM_REMOVE))
            {
                TranslateMessage(&msg);
                DispatchMessage(&msg);
            }
            else
            {
                GFX_Begin();
                {

                }
                GFX_End();
            }
        }
        GFX_Shutdown();
        return msg.wParam;
    }
```

If everything has gone according to plan, when you compile and execute the preceding code you should now be able to see the following screen.

Figure 3

Not very exciting is it? However, it is very useful as we now have the foundation for our 2D graphics engine, meaning we can easily use the 2D library to create primitives and bitmapped graphics on the screen.

Using the 2DLib Graphics Routines

Now we will cover all the graphical functions in the 2D library with an explanation of how to use them. Following that, we will cover a couple of examples in how you use them with the skeleton application.

Graphical Functions

Remember that all graphics functions must be placed between the GFX_Begin() and GFX_End() functions or the graphics will not be visible on the screen.

2D Positions on the Screen

For the x-coordinates, the values start from zero at the left-hand side of the application and end at the width of your application minus one. The y-coordinates start from zero at the top of your application and end at the height of your application minus one. The example that follows displays what the screen coordinates would be like for a 640 x 480 application in the format of (x, y).

Figure 4

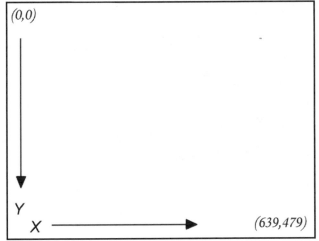

Use of Colors

Each primitive drawing function in the library has three parameters at the end that specify the red, green, and blue (RGB) values for what you wish to draw. These values range as integers from 0 to 255, where 0 is black and 255 is full brightness. Therefore, if you wanted your color to be bright red, you would use 255 red, 0 green, and 0 blue.

Plotting a Single Pixel

```
void GFX_Pixel(int x, int y, int r, int g, int b);
```

This function will display a single pixel on the screen at the specified (x, y) position. The position is specified by the first two parameters of the function, the first being x and the second being the y position. The final three parameters determine the color of the pixel in RGB format (see the information about colors in the previous paragraph).

Drawing a Line

```
void GFX_Line(int x1, int y1, int x2, int y2, int r, int g, int b);
```

This function draws a line between two points. The first two parameters are the (x, y) position of the first point. The next two parameters are the (x, y) position of the point we want to connect the first point to. The final three parameters specify the color in RGB format.

Drawing a Rectangle/Filled Rectangle

```
void GFX_Rect(int x1, int y1, int x2, int y2, int r, int g, int b);
```

```
void GFX_RectFill(int x1, int y1, int x2, int y2, int r, int g, int b);
```

These functions draw a rectangle based on the two points you specify. The first two parameters determine the top left corner for the rectangle. The next two specify the bottom right corner for the rectangle. Again, the final three parameters decide the color in RGB format.

The first function draws an outlined rectangle in the specified color, whereas the second draws a filled rectangle in the specified color.

Drawing a Triangle/Filled Triangle

```
void GFX_Tri(int x1, int y1, int x2, int y2, int x3, int y3, int r, int g, int b);
```

```
void GFX_TriFill(int x1, int y1, int x2, int y2, int x3, int y3, int r, int g,
int b);
```

These two primitive functions allow you to draw triangles and filled triangles on the screen. The first six parameters determine the three two-dimensional coordinates that are required to construct a triangle. The final three parameters then determine the RGB values the same way as the other primitive functions.

Graphic Loading Functions

Our 2D library has support for Windows bitmaps and 24-bit and 32-bit uncompressed Truevision Targa format. First, we need to declare a variable that will hold our graphic data. You do this as follows:

```
GFX_IMAGE2D my_image;
```

This line creates a variable called My_Image that you can use with the graphics loading commands in the library to load pictures from your hard drive in the application.

Next, you want to actually load an image in. Let's say we have an image called brick.bmp which is a Windows bitmap image. We would call the following function to load it into our My_Image variable. Notice you pass a pointer to the GFX_Image2D variable, followed by the filename of the graphic you wish to load.

```
GFX_LoadBitmap(&my_image, "brick.bmp");
```

The Truevision Targa loading function works in the same manner. If you have an image called phone.tga you would load it like this:

```
GFX_LoadTarga(&my_image, "phone.tga");
```

That is all there is to loading in graphics. Here are the prototypes for the graphics loading functions for your reference:

```
void GFX_LoadBitmap(GFX_IMAGE2D *pImage, char *filename);
```

```
void GFX_LoadTarga(GFX_IMAGE2D *pImage, char *filename);
```

Graphics Display (Blitting) Function

Once you have successfully loaded in your graphics, you use the following function to display them on the screen.

```
void GFX_Blit(GFX_IMAGE2D *pImage, int x, int y, int w, int h, float rotate);
```

The first parameter is a pointer to a GFX_Image2D. You simply pass a pointer to a graphic you have loaded using one of the loading functions explained previously. Next, you specify the (x, y) position using the second and third parameters of the function. The function also handles image scaling so you can state the width and height the image is to be drawn at on the screen. This is set in the forth and fifth parameters respectively. Finally, the function handles image rotation in degrees. Therefore, you can specify a floating-point value between 0.0 and 360.0 for the image to be drawn at (the image rotates around its center point).

For example, if you wanted to display an image you loaded into a My_Image variable at the point (25, 50) with a width of 100 and a height of 150 and no rotation, you would call the following function:

```
GFX_Blit(&my_image, 25, 50, 100, 150, 0.0);
```

If, however, you then decided you wanted it in the same position with the same dimensions, but at an angle of 30 degrees, the function would be as follows:

```
GFX_Blit(&my_image, 25, 50, 100, 150, 30.0);
```

That is all there is to the graphical side of the library. As you can see, there is nothing very complicated in it, and it simplifies many of the hard initialization procedures and other such things.

Keyboard Input Method

This is a very simple method of getting keyboard input. We would really recommend using a library such as DirectInput, but this method makes the process simple and it does what we require it to do for now.

To check a key on the keyboard, simply place an If statement after the GFX_End() as follows:

```
if(keys[VkKeyScan('a')])
{
    // place what is to be done here
}
```

The preceding If statement would determine if the "a" key had been pressed. The "a" can be replaced with any other character, symbol, or number from the keyboard. For example, if you wished to check if the "]" key had been pressed, you would use this statement:

```
if(keys[VkKeyScan(']')])
{
    // place what is to be done here
}
```

There are special cases such as the function keys (F1, F2, etc.) and other keys like the Spacebar and Return key. Following is a table containing most of these special cases and an If statement showing how to use a special key.

Table 1: Special Keys

Statement	Description
VK_F1	Function key F1
VK_F2	Function key F2
VK_F3	Function key F3
VK_F4	Function key F4
VK_F5	Function key F5
VK_F6	Function key F6
VK_F7	Function key F7
VK_F8	Function key F8
VK_F9	Function key F9
VK_F10	Function key F10
VK_F11	Function key F11
VK_F12	Function key F12
VK_INSERT	Insert key
VK_HOME	Home key
VK_PAGE_UP	Page Up key
VK_DELETE	Delete key
VK_END	End key
VK_PAGE_DOWN	Page Down key
VK_UP	Arrow key up
VK_DOWN	Arrow key down
VK_LEFT	Arrow key left
VK_RIGHT	Arrow key right
VK_ESCAPE	Escape key
VK_SPACE	Spacebar

Statement	Description
VK_CONTROL	Control key
VK_ALT	Alt key
VK_ADD	Numeric keypad + key
VK_SUBTRACT	Numeric keypad – key
VK_MULTIPLY	Numeric keypad * key
VK_DIVIDE	Numeric keypad / key
VK_EQUALS	= key
VK_TAB	Tab key

Unlike the other If statements where you use a function (VkKeyScan) to get the correct value for the character, you simply place in the VK_ value directly as follows:

```
if(keys[VK_SPACE])
{
    // place what is to be done here
}
```

The preceding example would check to see if the Spacebar had been pressed and if so, execute the code within the If statement.

2DLib Example 1 — Moving Primitives with the Cursor Keys

In this first example application, we create a program that allows the user to move a filled rectangle around the screen using the cursor keys, but not out of the borders of the application. In addition, the user will be able to select whether the rectangle is red, green, or blue by pressing r, g, or b, respectively. The complete code listing for this example is at the end of this section.

First, we must set up a project file for this application. This is done in exactly the same manner as the skeleton application that is explained earlier in this tutorial. Once we have the skeleton application running, the first thing we must do is create variables to store the position, dimensions, and color of the rectangle. We declare these globally as follows:

```
int rect_x, rect_y; // (x, y) position
int rect_w, rect_h; // width and height

float rect_r; // red color
float rect_g; // green color
float rect_b; // blue color
```

Next, subsequent to the initialization code for 2DLib, we want to set these variables for the rectangle. This is done as follows:

```
rect_x = 10;  // x position is 10
rect_y = 10;  // y position is 10
rect_w = 100; // width is 100 pixels
rect_h = 100; // height is 100 pixels

rect_r = 255.0; // red is full intensity
rect_g = 0.0;   // no blue
rect_b = 0.0;   // no green
```

Now, when we draw our rectangle it will appear at position (10, 10) and be 100 pixels wide and high. In addition, we have set the red value to maximum and green and blue to the minimum, making the rectangle appear a bright red color. In the drawing loop, we will then place the following function to draw it:

```
GFX_RectFill(rect_x, rect_y, rect_x+rect_w, rect_y+rect_h, rect_r, rect_g, rect_b);
```

This will draw the filled rectangle at the position we specified, using the values from the variables we declared before. For more information on this function, see the earlier section titled "Graphical Functions."

Finally, we wish to be able to move the rectangle around the screen so we need to have the correct keyboard code to do this. Here is what the movement code should look like:

```
if(keys[VK_UP])
{
    if(rect_y > 0)
        rect_y--;
}
if(keys[VK_DOWN])
{
    if(rect_y+rect_h < 480)
        rect_y++;
}
if(keys[VK_RIGHT])
{
    if(rect_x+rect_w < 640)
        rect_x++;
}
if(keys[VK_LEFT])
{
    if(rect_x > 0)
        rect_x--;
}
```

This simply adjusts the variables for the rectangle based on which arrow key the user presses on the keyboard. The colors work in a similar fashion; see the following code:

```
if(keys[VkKeyScan('r')])
{
    rect_r = 255.0;
    rect_g = 0.0;
    rect_b = 0.0;
}
if(keys[VkKeyScan('g')])
{
    rect_r = 0.0;
    rect_g = 255.0;
    rect_b = 0.0;
}
if(keys[VkKeyScan('b')])
{
    rect_r = 0.0;
    rect_g = 0.0;
    rect_b = 255.0;
}
```

This code checks whether r, g, or b has been pressed and if so, changes the rectangle variables to set the color respectively.

That covers everything for our first example. When you compile the code below you should be able to move the rectangle around with the arrow keys and also change the color with the r, g, and b keys.

Complete Code Listing for Example 1

```
#include <windows.h>
#include <gl/gl.h>
#include <gl/glu.h>
#include <gl/glaux.h>
#include <2dlib.h>

// APPLICATION SPECIFIC

int rect_x, rect_y; // (x, y) position
int rect_w, rect_h; // width and height

float rect_r; // red color
float rect_g; // green color
float rect_b; // blue color
```

```
// WINDOWS PROCEDURE

LRESULT CALLBACK WndProc(HWND hWnd, UINT uMsg, WPARAM wParam, LPARAM lParam)
{
    switch (uMsg)
    {
        case WM_CLOSE:
        {
            PostQuitMessage(0);
            return 0;
        }

        case WM_KEYDOWN:
        {
            keys[wParam] = TRUE;
            return 0;
        }

        case WM_KEYUP:
        {
            keys[wParam] = FALSE;
            return 0;
        }

        case WM_SIZE:
        {
            GFX_Resize(LOWORD(lParam),HIWORD(lParam));
            return 0;
        }
    }

    // Pass All Unhandled Messages To DefWindowProc
    return DefWindowProc(hWnd,uMsg,wParam,lParam);
}


// WINDOWS MESSAGE LOOP AND APPLICATION ENTRY POINT

int WINAPI WinMain(HINSTANCE hThisInst, HINSTANCE hPrevInst, LPSTR lpszArgs, int
nWinMode)
{

    MSG msg;

    // Initialise 2DLIB
    GFX_Init("2DLIB - Example 1", 640, 480, 16, 0, WndProc);
```

```
// Setup the Rectangle
rect_x = 10;  // x position is 10
rect_y = 10;  // y position is 10
rect_w = 100; // width is 100 pixels
rect_h = 100; // height is 100 pixels

rect_r = 255.0; // red is full intensity
rect_g = 0.0;   // no blue
rect_b = 0.0;   // no green

// Start the Windows Message Loop
while(msg.message != WM_QUIT)
{
    if(PeekMessage(&msg, NULL, 0, 0, PM_REMOVE))
    {
        TranslateMessage(&msg);
        DispatchMessage(&msg);
    }
    else
    {
        GFX_Begin();
        {
            // Draw the Rectangle
            GFX_RectFill(rect_x, rect_y, rect_x+rect_w, rect_y+rect_h,
            rect_r, rect_g, rect_b);
        }
        GFX_End();
    }

    // Check for Keyboard Input

    // -> Movement
    if(keys[VK_UP])
    {
        if(rect_y > 0)
            rect_y--;
    }
    if(keys[VK_DOWN])
    {
        if(rect_y+rect_h < 480)
            rect_y++;
    }
    if(keys[VK_RIGHT])
    {
        if(rect_x+rect_w < 640)
            rect_x++;
    }
```

```
        if(keys[VK_LEFT])
        {
            if(rect_x > 0)
                rect_x--;
        }

        // -> Colors
        if(keys[VkKeyScan('r')])
        {
            rect_r = 255.0;
            rect_g = 0.0;
            rect_b = 0.0;
        }
        if(keys[VkKeyScan('g')])
        {
            rect_r = 0.0;
            rect_g = 255.0;
            rect_b = 0.0;
        }
        if(keys[VkKeyScan('b')])
        {
            rect_r = 0.0;
            rect_g = 0.0;
            rect_b = 255.0;
        }
    }
    GFX_Shutdown();
    return msg.wParam;
}
```

2DLib Example 2 — Loading and Rotating Graphics

In this example we will load a single bitmap file, then display it twice on the screen and make the two copies rotate in opposite directions.

The first thing we must do is create our skeleton project as described earlier in this tutorial. Once we have this in place, we can begin by creating a variable that will hold the image and also another to hold the current angle in degrees.

```
GFX_IMAGE2D cdrom;
float rotation;
```

The preceding declarations are global and the first is used to store the image in a variable called cdrom. The second is used to store the angle in degrees the image is to be rotated at. To spin the second image in the opposite direction, we simply subtract the rotation value from 360 degrees.

Next, we need to load our graphic file into the application. In this case, the file is an image of a CD-ROM and is called cdrom.bmp. Therefore, to load it we would want to call the GFX_LoadBitmap() function as follows:

```
GFX_LoadBitmap(&cdrom, "cdrom.bmp");
```

This would load cdrom.bmp into the cdrom global variable. This is done after we initialize the 2D library. Once this is done we can then display the image on the screen using the following technique:

```
GFX_Blit(&cdrom, 32,  100, 256, 256, rotation);
GFX_Blit(&cdrom, 352, 100, 256, 256, 360-rotation);
```

These two functions are placed between the GFX_Begin() and GFX_End() functions as they display the image onto the screen. The first image is displayed at (32, 100) and the second is displayed at (352, 100). Both images are 256 x 256 pixels. Additionally, the first is rotated clockwise and the latter is rotated counterclockwise.

The only thing left to do now is adjust the rotation variable every time through the loop. This is simply done as follows:

```
rotation++;
if(rotation>360)
{
    rotation -= 360;
}
```

When the rotation value becomes greater than 360 degress, 360 is subtracted from the value.

That completes the second example. When you compile and execute the code listing that follows, you should see two CD-ROMs displayed on the screen spinning in opposite directions.

Complete Code Listing for Example 2

```
#include <windows.h>
#include <gl/gl.h>
#include <gl/glu.h>
#include <gl/glaux.h>
#include <2dlib.h>


// APPLICATION SPECIFIC

GFX_IMAGE2D cdrom; // variable to hold 'cdrom' graphic
float rotation;    // variable to hold current rotation value
```

```
// WINDOWS PROCEDURE
LRESULT CALLBACK WndProc(HWND hWnd, UINT uMsg, WPARAM wParam, LPARAM lParam)
{
    switch (uMsg)
    {
        case WM_CLOSE:
        {
            PostQuitMessage(0);
            return 0;
        }

        case WM_KEYDOWN:
        {
            keys[wParam] = TRUE;
            return 0;
        }

        case WM_KEYUP:
        {
            keys[wParam] = FALSE;
            return 0;
        }

        case WM_SIZE:
        {
            GFX_Resize(LOWORD(lParam),HIWORD(lParam));
            return 0;
        }
    }

    // Pass All Unhandled Messages To DefWindowProc
    return DefWindowProc(hWnd,uMsg,wParam,lParam);
}


// WINDOWS MESSAGE LOOP AND APPLICATION ENTRY POINT
int WINAPI WinMain(HINSTANCE hThisInst, HINSTANCE hPrevInst, LPSTR lpszArgs, int
nWinMode)
{

    MSG msg;

    // Initialise 2DLIB
    GFX_Init("2DLIB - Example 1", 640, 480, 16, 0, WndProc);

    // Load in the image
    GFX_LoadBitmap(&cdrom, "cdrom.bmp");
```

```
// Start the Windows Message Loop
while(msg.message != WM_QUIT)
{
    if(PeekMessage(&msg, NULL, 0, 0, PM_REMOVE))
    {
        TranslateMessage(&msg);
        DispatchMessage(&msg);
    }
    else
    {
        GFX_Begin();
        {
            GFX_Blit(&cdrom, 32,  100, 256, 256, rotation);
            GFX_Blit(&cdrom, 352, 100, 256, 256, 360-rotation);
        }
        GFX_End();

        rotation++;
        if(rotation>360)
        {
            rotation -= 360;
        }
    }

    // Check for Keyboard Input
}
GFX_Shutdown();
return msg.wParam;
}
```

Summary

In this tutorial, you learned how to create a simple 2D graphics application using our 2D openGL library. This knowledge is sufficient for you to understand the network game programming tutorials that are to follow, although we would recommend learning more about openGL and Direct3D as they are very useful pieces of knowledge. On a final note, it is also possible to add in openGL commands directly. The library creates an openGL window with a two-dimensional orthographic view; therefore you could, for example, change it to a perspective view and create a 3D application, but this is beyond the scope of these tutorials. The network code, however, is not tied to any one graphics library, so you can implement any style of game using the same network library whether it is 2D or 3D.

Creating Your Network Library

Introduction

In this tutorial we learn how to create the most essential part of our tutorial game: the network library. Obviously, we make a library of all the network code to gain access to it in every application we want. In the case of our tutorial game, we use the library in the game itself (client software) and in the server. Also, if we wanted to make any extra servers with different functionality than the normal game server, we would most likely want to use the same library for that, too.

We create the library so that it can be used under both Windows and Unix (Linux). The original idea is that the game (client) is run on Windows, and the server on Unix. But because of our platform-independent code, we do not have to worry about the network code if we want to change the platforms.

Why Create a Network Library of Our Own?

One big question arises when you start to think about creating your own network library. Why? Why would anyone want to make one by himself or herself, when there are perfectly good network libraries out there already? For example, why not use Microsoft's DirectPlay?

DirectPlay is an excellent library, and because it is solely designed for gaming, it is an excellent choice for a game programmer. But it has one major drawback: You do not have Unix connectivity with it. Now you may think that no one really needs that. Well, it is up to you if you want the Unix connectivity, but because Unix is an absolutely stable system it is the best choice for the server platform. There are some examples of bad experiences with not using any Unix operating system as the server platform in recent gaming history, so why repeat them? If you create your own network library using sockets, you can have full Unix connectivity if you want to. Plus, you will have a library that fits your needs exactly.

Planning the Structure

Before anything else we should take a moment to think about the structure of the library. We need to know all the facts of the library before we start to code it. If we started coding the library without any planning beforehand, we would most likely need to modify the structure many times before it met our requirements.

Let's look at some of the facts. Fact number one is that the library must be platform independent. This leads to a conclusion that it is best to divide the code platform by platform, so we will not mix the code together for the different platforms. Plus, we can easily add support for more platforms this way. The easiest and most clear way to divide the code is to store code for the different platforms in separate source files. This method requires one main source file that wraps up all the code and selects the correct functions to be run. Because our game needs to have only Windows and Unix support, we create three source files and their header files: netLib.cpp and netLib.h, netWinLib.cpp and netWinLib.h, and netLinuxLib.cpp and netLinuxLib.h. We also locate the files in separate directories so the directory structure stays clean and is easy to upgrade.

Fact number two is that the library must be protocol independent. Because the Sockets API is very flexible, we can easily write one code that works with multiple protocols. So there is no need to separate different protocol code in different files. We may need to write separate functions, though. We will learn how to do that in this tutorial.

A network library may vary in size, depending on the functionality we want, so it is a good idea to make the code as modular as possible. Therefore, we use the C++ class as the base of our library, each object being one connection on a client and one service on a server (with multiple connections). Other facts vary, and do not affect the structure of the library much.

Planning the Functionality

Knowing the basic functionality before starting to code is also a must. Of course, we could just write functions for sending and receiving data without anything extra, but what would that help? Nothing. We need to make the library as easy to use as possible, by moving all the complex network technology from the end programmer to the background. This way the end programmer can merely point and tell the library what to do. The end programmer should not have to worry about binding address information to a socket; that is a job for the network library. The end programmer should not have to understand the complex technical functionality of the network code. And most of all, the network library must take care of sending the data to the correct location.

Identifying Hosts

We need a system that identifies all the unique hosts on the network. In this network library we are about to create, we have a system of host ID numbers. They are unique only per server and more accurately per server socket. The server host ID is always zero (0). The first client to connect the server receives the ID number 1. The next client receives ID number 2 and so on. If client ID 1 disconnects, that ID number will be marked as free, and the next client to connect will receive the lowest free ID number (which is 1 in this case). Every host connected on the server can identify other hosts by this ID number.

Sending Data to Hosts

Sending data to hosts is not as straightforward as it may seem at first. This is because we need to decide if we want to let the clients send data between each other directly, without having the server as a router of any kind. To be able to send data directly between clients, all the clients need to know the address information of all the other clients. If there are a lot of clients in the network, it would consume vast amounts of memory and time (the address information must be sent via the network too). Also, the server cannot process the data that is sent between two clients. This is why we decided not to allow clients to exchange data directly.

To send data from client to client, the data is actually first sent to the server and the server will then resend the data to the destination after required processing. Now we can check if the data is acceptable, and the server can keep track of possible changes. For the end programmer it does not look any different sending data through a server or directly between two clients. You just enter the target host ID, and the network library will take care of delivering the data to the destination.

Building the Library

Now we will learn how to build the library file. This means that we will learn to set up the compiler so that it builds a library file for us, which can then be linked to other applications.

Windows

Building and compiling the library on Windows is very easy with Microsoft Visual C++ 6.0. Because we are building a library, there is no need (or no way) to link any extra libraries with it. All the linking of other libraries is done when we build the application that uses our library. But there is a way to make our library link other libraries automatically.

Because this network library requires the WinSock 2 library on Windows, we need to link it with the application. We could link it normally among the other libraries in Microsoft Visual C++ 6.0 settings, as shown in the following figure.

Figure 1

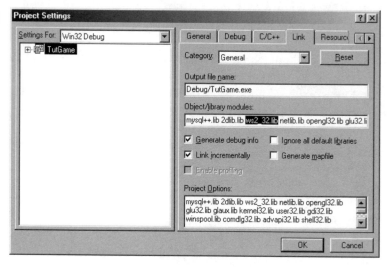

But we can also add the following line in our network library's header file to make the WinSock 2 library be linked automatically whenever our network library is linked:

```
#pragma comment (lib, "ws2_32.lib")
```

We must also define the constant WIN32, as shown in the following piece of code, to make the compiler compile the correct version of the source code:

```
#define WIN32
```

Or we can add it to the preprocessor list as shown in the following figure.

Figure 2

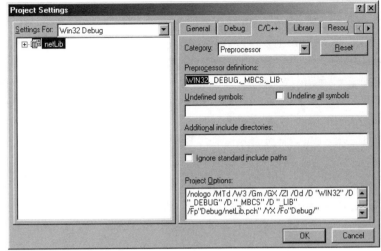

Unix/Linux

Building the library on Unix is a little bit more complicated, as is pretty much everything on Unix. We need to use the following makefile and a command line compiler:

```
C_LINK = -lpthread
C_ARGS = -Wall
CC = cc

all: netLib.o netLinuxLib.o
    ar q libnetLib.a netLib.o netLinuxLib.o

clean:
    rm -f *.o

netLib.o: netLib.cpp
    $(CC) $(C_ARGS) -c netLib.cpp

netLinuxLib.o: netLinuxLib.cpp
    $(CC) $(C_ARGS) $(C_LINK) -c netLinuxLib.cpp
```

Now all we need to do is run Make on the command line and the library is built.

NOTE Make sure you have enough rights to make the library on the Unix machine you use.

Creating Independent Code

In this section we discuss many things we need to know before we can make our code independent from various things, starting with operating systems and moving to communication protocols. Probably the biggest thing we discover is that we can actually run the very same code on different platforms. We use the same function calls, but the insides differ. To the end programmer it looks as if the code would be exactly the same, regardless of what system we are using.

Creating Definitions for Data Types

To create the new definitions we must know which platform is used for the build. This is very easy. You can either add a definition of the current platform in the beginning of your code, or you can use the preprocessor of the compiler. Both do the same thing really. If you want to use #define, just add this line when you are compiling under Windows:

```
#define WIN32
```

Now you do not have to add a define for Unix builds because you can simply comment out the definition of WIN32. This kind of system assumes that we going to use the code only on Windows and some other (unspecified) operating system. In our case the other operating system is Unix (or Linux). We could make definitions for all the operating systems we are going to support, but it is easier this way when we use only two known systems.

Using the preprocessor is even easier. Just add the string "WIN32" in the Windows version makefile (or workspace settings) preprocessor's list of definitions. Now you do not have to make any modifications to your code when you move from one platform to another. The makefile you use defines the platform for the code. Figure 3 (on the following page) shows the preprocessor screen of project settings in Microsoft Visual C++ 6.0. Notice the string "WIN32" in the first text box (preprocessor definitions).

But how do we check to see if the definition of WIN32 is there? Again, this is very simple:

```
#ifdef WIN32
    typedef int socklen_t; // will be run if we are on WIN32
#else
    typedef int SOCKET;      // will be run if we are not on WIN32
#endif
```

This small piece of code checks the platform used during the build. The compiler forgets the non-true statement, and it will not be added to the executable. Hence, it does not slow down the run-time process.

Figure 3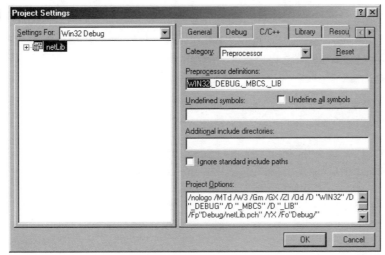

Protocol Independence

Making our application protocol independent is just as easy as making it operating system independent. We just need to define which protocol to use and then add the code to check the chosen protocol. Most socket functions work protocol independently, so there is no problem with them. We just need to remember that UDP does not have the concept of connections.

Transport Protocol Independence

When we create a socket, we do so as shown in the following code. We must define the Protocol variable beforehand, so the switch statement selects the correct function call for us.

```
// Check which protocol to use
switch(Protocol)
{
// TCP protocol
case NET_TCP:
    sock = socket(AF_INET, SOCK_STREAM, 0);
    break;

// UDP protocol
case NET_UDP:
    sock = socket(AF_INET, SOCK_DGRAM, 0);
    break;
}
```

Internet Protocol Independence

On Unix we can make our application independent of the Internet Protocol (IPv4/IPv6). For this we need to use the socket function GetAddrInfo, but because WinSock 2 does not have this function, we leave it out.

Log System

It is a good idea to log every happening somewhere, so we can see what exactly happened and when. For example, if something goes wrong we do not have to shut down the server to start investigating. We can first check the log file to see if that helps and then act upon that.

The following code listing shows the StartLog function, which is used to start the log system:

```
void StartLog(void)
{
    FILE *LogFile;

    time_t current = time(NULL);

    if((LogFile = fopen("netLib.log", "w")) != NULL)
    {
        fprintf(LogFile, "Log file started %s",
            ctime(&current));

        fclose(LogFile);
    }
}
```

The following piece of code is used to retrieve the current time. This information is written every time something is logged, so we know when it happened.

```
time_t current = time(NULL);
```

We open the file for writing and write the current time at the beginning of the file. Then we close the log file, so we can start adding text to it:

```
if((LogFile = fopen("netLib.log", "w")) != NULL)
{
    fprintf(LogFile, "Log file started %s", ctime(&current));

    fclose(LogFile);
}
```

The following code listing shows the LogString function, which is used to add a string to the log file:

```
void LogString(char *string, ...)
{
    char buf[1024];
    va_list ap;
    va_start(ap, string);
    vsprintf(buf, string, ap);
    va_end(ap);

    FILE *LogFile;

    time_t current = time(NULL);

    if((LogFile = fopen("netLib.log", "a")) != NULL)
    {
        fprintf(LogFile, "-> %s: %s", ctime(&current), buf);
        fprintf(LogFile, "\n");

        fclose(LogFile);
    }
}
```

First we will format the text so that we can add any variable values to it. The final string will be stored in the string buf:

```
char buf[1024];
va_list ap;
va_start(ap, string);
vsprintf(buf, string, ap);
va_end(ap);
```

Again we retrieve the current time to add a time stamp with each log string:

```
time_t current = time(NULL);
```

Then we open the log file for adding this time, so we will not rewrite the whole file. We write the time stamp and the string and follow it by a linefeed, so the user does not have to add the linefeed to the string every time. Once the string is added, we close the file:

```
if((LogFile = fopen("netLib.log", "a")) != NULL)
{
    fprintf(LogFile, "-> %s: %s", ctime(&current), buf);
    fprintf(LogFile, "\n");

    fclose(LogFile);
}
```

Getting Started

Let's get started. It is a good idea to start writing the code so that we can test it as soon as possible. It is very frustrating to write tons of code that possibly does not work at all. It is also much easier to debug the code if we notice when a bug appears (of course, we are aiming not to meet any critters). So we will start from scratch and move on to the final library step by step.

Setting Up Source and Header Files

Before we actually start coding the library, we need to set some things up in the source files and header files. In the main source file, netLib.cpp, we need to have the following build-time definition check the Windows version to make sure that WinSock 2 API is used instead of any older version:

```
#ifndef _WINSOCKAPI_
#define _WINSOCKAPI_
#endif
```

If we do not define _WinSockAPI_ before including windows.h, an old version of the WinSock header file will be included, and the build will fail. So the preceding piece of code is required for all WinSock 2 applications that include the windows.h header.

The beginning of netLib.cpp looks like this:

```
#ifdef WIN32
// Windows specific headers
    #ifndef _WINSOCKAPI_
    #define _WINSOCKAPI_
    #endif
    #include <windows.h>
    #include <winsock2.h>
#else
// UNIX specific headers
    #include <memory.h>
    #include <errno.h>
    #include <unistd.h>
    #include <sys/ioctl.h>
    #include <sys/socket.h>
    #include <sys/time.h>
    #include <sys/stat.h>
    #include <sys/types.h>
    #include <sys/wait.h>
    #include <netinet/in.h>
    #include <arpa/inet.h>
    #include <pthread.h>
```

```
        #include <signal.h>
#endif

// Common headers
#include <stdio.h>
#include <stdarg.h>
#include <stdlib.h>
#include <ctype.h>
#include <time.h>
#include "netLib.h"
```

As we can see in the preceding code, we have separate header files for Windows and Unix. Plus we have some common header files that both operating systems require. As we learned earlier in this chapter: When creating independent code, we use build-time definition checks to see what piece of code is to be linked and what is not, depending on the platform we are on.

NET_Socket Class

Now let's start with creating the base C++ class of the library. Each NET_Socket object is a separate connection on a client, and a separate multi-connection service on a server. We will be adding stuff to the class while we progress in this tutorial, so it is not complete in the beginning. As we need more functions and/or variables, we add them to the class. This first version will have only Windows and TCP support, and lacks some extra features. Thus, the class that is stored in netLib.h header file looks like this:

```
class NET_Socket
{
private:
    int GiveLocalIdTCP(void);
    void FindNextFreeHostIndex(void);

    // Server creation helper functions
    int CreateWinTCPServer(SOCKET listenSock);
    int CreateTCPServer(SOCKET sock);
    int CreateWinServer(int port);

#ifdef WIN32
    int WinHandleEvents(int id, LPWSANETWORKEVENTS NetworkEvents);
#endif

    void SendSystemMessage(NETMSG_GENERIC *Msg);

    HOSTID NextFreeHostIndex;
```

TUTORIAL 2

```cpp
public:
    NET_Socket();
    ~NET_Socket();

    // Uninitialization functions
    void CloseConnection(int id, int active);
    void Shutdown(void);

    // Miscellanous functions
    int SetNonBlocking(int id, u_long setBlocking);
    void AcceptConnection(void);
    int CreateServer(int port);
    int ConnectToServer(char *ipAddressString, int port);

    // Data reading / writing functions
    int Read(int id, char *buf, size_t count);
    int Write(int id, char *buf, size_t count);
    void WriteAll(char *buf, size_t count);

    int ReadFrom(SOCKET sock, char *buf, size_t count,
    struct sockaddr *sockAddr, socklen_t *sockLen,
    bool NonBlocking);

    int WriteTo(SOCKET sock, char *buf, size_t count,
    struct sockaddr *sockAddr, socklen_t sockLen);

    HOSTID GetNextFreeHostIndex(void) {return NextFreeHostIndex;}

    // Message processing functions
    void ProcessMessages(int id);

    int HandleSocketInputEvent(int id);

#ifdef WIN32
    HANDLE SocketOutputEvent;
#endif

    // Miscellanous variables
    SOCKET listenSocket;                    // Listening socket

    int localId;                            // Local host id
    bool Online;                            // Local online flag

    int RemoteHosts;                        // Amount of remote hosts
    RemoteHost_t *RemoteHost;
```

```
        int Port;                       // Port in use
};
```

We take a closer look at each of the functions and variables later in this tutorial. We see that there is a another class inside NET_Socket called RemoteHost. Obviously, this is used to store the information of the remote hosts, or connections. We call them remote hosts because when using UDP, we do not have a real connection. You probably noticed that the class has the suffix "_t". This means that this is the type definition, and it is not an object. Therefore, we can use the name "RemoteHost" for the object, and still keep the name of the class descriptive. The remote host class looks like this:

```
class RemoteHost_t
{
public:
        SOCKET socket;              // socket
        sockaddr_in inetSockAddr;   // socket address

#ifdef WIN32
        int addrLen;                // socket address length
#else
        socklen_t addrLen;          // socket address length
#endif

        bool online;                // host online flag
        bool thread;                // thread running flag
        bool NonBlocking;           // non-blocking flag

        int messageCounter;         // message buffer counter
        int bufsize;                // the length of the next message

        int lastMessageTime;        // seconds from last message

#ifdef WIN32
        HANDLE SocketInputEvent;
#endif

        void RecordMessage(void);
};
```

So when a new client connects a server, the server will add a new remote host to the list. The server can then look for address information, etc., of the remote host when it needs it. On a client there is only one remote host, which is the server. The remote hosts are indexed by the host ID number. So, if a client's host ID is 4, we can use that ID number directly as the index number to access the wanted remote host data.

Individual Setup Functions

There are some individual setup functions that are not in any class, but are very important for the library. These functions are:

```
int NET_Initialize(void);
int NET_InitializeWinSock(void);
void NET_Shutdown(void);
```

The NET_Initialize function is used to to initialize the library; it is a platform-independent function. This means that whatever the platform is, this function must be run before any other netLib function can be used. As we can see in the following code listing, this function currently has no use on Unix (other than starting the log system). But this function must exist to keep the source code platform independent. Also, we can add Unix code later if we need to. On Windows, this function runs a specific function to initialize the WinSock API. The following code listing is the first version of the NET_Initialize function. We will update this function later on.

```
int NET_Initialize(void)
{
    StartLog();

#ifdef WIN32
    return NET_InitializeWinSock();
#else
    return 0;
#endif
}
```

The NET_InitializeWinSock function, on the other hand, is used to initialize only WinSock API. The programmer using our library does not have to worry about this function, as the NET_Initialize function will automatically run this one if we are on Windows. More accurately speaking, the compiler will compile the source code so that this function will be run. We introduced and examined this function already in Chapter 5, "Basic Sockets Programming," so we will skip the explanation part here. See Chapter 5 for more information.

```
int NET_InitializeWinSock(void)
{
    WORD versionRequested;
    WSADATA wsaData;
    DWORD bufferSize = 0;

    LPWSAPROTOCOL_INFO SelectedProtocol;
    int NumProtocols;
```

```
// Start WinSock2. If it fails,
// we do not need to call WSACleanup()
versionRequested = MAKEWORD(2, 0);
int error = WSAStartup(versionRequested, &wsaData);

if(error)
{
    LogString("FATAL ERROR: WSAStartup failed
        (error = %d)", error);
    return 1;
}
else
{
    LogString("WSAStartup OK");

    // Confirm that the WinSock2 DLL
    // supports the exact version
    // we want. If not, call WSACleanup().
    if(LOBYTE(wsaData.wVersion) != 2 ||
    HIBYTE(wsaData.wVersion) != 0)
    {
        LogString("FATAL ERROR: WinSock2 DLL does not
            support the correct version (%d.%d)",
            LOBYTE(wsaData.wVersion),
            HIBYTE(wsaData.wVersion));

        WSACleanup();
        return 1;
    }
}

// Call WSAEnumProtocols to figure out how
// big of a buffer we need
NumProtocols = WSAEnumProtocols(NULL, NULL, &bufferSize);

if( (NumProtocols != SOCKET_ERROR) &&
    (WSAGetLastError() != WSAENOBUFS) )
{
    WSACleanup();
    return 1;
}

LogString("Protocol bufferSize = %d", bufferSize);

// Allocate a buffer, call
// WSAEnumProtocols to get an array of
// WSAPROTOCOL_INFO structs
```

TUTORIAL 2

```
        SelectedProtocol = (LPWSAPROTOCOL_INFO) malloc(bufferSize);

        if(SelectedProtocol == NULL)
        {
            WSACleanup();
            return 1;
        }

        // Allocate memory for protocol
        // list and define what protocols to look for
        int *protos = (int *) calloc(2, sizeof(int));

        protos[0] = IPPROTO_TCP;
        protos[1] = IPPROTO_UDP;

        NumProtocols = WSAEnumProtocols(protos,
            SelectedProtocol, &bufferSize);

        free(protos);
        protos = NULL;

        free(SelectedProtocol);
        SelectedProtocol = NULL;

        if(NumProtocols == SOCKET_ERROR)
        {
            LogString("FATAL ERROR: Didn't find any
                required protocols");
            WSACleanup();
            return 1;
        }

        return 0;
    }
```

The NET_Shutdown function is naturally used to shut down our network library. Like NET_Initialize, this function also currently has no real use on Unix. But again, it must exist in both operating systems' code to achieve full platform independence. On Windows this function will shut down the WinSock API. This function must be run to shut down the API; otherwise we may be interfering with the WinSock DLL registration process. The following code listing shows the first version of the NET_Shutdown function (we will update this function later):

```
void NET_Shutdown(void)
{
    LogString("Shutting down netLib");
```

```
#ifdef WIN32
    WSACleanup();
#endif
}
```

Dependence

We will now show you some functions that are dependent on the Windows operating system and TCP protocol. The complete library will have fully independent code, but we will first show you some dependent functions to make the advantages of the independent functions even more obvious.

IPv6 support had to be dropped from this library because it would require extra effort to make it work platform independent.

NET_Socket Class Initialization Functions

The NET_Socket class also has some functions used to initialize or uninitialize the library systems. Fortunately, the programmer using our library does not have to even know about two of these functions. These are the normal C++ class constructor and destructor functions: NET_Socket and ~NET_Socket. A constructor is a function that is run automatically each time a C++ object is created. We never run this function manually. So when we declare a NET_Socket object, the function runs. A destructor works similarly, but it is run when the object is destroyed. This happens when we exit the application. This is also a function that we never run manually.

Constructor

The following code listing shows the constructor function of NET_Socket class. This first version is very simple. The function just allocates memory for the RemoteHost structure. NET_Max_Connections is a constant value that is defined in netLib.h.

```
NET_Socket::NET_Socket()
{
    RemoteHost = (RemoteHost_t *) calloc(NET_MAX_CONNECTIONS,
        sizeof(RemoteHost_t));
}
```

Destructor

The destructor function shown in the following code listing is normally used to reset things to the state in which they were before the constructor function was run. So we now deallocate the memory we allocated in the constructor. In this first version we free the RemoteHost structure.

```
NET_Socket::~NET_Socket()
{
    if(RemoteHost)      free(RemoteHost);
}
```

Shutdown

Then there is a function called Shutdown, which is simply used to shut down the connection (or set of connections on a server) and release all memory we have allocated for it. The following code listing shows the Shutdown function:

```
void NET_Socket::Shutdown(void)
{
    LogString("Shutting down netLib object");

    // Loop through all remote hosts
    for(int id = 0; id < RemoteHosts; id++)
    {
        // If we are online, close the connection
        if(Online)
        {
            CloseConnection(id, 1);
        }

        // If input event handles exist, close them
        if(RemoteHost[id].SocketInputEvent)
        {
            CloseHandle(RemoteHost[id].SocketInputEvent);
            RemoteHost[id].SocketInputEvent = NULL;
        }
    }

    // Set us offline
    Online = 0;
}
```

Closing Connections

```
// If we are online, close the connection
if(Online)
{
    CloseConnection(id, 1);
}
```

The function loops through all the remote hosts, and the connections are closed using active closure. Active closure means that the host that starts the closure process sends the other host a message that the connection will be closed. Then the other host will close the connection as well. The CloseConnection function will be explained later in the tutorial.

Closing Input Event Handle

```
// If input event handles exist, close them if(RemoteHost[id].SocketInputEvent)
{
    CloseHandle(RemoteHost[id].SocketInputEvent);
    RemoteHost[id].SocketInputEvent = NULL;
}
```

We also check to see if the SocketInputEvent handles exist, and if they do, they are closed and set to NULL. SocketInputEvent indicates that a network event is incoming. The handle system will be explained later in the tutorial as well.

Setting the Local Host Offline

```
// Set us offline
Online = 0;
```

When we set the local online flag down (to 0), all running connection threads will stop. Also, no more connections will be accepted.

At this point, you may be wondering why we have two different uninitialization functions: ~NET_Socket and Shutdown. Well, the reason for this kind of system is to be able to shut down the connection or set of connections (= netLib socket) at run time and still be able to start using it afterwards. With the destructor, we cannot really do this because we are never running it manually. So for this we use the Shutdown function. However, we cannot use just the destructor function at the end of the application; it frees only the memory we have allocated, but does not close the connections or handles. So we need to run the Shutdown function at the end of every application and on every object we have.

Setting Blocking/Non-Blocking

We can set the input/output functions in the network library to work in blocking or non-blocking mode. To do this we set the remote host's option to either blocking or non-blocking. A blocking I/O function means that it does not return before it has, for example, received some data. A non-blocking function returns immediately no matter what happens.

```
int NET_Socket::SetNonBlocking(int id, u_long setBlocking)
{
    u_long set = setBlocking;
```

```
        // Copy the setting to the remote host structure
        RemoteHost[id].NonBlocking = (bool) setBlocking;

        // Set the socket option
        return ioctlsocket(RemoteHost[id].socket, FIONBIO, &set);
    }
```

Message System

This network library has a unique message system that makes our lives as programmers very easy. Let's see how each message is formed.

Generic Message

The following code shows the data structure of the generic message:

```
// netLib system message structures
typedef struct
{
    int type;          // Message type
    HOSTID toId;       // Destination host id
    HOSTID fromId;     // Source host id
} NETMSG_GENERIC;
```

The generic message consists of only the message header. The header holds the most important information of the message. The following information is stored in the message header:

- Message type. Used to identify each message.
- Destination host ID number.
- Source host ID number.

The message type is used to identify each message. Each message must be identified, so it can be processed correctly. The destination host ID number defines the host to which the message is going. Naturally the source host ID number defines where the message is coming from. This information is required for all kinds of actions, but mostly it is used to send the feedback to the correct host.

After the message header part, there is the message data part. The generic message does not have this data part at all. The data part is a user-defined group of user-defined data.

The following structure is an example of a message with the header part and the data part. The data part consists of an integer and a character.

```
typedef struct
{
    int type;          // Message type
```

```
    HOSTID toId;        // Destination host id
    HOSTID fromId;      // Source host id
    int number;
    char letter;
} NETMSG_EXAMPLE;
```

NOTE We must be aware that we cannot send pointers in the messages. Pointers are host-dependent information as they point to a location in the local computer memory. On a different computer, that same location may contain different information (and most likely does).

Confirmation Message

The following structure shows the confirmation message that is used to confirm that a local ID number has been successfully received when using the UDP protocol. Because UDP is an unreliable protocol, this kind of system is good to have.

```
// confirmation
typedef struct
{
    int conf;
} NETMSG_CONF;
```

This message has no header, because when we use this message, we know exactly when and from where to expect it.

Datasize Message

Because each message can vary in size, and because we need to know how many bytes to read off a socket, we need to be able to tell the other host in advance how many bytes to read. For this we have a message called "Datasize." This is a message that consists of the header and one integer that holds the length of the next message in bytes. This message structure is shown in the following code listing:

```
// used to send incoming data buffer's size
typedef struct
{
    int type;
    HOSTID toId;
    HOSTID fromId;
    int size;
} NETMSGDATA_DATASIZE;
```

So when we are sending normal data, we must first send a Datasize message to tell the other host how big the next message is. Because the Datasize message is always the same size, and because a normal message is always sent after a Datasize message, we know when to expect a Datasize message. Therefore, we can read the correct amount of bytes to get the Datasize message. And after we have the Datasize message, we know how many bytes to read to get the normal message.

Sending/Receiving Data

Our network library has its own functions to send and receive data. Let's have a look at them to see why we cannot just use plain socket functions.

Read Function

The following code listing shows the Read function. This is a platform-independent function; it works on both Unix and Windows.

```
int NET_Socket::Read(int id, char *buf, size_t count)
{
    size_t bytes_read = 0;
    int this_read = -1;

    // Blocking version
    if(!RemoteHost[id].NonBlocking)
    {
        while(bytes_read < count)
        {
            while(this_read < 0)
            {
                this_read = recv(RemoteHost[id].socket,
                    buf, count - bytes_read, 0);
            }

            if(this_read == 0)
            {
                return bytes_read;
            }

            bytes_read    += this_read;
            buf           += this_read;
        }
    }

    // Non-blocking version
    else
    {
        this_read = recv(RemoteHost[id].socket,
            buf, count - bytes_read, 0);
```

TUTORIAL 2

```
            if(this_read < 0)
            {
                 return this_read;
            }
            if(this_read == 0)
            {
                 return bytes_read;
            }

            bytes_read       += this_read;
            buf              += this_read;
     }

     return count;
}
```

We declare some variables at the beginning of the function. It is important to set the this_read variable to –1 in the beginning, because the function will loop as long as it is negative:

```
size_t bytes_read = 0;
int this_read = -1;
```

The function is divided into two parts: blocking and non-blocking. Depending on the socket's mode, we run the correct version.

```
// Blocking version
if(!RemoteHost[id].NonBlocking)
{
     ...
}

// Non-blocking version
else
{
     ...
}
```

We loop the Recv function as long as the function has read all the bytes it is supposed to read. When Recv returns a negative number (it is not reading anything), we wait for it to start reading incoming data.

```
while(bytes_read < count)
{
     while(this_read < 0)
     {
          ...
     }
}
```

We read the data from the remote host's socket. Because not all the data may be received by one call to Recv, we keep track of how many bytes there are still to read (count – bytes_read).

```
this_read = recv(RemoteHost[id].socket, buf,
    count - bytes_read, 0);
```

If Recv returns zero, it means the connection has been closed. We return the amount of bytes read and stop there:

```
if(this_read == 0)
{
    return bytes_read;
}
```

At the end of the loops we update the variables as shown in the following piece of code. We increase the bytes_read variable by the amount that we actually read, and move the pointer of the string buf to the correct place:

```
bytes_read      += this_read;
buf             += this_read;
```

The non-blocking version works similarly to the blocking one, but we do not check to see if all the data has been read or wait for some data to come in. The function will return even if there is no data coming in. The return value is –1 in this case. Other than that, this version does the same things as the blocking one. If the connection is closed, the function returns.

```
this_read = recv(RemoteHost[id].socket, buf,
    count - bytes_read, 0);

if(this_read < 0)
{
    return this_read;
}
if(this_read == 0)
{
    return bytes_read;
}

bytes_read      += this_read;
buf             += this_read;
```

ReadFrom Function

The ReadFrom function works pretty much the same way as the Read function in the network library. This time we are reading the data from a specific Internet address (defining a socket is not enough). The following code listing shows the ReadFrom function. This is also a platform-independent function.

```
int NET_Socket::ReadFrom(SOCKET sock, char *buf, size_t count, struct sockaddr
*sockAddr, socklen_t *sockLen, bool NonBlocking)
{
    size_t bytes_read = 0;
    int this_read = -1;

    // Blocking version
    if(!NonBlocking)
    {
        while(bytes_read < count)
        {
            while(this_read < 0)
            {
                this_read = recvfrom(sock, buf,
                    count - bytes_read, 0,
                    sockAddr, sockLen);
            }

            bytes_read    += this_read;
            buf           += this_read;
        }
    }

    // Non-blocking version
    else
    {
            this_read = recvfrom(sock, buf,
                count - bytes_read, 0, sockAddr, sockLen);
    }

    return count;
}
```

Like in the Read function, we declare some variables in the beginning of the function, as shown in the following piece of code. Again, the integer this_read must be negative from the beginning or the function will not work correctly.

```
size_t bytes_read = 0;
int this_read = -1;
```

The ReadFrom function is also divided into a blocking and non-blocking part. This time we must provide the blocking option as a parameter to the ReadFrom function, unlike with the Read function. The reason for this is that we do not pass the host ID number as a parameter, and therefore we cannot use the remote host structure to check if that connection is blocking or not.

```
// Blocking version
if(!NonBlocking)
{
      ...
}

// Non-blocking version
else
{
      ...
}
```

We block the RecvFrom socket function manually by looping the two loops as shown in the following piece of code. We loop as long as the amount of bytes read is smaller than the amount of bytes we are waiting for, and we loop as long as RecvFrom returns a negative number:

```
while(bytes_read < count)
{
    while(this_read < 0)
    {
          ...
    }
}
```

Now we read the data using the socket function RecvFrom. We must provide the exact address of the host we are reading from. Defining just the socket is not enough. We read only the bytes we have not already read.

```
this_read = recvfrom(sock, buf, count - bytes_read,
    0, sockAddr, sockLen);
```

To keep track of what we have already done, we update the variables shown in the following piece of code. The amount of bytes read (bytes_read) is increased by the amount the RecvFrom function read last time. Also, the data buffer pointer is moved by the same amount.

```
bytes_read    += this_read;
buf           += this_read;
```

The non-blocking version is very simple. All we do is call RecvFrom once, and then we are ready to move on. We do not care about reading all the data, if not all is read at once. Also, if there is nothing to read, the function returns and we are done.

```
this_read = recvfrom(sock, buf, count - bytes_read,
    0, sockAddr, sockLen);
```

Write Function

The Write function is used to send data to a remote host. The following code listing shows the Write function in its entirety. This function is designed for the TCP protocol, but later in this tutorial we will update this function to be protocol independent.

```
int NET_Socket::Write(int id, char *buf, size_t count)
{
    // If we are writing to all, use WriteAll function
    if(id == NETID_ALL)
    {
        WriteAll(buf, count);
        return count;
    }
    else
    {
        size_t bytes_sent = 0;
        int this_write = -1;

        LogString("Writing data to id %d, socket %d,
            data size %d (non-blocking = %d)",     id,
            RemoteHost[id].socket, count,
            RemoteHost[id].NonBlocking);

        // Blocking version
        if(!RemoteHost[id].NonBlocking)
        {
            while(bytes_sent < count)
            {
                this_write = send(RemoteHost[id].socket,
                    buf, count - bytes_sent, 0);

                if(this_write < 0)     return this_write;

                bytes_sent     += this_write;
                buf            += this_write;
            }
        }
    }

    // Non-blocking version
```

```
        else
        {
            this_write = send(RemoteHost[id].socket,
                buf,      count - bytes_sent, 0);

            if(this_write < 0)      return this_write;

            bytes_sent += this_write;
        }

        return bytes_sent;
    }
}
```

Before we send the data to the destination host, we check if the data is supposed to be sent to all remote hosts in the network. If this is the case, we use the WriteAll function, which is explained later in this tutorial.

```
// If we are writing to all, use WriteAll function
if(id == NETID_ALL)
{
    WriteAll(buf, count);
    return count;
}
```

We declare some variables in the beginning of the function again, as shown in the following piece of code. The integer this_write must be negative from the beginning to see if the function is sending anything or if the connection is still open:

```
size_t bytes_sent = 0;
int this_write = -1;
```

Similarly to the reading functions, the Write function is also divided into a blocking and non-blocking part. Here we check which version to use. We check if we have set the non-blocking option on for the remote host:

```
// Blocking version
if(!RemoteHost[id].NonBlocking)
{
    ...
}

// Non-blocking version
else
{
    ...
}
```

We block the Send function as long as it has not sent all the data:

```
while(bytes_sent < count)
{
    ...
}
```

Then we simply send the data using the socket function Send. We send only the data that has not already been sent in an earlier call to Send with the same buffer (therefore, the amount of bytes to send is count – bytes_sent). We store the amount of bytes written by this call to the integer this_write:

```
this_write = send(RemoteHost[id].socket, buf,
    count - bytes_sent, 0);
```

Then we check that the call to send was successful. If it returned a negative value, there was an error and we will stop running this function. If not, we update the variables for the next run of the loop. First, we increase the bytes_sent integer, and then we move the pointer of the data buffer:

```
if(this_write < 0)      return this_write;

bytes_sent      += this_write;
buf             += this_write;
```

The non-blocking version does nothing else than call the Send function once. After that it checks if there was an error and we are done. The non-blocking version does not check if all the data was sent:

```
this_write = send(RemoteHost[id].socket, buf,
    count - bytes_sent, 0);

if(this_write < 0)      return this_write;

bytes_sent += this_write;
```

WriteTo Function

The WriteTo function is used a bit differently than the plain Write function. This function also sends data to a remote host, but we need to specify the exact Internet address of the host along with the socket. This function is mostly used with the UDP protocol.

```
int NET_Socket::WriteTo(SOCKET sock, char *buf, size_t count, struct sockaddr
*sockAddr, socklen_t sockLen)
{
    size_t bytes_sent = 0;
    int this_write = -1;

    // Send all data
    while(bytes_sent < count)
```

```
    {
        // Send data
        this_write = sendto(sock, buf,
            count - bytes_sent, 0, sockAddr, sockLen);

        if(this_write < 0)      return this_write;

        // Update variables
        bytes_sent      += this_write;
        buf             += this_write;
    }

    return count;
}
```

Again, we declare these two variables as shown in the following piece of code. And again, the integer this_write must be negative from the beginning:

```
size_t bytes_sent = 0;
int this_write = -1;
```

We loop the SendTo function as long as all the data is sent. We need to keep in mind that all the data in the buffer is not always sent with just one call to the sending function:

```
// Send all data
while(bytes_sent < count)
{
    ...
}
```

Now we send the data using the socket SendTo function. We define the socket and the exact Internet address of the host. We send only the data that has not already been sent in an earlier call to this function.

```
// Send data
this_write = sendto(sock, buf, count - bytes_sent,
    0, sockAddr, sockLen);
```

After the call to SendTo, we check that there were no errors. If there were errors, we return immediately.

```
if(this_write < 0)      return this_write;
```

Then, we update the variables as shown in the following piece of code. The pointer of the buf string is moved and the bytes_sent integer is increased:

```
// Update variables
bytes_sent      += this_write;
buf             += this_write;
```

WriteAll Function

We have a dedicated function for sending data to all hosts at once, the WriteAll function. The following code listing shows this function. It works pretty much the same way as the normal data sending functions. There are some differences though. This function is designed to work only with TCP protocol.

```
void NET_Socket::WriteAll(char *buf, size_t count)
{
    size_t bytes_sent = 0;
    int this_write = -1;

    // If the local host is a client,
    // send the data first to the server
    if(localId != NETID_SERVER)
    {
        Write(NETID_SERVER, buf, count);
        return;
    }

    char *temp_buf = buf;

    // Loop through all possible remote hosts
    for(int id = 1; id < NET_MAX_CONNECTIONS; id++)
    {
        bytes_sent = 0;
        this_write = -1;
        buf = temp_buf;

        // If the remote host is not online
        // move on to the next host
        if(!RemoteHost[id].online) continue;

        // Blocking version
        if(!RemoteHost[id].NonBlocking)
        {
            while(bytes_sent < count)
            {
                while(this_write < 0)
                {
                    this_write = send(RemoteHost[id].socket,
                        buf,    count - bytes_sent, 0);
                }

                bytes_sent    += this_write;
                buf           += this_write;
            }
        }
```

```
    }

    // Non-blocking version
    else
    {
        this_write = send(RemoteHost[id].socket,
            buf,      count - bytes_sent, 0);

        bytes_sent      += this_write;
        buf             += this_write;
    }
  }
}
```

Declaring the variables for this function is similar to all I/O functions, as shown in the following code:

```
size_t bytes_sent = 0;
int this_write = -1;
```

Before anything else, we check to see if the local host that is trying to send data is a server. If it is not, we send the data to a server, which will then resend the data to all. After the function returns we are done here:

```
// If the local host is a client,
// send the data first to the server
if(localId != NETID_SERVER)
{
    Write(NETID_SERVER, buf, count);
    return;
}
```

Here we create a start pointer of the data buffer, so we can move the actual pointer to the beginning using this:

```
char *temp_buf = buf;
```

Then, we loop through all the possible remote hosts to send the data to each one. We start from index 1, because index 0 is the server (which is the local host):

```
// Loop through all possible remote hosts
for(int id = 1; id < NET_MAX_CONNECTIONS; id++)
{
    ...
}
```

Here in the beginning of the loop we reset the variables to what they were in the beginning, because each host must be treated equally. We move the pointer of the data buffer to the beginning of the data using the start pointer:

```
bytes_sent = 0;
this_write = -1;
buf = temp_buf;
```

Before we send the data, we make sure the host is online. If not, we move on to the next host:

```
// If the remote host is not online
// move on to the next host
if(!RemoteHost[id].online) continue;
```

As with some other data sending functions, WriteAll also is divided into blocking and non-blocking parts. Because they work exactly the same way here as they do in the other functions, we will skip the explanation part. See the Write function for more information.

```
// Blocking version
if(!RemoteHost[id].NonBlocking)
{
    while(bytes_sent < count)
    {
        while(this_write < 0)
        {
            this_write = send(RemoteHost[id].socket,
                buf,    count - bytes_sent, 0);
        }

        bytes_sent    += this_write;
        buf           += this_write;
    }
}

// Non-blocking version
else
{
    this_write = send(RemoteHost[id].socket, buf,
        count - bytes_sent, 0);

    bytes_sent    += this_write;
    buf           += this_write;
}
```

Host ID System

We need a system to keep track of all the hosts in the network. In this network library we have a host ID system, in which every host gets an ID number when connected to the server. The server host always has ID number 0. The first client to connect to the server is host number 1. The next client is host number 2, and so on. But when a client disconnects from the server, the ID number it had is marked free, so the next client to connect to the server may get the same ID number as the client that just disconnected. The ID number to give to a client is the first free ID number starting from 1. So, if there are, for example, five clients connected to a server and the clients have the ID numbers 1, 2, 3, 4, and 5, and client number 3 disconnects, that ID number is marked free. Now there are four clients connected to the server, but the clients have ID numbers 1, 2, 4, and 5. If a new client connects to the server now, it will get the first free ID number, which is 3 in this case.

Finding Next Free Host Index

The network library has a function to determine the next free ID number. The following code listing shows the FindNextFreeHostIndex function:

```
void NET_Socket::FindNextFreeHostIndex(void)
{
    RemoteHost_t *Host_ptr = RemoteHost;
    RemoteHost_t *Host_ptr_end = RemoteHost +
        NET_MAX_CONNECTIONS;

    for(int id = 0; Host_ptr < Host_ptr_end; Host_ptr++, id++)
    {
        if( (Host_ptr->online == 0) && (id != localId) )
        {
            NextFreeHostIndex = id;

            LogString("NextFreeHostIndex: %d", id);

            return;
        }
    }
}
```

The first thing to notice is that this function does not return anything. It just updates the NextFreeHostIndex integer of the NET_Socket object. If we run this function multiple times in a row, we would always get the same result if nothing else is happening in the background. This is because the next free host index value is determined from the list of remote hosts.

To gain the best possible performance, we use a pointer loop in this function. We set the start and end pointers in the beginning as shown in the following piece of code. Note that the end of the loop is not the current amount of remote hosts, but the maximum amount of remote hosts. This is because we can have any host ID between 1 and NET_Max_Connections taken and still have some free IDs in the middle.

```
RemoteHost_t *Host_ptr          = RemoteHost;
RemoteHost_t *Host_ptr_end      = RemoteHost + NET_MAX_CONNECTIONS;
```

Then we loop through all the possible remote hosts and check to see whether they are online. If the host we are looking at is not online, and the host number is not the same as the LocalId, we choose that number as the next free host index. Then we can stop looping because the result will not change any more.

```
for(int id = 0; Host_ptr < Host_ptr_end; Host_ptr++, id++)
{
    if( (Host_ptr->online == 0) && (id != localId) )
    {
        NextFreeHostIndex = id;

        return;
    }
}
```

Giving Local ID

Now we need to be able to give out the host IDs to the clients somehow. This is a job for the server, so when a new client connects to the server it will receive the local ID number before anything else is sent to it. The network library has a function called GiveLocalIdTCP to send the local ID number via TCP protocol. The following code listing shows this function:

```
int NET_Socket::GiveLocalIdTCP(void)
{
    NETMSG_GENERIC idMsg;

    idMsg.type     = NETMSG_GIVEID;
    idMsg.toId     = NextFreeHostIndex;
    idMsg.fromId   = NETID_SERVER;


    LogString("Sending localId number.. to:%d", NextFreeHostIndex);

    char *string;
    string =
        inet_ntoa(RemoteHost[NextFreeHostIndex].inetSockAddr.sin_addr);
```

```
LogString("Writing localId (TCP) to socket %d,
    addrLen %d ip %s", RemoteHost[NextFreeHostIndex].socket,
    RemoteHost[NextFreeHostIndex].addrLen, string);

Write(NextFreeHostIndex, (char *) &idMsg,
    sizeof(NETMSG_GENERIC));

LogString("localId number sent...");

return 0;
}
```

We send the local ID to the client using the generic message. We do not need any extra data members in the message, because the client can get the local ID number from the toId member. We set the type to NETMsg_GiveId, and the fromId number to NETId_Server. And because the client we are sending the message to has the ID number which is equal to NextFreeHostIndex, we set the toId to that index number:

```
NETMSG_GENERIC idMsg;

idMsg.type      = NETMSG_GIVEID;
idMsg.toId      = NextFreeHostIndex;
idMsg.fromId    = NETID_SERVER;
```

Then we simply send the message to the client. We do not need to send a Datasize message beforehand, because the client is expecting this message at the moment.

```
Write(NextFreeHostIndex, (char *) &idMsg, sizeof(NETMSG_GENERIC));
```

Creating the Server

The most important part of our network library is the server system. If we do not have a server, we do not have any use for clients. If the server is bad, every client will be affected. Let's see how to create the server.

CreateServer Function

We have divided the server creation into fragments to have full platform independence. First, there is the wrapper function, which defines the function to be run based on what operating system we are using. The following code listing shows the first version of this wrapper function. Since we are still showing you only the Windows and TCP code, this function does not wrap anything yet.

```
int NET_Socket::CreateServer(int port)
```

```
{
    LogString("CreateServer()");

    int ret = 0;

    // Set the local host online and set the local id number
    Port     = port;
    Online   = 1;
    localId  = NETID_SERVER;

    ret = CreateWinServer(port);

    return ret;
}
```

We set the NET_Socket object variables as shown in the following code listing. The port number is copied from the one we provide to the CreateServer function. The online flag is set up to keep all threads running. Lastly, the localId number is set to NETID_Server to indicate that this host is a server.

```
// Set the local host online and set the local id number
Port     = port;
Online   = 1;
localId  = NETID_SERVER;
```

Then, we run the function to create a Windows server. Because we are only showing the Windows code so far, we do not really wrap any code here yet.

```
ret = CreateWinServer(port, Protocol);
```

CreateWinServer Function

You can see in the preceding function that a function called CreateWinServer is run next. Let's take a look at that function:

```
int NET_Socket::CreateWinServer(int port)
{
    struct sockaddr *servAddr;
    struct sockaddr_in *inetServAddr;
    SOCKET sock;

    LogString("CreateWinServer()");

    // Create TCP socket
    sock = socket(AF_INET, SOCK_STREAM, 0);

    if(sock == INVALID_SOCKET)
    {
```

```
        LogString("ERROR: socket() failed at
            CreateWinServer (sock: %d)", sock);
        return -1;
    }

    // Allocate memory for address structure
    servAddr = (struct sockaddr *) malloc(sizeof(sockaddr));

    if(!servAddr) return -1;

    memset((char *) servAddr, 0, sizeof(sockaddr));

    // Fill the address structure
    servAddr->sa_family      = (u_short) AF_INET;
    inetServAddr             = (struct sockaddr_in *) servAddr;
    inetServAddr->sin_port   = htons((u_short) port);

    // Bind address information to the socket
    int error = bind(sock, servAddr, sizeof(sockaddr));

    if(error == SOCKET_ERROR)
    {
        free(servAddr);
        return -1;
    }

    char *string;
    string = inet_ntoa(inetServAddr->sin_addr);

    LogString("Creating server on socket %d, addrLen %d, ip %s,
        port %d", sock, sizeof(inetServAddr), string,
        ntohs(inetServAddr->sin_port));

    // Free address structure memory
    free(servAddr);
    servAddr = NULL;

    // Will run CreateWinTCPServer
    return CreateTCPServer(sock);

    return -1;
}
```

Notice that we have finally reached the level where we actually start running sockets code. Let's see what we are doing here:

```
// Create TCP socket
```

```
sock = socket(AF_INET, SOCK_STREAM, 0);

if(sock == INVALID_SOCKET)
{
    return -1;
}
```

As we have already learned, we need to create the socket before anything else. Here we create a stream socket (TCP). After the call to the socket function, we check whether the call returned a valid socket.

NOTE   Here we use the constant INVALID_SOCKET, which works only with WinSock. On Unix, we would use the value −1. In the complete library we have wrapped these two values under one constant, so it is not a problem.

After we create the socket, we fill the address information to be bound to that socket. We allocate memory for the address structure, check if it was successful, and set the memory to zero. Then, we fill the structure with the required information. The protocol family is AF_INET, because we will be using IPv4. The port number must be converted from host byte order to network byte order. Then, we bind the address information to the socket and check that everything went fine. If not, we free the address structure memory and end running the function.

```
// Allocate memory for address structure
servAddr = (struct sockaddr *) malloc(sizeof(sockaddr));

if(!servAddr) return -1;

memset((char *) servAddr, 0, sizeof(sockaddr));

// Fill the address structure
servAddr->sa_family     = (u_short) AF_INET;
inetServAddr            = (struct sockaddr_in *) servAddr;
inetServAddr->sin_port  = htons((u_short) port);

// Bind address information to the socket
int error = bind(sock, servAddr, sizeof(sockaddr));

if(error == SOCKET_ERROR)
{
        LogString("ERROR: bind() failed at CreateWinServer");
    free(servAddr);
    return -1;
}
```

```
// Free address structure memory
free(servAddr);
servAddr = NULL;
```

Lastly, we run the TCP server creation function. We are not really wrapping any functions yet as UDP code is not explained yet.

```
// Will run CreateWinTCPServer
return CreateTCPServer(sock);
```

CreateTCPServer Function

This function is another wrapper, but as we are explaining only Windows code right now, we are not really wrapping anything.

```
int NET_Socket::CreateTCPServer(SOCKET listenSock)
{
    LogString("CreateTCPServer()");

    return CreateWinTCPServer(listenSock);
}
```

CreateWinTCPServer Function

```
int NET_Socket::CreateWinTCPServer(SOCKET listenSock)
{
    LogString("CreateWinTCPServer()");

    // Set up a Windows message to notify
    // of an incoming connection
    WSAAsyncSelect(listenSock, hWnd_netLib, USMSG_ACCEPT, FD_ACCEPT);

    // Start listening for incoming connections
    int error = listen(listenSock, NET_MAX_CONNECTIONS);

    if(error == SOCKET_ERROR)
    {
        LogString("ERROR: listen() error at
            CreateWinTCPServer");
        return -1;
    }

    // Copy socket descriptor to the object
    listenSocket = listenSock;

    return 0;
}
```

The following function call makes WinSock send a message to the hWnd_netLib window when there is an incoming connection on the provided socket. The message is a user-defined message, USMsg_Accept, which we have defined in netLib.h.

```
// Set up a Windows message to notify of an incoming connection
WSAAsyncSelect(listenSock, hWnd_netLib, USMSG_ACCEPT, FD_ACCEPT);
```

When a server accepts a connection with a client, this Windows message is sent to the window. Then we can run our connection accept function, which is explained later in this tutorial.

Next we set the socket to listen for incoming connections. We set the backlog value of the Listen function to NET_Max_Connections, which is defined in netLib.h. Then, we check to see if any errors occurred. If none did, we set the NET_Socket object's listenSocket variable to match the socket we just set up to listen for incoming connections. Now we can use this socket descriptor elsewhere, too.

```
// Start listening for incoming connections
int error = listen(listenSock, NET_MAX_CONNECTIONS);

if(error == SOCKET_ERROR)
{
    return -1;
}

// Copy socket descriptor to the object
listenSocket = listenSock;
```

Accepting a Connection

Now that we have our server up and running, we can start accepting the connection requests. The following function is run when the USMsg_Accept message is sent to the hWnd_netLib window. It means that there is an incoming connection that needs to be accepted. So let's see what we do when we accept a connection:

```
void NET_Socket::AcceptConnection(void)
{
    SOCKET connectSock = INVALID_SOCKET;
    struct sockaddr_in clientAddr;
    socklen_t clientLen;

    // Loop as long as the connection has not been accepted
    while(connectSock == INVALID_SOCKET)
    {
        clientLen = sizeof(clientAddr);
```

```
        connectSock = accept(listenSocket,
            (struct sockaddr *) &clientAddr, &clientLen);
    }

    LogString("Accepted a connection");
    LogString("Connection on socket %d", connectSock);

    // Update the next free host index number
    FindNextFreeHostIndex();

    // Set the socket non-blocking
    SetNonBlocking(NextFreeHostIndex, 1);

    // Create input event handle
    RemoteHost[NextFreeHostIndex].SocketInputEvent =
        CreateEvent(NULL, FALSE, FALSE, NULL);

    // Fill remote host information
    RemoteHost[NextFreeHostIndex].socket = connectSock;
    RemoteHost[NextFreeHostIndex].inetSockAddr = clientAddr;
    RemoteHost[NextFreeHostIndex].addrLen = clientLen;
    RemoteHost[NextFreeHostIndex].online = 1;
    RemoteHosts++;

    // Give local id number to the client
    GiveLocalIdTCP();

    // Fill parameter information for the thread
    param.id                = NextFreeHostIndex;
    param.netParamSocket    = this;

    // Start the IO thread
    // Stop notifying for incoming connections on this socket
    WSAAsyncSelect(connectSock, hWnd_netLib, 0, 0);

    // Monitor incoming network events
        WSAEventSelect(connectSock,
        RemoteHost[NextFreeHostIndex].SocketInputEvent,
        FD_READ);

    // Create the thread
    DWORD threadId;

    HANDLE threadHandle = CreateThread(NULL, 0,
        (LPTHREAD_START_ROUTINE) NET_WinIOThreadFunc,
        (void *) &param, 0, &threadId);
}
```

As shown in the following piece of code, we poll the Accept function as long as it does not return a valid socket descriptor. When the Accept function does return a valid socket, it means that the connection has been succesfully accepted and that it is open. The variables we provide as parameters to the function will be filled with correct information. The address information of the client will be stored in clientAddr, and the length of that structure in clientLen. But because clientLen is a value-result argument, we need to fill it before we call Accept too. The function will update the value then.

```
// Loop as long as the connection has not been accepted
while(connectSock == INVALID_SOCKET)
{
    clientLen = sizeof(clientAddr);
    connectSock = accept(listenSocket,
            (struct sockaddr *) &clientAddr, &clientLen);
}
```

After the connection has been accepted, we start setting up the server process thread. First, we seek the next free host index for the client. This function does not return the value; it updates the NextFreeHostIndex variable stored in the NET_Socket object. So we can always determine the next free host index by looking at the variable. But to make sure the variable is up to date, we must run this function. Remember that this number is not the number of hosts. This number could be anything from 1 to the amount of remote hosts on the server because each index will be used again if a client disconnects from the server.

```
// Update the next free host index number
FindNextFreeHostIndex();
```

Next, we set the remote host's socket non-blocking. After calling this function, we must manually loop some of the socket functions if they have time as a factor. This also gives more control over the functions because we can easily break up the loops if we need to do so.

```
// Set the socket non-blocking
SetNonBlocking(NextFreeHostIndex, 1);
```

Then we create the socket input event handle, which is required for Windows code:

```
// Create input event handle
RemoteHost[NextFreeHostIndex].SocketInputEvent =
        CreateEvent(NULL, FALSE, FALSE, NULL);
```

Now we fill the remote host information. We use the NextFreeHostIndex index number we retrieved by using the FindNextFreeHostIndex function. The socket descriptor of the remote host is the socket descriptor that Accept returned.

Similarly, the address information structure and length of the structure are the ones that Accept filled. Then we set the host's online flag so the thread will keep running once it has been started. Last, but not least, we increase the total amount of remote hosts on the server. Note that this number is NET_Socket dependent. So if one server machine has more than one NET_Socket service running, each of them have their own amount of remote hosts (and their data of course).

```
// Fill remote host information
RemoteHost[NextFreeHostIndex].socket = connectSock;
RemoteHost[NextFreeHostIndex].inetSockAddr = clientAddr;
RemoteHost[NextFreeHostIndex].addrLen = clientLen;
RemoteHost[NextFreeHostIndex].online = 1;
RemoteHosts++;
```

Now that we have filled the remote host information, we can send the local ID number to the client. This function is explained later in this tutorial.

```
// Give local id number to the client
GiveLocalIdTCP();
```

We have a special thread parameter structure to store the parameters we need to pass to the I/O thread. Here we fill the correct information to it. The ID number is the NextFreeHostIndex, which is not updated after the first call to it, because we need to use the same value here. The second parameter is a pointer to the NET_Socket object. So we pass a pointer to the current object to it by using the this pointer:

```
// Fill parameter information for the thread
param.id              = NextFreeHostIndex;
param.netParamSocket  = this;
```

Now we can start the server's input/output thread to finally start to process user-defined data. First, we stop notifying for incoming connections on the connected socket because we have already run the Accept function (or we are running it as we speak). Then we set the socket input event handle to handle all network events. So now we can see when there is data incoming to the socket by looking at the socket input event handle. These last two actions are done only on Windows. We learn the Unix way later in this tutorial.

Next, we create the thread. We pass the correct parameters to it by defining the thread routine function (NET_WinIOThreadFunc), and the parameters we pass to that function (param). The thread is now running.

```
// Start the IO thread
DWORD threadId;

// Stop notifying for incoming connections on this socket
WSAAsyncSelect(connectSock, hWnd_netLib, 0, 0);
```

```
// Set socket input event handle to handle network events
WSAEventSelect(connectSock,
    RemoteHost[NextFreeHostIndex].SocketInputEvent,
    FD_READ);

// Create the thread
HANDLE threadHandle = CreateThread(NULL, 0,
    (LPTHREAD_START_ROUTINE) NET_WinIOThreadFunc,
    (void *) &param, 0, &threadId);
```

Connecting to the Server

Now let's see how to connect to the server we created using the network library functions. Again, it is a good idea to make things as easy as possible for the end programmer. We have only one function that the programmer needs to call to connect to the server. Let's see what this involves.

ConnectToServer Function

ConnectToServer is the only function the end programmer needs to call to connect to the server. We need to know the IP address and the port of the server process. The following code listing shows the first version (TCP dependent) of ConnectToServer:

```
int NET_Socket::ConnectToServer(char *addressText, int port)
{
    SOCKET sock;
    struct sockaddr_in inetServAddr;

    NETMSGDATA_DATASIZE DataMsg;
    memset(&DataMsg, 0, sizeof(NETMSGDATA_DATASIZE));

    // TCP protocol
    sock = socket(AF_INET, SOCK_STREAM, 0);

    if(sock == INVALID_SOCKET)
    {
        return -1;
    }

    // Create inet_addr from the IP number
    u_long inetAddr = inet_addr(addressText);

    // Fill the address information
    memset((char *) &inetServAddr, 0, sizeof(inetServAddr));
```

```c
inetServAddr.sin_family        = AF_INET;
inetServAddr.sin_port          = htons((u_short) port);
inetServAddr.sin_addr.s_addr   = inetAddr;

// Connect
int error = connect(sock, (struct sockaddr *) &inetServAddr,
    sizeof(inetServAddr));

if(error != 0)
{
    LogString("ERROR: connect() error (error = %d)", error);

    return INVALID_SOCKET;
}

// Create Win32 socket input event handle
RemoteHost[NETID_SERVER].SocketInputEvent =
    CreateEvent(NULL, FALSE, FALSE, NULL);

// Fill remote host (server) info
RemoteHost[NETID_SERVER].socket          = sock;
RemoteHost[NETID_SERVER].inetSockAddr    = inetServAddr;
RemoteHost[NETID_SERVER].addrLen         = (socklen_t)
    sizeof(inetServAddr);
RemoteHost[NETID_SERVER].online          = 1;
RemoteHosts++;

char *string;
string =
    inet_ntoa(RemoteHost[NETID_SERVER].inetSockAddr.sin_addr);

LogString("Sending knock to socket %d, ip: %s, port %d",
    RemoteHost[NETID_SERVER].socket, string,
    ntohs(RemoteHost[NETID_SERVER].inetSockAddr.sin_port));

NETMSG_GENERIC *Msg;
char *recvbuf;

recvbuf = (char *) malloc(NET_BUFFSIZE);
memset((char *) recvbuf, 0, sizeof(char));

LogString("Waiting for localId");

// Set the remote host (server) non-blocking
SetNonBlocking(NETID_SERVER, 1);

int counter = 0;
```

```
// Loop while we do not have a local ID number
while(localId < 1)
{
    counter++;

    // Check if we are here too long
    // we probably cannot connect to anywhere.
    if(counter == 100000)
    {
        LogString("ERROR: We were waiting for localId
            for too long");

        return NET_INVALID_SOCKET;
    }

    struct sockaddr_in newAddr;
    socklen_t newLen = sizeof(newAddr);

    memset((char *) recvbuf, 0, sizeof(char));

    // Read data from the server
    if(ReadFrom(RemoteHost[NETID_SERVER].socket, recvbuf,
        sizeof(NETMSGDATA_DATASIZE),
        (struct sockaddr *) &newAddr,
        &newLen, 1))
    {
        Msg = (NETMSG_GENERIC *) recvbuf;

        switch(Msg->type)
        {
        // Got local ID number
        case NETMSG_GIVEID:
            NETMSGDATA_DATASIZE *idMsg;
            idMsg = (NETMSGDATA_DATASIZE *) Msg;

            // Set the local ID number
            localId = idMsg->toId;

            string =
                inet_ntoa(RemoteHost[NETID_SERVER].inetSockAddr.sin_addr);

            LogString("The server is now on socket %d, ip %s, port %d",
                RemoteHost[NETID_SERVER].socket, string,
                ntohs(RemoteHost[NETID_SERVER].inetSockAddr.sin_port));

            break;
```

```
            default:
                continue;
            }
        }
    }

    free(recvbuf);
    recvbuf = NULL;

    LogString("Got localId %d", localId);

    // Set the local host online
    Online = 1;

    FindNextFreeHostIndex();

    param.id                = NETID_SERVER;
    param.netParamSocket     = this;

    // Start the IO thread
    WSAAsyncSelect(sock, hWnd_netLib, 0, 0);

    WSAEventSelect(sock, RemoteHost[NETID_SERVER].SocketInputEvent,
        FD_READ);

    DWORD threadId;

    HANDLE threadHandle = CreateThread(NULL, 0,
        (LPTHREAD_START_ROUTINE) NET_WinIOThreadFunc,
        (void *) &param, 0, &threadId);

    // Wait for the thread to start
    while(!RemoteHost[NETID_SERVER].thread);

    return 0;
}
```

First, we need to create the TCP socket that we will use to connect the server. In this first version, we simply create an IPv4 stream socket, and then check that it was created successfully. If not, the function returns.

```
// TCP protocol
sock = socket(AF_INET, SOCK_STREAM, 0);

if(sock == INVALID_SOCKET)
```

```
{
    return -1;
}
```

Next, we fill the address information structure of the server. Before we can fill the structure, we need to create the Internet address from the IP address we passed in as a parameter to this function.

Then we fill the structure to use IPv4 (AF_INET), the port that we also passed in as a parameter, and the Internet address we just created:

```
// Create inet_addr from the IP number
u_long inetAddr = inet_addr(addressText);

// Fill the address information
memset((char *) &inetServAddr, 0, sizeof(inetServAddr));
inetServAddr.sin_family      = AF_INET;
inetServAddr.sin_port        = htons((u_short) port);
inetServAddr.sin_addr.s_addr = inetAddr;
```

We then connect the server using the socket function Connect. Note that this can be done only with the TCP protocol. We use the address information structure we just filled and the socket we created at the beginning of the function. After the call to Connect, we check that everything went correctly. If not, the function returns.

```
// Connect
int error = connect(sock,
    (struct sockaddr *) &inetServAddr, sizeof(inetServAddr));

if(error != 0)
{
    LogString("ERROR: connect() error (error = %d)", error);

    return INVALID_SOCKET;
}
```

After we know that Connect returned successfully, we create the socket input event handle to monitor input events. This works only on Win32 systems.

```
// Create Win32 socket input event handle
RemoteHost[NETID_SERVER].SocketInputEvent =
    CreateEvent(NULL, FALSE, FALSE, NULL);
```

Then, we fill in the server host info in the remote host structure and increase the amount of remote hosts. But because a client cannot have more than one remote host at a time, this is not really necessary.

```
// Fill remote host (server) info
RemoteHost[NETID_SERVER].socket        = sock;
RemoteHost[NETID_SERVER].inetSockAddr  = inetServAddr;
```

```
RemoteHost[NETID_SERVER].addrLen          = (socklen_t)
    sizeof(inetServAddr);
RemoteHost[NETID_SERVER].online           = 1;
RemoteHosts++;
```

We need to set up a receive buffer to receive the local ID number from the server. The following piece of code shows this. We allocate some memory for the buffer. NET_BuffSize is defined in netLib.h. After that, we set the memory to zero.

```
char *recvbuf;

recvbuf = (char *) malloc(NET_BUFFSIZE);
memset((char *) recvbuf, 0, sizeof(char));
```

We set the server host socket non-blocking, as shown in the following piece of code:

```
// Set the remote host (server) non-blocking
SetNonBlocking(NETID_SERVER, 1);
```

We need to wait to receive the local ID number because we really cannot move on without it, and we cannot be sure how long it takes for the server to send it to us. We loop here as long as we do not have a unique ID.

```
int counter = 0;

// Loop while we do not have a local ID number
while(localId < 1)
{
    ...
}
```

We cannot wait for the local ID number forever, so here we check if the counter limit has been reached. If it has been reached, the function returns an error.

```
counter++;

// Check if we are here too long
// we probably cannot connect to anywhere.
if(counter == 100000)
{
    LogString("ERROR: We were waiting for localId
        for too long");

    return NET_INVALID_SOCKET;
}
```

We read any incoming data from the server next, but we are really expecting only the local ID number. We use a non-blocking function to be able to loop all the time.

```
// Read data from the server
if(ReadFrom(RemoteHost[NETID_SERVER].socket, recvbuf,
     sizeof(NETMSGDATA_DATASIZE),
     (struct sockaddr *) &newAddr,
     &newLen, 1))
{
    ...
}
```

Once we receive something we process it as shown in the following code. Because we are expecting only the local ID message, we discard any other message. If we do receive the NETMsg_GiveID message, we retrieve the local ID number from the destination host number (toId):

```
Msg = (NETMSG_GENERIC *) recvbuf;

switch(Msg->type)
{
// Got local ID number
case NETMSG_GIVEID:
    NETMSGDATA_DATASIZE *idMsg;
    idMsg = (NETMSGDATA_DATASIZE *) Msg;

    // Set the local ID number
    localId = idMsg->toId;

    string =
        inet_ntoa(RemoteHost[NETID_SERVER].inetSockAddr.sin_addr);

    LogString("The server is now on socket %d, ip %s, port %d",
        RemoteHost[NETID_SERVER].socket, string,
        ntohs(RemoteHost[NETID_SERVER].inetSockAddr.sin_port));

    break;

default:
    continue;
}
```

Once we are sure we are connected to the server, we set the local host online flag up. This keeps the threads running, etc. We also update the next free host index number. The next thing we do is start the thread for the server host, so we set up the parameter structure for the thread function here, too. The host ID number is naturally the one dedicated to all servers: NETID_Server which is actually (0) and the NET_Socket pointer is set to point to the current object.

```
// Set the local host online
Online = 1;

FindNextFreeHostIndex();

param.id              = NETID_SERVER;
param.netParamSocket  = this;
```

Next we start the input/output thread for the server host. We set the socket to inform us of all events to the socket input event and then start the thread with the parameters we filled in to the parameter structure:

```
// Start the IO thread

WSAAsyncSelect(sock, hWnd_netLib, 0, 0);

WSAEventSelect(sock, RemoteHost[NETID_SERVER].SocketInputEvent,
    FD_READ);

DWORD threadId;

HANDLE threadHandle = CreateThread(NULL, 0,
    (LPTHREAD_START_ROUTINE) NET_WinIOThreadFunc,
    (void *) &param, 0, &threadId);
```

Finally, we wait for the thread to start, to make sure the function does not return before everything is set:

```
// Wait for the thread to start
while(!RemoteHost[NETID_SERVER].thread);
```

CloseConnection Function

Once we have successfully connected to the server, we probably want to disconnect from it at some point. For this, the network library has one easy-to-use function, called CloseConnection. The following code listing shows this function. We need to define the host ID to close the connection with, and we need to define if we initiated the closure. If we initiate the closure, a message is sent to the other host to tell it to close the connection, too.

```
void NET_Socket::CloseConnection(int id, int active)
{
    // If the remote host is offline, there is
    // no point in closing the connection
    if(!RemoteHost[id].online)
    {
        LogString("Trying to close connection %d,
            but RemoteHost is not online", id);
```

```
            return;
    }

    LogString("Closing connection %d", id);

    // Send CLOSE_CONNECTION message only
    // if this is an active closure
    // (this host initiates the closure)
    if(active)
    {
        NETMSG_GENERIC Msg;
        NETMSGDATA_DATASIZE DataMsg;
        memset(&DataMsg, 0, sizeof(NETMSGDATA_DATASIZE));

        DataMsg.type = NETMSG_DATASIZE;
        DataMsg.size = sizeof(NETMSG_GENERIC);

        Msg.type      = NETMSG_CLOSE_CONNECTION;
        Msg.fromId    = localId;
        Msg.toId      = id;

        Write(id, (char *) &DataMsg, sizeof(NETMSGDATA_DATASIZE));
        Write(id, (char *) &Msg, sizeof(NETMSG_GENERIC));
    }

    struct linger Ling;

    Ling.l_onoff = 1;
    Ling.l_linger = 0;

    setsockopt(RemoteHost[id].socket, SOL_SOCKET, SO_LINGER,
            (const char *) &Ling, sizeof(struct linger));

    // Close the socket
    shutdown(RemoteHost[id].socket, SD_BOTH);

    int ret = WSAEWOULDBLOCK;

    while(ret == WSAEWOULDBLOCK)
        ret = closesocket(RemoteHost[id].socket);

    RemoteHost[id].socket = 0;

    // if we are closing connection to the server,
    // we will not be online anymore
    if(id == NETID_SERVER)
    {
```

```
            Online          = 0;
            localId         = NETID_UNKNOWN;
    }


    // because the remote host list cannot
    // be resorted, mark this connection offline
    // and decrease RemoteHosts amount
    RemoteHost[id].online = 0;
    RemoteHosts--;

    FindNextFreeHostIndex();

    LogString("Disconnected: NextFreeHostIndex %d",
        NextFreeHostIndex);
}
```

Before closing any connection it is a good idea to check if the connection is already closed. This is what we do here. If the remote host's online flag is down, we do not attempt to close the connection.

```
// If the remote host is offline, there is
// no point in closing the connection
if(!RemoteHost[id].online)
{
    LogString("Trying to close connection %d,
        but RemoteHost is not online", id);
    return;
}
```

Now we check to see if this is an active closure. Active closure means that the local host is the one initiating the closure operation. If the local host is initiating the closure, it must inform the other host so it knows to close the connection, too.

All we do is simply send a normal message to the remote host to tell it that we are closing the connection. There is no need for extra data in the message (only the header is sent) because this is a notification only.

```
// Send CLOSE_CONNECTION message only
// if this is an active closure
// (this host initiates the closure)
if(active)
{
    NETMSG_GENERIC Msg;
    NETMSGDATA_DATASIZE DataMsg;
    memset(&DataMsg, 0, sizeof(NETMSGDATA_DATASIZE));

    DataMsg.type = NETMSG_DATASIZE;
    DataMsg.size = sizeof(NETMSG_GENERIC);
```

```
    Msg.type        = NETMSG_CLOSE_CONNECTION;
    Msg.fromId      = localId;
    Msg.toId        = id;

    Write(id, (char *) &DataMsg, sizeof(NETMSGDATA_DATASIZE));
    Write(id, (char *) &Msg, sizeof(NETMSG_GENERIC));
}
```

Now that the notification has been sent (if active closure), we can close the
socket. We do not just close the socket with one call to CloseSocket, but instead
we linger on the call to make sure all the outgoing data is sent before the socket is
closed:

```
struct linger Ling;

Ling.l_onoff = 1;
Ling.l_linger = 0;

setsockopt(RemoteHost[id].socket, SOL_SOCKET, SO_LINGER,
      (const char *) &Ling, sizeof(struct linger));

// Close the socket
shutdown(RemoteHost[id].socket, SD_BOTH);

int ret = WSAEWOULDBLOCK;

while(ret == WSAEWOULDBLOCK)
      ret = closesocket(RemoteHost[id].socket);

RemoteHost[id].socket = 0;
```

If the local host is a client and it is closing the connection to the server, the host is
set offline as shown in the following code. The local ID number is set to unknown
because we are not part of any network anymore:

```
// if we are closing connection to the server,
// we will not be online anymore
if(id == NETID_SERVER)
{
    Online        = 0;
    localId       = NETID_UNKNOWN;
}
```

Because we cannot re-sort the remote host list, we simply set the online flag of
the host down and decrease the amount of remote hosts. Now we know that this
ID is free to be used again.

```
// because the remote host list cannot
// be resorted, mark this connection offline
// and decrease RemoteHosts amount
RemoteHost[id].online = 0;
RemoteHosts--;
```

Lastly, we update the next free host index number, because it may have changed when the connection closed:

```
FindNextFreeHostIndex();
```

Multithreading

We have one function that the server is running for each client at the same time, and that each client is running for the server. This is the NET_WinIOThreadFunc function; it is the multithread routine function. The purpose of this function is to process each incoming event from a remote host. Because each host will have its own thread running, multiple incoming events can be processed at a time. The following code listing shows this function:

```
void NET_WinIOThreadFunc(void *ParamPtr)
{
    DWORD waitStatus;

    // Copy the parameter info into more easy to use variables
    NET_Socket *netSock = ((threadParam_t *)
        ParamPtr)->netParamSocket;
    int id = ((threadParam_t *) ParamPtr)->id;

    if(netSock == NULL)
        return;

    WSAEVENT EventArray[1];

    // Fill EventArray with SocketInputEvent
    EventArray[0] = netSock->RemoteHost[id].SocketInputEvent;

    LogString("------ Entering Windows IO thread loop ------");

    // Set the thread flag up to mark that the thread is running
    netSock->RemoteHost[id].thread = 1;

    // Keep thread running as long as the remote host is online
    while(netSock->RemoteHost[id].online)
    {
        // Wait for an event
        waitStatus = WSAWaitForMultipleEvents(1, EventArray,
```

```
                FALSE, NET_IOTIMEOUT, FALSE);

        switch(waitStatus)
        {
        case WSA_WAIT_FAILED:
            // A fatal error
            break;

        case WAIT_IO_COMPLETION:
            // Keep looping
            continue;

        case WSA_WAIT_TIMEOUT:
            // Timeout elapsed
            continue;

        // Input
        case WSA_WAIT_EVENT_0:
            if(netSock->HandleSocketInputEvent(id) == NET_OK)
            {
                continue;
            }
            else
            {
                LogString("HandleSocketInputEvent error");

                netSock->RemoteHost[id].online = 0;
                break;
            }

        default:
            continue;
        }

        break;
    }

    // Set the thread flag down to mark that
    // the thread is not running
    netSock->RemoteHost[id].thread = 0;

    // Thread is ending because the
    // connection was closed or an error occurred
    LogString("------ Exiting Windows IO thread loop ------");
    return;
}
```

As we can pass only one parameter to the thread routine function, we pass a pointer of a structure to it that actually holds two parameters. These two parameters are a pointer to a NET_Socket object and a host ID number. Here we copy the parameter info from the structure variables that are easier to use. Now we can simply use the integer id instead of ((threadParam_t *) ParamPtr)->id:

```
// Copy the parameter info into more easy to use variables
NET_Socket *netSock = ((threadParam_t *)
    ParamPtr)->netParamSocket;
int id = ((threadParam_t *) ParamPtr)->id;
```

Next, we fill the event array for WinSock's WSAWaitForMultipleEvents function. As we want to see only if there are incoming events, we can create an array with only one member, which is the socket input event handle:

```
WSAEVENT EventArray[1];

// Fill EventArray with SocketInputEvent
EventArray[0] = netSock->RemoteHost[id].SocketInputEvent;
```

Here we set the thread flag of the remote host up to indicate that the thread of this host is running. The network library uses this flag to see if the thread really is running and acts accordingly.

```
// Set the thread flag up to mark that the thread is running
netSock->RemoteHost[id].thread = 1;
```

This is a very important part of the thread routine function. The following While statement keeps the thread alive as long as the remote host's online flag is up. So when we set this flag down, the thread will stop and we cannot receive any more data from that host.

```
// Keep thread running as long as the remote host is online
while(netSock->RemoteHost[id].online)
{
    ...
}
```

Once the thread loop is running, we start to wait for events; in this case, only for incoming network events. As you can see from the prefix "WS," WSAWaitForMultipleEvents is a WinSock function only. The first parameter we pass to it defines the number of events to wait for, which is only one in our case. The second parameter is a pointer to the event array itself, which we filled earlier. The third parameter defines whether we want to wait for all the events before we continue. We have set it to FALSE, but in this case when we are waiting for only one event, it does not really matter. The fourth parameter defines the timeout value in milliseconds. If no event occurs during that time, the function will return. We can set this to WSA_Infinite to make the function never return if no events occur. We have no use for the last parameter so we set it to FALSE. The function return value indicates the event that occurred.

```
// Wait for an event
waitStatus = WSAWaitForMultipleEvents(1, EventArray, FALSE,
    NET_IOTIMEOUT, FALSE);
```

We use a switch statement to check which event occurred. Although we are only waiting for incoming network events, there may be some system events happening as well. So, we check to see if these happened before we check for the network events.

First, determine if there was an error. For this we check if WSAWaitForMultipleEvents returned WSA_Wait_Failed, and if it did, we break up the thread loop and the connection to the remote host will be cut off.

Then, we check to see if an input/output process is waiting for completion by checking for return value Wait_IO_Completion. If this is the case, we continue to loop the thread loop.

Lastly, we check that the timeout value elapsed by checking if the return value is WSA_Wait_Timeout. This could be left out because there is nothing happening if this case occurs, but it is good to have it already there if we need to add something to it later. So for now, we continue the loop:

```
switch(waitStatus)
{
case WSA_WAIT_FAILED:
    // A fatal error
    break;

case WAIT_IO_COMPLETION:
    // Keep looping
    continue;

case WSA_WAIT_TIMEOUT:
    // Timeout elapsed
    continue;

    ...

}
```

Next, we check to see if there is an incoming event to be processed. We do this by checking if WSAWaitForMultipleEvents returned WSA_Wait_Event_0. If we had more than one event to wait for, the next event in the event array would return WSA_Wait_Event_0 + 1 and so on.

Now that we can see that there is a network input event incoming, we run HandleSocketInputEvent to handle this event. We pass the host ID number as a parameter to it, so it handles the correct host's events. If this function returns an error, we break up the loop and disconnect from the host.

```
// Input
case WSA_WAIT_EVENT_0:
    if(netSock->HandleSocketInputEvent(id) == NET_OK)
    {
        continue;
    }
    else
    {
        LogString("HandleSocketInputEvent error");

        netSock->RemoteHost[id].online = 0;
        break;
    }
```

Once the thread loop returns, we set the thread flag of the remote host down, so the network library will know elsewhere that the thread is not running:

```
// Set the thread flag down to mark that the thread is not running
netSock->RemoteHost[id].thread = 0;
```

Handling Network Events

To handle the incoming network input events we use a function called Handle-SocketInputEvent. It is part of the NET_Socket class, so each NET_Socket object has its own copy of this. However, we need to pass the host ID number as a parameter to it, because each NET_Socket object may have more than one remote host. The following code listing shows the function:

```
int NET_Socket::HandleSocketInputEvent(int id)
{
    WSANETWORKEVENTS networkEvents;

    // Find out what happened and act accordingly
    int result = WSAEnumNetworkEvents(RemoteHost[id].socket,
        RemoteHost[id].SocketInputEvent, &networkEvents);

    if(result == SOCKET_ERROR)
    {
        LogString("WSAEnumNetworkEvents error");

        // A fatal error.
        return FALSE;
    }
    else
```

```
    {
        // handle all of the network events on the given socket
        return WinHandleEvents(id, &networkEvents);
    }
}
```

Now that we know that something happened on the socket, we should find out what it is. For this we use the WSAEnumNetworkEvents function to enumerate the network events. We pass the socket descriptor and the socket input event handle as parameters to the function. The function determines what happened using these parameters and returns the information to the third parameter and the normal return value. We then check if the function returned successfully. If it did not, HandleSocketInputEvent returns with an error value.

```
WSANETWORKEVENTS networkEvents;

// Find out what happened and act accordingly
int result = WSAEnumNetworkEvents(RemoteHost[id].socket,
    RemoteHost[id].SocketInputEvent, &networkEvents);

if(result == SOCKET_ERROR)
{
    LogString("WSAEnumNetworkEvents error");

    // A fatal error.
    return FALSE;
}
```

If everything went fine, we handle the events by calling the WinHandleEvents function. We pass the host ID number and the NetworkEvents pointer to the function. The return value of the WinHandleEvents function is also the return value of HandleSocketInputEvent.

```
// handle all of the network events on the given socket
return WinHandleEvents(id, &networkEvents);
```

WinHandleEvents Function

The following code listing shows the WinHandleEvents function:

```
int NET_Socket::WinHandleEvents(int id, LPWSANETWORKEVENTS NetworkEvents)
{
    if(NetworkEvents->lNetworkEvents & FD_READ)
    {
        // An FD_READ event has occurred on the connected socket
        if(NetworkEvents->iErrorCode[FD_READ_BIT] ==
            WSAENETDOWN)
        {
```

```
            LogString("ERROR: WSAENETDOWN at WinHandleEvents");

            // There's an error
            return NET_ERROR;
        }
        else
        {
            // Read data off the socket
            ProcessMessages(id);

            return NET_OK;
        }
    }

    return NET_OK;
}
```

First, we check to see if an FD_Read event has occurred. This happens when there is an incoming input event from the remote host. We determine if the FD_Read bit of NetworkEvents->lNetworkEvents is 1. Obviously, as we are not expecting any other event than an incoming input event, we do not check for any other bits.

```
if(NetworkEvents->lNetworkEvents & FD_READ)
{
    ...
}
```

Now we need to determine whether the network is still up. We can do this by looking at the NetworkEvents structure again. This time we see if iErrorCode[FD_READ_BIT] is WSAENetDown. If it is, it means that the network is down and we cannot read the data from the socket. When this happens, we return NET_Error, and we are done here. But if WSAENetDown does not happen, we can read the socket and keep on processing the data.

```
// An FD_READ event has occurred on the connected socket
if(NetworkEvents->iErrorCode[FD_READ_BIT] == WSAENETDOWN)
{
    // There's an error
    return NET_ERROR;
}
```

So, assuming that the network is still up and we can process the data, we run the ProcessMessages function and pass the host ID number to it, so the data is read from the correct socket. After this function returns, we can return NET_OK from WinHandleEvents as well.

```
// Read data off the socket
```

```
    ProcessMessages(id);

    return NET_OK;
```

ProcessMessages Function

The ProcessMessages function is a function that receives data and processes system-level messages, such as incoming data's Datasize and CloseConnection messages. It also calls the function that processes the user-level messages in the application itself. This function is NET_HandleMessages. It is an external function that must be declared in every netLib application. The following code listing shows ProcessMessages in its entirety:

```
void NET_Socket::ProcessMessages(int id)
{
    NETMSG_GENERIC *Msg;

    char buf[NET_BUFFSIZE];
    strcpy(buf, "");

    if(RemoteHost[id].messageCounter == 0)
    {
        RemoteHost[id].bufsize = sizeof(NETMSGDATA_DATASIZE);
    }

    LogString("Reading from socket: %d (id: %d) bufsize: %d",
        RemoteHost[id].socket, id, RemoteHost[id].bufsize);

    if(ReadFrom(RemoteHost[id].socket, buf,
        RemoteHost[id].bufsize, (struct sockaddr *)
        &RemoteHost[id].inetSockAddr, &RemoteHost[id].addrLen,
        RemoteHost[id].NonBlocking))
    {
        LogString("Going to record message");

        RemoteHost[id].RecordMessage();

        Msg = (NETMSG_GENERIC *) buf;
        if(Msg == NULL) return;

        LogString("Message info: toId: %d, fromId: %d, type: %d,
            bufsize: %d", Msg->toId, Msg->fromId, Msg->type,
            RemoteHost[id].bufsize);

        // Check if we should re-send NETID_ALL message.
        // Only server can do this.
        if( (localId == NETID_SERVER) &&
```

TUTORIAL 2

```
                    (Msg->toId == NETID_ALL) )
          {
                Write(NETID_ALL, buf, bufsize);
                return;
          }

          LogString("(Msg->type: %d)", Msg->type);

          switch(Msg->type)
          {
          case NETMSG_DATASIZE:
                NETMSGDATA_DATASIZE *DataMsg;
                DataMsg = (NETMSGDATA_DATASIZE *) Msg;

                LogString("Got datasize");

                RemoteHost[id].bufsize = DataMsg->size;
                break;

          case NETMSG_CLOSE_CONNECTION:
                LogString("Got NETMSG_CLOSE_CONNECTION message");

                CloseConnection(Msg->fromId, 0);
                break;

          default:
                LogString("Going to run NET_HandleMessages()");

                NET_HandleMessages(Msg);
                break;
          }
     }
}
```

At the beginning of this function we declare the variables we are going to use. The generic network message Msg is used to retrieve the message type from the data buffer. The buf string is used to store the data we receive. The size of this buffer (NET_BuffSize) is defined in netLib.h. We then make sure that the string is empty by using Strcpy to make it empty:

```
NETMSG_GENERIC *Msg;

char buf[NET_BUFFSIZE];
strcpy(buf, "");
```

Because we need to know the size of the data before we receive it, we send the Datasize message before every "normal" message. We know the size of the

Datasize message, so all we need to determine is when we are receiving a Datasize message and when we are receiving a normal message. For this, we have a message counter for each remote host. This counter is an integer which is either zero or one, depending on which message we are going to receive next. When the counter is zero, the next message will be a Datasize message. When it is one, it will be a "normal" message. So, when the next message is going to be a Datasize message, we set the size of the buffer to the size of the Datasize message. Then, when we receive the Datasize message, we get the information of the next message's size and set the buffer accordingly.

In the following piece of code we check if the next message will be a Datasize message. If yes, we set the correct buffer size.

```
if(RemoteHost[id].messageCounter == 0)
{
    RemoteHost[id].bufsize = sizeof(NETMSGDATA_DATASIZE);
}
```

Now we get to the fun part: receiving data! We use the ReadFrom function here, because that way it does not matter if we are using TCP or UDP. The parameters we pass to it are retrieved from the remote host structure, so we read the data from the correct place and in the correct way.

```
if(ReadFrom(RemoteHost[id].socket, buf, RemoteHost[id].bufsize,
    (struct sockaddr *) &RemoteHost[id].inetSockAddr,
    &RemoteHost[id].addrLen, RemoteHost[id].NonBlocking))
{
    ...
}
```

We record the message once we have read it to the buffer. Recording the message means that the message counter is updated. Now we know to expect a correct type of message again.

```
RemoteHost[id].RecordMessage();
```

Now that we have the data in the buffer, it would be nice to have it in a format that we could understand better, so we cast it into a different type. We make the generic message Msg point to the data buffer so we can check the message type. After typecasting the operation, we make sure that the message is not empty. If it is, the function returns.

```
Msg = (NETMSG_GENERIC *) buf;
if(Msg == NULL) return;
```

Before we check the type of the message and process it any further, we check if the message is supposed to be delivered to all clients. This is done only on server hosts. If the data is addressed to all clients, we resend the data to all clients without processing it anymore on the local host. After that, the function returns because nothing else is to be done.

```
// Check if we should re-send NETID_ALL message.
// Only server can do this.
if( (localId == NETID_SERVER) && (Msg->toId == NETID_ALL) )
{
    Write(NETID_ALL, buf, bufsize);
    return;
}
```

Now we check the type of the message and process it accordingly. There are two types of system messages, which are explained next.

In case of a Datasize message (NETMsg_Datasize), we typecast the generic message into a Datasize message and retrieve the actual data from it. The data of a Datasize message is the length of the next message to be received.

In case of a CloseConnection message, we simply close the connection with the host from which we received the message. We do a passive closure, which means that we do not send the other host any indication that we are closing the connection, as the other host just did it.

In addition to system messages, there are user-defined messages. The network library will not process these, as this is a job for the network application the user is developing. The library calls the external function that each netLib application must have. We explain the usage of this function later in this tutorial.

```
switch(Msg->type)
{
case NETMSG_DATASIZE:
    NETMSGDATA_DATASIZE *DataMsg;
    DataMsg = (NETMSGDATA_DATASIZE *) Msg;

    LogString("Got datasize");

    RemoteHost[id].bufsize = DataMsg->size;
    break;

case NETMSG_CLOSE_CONNECTION:
    LogString("Got NETMSG_CLOSE_CONNECTION message");
    CloseConnection(Msg->fromId, 0);
    break;

default:
    LogString("Going to run NET_HandleMessages()");
    NET_HandleMessages(Msg);
    break;
}
```

Message Recording

As we learned in the previous section, the network library keeps track of what kind of message it is about to receive next. The reason for this kind of system is that we need to know how many bytes we are going to receive. Because we know that the first message we receive is the Datasize message, and because we know the size of that message, we know how many bytes to receive when we are receiving the very first message. Then, when we do receive the Datasize message, we get the length of the next message to be received, and we can set the ReadFrom function to read that known amount of bytes.

The following function is used to update the message counter:

```
void RemoteHost_t::RecordMessage(void)
{
    messageCounter++;
    messageCounter = messageCounter % 2;
}
```

As you can see, this function is very simple. All it does is increase the integer MessageCounter, and then set it to the modulus found by dividing the MessageCounter variable by 2. That way the MessageCounter variable is always zero or one: Datasize or normal message.

It is very important to have a unique message counter for each remote host. If we had only one counter and multiple remote hosts, we might receive multiple messages of the same type in a row, and the counter would be useless.

Complete Independent Version

Now you have seen how to create a network library for Windows and TCP protocol. This is how development of a network library could go if you are starting from scratch. First, you create a working version for one operating system and one protocol, and then you start adding more functionality and support for other platforms and protocols.

So what we are going to do next is add support for the Unix operating system and UDP protocol. As this was the original idea, it is rather easy to add in the support for both. The code we will introduce to you next is the final, complete independent network library. Most of the functions are the same as we have already seen, but they have more functionality now and, of course, are platform and protocol independent.

NET_Socket Class

The following code listing shows the complete NET_Socket class. It will not change again. This is the result of our design in the beginning.

```
class NET_Socket
{
private:
    int GiveLocalIdTCP(void);
    void FindNextFreeHostIndex(void);

    // Server creation helper functions
    int CreateUnixTCPServer(SOCKET listenSock);
    int CreateWinTCPServer(SOCKET listenSock);
    int CreateUnixUDPServer(SOCKET sock);
    int CreateWinUDPServer(SOCKET sock);
    int CreateTCPServer(SOCKET sock);
    int CreateUDPServer(SOCKET sock);
    int CreateUnixServer(int port, int Protocol);
    int CreateWinServer(int port, int Protocol);

#ifdef WIN32
    int WinHandleEvents(int id, LPWSANETWORKEVENTS NetworkEvents);
#endif

    void SendSystemMessage(NETMSG_GENERIC *Msg);

    HOSTID NextFreeHostIndex;

public:
    NET_Socket();
    ~NET_Socket();

    // Uninitialization functions
    void CloseConnection(int id, int active);
    void Shutdown(void);

    // Miscellaneous functions
    int SetNonBlocking(int id, u_long setBlocking);
    int GiveLocalIdUDP(sockaddr_in clientAddr);
    void AcceptConnection(void);
    int CreateServer(int port, int Protocol);
    int ConnectToServer(char *ipAddressString,
        int port, int Protocol);

    // Data reading / writing functions
    int ReadToBuffer(HOSTID id, size_t count,
```

```
        bool NonBlocking);

    int Read(int id, char *buf, size_t count);
    int Write(int id, char *buf, size_t count);
    void WriteAll(char *buf, size_t count);

    int ReadFrom(SOCKET sock, char *buf, size_t count,
        struct sockaddr *sockAddr, socklen_t *sockLen,
        bool NonBlocking);

    int WriteTo(SOCKET sock, char *buf, size_t count,
            struct sockaddr *sockAddr, socklen_t sockLen);

    HOSTID GetNextFreeHostIndex(void) {return NextFreeHostIndex;}

    // Message processing functions
    void ProcessMessageBuffer(int id);
    void ProcessMessages(int id);

    int HandleSocketInputEvent(int id);
    int HandleSocketOutputEvent(int id);

#ifdef WIN32
    HANDLE SocketOutputEvent;
#endif

    // Miscellanous variables
    SOCKET listenSocket;                // Listening socket

    int localId;                        // Local host id
    bool Online;                        // Local online flag

    int RemoteHosts;                    // Amount of remote hosts
    RemoteHost_t *RemoteHost;

    int Port; // Port in use
};
```

Constructor/Destructor

We update the constructor and destructor functions to allocate and free memory for our message buffer. The message buffer system will be explained later in this tutorial.

```
NET_Socket::NET_Socket()
{
    RemoteHost = (RemoteHost_t *) calloc(NET_MAX_CONNECTIONS,
```

```
                    sizeof(RemoteHost_t));

        for(int i = 0; i < NET_MAX_CONNECTIONS; i++)
        {
            RemoteHost[i].InMessageBuffer =
                  (MessageBuffer_t *) calloc(NET_MESSAGE_BUFFER,
                  sizeof(MessageBuffer_t));
        }
    }

    NET_Socket::~NET_Socket()
    {
        for(int i = 0; i < NET_MAX_CONNECTIONS; i++)
        {
            if(RemoteHost[i].InMessageBuffer)
                  free(RemoteHost[i].InMessageBuffer);
        }

        if(RemoteHost) free(RemoteHost);
    }
```

RemoteHost Class

Here is the updated remote host class. The only new things are the message
buffer and the message buffer counter:

```
class RemoteHost_t
{
public:
    SOCKET socket;              // socket
    sockaddr_in inetSockAddr;   // socket address

#ifdef WIN32
    int addrLen;                // socket address length
#else
    socklen_t addrLen;          // socket address length
#endif

    bool online;                // host online flag
    bool thread;                // thread running flag
    bool NonBlocking;           // non-blocking flag

    int messageCounter;         // message buffer counter
    int bufsize;                // the length of the next message

    int lastMessageTime;        // seconds from last message
```

```
        int InMessages;                // Input buffer messages
        MessageBuffer_t *InMessageBuffer;

#ifdef WIN32
        HANDLE SocketInputEvent;
#endif

        void RecordMessage(void);
};
```

Initializing/Uninitializing

We update various functions to be platform and protocol independent, and the following two functions are no exception. We add the #ifdefs to determine if WinSock should be initialized or unitialized.

```
int NET_Initialize(void)
{
        StartLog();

#ifdef WIN32
        return NET_InitializeWinSock();
#else
        return 0;
#endif
}


void NET_Shutdown(void)
{
        LogString("Shutting down netLib");

#ifdef WIN32
        WSACleanup();
#endif
}
```

Blocking/Non-blocking I/O

The following function sets the I/O mode of the remote host. We explained this function earlier in this tutorial, but it has some changes in this complete version.

```
int NET_Socket::SetNonBlocking(int id, u_long setBlocking)
{
        u_long set = setBlocking;
```

```
        // Copy the setting to the remote host structure
        RemoteHost[id].NonBlocking = (bool) setBlocking;

        // Set the socket option
#ifdef WIN32
        return ioctlsocket(RemoteHost[id].socket, FIONBIO, &set);
#else
        return ioctl(RemoteHost[id].socket, FIONBIO, &set);
#endif
}
```

The following piece of code shows the only thing that has changed in this function compared to the first version. Here we wrap and call the correct function depending on what platform we are on. The functions are exactly the same, although they have slightly different names.

```
        // Set the socket option
#ifdef WIN32
        return ioctlsocket(RemoteHost[id].socket, FIONBIO, &set);
#else
        return ioctl(RemoteHost[id].socket, FIONBIO, &set);
#endif
```

Sending/Receiving Data

In this complete version of the library, we have updated pretty much every function. Sending and receiving data are no exceptions. Let's take a look at the functions again.

Read Function

```
int NET_Socket::Read(int id, char *buf, size_t count)
{
    size_t bytes_read = 0;
    int this_read = -1;

    // Blocking version
    if(!RemoteHost[id].NonBlocking)
    {
        while(bytes_read < count)
        {
            while(this_read < 0)
            {
                // Check whether to use the address
                // information or socket only
                if(RemoteHost[id].addrLen != (socklen_t) NULL)
                {
```

```
                    this_read =
                        recvfrom(RemoteHost[id].socket,
                        buf, count - bytes_read,
                        0, (struct sockaddr *)
                        &RemoteHost[id].inetSockAddr,
                        &RemoteHost[id].addrLen);
                }
                else
                {
                    this_read = recv(RemoteHost[id].socket,
                        buf, count - bytes_read, 0);
                }
            }

            if(this_read == 0)
            {
                return bytes_read;
            }

            bytes_read      += this_read;
            buf             += this_read;
        }
    }

    // Non-blocking version
    else
    {
        // Check whether to use the address
        // information or socket only
        if(RemoteHost[id].addrLen != (socklen_t) NULL)
        {
            this_read = recvfrom(RemoteHost[id].socket,
                buf, count - bytes_read,      0,
                 (struct sockaddr *)
                &RemoteHost[id].inetSockAddr,
                &RemoteHost[id].addrLen);
        }
        else
        {
            this_read = recv(RemoteHost[id].socket, buf,
                count - bytes_read, 0);
        }

        if(this_read < 0)
        {
            return this_read;
        }
```

LIVERPOOL JOHN MOORES UNIVERSITY
LEARNING & INFORMATION SERVICES

```
        if(this_read == 0)
        {
             return bytes_read;
        }

        bytes_read      += this_read;
        buf             += this_read;
    }

    return count;
}
```

The only change in this function compared to the function we explained earlier in this tutorial is shown in the following code. We determine if the address structure length is set to see if the address information of the remote host is set. If it is, we use RecvFrom instead of Recv. This way we have a protocol-independent function in our hands. We can use this with both TCP and UDP.

```
// Check whether to use the address
// information or socket only
if(RemoteHost[id].addrLen != (socklen_t) NULL)
{
    ...
}
else
{
    ...
}
```

ReadFrom Function

This function is unchanged from to the earlier version. We have this function so we are able to directly use the RecvFrom function if we need to. With the Read function we might end up using either Recv or RecvFrom.

```
int NET_Socket::ReadFrom(SOCKET sock, char *buf, size_t count, struct sockaddr
*sockAddr, socklen_t *sockLen, bool NonBlocking)
{
    size_t bytes_read = 0;
    int this_read = -1;

    // Blocking version
    if(!NonBlocking)
    {
        while(bytes_read < count)
        {
            while(this_read < 0)
```

```
            {
                this_read = recvfrom(sock, buf,
                    count - bytes_read, 0, sockAddr,
                    sockLen);
            }

            bytes_read      += this_read;
            buf             += this_read;
        }
    }

    // Non-blocking version
    else
    {
        this_read = recvfrom(sock, buf, count - bytes_read,
            0, sockAddr, sockLen);
    }

    return count;
}
```

Write Function

This function also has some changes. It is now a protocol-independent function like the Read function.

```
int NET_Socket::Write(int id, char *buf, size_t count)
{
    // If we are writing to all, use WriteAll function
    if(id == NETID_ALL)
    {
        WriteAll(buf, count);
        return count;
    }
    else
    {
        size_t bytes_sent = 0;
        int this_write = -1;

        LogString("Writing data to id %d, socket %d,
            data size %d (non-blocking = %d)",
            id, RemoteHost[id].socket, count,
            RemoteHost[id].NonBlocking);

        // Blocking version
        if(!RemoteHost[id].NonBlocking)
        {
```

```
        while(bytes_sent < count)
        {
            // Check whether to use the address
            // information or socket only
            if(RemoteHost[id].addrLen != (socklen_t) NULL)
            {
                this_write =
                    sendto(RemoteHost[id].socket, buf,
                    count - bytes_sent, 0,
                    (struct sockaddr *)
                    &RemoteHost[id].inetSockAddr,
                    RemoteHost[id].addrLen);
            }
            else
            {
                this_write =
                    sendto(RemoteHost[id].socket, buf,
                    count - bytes_sent, 0, NULL,
                    (socklen_t) NULL);
            }

            if(this_write < 0)      return this_write;

            bytes_sent      += this_write;
            buf             += this_write;
        }
    }

    // Non-blocking version
    else
    {
        // Check whether to use the address
        // information or socket only
        if(RemoteHost[id].addrLen != (socklen_t) NULL)
        {
            this_write = sendto(RemoteHost[id].socket,
                buf, count - bytes_sent, 0,
                (struct sockaddr *)
                &RemoteHost[id].inetSockAddr,
                RemoteHost[id].addrLen);
        }
        else
        {
            this_write = sendto(RemoteHost[id].socket,
                buf, count - bytes_sent, 0, NULL,
                (socklen_t) NULL);
        }
```

```
            if(this_write < 0)      return this_write;

            bytes_sent += this_write;
        }

        return bytes_sent;
    }
}
```

The following code is the only thing that has changed in this function. We now determine if we should use the address information, and therefore SendTo instead of Send, or just the socket. This change is made to both blocking and non-blocking versions.

```
// Check whether to use the address
// information or socket only
if(RemoteHost[id].addrLen != (socklen_t) NULL)
{
    ...
}
else
{
    ...
}
```

WriteTo Function

Like the ReadFrom function, this function has no changes either. WriteTo exists to be able to use the SendTo function whenever we want.

```
int NET_Socket::WriteTo(SOCKET sock, char *buf, size_t count, struct sockaddr
*sockAddr, socklen_t sockLen)
{
    size_t bytes_sent = 0;
    int this_write = -1;

    // Send all data
    while(bytes_sent < count)
    {
        // Send data
        this_write = sendto(sock, buf,
            count - bytes_sent, 0, sockAddr, sockLen);

        if(this_write < 0)      return this_write;

        // Update variables
        bytes_sent     += this_write;
```

```
            buf              += this_write;
        }

        return count;
    }
```

WriteAll Function

This function has also been updated to be protocol independent.

```
void NET_Socket::WriteAll(char *buf, size_t count)
{
    size_t bytes_sent = 0;
    int this_write = -1;

    // If the local host is a client,
    // send the data first to the server
    if(localId != NETID_SERVER)
    {
        Write(NETID_SERVER, buf, count);
        return;
    }

    char *temp_buf = buf;

    // Loop through all possible remote hosts
    for(int id = 1; id < NET_MAX_CONNECTIONS; id++)
    {
        bytes_sent = 0;
        this_write = -1;
        buf = temp_buf;

        // If the remote host is not online,
        // move on to the next host
        if(!RemoteHost[id].online) continue;

        // Blocking version
        if(!RemoteHost[id].NonBlocking)
        {
            while(bytes_sent < count)
            {
                while(this_write < 0)
                {
                    // Check whether to use the address
                    // information or socket only
                    if(RemoteHost[id].addrLen !=
                        (socklen_t) NULL)
```

```
                    {
                        this_write =
                            sendto(RemoteHost[id].socket,
                            buf, count - bytes_sent, 0,
                            (struct sockaddr *)
                            &RemoteHost[id].inetSockAddr,
                            RemoteHost[id].addrLen);
                    }
                    else
                    {
                        this_write =
                            sendto(RemoteHost[id].socket,
                            buf, count - bytes_sent, 0,
                            NULL, (socklen_t) NULL);
                    }
                }

                bytes_sent      += this_write;
                buf             += this_write;
            }
        }

        // Non-blocking version
        else
        {
            // Check whether to use the address
            // information or socket only
            if(RemoteHost[id].addrLen != (socklen_t) NULL)
            {
                this_write = sendto(RemoteHost[id].socket,
                    buf, count - bytes_sent, 0,
                    (struct sockaddr *)
                    &RemoteHost[id].inetSockAddr,
                    RemoteHost[id].addrLen);
            }
            else
            {
                this_write = sendto(RemoteHost[id].socket,
                    buf, count - bytes_sent, 0, NULL,
                    (socklen_t) NULL);
            }

            bytes_sent      += this_write;
            buf             += this_write;
        }
    }
}
```

The following code is the only change in this function. We determine if we should use the socket address instead of the plain socket to send the data. Both blocking and non-blocking functions have this change.

```
// Check whether to use the address
// information or socket only
if(RemoteHost[id].addrLen != (socklen_t) NULL)
{
    ...
}
else
{
    ...
}
```

Message Buffer System

In this complete version, we use a message buffering system that buffers only the incoming messages on each host. This is not an essential system, so we do not put too much effort into the Unix version of this buffering system. The Unix version is merely a temporary storage for the message that just arrived; it is processed immediately after that. So the buffer on Unix holds only one message at a time.

On Windows the buffer actually works because it is much easier to make it work on Windows. When a message is coming in, the network library reads the data to the buffer and increases the counter of buffered messages. Some memory is allocated for the message also. If another message comes in before the system has processed the buffer, it will be added to the buffer right after the first one. And the counter is increased again. Now, the first message in the buffer is always the one we have received first, so we also process that first. When a message in the buffer is processed, the counter is decreased and the memory is freed.

The system on Windows works so that if there are multiple messages incoming in a row, they are read to the buffer and the system does not have time to process them (because it is all done in the same loop basically). Once there are no incoming messages, the system reaches the point in the loop where it starts to process the buffer. So the idea of the buffer is to make sure no messages are lost if multiple messages are coming in at almost the same time from the same host.

Message Buffer Class

The following piece of code shows the message buffer class:

```
// Message buffer class
class MessageBuffer_t
{
public:
    int id;                          // destination host id
    char buf[NET_BUFFSIZE];          // the message data itself
    size_t count;                    // length of the data
    SOCKET socket;                   // socket
    struct sockaddr_in sockAddr;     // socket address
    socklen_t sockLen;               // socket address length
    bool processing;                 // buffer being processed flag
};
```

ReadToBuffer Function

To read data to the buffer, we create the following function. ReadToBuffer is a simple function that reads data normally, but instead of processing it immediately, it is stored in the buffer.

```
int NET_Socket::ReadToBuffer(HOSTID id, size_t count, bool NonBlocking)
{
    RemoteHost[id].InMessageBuffer[RemoteHost[id].InMessages].sockLen =
    sizeof(RemoteHost[id].inetSockAddr);

    RemoteHost[id].InMessageBuffer[RemoteHost[id].InMessages].count = count;

    LogString("Going to read data to buffer");

    // Read data
    int ret = ReadFrom(RemoteHost[id].socket,
    RemoteHost[id].InMessageBuffer[RemoteHost[id].InMessages].buf, count,
    (struct sockaddr *)
    &RemoteHost[id].InMessageBuffer[RemoteHost[id].InMessages].sockAddr,
    &RemoteHost[id].InMessageBuffer[RemoteHost[id].InMessages].sockLen,
    NonBlocking);

    // Check everything is ok
    if((unsigned int) ret == count)
    {
        RemoteHost[id].InMessages++;

        LogString("++++++++ InMessages: %d",
            RemoteHost[id].InMessages);
    }
```

```
        return ret;
    }
```

First we read the data to the buffer. Before we can call ReadFrom we must first set the socket length because it is a value-result argument. We use the ReadFrom function to assure full protocol independence.

```
RemoteHost[id].InMessageBuffer[RemoteHost[id].InMessages].sockLen =
sizeof(RemoteHost[id].inetSockAddr);

RemoteHost[id].InMessageBuffer[RemoteHost[id].InMessages].count = count;

LogString("Going to read data to buffer");

// Read data
int ret = ReadFrom(RemoteHost[id].socket,
RemoteHost[id].InMessageBuffer[RemoteHost[id].InMessages].buf, count,
(struct sockaddr *) &RemoteHost[id].InMessageBuffer[RemoteHost[id].InMessages]
.sockAddr,&RemoteHost[id].InMessageBuffer[RemoteHost[id].InMessages].sockLen,
NonBlocking);
```

Then we need to check if the data was read in successfully. If it was, we can increase the buffer counter. If not, we do not increase the counter.

```
// Check everything is ok
if((unsigned int) ret == count)
{
    RemoteHost[id].InMessages++;

    LogString("++++++++ InMessages: %d",
        RemoteHost[id].InMessages);
}
```

ProcessMessageBuffer Function

The ProcessMessageBuffer function calls the ReadToBuffer function. This is the function that is called when there is any incoming data. Note that this function does not process the message data.

```
void NET_Socket::ProcessMessageBuffer(int id)
{
    NETMSG_GENERIC *Msg;

    // Next message is datasize?
    if(RemoteHost[id].messageCounter == 0)
    {
        RemoteHost[id].bufsize = sizeof(NETMSGDATA_DATASIZE);
```

```
}

LogString("Reading from socket: %d (id: %d) bufsize: %d",
    RemoteHost[id].socket, id, RemoteHost[id].bufsize);

// Read data to buffer
if(ReadToBuffer(RemoteHost[id].socket,
    RemoteHost[id].bufsize, 0))
{
    RemoteHost[id].InMessageBuffer[0].processing = TRUE;

    // Record message
    RemoteHost[id].RecordMessage();

    // Cast a pointer to the first message in the buffer
    Msg = (NETMSG_GENERIC *) InMessageBuffer[0].buf;
    if(Msg == NULL) return;

    LogString("(Msg->type: %d) (Msg->fromId: %d)
        (Msg->toId: %d)", Msg->type, Msg->fromId,
        Msg->toId);

    // Check the type of the message
    switch(Msg->type)
    {
    // Datasize message
    case NETMSG_DATASIZE:
        NETMSGDATA_DATASIZE *DataMsg;
        DataMsg = (NETMSGDATA_DATASIZE *) Msg;

        // Check if the buffer size does not match
        // the datasize message size
        if(RemoteHost[id].bufsize !=
        sizeof(NETMSGDATA_DATASIZE))
        {
            LogString("Got datasize with wrong bufsize.
                Recovering");

            // Record message
            RemoteHost[id].RecordMessage();
        }

        // Check if we should resend NETID_ALL message.
        // Only server can do this.
        if( (localId == NETID_SERVER) &&
            (Msg->toId == NETID_ALL) )
        {
```

```
                    LogString("Before calling Write (all,
                        datasize), bufsize: %d",
                        RemoteHost[id].bufsize);
                    Write(NETID_ALL,
                        RemoteHost[id].InMessageBuffer[0].buf,
                        RemoteHost[id].bufsize);
                }

                // Next buffer size
                RemoteHost[id].bufsize = DataMsg->size;

                LogString("Going to free buffer memory
                        (datasize) datasize: %d", DataMsg->size);

                // Remove the processed message
                for(int i = 0;  i < RemoteHost[id].InMessages; i++)
                {
                    memcpy(&RemoteHost[id].InMessageBuffer[i],
                        &RemoteHost[id].InMessageBuffer[i+1],
                        sizeof(MessageBuffer_t));
                }

                RemoteHost[id].InMessages--;

                LogString("-------- %d InMessages: %d", id,
                        RemoteHost[id].InMessages);

                break;
            }

            RemoteHost[id].InMessageBuffer[0].processing = FALSE;
        }
    }
```

As in the earlier version of the ProcessMessages function, we need to keep track of what type of message to expect next. At the very beginning of the function we determine if the next message is supposed to be a Datasize message, and then set the buffer size to match the size of a Datasize message:

```
// Next message is datasize?
if(RemoteHost[id].messageCounter == 0)
{
    RemoteHost[id].bufsize = sizeof(NETMSGDATA_DATASIZE);
}
```

Next we read the data to the buffer using the buffer size that was defined earlier by the expectation of what message will be received next.

```
// Read data to buffer
if(ReadToBuffer(RemoteHost[id].socket, RemoteHost[id].bufsize, 0))
{
    ...
}
```

Because we want to check the type of the first message in the buffer, we cast a generic message pointer to it:

```
// Cast a pointer to the first message in the buffer
Msg = (NETMSG_GENERIC *) RemoteHost[id].InMessageBuffer[0].buf;
if(Msg == NULL) return;
```

We need to determine if the message we received is a Datasize message, so we check the type of each received message here. If the message is a Datasize message, we process it immediately.

```
// Check the type of the message
switch(Msg->type)
{
// Datasize message
case NETMSG_DATASIZE:
        ...
}
```

It is possible that sometimes we miss a message, which leads us to a situation where we are expecting the wrong type of message. Here we check if the message we received really is a Datasize message by looking at the size of the message. If it is not, we record the message to catch up with the messages.

```
// Check if the buffer size does not match
// the datasize message size
if(RemoteHost[id].bufsize != sizeof(NETMSGDATA_DATASIZE))
{
    LogString("Got datasize with wrong bufsize. Recovering");

    // Record message
    RemoteHost[id].RecordMessage();
}
```

Then we check if the local host is a server, and if it is, we check if the Datasize message is to be sent to all hosts. If yes, we resend the data to all.

```
// Check if we should resend NETID_ALL message.
// Only server can do this.
if( (localId == NETID_SERVER) && (Msg->toId == NETID_ALL) )
{
    LogString("Before calling Write (all, datasize),
        bufsize: %d", RemoteHost[id].bufsize);
```

```
        Write(NETID_ALL, RemoteHost[id].InMessageBuffer[0].buf,
            RemoteHost[id].bufsize);
    }
```

We get the size of the next incoming message from the data of the Datasize message:

```
// Next buffer size
RemoteHost[id].bufsize = DataMsg->size;
```

After we have processed the Datasize message, we must remove it from the buffer so it is not processed anymore. First, we copy all the messages in the buffer one position forward and decrease the buffer counter:

```
// Remove the processed message
for(int i = 0;  i < RemoteHost[id].InMessages; i++)
{
    memcpy(&RemoteHost[id].InMessageBuffer[i],
        &RemoteHost[id].InMessageBuffer[i+1],
        sizeof(MessageBuffer_t));
}

RemoteHost[id].InMessages--;
```

ProcessMessages Function

This function processes the message data from the messages in the buffer:

```
void NET_Socket::ProcessMessages(int id)
{
    // If no messages in the buffer, return
    if(RemoteHost[id].InMessages < 1)
        return;

    // If the message is being processed already, return
    if(InMessageBuffer[0].processing == TRUE)
        return;

    LogString("!!! Going to process buffer !!!");

    // Mark that this message is being processed
    InMessageBuffer[0].processing = TRUE;

    NETMSG_GENERIC *Msg;

    // Message size
    int bufsize = RemoteHost[id].InMessageBuffer[0].count;

    // Cast a message pointer
```

```
Msg = (NETMSG_GENERIC *) InMessageBuffer[0].buf;

// Make sure this is not a Datasize message
if(Msg->type == NETMSG_DATASIZE)
{
    RemoteHost[id].InMessageBuffer[0].processing = FALSE;
    return;
}

// Check if we should resend NETID_ALL message.
// Only server can do this.
if( (localId == NETID_SERVER) && (Msg->toId == NETID_ALL) )
{
    Write(NETID_ALL, RemoteHost[id].InMessageBuffer[0].buf,
        bufsize);
    goto freeBuffer;
}

// Check message type
switch(Msg->type)
{
// Close connection
case NETMSG_CLOSE_CONNECTION:
    LogString("Got NETMSG_CLOSE_CONNECTION message");
    CloseConnection(Msg->fromId, 0);
    break;

// User message
default:
    LogString("Going to run NET_HandleMessages()");
    NET_HandleMessages(Msg);
    break;
}

freeBuffer:

    LogString("Going to free buffer memory");

    // Mark that the message is not being processed
    RemoteHost[id].InMessageBuffer[0].processing = FALSE;

    // Remove processed message
    for(int i = 0;  i < RemoteHost[id].InMessages; i++)
    {
        memcpy(&RemoteHost[id].InMessageBuffer[i],
            &RemoteHost[id].InMessageBuffer[i+1],
            sizeof(MessageBuffer_t));
```

```
        }

        RemoteHost[id].InMessages--;

        LogString("-------- InMessages: %d",
            RemoteHost[id].InMessages);
        LogString("Message handling ends");
    }
```

Buffered Function Calls

There are two functions that need to be modified so the buffered message system works correctly. One function is WinHandleEvents, the function that handles the messages on Windows. The other is NET_UnixIOThreadFunc, the Unix function that also handles messages.

WinHandleEvents Function (Win32)

The following code listing shows the WinHandleEvents function:

```
int NET_Socket::WinHandleEvents(int id, LPWSANETWORKEVENTS NetworkEvents)
{
    if(NetworkEvents->lNetworkEvents & FD_READ)
    {
        // An FD_READ event has occurred
        // on the connected socket
        if(NetworkEvents->iErrorCode[FD_READ_BIT] ==
            WSAENETDOWN)
        {
            LogString("ERROR: WSAENETDOWN at WinHandleEvents");

            // There's an error
            return NET_ERROR;
        }
        else
        {
            // Read data off the socket
            ProcessMessageBuffer(id);

            return NET_OK;
        }
    }

    return NET_OK;
}
```

Platform-Dependent Functions

The netLib.h header file declares four prototypes for platform-dependent functions as shown in the following piece of code. One of them we have already seen, the NET_WinIOThreadFunc function. As you can see, we have used #ifdefs to create platform-independent code. Now we can compile the code on Windows and Unix without any modifications.

```
// Platform-dependent function prototypes
#ifdef WIN32
    void NET_WinIOThreadFunc(void *ParamPtr);
    void NET_WinUDPServerIOThreadFunc(void *ParamPtr);
#else
    void *NET_UnixIOThreadFunc(void *ParamPtr);
    void *NET_UnixUDPServerIOThreadFunc(void *ParamPtr);
#endif
```

So we need four platform/protocol-dependent functions in the library:

- NET_WinIOThreadFunc — Windows I/O thread function
- NET_WinUDPServerIOThreadFunc — Windows UDP server I/O thread function
- NET_UnixIOThreadFunc — Unix I/O thread function
- NET_UnixUDPServerIOThreadFunc — Unix UDP server I/O thread function

NET_WinIOThreadFunc (Win32)

We have already examined this function earlier in this tutorial, but we make some changes to it now:

```
void NET_WinIOThreadFunc(void *ParamPtr)
{
    DWORD waitStatus;

    // Copy the parameter info into more easy to use variables
    NET_Socket *netSock =
        ((threadParam_t *) ParamPtr)->netParamSocket;
    int id = ((threadParam_t *) ParamPtr)->id;

    if(netSock == NULL)
        return;

    WSAEVENT EventArray[1];

    // Fill EventArray with SocketInputEvent
    EventArray[0] = netSock->RemoteHost[id].SocketInputEvent;
```

LIVERPOOL
JOHN MOORES UNIVERSITY
AVRIL ROBARTS LRC
TEL. 0151 231 4022

```
LogString("------ Entering Windows IO thread loop ------");

// Set the thread flag up to mark that the thread is running
netSock->RemoteHost[id].thread = 1;

// Keep thread running as long as the remote host is online
while(netSock->RemoteHost[id].online)
{
    // Wait for an event
    waitStatus = WSAWaitForMultipleEvents(1, EventArray,
        FALSE, NET_IOTIMEOUT, FALSE);

    // Process messages in the buffer
    netSock->ProcessMessages(id);

    switch(waitStatus)
    {
    case WSA_WAIT_FAILED:
        // A fatal error
        break;

    case WAIT_IO_COMPLETION:
        // Keep looping
        continue;

    case WSA_WAIT_TIMEOUT:
        // Timeout elapsed
        continue;

    // Input
    case WSA_WAIT_EVENT_0:
        LogString("Input event (id: %d)", id);

        if(netSock->HandleSocketInputEvent(id) == NET_OK)
        {
            continue;
        }
        else
        {
            LogString("HandleSocketInputEvent error");

            netSock->RemoteHost[id].online = 0;
            break;
        }

    default:
        continue;
```

```
        }

        break;
    }

    // Set the thread flag down to mark
    // that the thread is not running
    netSock->RemoteHost[id].thread = 0;

    // Thread is ending because the
    // connection was closed or an error occurred
    LogString("------ Exiting Windows IO thread loop ------");
    return;
}
```

The only change we have made to this function is that we have added the following piece of code to process the messages in the message buffer. This function is called every time the function loops, so the buffer is monitored if there is anything to process. If the buffer is empty, ProcessMessages returns immediately, as we will see later in this tutorial.

```
// Process messages in the buffer
netSock->ProcessMessages(id);
```

NET_WinUDPServerIOThreadFunc (Win32)

The following function is a very important part of the network library's knocking system. This function is a thread routine function that polls for the knock from the client, and acts accordingly when it happens. After that, this thread is closed and a new thread for the client is started.

```
void NET_WinUDPServerIOThreadFunc(void *ptr)
{
    struct sockaddr_in clientAddr;
    socklen_t clientLen = sizeof(clientAddr);

    // Define the buffer size
    int bufsize = sizeof(NETMSG_GENERIC);

    // Allocate memory for receive buffer
    char *recvbuf = (char *) malloc(NET_BUFFSIZE);

    // Cast a NET_Socket pointer
    NET_Socket *netSock = (NET_Socket *) ptr;

    // Create the socket input event handle
    HANDLE SocketInputEvent =
```

```
            CreateEvent(NULL, FALSE, FALSE, NULL);

    // Monitor incoming network events
    WSAEventSelect(netSock->listenSocket, SocketInputEvent,
        FD_READ);

    WSAEVENT EventArray[1];
    EventArray[0] = SocketInputEvent;

    NETMSG_GENERIC *Msg;

    LogString("Entering knock listening thread loop");

    int ok = 0;

    // Loop to wait for knock message
    while(!ok)
    {
        int waitStatus = WSAWaitForMultipleEvents(1, EventArray,
            FALSE, WSA_INFINITE, FALSE);

        switch(waitStatus)
        {

        case WSA_WAIT_FAILED:
            // A fatal error
            return;

        case WAIT_IO_COMPLETION:
            // Continue to loop
            continue;

        case WSA_WAIT_EVENT_0:
            // Incoming network event, break up to continue
            break;

        default:
            continue;
        }

        memset((char *) recvbuf, 0, sizeof(char));

        // Read incoming data
        if(netSock->ReadFrom(netSock->listenSocket, recvbuf,
            bufsize, (struct sockaddr *) &clientAddr,
            &clientLen, 1))
        {
```

```
Msg = (NETMSG_GENERIC *) recvbuf;

switch(Msg->type)
{
// Knock message
case NETMSG_KNOCK:
    LogString("socket %d, clientLen %d
        knocking...", netSock->listenSocket,
        clientLen);

    char *string;
    string = inet_ntoa(clientAddr.sin_addr);

    LogString("Socket %d, addrLen %d, ip %s,
        port %d knocking", netSock->listenSocket,
        sizeof(clientAddr),      string,
        ntohs(clientAddr.sin_port));

    // Copy the address information to the
    // remote host structure
    netSock->RemoteHost[netSock->
        GetNextFreeHostIndex()].inetSockAddr = clientAddr;
    netSock->RemoteHost[netSock->
        GetNextFreeHostIndex()].addrLen = clientLen;

    // Close the listening socket
    closesocket(netSock->listenSocket);

    // Create a new socket
    SOCKET newSocket = socket(AF_INET,
        SOCK_DGRAM, 0);

    struct sockaddr_in inetNewServAddr;

    // Fill address information
    memset((char *) &inetNewServAddr, 0,
        sizeof(inetNewServAddr));

    inetNewServAddr.sin_family = AF_INET;
    inetNewServAddr.sin_port = htons(0);
    inetNewServAddr.sin_addr.s_addr =
        htonl(INADDR_ANY);

    // Bind the new socket
    int error = bind(newSocket,
        (struct sockaddr *) &inetNewServAddr,
        sizeof(inetNewServAddr));
```

TUTORIAL 2

```
string =
    inet_ntoa(netSock->RemoteHost[netSock->
    GetNextFreeHostIndex()].inetSockAddr.sin_addr);

struct sockaddr_in newAddr;
socklen_t newLen = sizeof(newAddr);

// Get the new local address
getsockname(newSocket,
    (struct sockaddr *) &newAddr, &newLen);

LogString("Creating child to serve socket %d,
    addrLen %d, ip %s, port %d", newSocket,
    sizeof(netSock->RemoteHost[netSock->
    GetNextFreeHostIndex()].inetSockAddr),
    string, ntohs(newAddr.sin_port));

if(error == -1)
{
    LogString("ERROR: bind() failed at
        NET_WinUDPServerIOThreadFunc");
    return;
}

// Monitor incoming network events
WSAEventSelect(newSocket,
    netSock->RemoteHost[netSock->
    GetNextFreeHostIndex()].SocketInputEvent,
    FD_READ);

// Copy the new socket to the remote host
netSock->RemoteHost[netSock->
GetNextFreeHostIndex()].socket = newSocket;

// Give local ID number to client
int idError = netSock->GiveLocalIdUDP(netSock->
RemoteHost[netSock->GetNextFreeHostIndex()].inetSockAddr);

if(idError)
{
    return;
}

// Fill thread parameters
winParam.id = netSock->GetNextFreeHostIndex();
winParam.netParamSocket = netSock;
```

```
                    DWORD threadId;

                    // Create the thread
                    HANDLE threadHandle = CreateThread(NULL, 0,
                        (LPTHREAD_START_ROUTINE)
                        NET_WinIOThreadFunc,
                        (void *) &winParam, 0, &threadId);

                    ok = 1;

                    break;
                }
            }
        }

        LogString("Exiting knock listening thread loop");

        free(recvbuf);
        recvbuf = NULL;

        // Start the server again
        netSock->CreateServer(netSock->Port, NET_UDP);
    }
```

First, we declare some variables, which will be used in the function. Because clientLen is a value-result variable, it must be set to the size of the address structure in the beginning. The buffer size variable is set to the size of a generic message because we are expecting only a knock message here. A knock message is a normal generic message because all it does is notify the server of a new client (no extra data is required). Then we cast a NET_Socket pointer from the parameter. And because this is a Win32 function, we need to have the socket input event handle to know when there are incoming events.

```
struct sockaddr_in clientAddr;
socklen_t clientLen = sizeof(clientAddr);

// Define the buffer size
int bufsize = sizeof(NETMSG_GENERIC);

// Allocate memory for receive buffer
char *recvbuf = (char *) malloc(NET_BUFFSIZE);

// Cast a NET_Socket pointer
NET_Socket *netSock = (NET_Socket *) ptr;

// Create the socket input event handle
HANDLE SocketInputEvent = CreateEvent(NULL, FALSE, FALSE, NULL);
```

We make the socket input event notify us of all network events as shown in the following piece of code. Then we put the input event handle into the event array.

```
// Monitor for all network events
WSAEventSelect(netSock->listenSocket, SocketInputEvent,
    FD_READ);

WSAEVENT EventArray[1];
EventArray[0] = SocketInputEvent;
```

The next thing we do is start a loop to wait for the knock message. We will loop here as long as any client is sending the knock message.

```
while(!ok)
{
    ...
}
```

In the beginning of the loop we start to wait for incoming events by monitoring the event array (which holds only the input event handle):

```
int waitStatus = WSAWaitForMultipleEvents(1, EventArray, FALSE, NET_IOTIMEOUT,
FALSE);
```

Then we process the events that occur. This is an "artificial" loop because we will not move on in the function until we receive any input event. If this happens, the switch statement stops instead of continuing to loop again and the function continues running.

```
switch(waitStatus)
{

case WSA_WAIT_FAILED:
    // A fatal error
    return;

case WAIT_IO_COMPLETION:
    // Continue to loop
    continue;

case WSA_WAIT_EVENT_0:
    // Incoming network event, break up to continue
    break;

default:
    continue;
}
```

We read the incoming data immediately after we know that there is an incoming event. We use the listening socket and we store the client's address information in this non-blocking call to our ReadFrom function:

```
// Read incoming data
if(netSock->ReadFrom(netSock->listenSocket, recvbuf,
    bufsize, (struct sockaddr *) &clientAddr,
    &clientLen, 1))
{
    ...
}
```

Next, we check what we received. We cast a generic message pointer to the receive buffer and check the type of the message. In this case we are waiting for only a knock message, but we need to make sure that the message really is that. If it is not, nothing happens.

```
Msg = (NETMSG_GENERIC *) recvbuf;

switch(Msg->type)
{
    ...
}
```

We copy the client's address information (which we got from ReadFrom) to the remote host structure. The length of the address is also copied.

```
// Copy the address information to the
// remote host structure
netSock->RemoteHost[netSock->GetNextFreeHostIndex()].inetSockAddr
    = clientAddr;
netSock->RemoteHost[netSock->GetNextFreeHostIndex()].addrLen =
    clientLen;
```

Now we can close the listening socket and create a new socket for the connection:

```
// Close the listening socket
closesocket(netSock->listenSocket);

// Create a new socket
SOCKET newSocket = socket(AF_INET, SOCK_DGRAM, 0);
```

Each new child process has its own port on the server, so we fill the new server address structure with "unknown" information. An ephemeral port and an InAddr_Any IP address is put into the structure, so a call to Bind will fill the information for us.

```
struct sockaddr_in inetNewServAddr;
```

```
// Fill address information
memset((char *) &inetNewServAddr, 0, sizeof(inetNewServAddr));

inetNewServAddr.sin_family = AF_INET;
inetNewServAddr.sin_port = htons(0);
inetNewServAddr.sin_addr.s_addr = htonl(INADDR_ANY);
```

Then, we bind the socket to the "unknown" address information, and this information is filled in for us. Then we retrieve the new address information of the service to the NewAddr structure, and make sure the call to Bind was successful.

```
// Bind the new socket
int error = bind(newSocket, (struct sockaddr *) &inetNewServAddr,
sizeof(inetNewServAddr));

…

// Get the new local address
getsockname(newSocket, (struct sockaddr *) &newAddr, &newLen);

…

if(error == -1)
{
    LogString("ERROR: bind() failed at
        NET_WinUDPServerIOThreadFunc");
    return;
}
```

Next, we start to handle the new socket as the remote host's own socket. First, we make WinSock monitor all the network events on it and inform them of the socket input event handle. After that, we copy the new socket descriptor to the remote host structure.

```
// Monitor all incoming events
WSAEventSelect(newSocket,
netSock->RemoteHost[netSock->GetNextFreeHostIndex()].SocketInputEvent, FD_READ);

// Copy the new socket to the remote host
netSock->RemoteHost[netSock->GetNextFreeHostIndex()].socket = newSocket;
```

Now that we have the host information in the remote host structure, we can send the local ID number to the remote host. We check that the call to GiveLocal-IdUDP was successful before we move on:

```
// Give local ID number to client
int idError = netSock->GiveLocalIdUDP(netSock->
RemoteHost[netSock->GetNextFreeHostIndex()].inetSockAddr);
```

```
if(idError)
{
    return;
}
```

Now everything is ready for the input/output thread to be started. The connection is set up and the remote host (client) has the local ID number. We start the thread, passing the parameters from the parameter structure that we first fill with the correct information. The ID number is the next free host index value (this new client), and the NET_Socket pointer is the pointer we used throughout the function.

```
// Fill thread parameters
winParam.id = netSock->GetNextFreeHostIndex();
winParam.netParamSocket = netSock;

DWORD threadId;

// Create the thread
HANDLE threadHandle = CreateThread(NULL, 0,
    (LPTHREAD_START_ROUTINE)
    NET_WinIOThreadFunc,
    (void *) &winParam, 0, &threadId);
```

Finally, we end the knock loop by setting the ok flag up. This also means that the UDP knock thread ends.

```
ok = 1;
```

We must restart the server to be able to connect with more clients. We start the server in the well-known port, so the clients know where to connect to.

```
// Start the server again
netSock->CreateServer(netSock->Port, NET_UDP);
```

NET_UnixIOThreadFunc (Unix)

NET_UnixIOThreadFunc is a Unix version of the input/output function we have already examined for Windows. This function notices when there are incoming events and starts processing them then.

```
void *NET_UnixIOThreadFunc(void *ParamPtr)
{
    // Copy the parameter info into more easy to use variables
    NET_Socket *netSock =
        ((threadParam_t *) ParamPtr)->netParamSocket;
    int id = ((threadParam_t *) ParamPtr)->id;

    int maxfd = netSock->RemoteHost[id].socket;
```

```
    fd_set allset;

    // Reset socket event system
    FD_ZERO(&allset);
    FD_SET(netSock->RemoteHost[id].socket, &allset);

    LogString("---- Entering Unix IO thread loop ----");

    // Set the thread flag up to mark that the thread is running
    netSock->RemoteHost[id].thread = 1;

    // Keep thread running as long as the remote host is online
    while(netSock->RemoteHost[id].online)
    {
        // Monitor for incoming events
        fd_set reading = allset;
        int nready = select(maxfd + 1, &reading,
            NULL, NULL, NULL);

        // Check if there is an incoming event
        if(nready)
        {
            // Read data to the buffer
            netSock->ProcessMessageBuffer(id);

            // If message buffer is not empty,
            // process the messages in the buffer
            if(netSock->RemoteHost[id].InMessages)
            {
                LogString("Going to process buffer !!!!");
                netSock->ProcessMessages(id);
            }
        }
    }

    // Set the thread flag down to mark
    // that the thread is not running
    netSock->RemoteHost[id].thread = 0;

    // Thread is ending because the connection
    // was closed or an error occurred
    LogString("---- Exiting Unix IO thread loop ----");
    return (NULL);
}
```

First, we copy the parameters into variables that are easier to use. We cast a new pointer to the NET_Socket and copy the ID number into integer id.

```
// Copy the parameter info into more easy to use variables
NET_Socket *netSock =
        ((threadParam_t *) ParamPtr)->netParamSocket;
int id = ((threadParam_t *) ParamPtr)->id;
```

We set up the event monitoring by first creating some variables and resetting them, as shown in the following code:

```
int maxfd = netSock->RemoteHost[id].socket;
fd_set allset;

// Reset socket event system
FD_ZERO(&allset);
FD_SET(netSock->RemoteHost[id].socket, &allset);
```

Like in the Windows version, we need to set the remote host's thread flag up here. This indicates that the thread is running. We need this information elsewhere in the library.

```
// Set the thread flag up to mark that the thread is running
netSock->RemoteHost[id].thread = 1;
```

We loop the thread as long as the remote host online flag is up:

```
// Keep thread running as long as the remote host is online
while(netSock->RemoteHost[id].online)
{
    ...
}
```

Now we start monitoring for incoming events by using the socket function Select. It will return a value larger than zero if there is an incoming event. The return value of Select tells us how many sockets have incoming data, and therefore, if it is larger than zero, we know there is data to read.

```
// Monitor for incoming events
fd_set reading = allset;
int nready = select(maxfd + 1, &reading, NULL, NULL, NULL);
```

To see if there is an incoming event, we check to see if the Select function return value is larger than zero (there is a socket with incoming data). If it is, we read the data to the input buffer and then process the buffer right away. This means that the buffer is merely a temporary storage for the data on our Unix version of the network library. On Windows, the buffer actually works by adding in more than one message at a time. Because of system differences, it is much easier to make the buffer work like this on Unix.

```
// Check if there is an incoming event
if(nready)
```

```
    {
        // Read data to the buffer
        netSock->ProcessMessageBuffer(id);

        // If message buffer is not empty,
        // process the messages in the buffer
        if(netSock->RemoteHost[id].InMessages)
        {
            LogString("Going to process buffer !!!!");
            netSock->ProcessMessages(id);
        }
    }
}
```

When the thread loop terminates, we set the thread flag of the remote host down to keep the system aware of the situation:

```
// Set the thread flag down to mark
// that the thread is not running
netSock->RemoteHost[id].thread = 0;
```

NET_UnixUDPServerIOThreadFunc (Unix)

This is a Unix version of the UDP server thread function. This function polls the knock message to be received from any client and then creates a child process for that client. This function is similar to NET_WinUDPServerIOThreadFunc, but has some differences.

```
void *NET_UnixUDPServerIOThreadFunc(void *ptr)
{
    struct sockaddr_in clientAddr;
    socklen_t clientLen = sizeof(clientAddr);

    // Define the buffer size
    int bufsize = sizeof(NETMSG_GENERIC);

    // Allocate memory for receive buffer
    char *recvbuf = (char *) malloc(NET_BUFFSIZE);

    // Cast a NET_Socket pointer
    NET_Socket *netSock = (NET_Socket *) ptr;

    NETMSG_GENERIC *Msg;

    LogString("Entering knock listening thread loop");

    int ok = 0;

    // Loop to wait for knock message
```

```
while(!ok)
{
    memset((char *) recvbuf, 0, sizeof(char));

    // Set the socket non-blocking
    u_long set = 0;
    ioctl(netSock->listenSocket, FIONBIO, &set);

    // Read incoming data
    if(netSock->ReadFrom(netSock->listenSocket,
        recvbuf, bufsize, (struct sockaddr *) &clientAddr,
        &clientLen, 1))
    {
        Msg = (NETMSG_GENERIC *) recvbuf;

        switch(Msg->type)
        {
        // Knock message
        case NETMSG_KNOCK:
            LogString("socket %d,
                clientLen %d knocking...",
                netSock->listenSocket, clientLen);

            char *string;
            string = inet_ntoa(clientAddr.sin_addr);

            LogString("Socket %d, addrLen %d,
                ip %s, port %d knocking",
                netSock->listenSocket,
                sizeof(clientAddr),
                string, ntohs(clientAddr.sin_port));

            // Copy the address information to the
            // remote host structure
            netSock->RemoteHost[netSock->
            GetNextFreeHostIndex()].inetSockAddr = clientAddr;
            netSock->RemoteHost[netSock->
            GetNextFreeHostIndex()].addrLen = clientLen;

            // Close the listening socket
            close(netSock->listenSocket);

            // Create a new socket
            SOCKET newSocket = socket(AF_INET,
                SOCK_DGRAM, 0);

            struct sockaddr_in inetNewServAddr;
```

```
// Fill address information
memset((char *) &inetNewServAddr,
    0, sizeof(inetNewServAddr));
inetNewServAddr.sin_family = AF_INET;
inetNewServAddr.sin_port = htons(0);
inetNewServAddr.sin_addr.s_addr = htonl(INADDR_ANY);

// Bind the new socket
int error = bind(newSocket,
    (struct sockaddr *) &inetNewServAddr,
    sizeof(inetNewServAddr));

if(error == -1)
{
    LogString("ERROR: bind() failed at
        NET_UnixUDPServerIOThreadFunc");
}

string = inet_ntoa(netSock->RemoteHost[netSock->
GetNextFreeHostIndex()].inetSockAddr.sin_addr);

struct sockaddr_in newAddr;
socklen_t newLen = sizeof(newAddr);

// Get the new local address
getsockname(newSocket,
    (struct sockaddr *) &newAddr, &newLen);

LogString("Creating child to serve socket %d,
    addrLen %d, ip %s, port %d", newSocket,
    sizeof(netSock->RemoteHost[netSock->
    GetNextFreeHostIndex()].inetSockAddr),
    string, ntohs(newAddr.sin_port));

netSock->RemoteHost[netSock->
GetNextFreeHostIndex()].socket = newSocket;

// Give local ID number to client
int idError = netSock->GiveLocalIdUDP(netSock->
RemoteHost[netSock->GetNextFreeHostIndex()].inetSockAddr);

if(idError)
{
    return 0;
}
```

```
                // Fill thread parameters
                unixParam.id= netSock->GetNextFreeHostIndex();
                unixParam.netParamSocket      = netSock;

                // Create the thread
                pthread_t threadId;
                pthread_create(&threadId, NULL,
                    NET_UnixIOThreadFunc,
                    (void *) &unixParam);

                ok = 1;

                break;
            }
        }
    }

    LogString("Exiting knock listening thread loop");

    free(recvbuf);
    recvbuf = NULL;

    // Start the server again
    netSock->CreateServer(netSock->Port, NET_UDP);

    return 0;
}
```

The first thing that is different in the Unix version from the Windows version is
that the loop where we wait for the knock message loops all the time, reading any
incoming data:

```
// Loop to wait for knock message
while(!ok)
{
    …
}
```

Before we read anything from the socket, we set it non-blocking so that the
ReadFrom call returns even if there is nothing incoming:

```
// Set the socket non-blocking
u_long set = 0;
ioctl(netSock->listenSocket, FIONBIO, &set);
```

The last thing that is slightly different from the Windows version is creating the
input/output thread, as shown in the following code. We fill in the parameters as
we do on the Windows version, but we create the thread using Unix's own thread

creation functions (as we create the thread with Window's own functions on the Windows version):

```
// Fill thread parameters
unixParam.id = netSock->GetNextFreeHostIndex();
unixParam.netParamSocket = netSock;

// Create the thread
pthread_t threadId;
pthread_create(&threadId, NULL, NET_UnixIOThreadFunc, (void *) &unixParam);
```

Give Local ID Number

We have two functions in the complete library to send the local ID number to the new client. There is a version for each of the protocols.

GiveLocalIdTCP Function

We have already explained this function, so we will not explain it here.

```
int NET_Socket::GiveLocalIdTCP(void)
{
    NETMSG_GENERIC idMsg;

    idMsg.type      = NETMSG_GIVEID;
    idMsg.toId      = NextFreeHostIndex;
    idMsg.fromId    = NETID_SERVER;

    LogString("Sending localId number.. to:%d",
        NextFreeHostIndex);

    char *string;
    string =
        inet_ntoa(RemoteHost[NextFreeHostIndex].inetSockAddr.sin_addr);

    LogString("Writing localId (TCP) to socket %d,
        addrLen %d ip %s", RemoteHost[NextFreeHostIndex].socket,
        RemoteHost[NextFreeHostIndex].addrLen, string);

    Write(NextFreeHostIndex, (char *) &idMsg,
        sizeof(NETMSG_GENERIC));

    LogString("localId number sent...");

    return 0;
}
```

GiveLocalIdUDP Function

The following function is used with UDP:

```cpp
int NET_Socket::GiveLocalIdUDP(sockaddr_in clientAddr)
{
    char *buf;
    buf = (char *) calloc(NET_BUFFSIZE, sizeof(char));

    NETMSG_CONF *Msg;

    // Note that FindNextFreeHostIndex()
    // is run when creating the UDP server

    // Fill remote host info from the parameter
    RemoteHost[NextFreeHostIndex].inetSockAddr = clientAddr;
    RemoteHost[NextFreeHostIndex].addrLen = sizeof(clientAddr);
    RemoteHosts++;

    NETMSG_GENERIC idMsg;

    // Fill message data
    idMsg.type    = NETMSG_GIVEID;
    idMsg.toId    = NextFreeHostIndex;
    idMsg.fromId  = NETID_SERVER;

    char *string;
    string =
        inet_ntoa(RemoteHost[NextFreeHostIndex].inetSockAddr.sin_addr);

    LogString("Writing localId %d (UDP) to socket %d,
        addrLen %d, ip %s, port %d", NextFreeHostIndex,
        RemoteHost[NextFreeHostIndex].socket,
        RemoteHost[NextFreeHostIndex].addrLen, string,
        ntohs(RemoteHost[NextFreeHostIndex].inetSockAddr.sin_port));

    // Send data
    WriteTo(RemoteHost[NextFreeHostIndex].socket,
        (char *) &idMsg, sizeof(NETMSGDATA_DATASIZE),
        (struct sockaddr *) &clientAddr, sizeof(clientAddr));

    int counter = 0;

    // Loop while the remote host is marked offline
    while(RemoteHost[NextFreeHostIndex].online == 0)
    {
        // Check if we've been waiting for too long
```

```
        if(counter == 100000)
        {
            RemoteHosts--;
            return 1;
        }

        // Read confirmation data
        if(ReadFrom(RemoteHost[NextFreeHostIndex].socket,
            buf, sizeof(NETMSG_CONF), (struct sockaddr *)
            &RemoteHost[NextFreeHostIndex].inetSockAddr,
            &RemoteHost[NextFreeHostIndex].addrLen, 1))
        {
            Msg = (NETMSG_CONF *) buf;

            // If the confirmation matches the ID number
            // everything is ok
            if(Msg->conf == NextFreeHostIndex)
            {
                RemoteHost[NextFreeHostIndex].online = 1;

                LogString("Got confirmation of localId
                    (Msg->conf: %d)", Msg->conf);
            }
        }
    }

    return 0;
}
```

We fill in the remote host address info from the parameter we pass to the function. That is the client's address, which will receive the ID number. Plus, we increase the amount of remote hosts on the local host.

```
// Fill remote host info from the parameter
RemoteHost[NextFreeHostIndex].inetSockAddr = clientAddr;
RemoteHost[NextFreeHostIndex].addrLen = sizeof(clientAddr);
RemoteHosts++;
```

Then we fill the actual message data. We set the message type to NETMSG_GiveID, because we are giving an ID number. The destination host ID is the next free host index and the source host ID is the local ID number, which is NETID_Server in this case. There is no need for any extra data, because the remote host can get the local ID number from the destination ID number (toId).

```
NETMSG_GENERIC idMsg;

// Fill message data
```

```
idMsg.type    = NETMSG_GIVEID;
idMsg.toId    = NextFreeHostIndex;
idMsg.fromId  = NETID_SERVER;
```

After that we just send the data using the WriteTo function. We send the data to the address we passed in as a parameter to the GiveLocalIdUDP function:

```
// Send data
WriteTo(RemoteHost[NextFreeHostIndex].socket, (char *) &idMsg,
    sizeof(NETMSGDATA_DATASIZE), (struct sockaddr *) &clientAddr, sizeof(clientAddr));
```

We wait and loop here as long as the remote host is marked offline or the counter has reached its limit. If the counter reaches the limit, we decrease the amount of remote hosts, because we increased it earlier in this function.

```
int counter = 0;

// Loop while the remote host is marked offline
while(RemoteHost[NextFreeHostIndex].online == 0)
{
    // Check if we've been waiting for too long
    if(counter == 100000)
    {
        RemoteHosts--;
        return 1;
    }

    ...

}
```

Each time we loop, we try to read the confirmation from the remote host. This must be a non-blocking call so the ReadFrom function returns even if there is nothing to read.

```
// Read confirmation data
if(ReadFrom(RemoteHost[NextFreeHostIndex].socket, buf,
    sizeof(NETMSG_CONF), (struct sockaddr *)
    &RemoteHost[NextFreeHostIndex].inetSockAddr,
    &RemoteHost[NextFreeHostIndex].addrLen, 1))
{

    ...

}
```

When we do receive something from the client, we ensure that the data is correct. We check that the confirmation number we received equals the local ID number we sent to the client. If it does, we know that the client received the ID number correctly. Then, we can set the remote host's online flag up.

```
// If the confirmation matches the ID number
// everything is ok
if(Msg->conf == NextFreeHostIndex)
{
     RemoteHost[NextFreeHostIndex].online = 1;

     LogString("Got confirmation of localId
           (Msg->conf: %d)", Msg->conf);
}
```

Creating a Server

Now let's see how we create the servers using platform- and protocol-independent code. We define the protocol to use in the call to the CreateServer function, and everything is set up so that everything else works using that protocol. So, basically, we do not have to worry about the protocol anymore after we have chosen it in the call to the following function.

CreateServer Function

The following function is the main level of this multi-level function. This is the function that the user will call when a server is created. This is the only function that must be called. As you can see in the following code, the port and the protocol must be passed in as a parameter to this function. The protocol is either NET_TCP or NET_UDP.

```
int NET_Socket::CreateServer(int port, int Protocol)
{
     LogString("CreateServer()");

     int ret = 0;

     // Set the local host online and set the local id number
     Port      = port;
     Online    = 1;
     localId   = NETID_SERVER;

#ifdef WIN32
     ret = CreateWinServer(port, Protocol);
#else
     ret = CreateUnixServer(port, Protocol);
#endif

     return ret;
}
```

This part of the function is the only part that has changed from the earlier Windows/TCP-only function (plus the protocol parameter). This wraps the platform-dependent functions to be called depending on what operating system we are compiling the code on.

```
#ifdef WIN32
    ret = CreateWinServer(port, Protocol);
#else
    ret = CreateUnixServer(port, Protocol);
#endif
```

CreateWinServer Function

This function is the Windows version of our server creation function. It now supports both protocols. This is the second level of this multi-level protocol.

```
int NET_Socket::CreateWinServer(int port, int Protocol)
{
    struct sockaddr *servAddr;
    struct sockaddr_in *inetServAddr;
    SOCKET sock;

    LogString("CreateWinServer()");

    // Check which protocol we are using
    switch(Protocol)
    {
    case NET_TCP:
        // Create TCP socket
        sock = socket(AF_INET, SOCK_STREAM, 0);
        break;

    case NET_UDP:
        // Create UDP socket
        sock = socket(AF_INET, SOCK_DGRAM, 0);
        break;
    }

    if(sock == NET_INVALID_SOCKET)
    {
        LogString("ERROR: socket() failed at
            CreateWinServer (sock: %d)", sock);
        return -1;
    }

    // Allocate memory for address structure
    servAddr = (struct sockaddr *) malloc(sizeof(sockaddr));
```

```
if(!servAddr) return -1;

memset((char *) servAddr, 0, sizeof(sockaddr));

// Fill the address structure
servAddr->sa_family    = (u_short) AF_INET;
inetServAddr           = (struct sockaddr_in *) servAddr;
inetServAddr->sin_port = htons((u_short) port);

// Bind address information to the socket
int error = bind(sock, servAddr, sizeof(sockaddr));

if(error == SOCKET_ERROR)
{
    LogString("ERROR: bind() failed at CreateWinServer");
    free(servAddr);
    return -1;
}

char *string;
string = inet_ntoa(inetServAddr->sin_addr);

LogString("Creating server on socket %d,
    addrLen %d, ip %s, port %d",
    sock, sizeof(inetServAddr),
    string, ntohs(inetServAddr->sin_port));

// Free address structure memory
free(servAddr);
servAddr = NULL;

switch(Protocol)
{
case NET_TCP:
    // Will run CreateWinTCPServer
    return CreateTCPServer(sock);
    break;

case NET_UDP:
    // Will run CreateWinUDPServer
    return CreateUDPServer(sock);
    break;
}

    return -1;
}
```

The first change to the TCP-only function is that now we check which protocol to use, and then create the socket accordingly. This is shown in the following piece of code:

```
// Check which protocol we are using
switch(Protocol)
{
case NET_TCP:
    // Create TCP socket
    sock = socket(AF_INET, SOCK_STREAM, 0);
    break;

case NET_UDP:
    // Create UDP socket
    sock = socket(AF_INET, SOCK_DGRAM, 0);
    break;
}
```

The other change that may go unnoticed is the constant for invalid sockets. In the Windows-only version we used the WinSock constant INVALID_SOCKET, but now we use our own constant NET_INVALID_SOCKET. This constant wraps the correct value depending on what platform we are using.

```
if(sock == NET_INVALID_SOCKET)
{
    ...
}
```

Lastly, we call the third-level function of this multi-level function to create the server using the correct protocol:

```
switch(Protocol)
{
case NET_TCP:
    // Will run CreateWinTCPServer
    return CreateTCPServer(sock);
    break;

case NET_UDP:
    // Will run CreateWinUDPServer
    return CreateUDPServer(sock);
    break;
}
```

TUTORIAL 2

CreateUnixServer Function

This is the Unix version of the second-level server creation function. This function works similarly to the Windows version.

```
int NET_Socket::CreateUnixServer(int port, int Protocol)
{
    struct sockaddr_in inetServAddr;
    SOCKET sock;

    LogString("CreateUnixServer()");

    switch(Protocol)
    {
    case NET_TCP:
        sock = socket(AF_INET, SOCK_STREAM, 0);
        break;

    case NET_UDP:
        sock = socket(AF_INET, SOCK_DGRAM, 0);
        break;
    }

    // Fill the address structure.
    memset((char *) &inetServAddr, 0, sizeof(inetServAddr));
    inetServAddr.sin_family = AF_INET;
    inetServAddr.sin_port = htons((u_short) port);
    inetServAddr.sin_addr.s_addr = htonl(INADDR_ANY);

    // Retrieve the IP address string
    char *string;
    string = inet_ntoa(inetServAddr.sin_addr);

    LogString("Creating server on socket %d,
        addrLen %d, ip %s, port %d",
        sock, sizeof(inetServAddr),
        string, ntohs(inetServAddr.sin_port));

    int error = bind(sock, (struct sockaddr *) &inetServAddr,
        sizeof(inetServAddr));

    if(error == -1)
    {
        LogString("ERROR: bind() failed at CreateUnixServer");
        return -1;
    }
```

```
        switch(Protocol)
        {
        case NET_TCP:
            // Will run CreateUnixTCPServer
            return CreateTCPServer(sock);
            break;

        case NET_UDP:
            // Will run CreateUnixUDPServer
            return CreateUDPServer(sock);
            break;
        }

        return -1;
    }
```

CreateTCPServer and CreateUDPServer Functions

These two functions are the third level of the server creation function complex.
They wrap the correct function depending on what platform we are using.

```
    int NET_Socket::CreateTCPServer(SOCKET listenSock)
    {
        LogString("CreateTCPServer()");

#ifdef WIN32
        return CreateWinTCPServer(listenSock);
#else
        return CreateUnixTCPServer(listenSock);
#endif
    }


    int NET_Socket::CreateUDPServer(SOCKET listenSock)
    {
        LogString("CreateUDPServer()");

#ifdef WIN32
        return CreateWinUDPServer(listenSock);
#else
        return CreateUnixUDPServer(listenSock);
#endif
    }
```

CreateWinTCPServer Function

This is a function that we have already explained earlier in this tutorial. The purpose of this function is to create a TCP server.

```
int NET_Socket::CreateWinTCPServer(SOCKET listenSock)
{
    LogString("CreateWinTCPServer()");

    // Set up a Windows message to
    // notify of an incoming connection
    WSAAsyncSelect(listenSock, hWnd_netLib, USMSG_ACCEPT,
        FD_ACCEPT);

    // Start listening for incoming connections
    int error = listen(listenSock, NET_MAX_CONNECTIONS);

    if(error == SOCKET_ERROR)
    {
        LogString("ERROR: listen() error at
            CreateWinTCPServer");
        return -1;
    }

    // Copy socket descriptor to the object
    listenSocket = listenSock;

    return 0;
}
```

CreateUnixTCPServer Function

This function is the Unix version of the final level server creation function. It creates a TCP server that listens for incoming connections.

```
int NET_Socket::CreateUnixTCPServer(SOCKET listenSock)
{
    SOCKET connectSock = NET_INVALID_SOCKET;

    LogString("CreateUnixTCPServer()");

    int error = listen(listenSock, NET_MAX_CONNECTIONS);

    if(error == -1)
    {
        LogString("ERROR: listen() error at
            CreateUnixTCPServer");
        return 1;
```

```
        }

        listenSocket = listenSock;

        pthread_t threadId;

        pthread_create(&threadId, NULL,
            NET_UnixPollAcceptFunc, (void *) this);

        return 0;
    }
```

The only new thing in this function is that it polls for the accept connection function to be called. On Windows the system sends a message to the main window to
tell it that the Accept function should be called, but on Unix we poll for it
constantly.

```
pthread_create(&threadId, NULL,
    NET_UnixPollAcceptFunc, (void *) this);
```

NET_UnixPollAcceptFunc Function

This function polls (waits for) incoming connections. If a connection is incoming,
the accept() function is run. This is a socket function that is required for all TCP
connections.

```
void *NET_UnixPollAcceptFunc(void *ptr)
{
    int maxfd;
    fd_set allset;

    // Cast a pointer
    NET_Socket *netSock = (NET_Socket *) ptr;

    maxfd = netSock->listenSocket;

    // Reset all bits
    FD_ZERO(&allset);
    FD_SET(netSock->listenSocket, &allset);

    // Loop while we are online
    while(netSock->Online)
    {
        fd_set acc = allset;
        int nready = select(maxfd + 1, &acc, NULL, NULL, NULL);

        // Check if we should accept
        if(nready)
```

```
            {
                    netSock->AcceptConnection();
            }
        }

        return 0;
}
```

We reset the socket descriptor's I/O bits before we check if any of them are up:

```
// Reset all bits
FD_ZERO(&allset);
FD_SET(netSock->listenSocket, &allset);
```

We loop the poll function as long as the server is online:

```
// Loop while we are online
while(netSock->Online)
{
    …
}
```

Next, we check to see if there are any sockets with incoming events, and if so, we call the AcceptConnection function:

```
fd_set acc = allset;
int nready = select(maxfd + 1, &acc, NULL, NULL, NULL);

// Check if we should accept
if(nready)
{
    netSock->AcceptConnection();
}
```

CreateWinUDPServer Function

This is a Windows/UDP version of the last level server creation function. It starts the thread to listen to incoming hosts.

```
int NET_Socket::CreateWinUDPServer(SOCKET sock)
{
    LogString("CreateWinUDPServer()");

    listenSocket = sock;

    // Make sure no system message is sent
    WSAAsyncSelect(listenSocket, hWnd_netLib, 0, 0);

    FindNextFreeHostIndex();
```

```
    // Create socket input event and copy the socket
    RemoteHost[NextFreeHostIndex].SocketInputEvent =
        CreateEvent(NULL, FALSE, FALSE, NULL);
    RemoteHost[NextFreeHostIndex].socket = listenSocket;

    // Create the thread
    DWORD threadId;

    HANDLE threadHandle = CreateThread(NULL, 0,
        (LPTHREAD_START_ROUTINE) NET_WinUDPServerIOThreadFunc,
        (void *) this, 0, &threadId);

    return 0;
}
```

We copy the parameter socket to the NET_Socket object by copying it to the listening socket. Now we know that this is the listening socket's descriptor everywhere in the library.

```
    listenSocket = sock;
```

Then we make sure that no system messages are sent to the main window if a network event occurs. This is because we do not need this information.

```
    // Make sure no system message is sent
    WSAAsyncSelect(listenSocket, hWnd_netLib, 0, 0);
```

The remote host structure is kept up to date by creating the socket input event and copying the socket descriptor to it:

```
    // Create socket input event and copy the socket
    RemoteHost[NextFreeHostIndex].SocketInputEvent =
        CreateEvent(NULL, FALSE, FALSE, NULL);
    RemoteHost[NextFreeHostIndex].socket = listenSocket;
```

Then we create the I/O thread that runs the NET_WinUDPServerIOThreadFunc. We explained this function earlier in this tutorial.

```
    // Create the thread
    DWORD threadId;

    HANDLE threadHandle = CreateThread(NULL, 0,
        (LPTHREAD_START_ROUTINE) NET_WinUDPServerIOThreadFunc,
        (void *) this, 0, &threadId);
```

CreateUnixUDPServer Function

This is the Unix version of the last level server creation function.

```
    int NET_Socket::CreateUnixUDPServer(SOCKET sock)
```

```
    {
        LogString("CreateUnixUDPServer()");

        listenSocket = sock;

        FindNextFreeHostIndex();

        // Copy the socket
        RemoteHost[NextFreeHostIndex].socket = listenSocket;

        // Create the thread
        pthread_t threadId;
        pthread_create(&threadId, NULL,
            NET_UnixUDPServerIOThreadFunc, (void *) this);

        return 0;
    }
```

We update the remote host structure like we did on the Windows version, but this time we do not create the socket input event handle, because Unix does not have them.

```
// Copy the socket
RemoteHost[NextFreeHostIndex].socket = listenSocket;
```

And finally, we create the I/O thread as we did in Windows:

```
// Create the thread
pthread_t threadId;
pthread_create(&threadId, NULL,
    NET_UnixUDPServerIOThreadFunc, (void *) this);
```

AcceptConnection Function

When we want to accept a TCP connection, we call the following function. This is the same function we explained earlier, but there are some changes that make this function platform independent. This function is not used with the UDP protocol.

One change in this function is that we use #ifdefs to identify which lines to call on which operating system:

```
void NET_Socket::AcceptConnection(void)
{
    SOCKET connectSock = NET_INVALID_SOCKET;
    struct sockaddr_in clientAddr;
    socklen_t clientLen;

    // Loop as long as the connection has not been accepted
    while(connectSock == NET_INVALID_SOCKET)
```

```
    {
        clientLen = sizeof(clientAddr);
        connectSock = accept(listenSocket,
            (struct sockaddr *) &clientAddr, &clientLen);
    }

    LogString("Accepted a connection");
    LogString("Connection on socket %d", connectSock);

    // Update the next free host index number
    FindNextFreeHostIndex();

    // Set the socket non-blocking
    SetNonBlocking(NextFreeHostIndex, 1);

#ifdef WIN32
    // Create input event handle
    RemoteHost[NextFreeHostIndex].SocketInputEvent =
        CreateEvent(NULL, FALSE, FALSE, NULL);
#endif

    // Fill remote host information
    RemoteHost[NextFreeHostIndex].socket = connectSock;
    RemoteHost[NextFreeHostIndex].inetSockAddr = clientAddr;
    RemoteHost[NextFreeHostIndex].addrLen = clientLen;
    RemoteHost[NextFreeHostIndex].online = 1;
    RemoteHosts++;

    // Give local id number to the client
    GiveLocalIdTCP();

    // Fill parameter information for the thread
    param.id             = NextFreeHostIndex;
    param.netParamSocket = this;

// Start the IO thread
#ifdef WIN32
    // Stop notifying for incoming connections on this socket
    WSAAsyncSelect(connectSock, hWnd_netLib, 0, 0);

    // Monitor incoming network events
    WSAEventSelect(connectSock,
        RemoteHost[NextFreeHostIndex].SocketInputEvent,
        FD_READ);

    DWORD threadId;
```

```
        // Create the thread
        HANDLE threadHandle = CreateThread(NULL, 0,
            (LPTHREAD_START_ROUTINE) NET_WinIOThreadFunc,
            (void *) &param, 0, &threadId);

#else
    pthread_t threadId;

    // Create the thread
    pthread_create(&threadId, NULL, NET_UnixIOThreadFunc,
        (void *) &param);
#endif
    }
```

Notice that we use our own constant for the invalid sockets throughout the function now. This is to make the function platform independent.

```
SOCKET connectSock = NET_INVALID_SOCKET;
```

Connecting to a Server

The final library has the same system for connecting the server as does the first version we discussed earlier in this tutorial. One difference is that we need to define which protocol to use.

ConnectToServer Function

The following code listing shows the updated ConnectToServer function. We must pass the protocol to use as a parameter: NET_TCP for TCP and NET_UDP for UDP.

Like with the AcceptConnection function, this function also uses #ifdefs to gain platform independence.

```
int NET_Socket::ConnectToServer(char *addressText, int port, int Protocol)
{
    SOCKET sock;
    struct sockaddr_in inetServAddr;

    NETMSGDATA_DATASIZE DataMsg;
    memset(&DataMsg, 0, sizeof(NETMSGDATA_DATASIZE));

    // Check which protocol to use
    switch(Protocol)
    {
    // TCP protocol
    case NET_TCP:
        sock = socket(AF_INET, SOCK_STREAM, 0);
```

```
        break;

    // UDP protocol
    case NET_UDP:
        sock = socket(AF_INET, SOCK_DGRAM, 0);
        break;

    default:
        return NET_INVALID_PROTOCOL;
    }

    if(sock == NET_INVALID_SOCKET)
    {
        return -1;
    }

    // Create inet_addr from the IP number
    u_long inetAddr = inet_addr(addressText);

    // Fill the address information
    memset((char *) &inetServAddr, 0, sizeof(inetServAddr));
    inetServAddr.sin_family        = AF_INET;
    inetServAddr.sin_port          = htons((u_short) port);
    inetServAddr.sin_addr.s_addr   = inetAddr;

    // Connect using TCP
    if(Protocol == NET_TCP)
    {
        int error = connect(sock,
            (struct sockaddr *) &inetServAddr,
            sizeof(inetServAddr));

        // This works only when using TCP
        if(error != 0)
        {
            LogString("ERROR: connect()
                error (error = %d)", error);

            return NET_INVALID_SOCKET;
        }
    }

#ifdef WIN32
    // Create Win32 socket input event handle
    RemoteHost[NETID_SERVER].SocketInputEvent =
        CreateEvent(NULL, FALSE, FALSE, NULL);
#endif
```

```
// Fill remote host (server) info
RemoteHost[NETID_SERVER].socket = sock;
RemoteHost[NETID_SERVER].inetSockAddr = inetServAddr;
RemoteHost[NETID_SERVER].addrLen =
    (socklen_t) sizeof(inetServAddr);
RemoteHost[NETID_SERVER].online = 1;
RemoteHosts++;

char *string;
string =
    inet_ntoa(RemoteHost[NETID_SERVER].inetSockAddr.sin_addr);

LogString("Sending knock to socket %d, ip: %s, port %d",
    RemoteHost[NETID_SERVER].socket, string,
    ntohs(RemoteHost[NETID_SERVER].inetSockAddr.sin_port));

// Knock if using UDP
if(Protocol == NET_UDP)
{
    NETMSG_GENERIC KnockMsg;

    // Fill the message data
    KnockMsg.type      = NETMSG_KNOCK;
    KnockMsg.toId      = NETID_SERVER;
    KnockMsg.fromId    = NETID_UNKNOWN;

    DataMsg.type = NETMSG_DATASIZE;
    DataMsg.size = sizeof(NETMSG_GENERIC);

    char *string;
    string =
        inet_ntoa(RemoteHost[NETID_SERVER].inetSockAddr.sin_addr);

    LogString("Writing knock to socket %d,
        addrLen %d ip %s", RemoteHost[NETID_SERVER].socket,
        RemoteHost[NETID_SERVER].addrLen, string);

    // Write the knock message
    int bytes = WriteTo(RemoteHost[NETID_SERVER].socket,
        (char *) &KnockMsg, sizeof(NETMSG_GENERIC),
        (struct sockaddr *)
        &RemoteHost[NETID_SERVER].inetSockAddr,
        sizeof(RemoteHost[NETID_SERVER].inetSockAddr));

    if(!bytes) return NET_INVALID_SOCKET;
}
```

```
NETMSG_GENERIC *Msg;
char *recvbuf;

recvbuf = (char *) malloc(NET_BUFFSIZE);
memset((char *) recvbuf, 0, sizeof(char));

LogString("Waiting for localId");

// Set the remote host (server) non-blocking
SetNonBlocking(NETID_SERVER, 1);

int counter = 0;

// Loop while we do not have a local ID number
while(localId < 1)
{
    counter++;

    // Check if we are here too long,
    // we probably cannot connect to anywhere.
    if(counter == 100000)
    {
        LogString("ERROR: We were waiting for
            localId for too long");

        return NET_INVALID_SOCKET;
    }

    struct sockaddr_in newAddr;
    socklen_t newLen = sizeof(newAddr);

    memset((char *) recvbuf, 0, sizeof(char));

    // Read data from the server
    if(ReadFrom(RemoteHost[NETID_SERVER].socket, recvbuf,
        sizeof(NETMSGDATA_DATASIZE),
        (struct sockaddr *) &newAddr,
        &newLen, 1))
    {
        Msg = (NETMSG_GENERIC *) recvbuf;

        // Update server's address
        if(Protocol == NET_UDP)
        {
            RemoteHost[NETID_SERVER].inetSockAddr =
                newAddr;
```

```
            RemoteHost[NETID_SERVER].addrLen = newLen;
        }

    switch(Msg->type)
    {
    // Got local ID number
    case NETMSG_GIVEID:
        NETMSGDATA_DATASIZE *idMsg;
        idMsg = (NETMSGDATA_DATASIZE *) Msg;

        // Set the local ID number
        localId = idMsg->toId;

        string =
            inet_ntoa(RemoteHost[NETID_SERVER].inetSockAddr.sin_addr);

        LogString("The server is now on socket %d,
            ip %s, port %d",
            RemoteHost[NETID_SERVER].socket, string,
            ntohs(RemoteHost[NETID_SERVER].inetSockAddr.sin_port));

        NETMSG_CONF ConfMsg;
        ConfMsg.conf = localId;

        // If using UDP, send confirmation
        // of local ID number
        if(Protocol == NET_UDP)
        {
            LogString("Writing confirmation of
                localId (localId: %d)", localId);

            WriteTo(RemoteHost[NETID_SERVER].socket,
                (char *) &ConfMsg,
                sizeof(NETMSG_CONF),
                (struct sockaddr *)
                &RemoteHost[NETID_SERVER].inetSockAddr,
                sizeof(RemoteHost[NETID_SERVER].inetSockAddr));
        }

        break;

    default:
        continue;
    }
  }
}
```

```
        free(recvbuf);
        recvbuf = NULL;

        LogString("Got localId %d", localId);

        // Set the local host online
        Online = 1;

        FindNextFreeHostIndex();

        param.id                = NETID_SERVER;
        param.netParamSocket    = this;

// Start the IO thread
#ifdef WIN32
    WSAAsyncSelect(sock, hWnd_netLib, 0, 0);

    WSAEventSelect(sock,
        RemoteHost[NETID_SERVER].SocketInputEvent,
        FD_READ);

    DWORD threadId;

    HANDLE threadHandle = CreateThread(NULL, 0,
        (LPTHREAD_START_ROUTINE) NET_WinIOThreadFunc,
        (void *) &param, 0, &threadId);

#else
    pthread_t threadId;

    pthread_create(&threadId, NULL, NET_UnixIOThreadFunc,
        (void *) &param);
#endif

    // Wait for the thread to start
    while(!RemoteHost[NETID_SERVER].thread);

    return 0;
}
```

To make this function protocol independent, we check which protocol to use to create the socket:

```
// Check which protocol to use
switch(Protocol)
{
// TCP protocol
```

```
case NET_TCP:
    sock = socket(AF_INET, SOCK_STREAM, 0);
    break;

// UDP protocol
case NET_UDP:
    sock = socket(AF_INET, SOCK_DGRAM, 0);
    break;

default:
    return NET_INVALID_PROTOCOL;
}
```

If we use the TCP protocol, we call the Connect socket function. This establishes the connection with the server.

```
// Connect using TCP
if(Protocol == NET_TCP)
{
    int error = connect(sock,
        (struct sockaddr *) &inetServAddr,
        sizeof(inetServAddr));

    // This works only when using TCP
    if(error != 0)
    {
        LogString("ERROR: connect() error (error = %d)", error);

        return NET_INVALID_SOCKET;
    }
}
```

If the UDP protocol is used, we send the knock message now as shown in the following code. The knock message is used to notify the server of our presence. We set the source host ID to unknown, because we have not received the local ID number yet.

```
// Knock if using UDP
if(Protocol == NET_UDP)
{
    NETMSG_GENERIC KnockMsg;

    // Fill the message data
    KnockMsg.type     = NETMSG_KNOCK;
    KnockMsg.toId     = NETID_SERVER;
    KnockMsg.fromId   = NETID_UNKNOWN;

    DataMsg.type = NETMSG_DATASIZE;
```

```
        DataMsg.size = sizeof(NETMSG_GENERIC);

        char *string;
        string =
            inet_ntoa(RemoteHost[NETID_SERVER].inetSockAddr.sin_addr);

        LogString("Writing knock to socket %d,
            addrLen %d ip %s", RemoteHost[NETID_SERVER].socket,
            RemoteHost[NETID_SERVER].addrLen, string);

        // Write the knock message
        int bytes = WriteTo(RemoteHost[NETID_SERVER].socket,
            (char *) &KnockMsg, sizeof(NETMSG_GENERIC),
            (struct sockaddr *)
            &RemoteHost[NETID_SERVER].inetSockAddr,
            sizeof(RemoteHost[NETID_SERVER].inetSockAddr));

        if(!bytes) return NET_INVALID_SOCKET;
    }
```

Because UDP is an unreliable protocol, it is a good idea to send a confirmation of received data. We do this here by sending confirmation of receiving the local ID number. Note that this is done only with the UDP protocol; there is no need to do this with TCP.

```
    // If using UDP, send confirmation
    // of local ID number
    if(Protocol == NET_UDP)
    {
        LogString("Writing confirmation of localId (localId: %d)",
            localId);

        WriteTo(RemoteHost[NETID_SERVER].socket, (char *) &ConfMsg,
            sizeof(NETMSG_CONF), (struct sockaddr *)
            &RemoteHost[NETID_SERVER].inetSockAddr,
            sizeof(RemoteHost[NETID_SERVER].inetSockAddr));
    }
```

CloseConnection Function

We need to close the connection we have established. We explained this function earlier in this tutorial, but this new version has been updated to make it platform independent:

```
    void NET_Socket::CloseConnection(int id, int active)
    {
        // If the remote host is offline, there is
        // no point in closing the connection
```

```
        if(!RemoteHost[id].online)
        {
            LogString("Trying to close connection %d,
                but RemoteHost is not online", id);
            return;
        }

        LogString("Closing connection %d", id);

        // Send CLOSE_CONNECTION message only
        // if this is an active closure
        // (this host initiates the closure)
        if(active)
        {
            NETMSG_GENERIC Msg;
            NETMSGDATA_DATASIZE DataMsg;
            memset(&DataMsg, 0, sizeof(NETMSGDATA_DATASIZE));

            DataMsg.type = NETMSG_DATASIZE;
            DataMsg.size = sizeof(NETMSG_GENERIC);

            Msg.type    = NETMSG_CLOSE_CONNECTION;
            Msg.fromId  = localId;
            Msg.toId    = id;

            Write(id, (char *) &DataMsg,
                sizeof(NETMSGDATA_DATASIZE));
            Write(id, (char *) &Msg, sizeof(NETMSG_GENERIC));
        }

        struct linger Ling;

        Ling.l_onoff = 1;
        Ling.l_linger = 0;

        setsockopt(RemoteHost[id].socket, SOL_SOCKET, SO_LINGER,
            (const char *) &Ling, sizeof(struct linger));

        // Close the socket
#ifdef WIN32
        shutdown(RemoteHost[id].socket, SD_BOTH);

        int ret = WSAEWOULDBLOCK;

        while(ret == WSAEWOULDBLOCK)
            ret = closesocket(RemoteHost[id].socket);
#else
```

```
        shutdown(RemoteHost[id].socket, SHUT_RDWR);

        int ret = -1;

        while(ret == -1)
            close(RemoteHost[id].socket);
#endif
        RemoteHost[id].socket = 0;

        // if we are closing connection to the server,
        // we will not be online anymore
        if(id == NETID_SERVER)
        {
            Online        = 0;
            localId       = NETID_UNKNOWN;
        }

        // because the remote host list cannot
        // be resorted, mark this connection offline
        // and decrease RemoteHosts amount
        RemoteHost[id].online = 0;
        RemoteHosts--;

        FindNextFreeHostIndex();

        LogString("Disconnected: NextFreeHostIndex %d",
            NextFreeHostIndex);
    }
```

The two minor changes in this function compared to the earlier version are that now we close the socket using the correct function depending on what operating system we are using, and we pass the correct constant to the shutdown function, also depending on the operating system. This is shown in the following piece of code. The functions do the same thing although they have slightly different names.

```
        // Close the socket
#ifdef WIN32
        shutdown(RemoteHost[id].socket, SD_BOTH);

        int ret = WSAEWOULDBLOCK;

        while(ret == WSAEWOULDBLOCK)
            ret = closesocket(RemoteHost[id].socket);
#else
        shutdown(RemoteHost[id].socket, SHUT_RDWR);
```

```
        int ret = -1;

        while(ret == -1)
            close(RemoteHost[id].socket);
#endif
```

Shutdown Function

The final function we call when we are closing a NET_Socket object is this one. It shuts down the connection. This function is also updated to be platform independent. The only change is that now we check to see if we are on Windows; if we are, we close the socket input event handle.

```
void NET_Socket::Shutdown(void)
{
    LogString("Shutting down netLib object");

    // Loop through all remote hosts
    for(int id = 0; id < RemoteHosts; id++)
    {
        // If we are online, close the connection
        if(Online)
        {
            CloseConnection(id, 1);
        }

#ifdef WIN32
        // If input event handles exist, close them
        if(RemoteHost[id].SocketInputEvent)
        {
            CloseHandle(RemoteHost[id].SocketInputEvent);
            RemoteHost[id].SocketInputEvent = NULL;
        }
#endif
    }

    // Set us offline
    Online = 0;
}
```

Final Thoughts

This network library we have created is not even close to perfect. It is supposed to be a stepping stone for your own ideas and your own network libraries. For example, this library does not authenticate users or hosts in any way. Any TCP socket application can connect to the TCP server we create using this library. Of course, the client that connects to the server needs to know what data to send to it after the connection, but the connection can be established without any problems.

So keep your brain working and use this library as a reference for your solutions.

Summary

We have now learned how to create a network library from scratch. First, we created a Windows/TCP-only protocol to show how easy it really is to modify the code to make it platform/protocol independent. Please do not settle for the functions and solutions given here, but explore new ideas and ways to make something useful.

TUTORIAL 2

Creating the Login System

Introduction

This tutorial explains how we create the login system for our tutorial game. First, we create the MySQL database in which to store our user accounts, then we move onto creating our game interface and basic server application, which will allow users to create new accounts and login to accounts they have created previously. In later tutorials, this login system is used to log players into the game lobby, in which the player will be able to create and join games online.

Creating the Database

As this is the first time we have been required to store information, we must first create a database to store the tables required for our tutorial game. We will call our database onlinedata as it will contain all the data for the online game. To create this database, go to the MySQL console and type in the following command (followed by Return):

```
mysql> CREATE DATABASE onlinedata;
```

Remember that every time you wish to execute a command on the onlinedata database, you need to tell MySQL to use the database. This is done with the following command:

```
mysql> USE onlinedata;
```

Now that we have a database to store our tables in, we need to decide what information we must store about the players in the game. Here is a list of the information we will require for the player's accounts:

- A unique identification number
- A nickname (for the login)
- The player's first name
- The player's last name
- The player's age
- The gender of the player
- The password the player will use to login
- The date the player last logged into the game
- A variable to determine whether the player is currently logged in
- The player's e-mail address

In our tutorial game, the table that will hold this information will be named playerdata. We now need to create this table in MySQL. This can be done with the following MySQL command:

```
mysql> CREATE TABLE playerdata (
mysql> id INT auto_increment,
mysql> nickname VARCHAR(30),
mysql> firstname VARCHAR(50),
mysql> surname VARCHAR(50),
mysql> age INT,
mysql> gender VARCHAR(10),
mysql> password VARCHAR(50),
mysql> lastlogin TIMESTAMP,
mysql> online INT,
mysql> email VARCHAR(150),
mysql> PRIMARY KEY(id));
```

Once our table has been created, it is a good idea to use the Describe command to check that our table was created as we intended. To describe our playerdata table we use the following command:

```
mysql> DESCRIBE playerdata;
```

When we execute the Describe command, we expect the following output from the MySQL console.

Figure 1

That is all we are required to do from the MySQL console. We now have our table available for use by our login system, which we are going to create over the next few sections.

Creating Our Basic Client Application

We now wish to create a blank application to which we can add the login system. The blank application will evolve into the game lobby in later chapters, but for now will remain as a simple blank window.

First though, we must create our workspace in Visual Studio. Select New... from the main Visual Studio menu and create an empty Win32 Application project. (More detailed information on this stage can be found in Chapter 1.)

Next, we need to add the correct libraries we require into our newly created workspace. To do this, select Project..., Settings from the main Visual Studio menu. Then select the Link tab in the dialog, which appears in the middle of the screen. Also ensure that the top-right pull-down box is set to All Configurations, then add the following libraries before kernel32.lib in the Object/Library Modules edit box.

```
netlib.lib 2dlib.lib opengl32.lib glu32.lib glaux.lib
```

When you enter these libraries, the dialog should look like Figure 2.

Figure 2

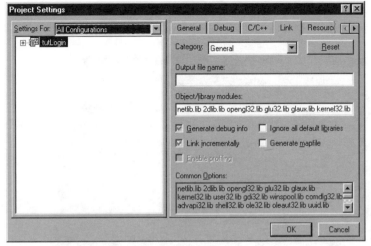

What we have done here is added the netLib, 2DLib, and openGL libraries into our project. You also need to ensure that you have added the appropriate directories for these libraries into the Visual Studios directory list; see Chapter 1 for more details on this.

Once this information is added, we can then add our main source and header file to our workspace. Select New... from the main menu again, but this time add a C++ source file and name it main.cpp. Repeat this process again, but this time add a C++ header file called main.h.

Let's now create our main application window. We first need the following header files at the top of our main.cpp file:

```
#include <netLib.h>
#include <windows.h>
#include <gl/gl.h>
#include <gl/glu.h>
#include <gl/glaux.h>
#include <2dlib.h>

#include "main.h"
```

First is our header file for the network library we created in the previous tutorial. Next is the standard Windows header file, windows.h, which contains pretty much everything we require to use the Win32 API. The next four are required by the openGL library and also our 2DLib library. Then we have the header specific to our application, which in this case is main.h.

Now we need to declare two global variables as follows:

```
// GLOBAL VARIABLES
HWND hWnd_Application;
HINSTANCE hInst;
```

The first variable is used to store the window handle of our main application so we can manipulate it after we create it. The second variable is a copy of the application's instance, which we use later in the creation of dialogs.

Note that we also extern these global variables in the main.h header file as follows so we can access them from other files in the project:

```
// GLOBAL VARIABLES
extern HWND hWnd_Application;
extern HINSTANCE hInst;
```

Next, we need to create a Windows procedure for the main application window. This processes all the messages that are sent to the main window and will also set the keypresses array that is contained within the 2DLib library. Here is the code we require for the Windows procedure for our main application window:

```
// WINDOWS PROCEDURE
LRESULT CALLBACK ApplicationProc(HWND hWnd, UINT uMsg, WPARAM wParam, LPARAM lParam)
{
    switch (uMsg)
    {
        case WM_CLOSE:
        {
            PostQuitMessage(0);
            return 0;
        }

        case WM_KEYDOWN:
        {
            keys[wParam] = TRUE;
            return 0;
        }

        case WM_KEYUP:
        {
            keys[wParam] = FALSE;
            return 0;
        }
    }

    // Pass All Unhandled Messages To DefWindowProc
    return DefWindowProc(hWnd,uMsg,wParam,lParam);
}
```

We will be adding more to this procedure in later tutorials, but this is all we require at this stage to create the basic application. This procedure handles three different Windows messages. The first is the WM_CLOSE message that tells the application to quit if the Close button (x) is pressed. The WM_KEYDOWN and

WM_KEYUP messages are used to set the correct values in the keys array that is stored internally in the 2DLib library. All other unhandled messages are returned to the default Windows procedure (which is handled internally within the operating system).

Finally, we need to create our application entry point, which is our WinMain function. We start the function with the following code:

```
// WINDOWS MESSAGE LOOP AND APPLICATION ENTRY POINT
int WINAPI WinMain(HINSTANCE hThisInst, HINSTANCE hPrevInst, LPSTR lpszArgs, int
nWinMode)
{
```

This is simply the entry point to our application, i.e., the first function that will be run when our program is executed. Next we create two local variables, the first to store our Windows messages locally and the second to set up the parameters for our Windows class. We declare these as follows:

```
MSG msg;
WNDCLASSEX wcl;
```

Next, we must set up our Windows class, using the wcl variable. This is done with the following code:

```
// Create our Main Window
wcl.cbSize = sizeof(WNDCLASSEX);

wcl.hInstance = hThisInst;
wcl.lpszClassName = "ArmyWar";
wcl.lpfnWndProc = ApplicationProc;
wcl.style = 0;

wcl.hIcon = LoadIcon(NULL, IDI_APPLICATION);
wcl.hIconSm = LoadIcon(NULL, IDI_WINLOGO);
wcl.hCursor = LoadCursor(NULL, IDC_ARROW);

wcl.lpszMenuName = NULL;
wcl.cbClsExtra = 0;
wcl.cbWndExtra = 0;

wcl.hbrBackground = (HBRUSH) GetStockObject(LTGRAY_BRUSH);
```

This will give us a very standard looking gray window with a standard icon. Also note that we have assigned the ApplicationProc procedure, which we created previously as the procedure for this window; hence, messages from this window will be processed by the ApplicationProc procedure.

Now that we have our application window class set up, we need to register the class before we can create the window. This is done with the following code. Note also that we have named the class "ArmyWar."

```
if(!RegisterClassEx(&wcl)) return 0;
```

Now that our class is registered, we can go ahead and create the window. This is done with the following code segment:

```
hWnd_Application = CreateWindow(
    "ArmyWar",
    "ARMY WAR Online",
    WS_OVERLAPPEDWINDOW,
    CW_USEDEFAULT,
    CW_USEDEFAULT,
    CW_USEDEFAULT,
    CW_USEDEFAULT,
    HWND_DESKTOP,
    NULL,
    hThisInst,
    NULL
    );
```

The first parameter of this function is the class name, which is ArmyWar in this case. The second is the title of our window, which we have set to be ARMY WAR Online. The third parameter specifies what type of window is to be created; in this case we require a standard overlapped window. The next four parameters specify where the window is to be placed on the screen; here, we have told Windows to place the window in the default position with a default size. This will be changed in later tutorials. Next, we have the handle to the parent window, which is the desktop in this case. Then we have the parameter to specify a menu for the window, which we do not currently have, so we leave this as NULL. Next is the instance, which we get from a parameter passed into the WinMain function. Finally, we have a pointer for applications that require a multiple document interface, which we do not, so we leave this as NULL. Note that the CreateWindow function returns a handle to the window it creates, so we store this in the hWnd_Application variable, which we previously declared as a global variable.

Next, we wish to make our main application window visible, so we want to show and update our window with the following code segment:

```
ShowWindow(hWnd_Application, nWinMode);
UpdateWindow(hWnd_Application);
```

Note that we use the handle to our window (hWnd_Application) with these functions to specify which window we are referring to. The nWinMode is simply one of the parameters taken from the WinMain function.

Now we assign the instance variable, which was passed into the WinMain function to the global variable we declared earlier. This is simply to allow other functions in the project access to the application instance without the need to pass it directly into the function that requires it. Here is the code that assigns the instance to our global hInst variable.

```
// Set Global Instance Variable
hInst = hThisInst;
```

Next, we create our message pump, which loops until the application receives a quit message from Windows. Here is the code segment for our message loop:

```
// Start the Windows Message Loop
while(msg.message != WM_QUIT)
{
    if(PeekMessage(&msg, NULL, 0, 0, PM_REMOVE))
    {
        TranslateMessage(&msg);
        DispatchMessage(&msg);
    }
    else
    {
    }
}
```

This will loop indefinitely, receiving and processing messages, until the application receives a WM_QUIT message. If you remember from our Windows procedure, which we created previously, it sends a quit message when the user tries to close the application, and therefore breaks out of the loop.

Finally, when the application quits, we return the wParam of the WM_QUIT message back to Windows, as it contains the exit code. Here is the code segment that completes the WinMain function:

```
    return msg.wParam;
}
```

Here is the complete listing of the code from the main.cpp file for your reference.

```
#include <netlib.h>
#include <windows.h>
#include <gl/gl.h>
#include <gl/glu.h>
#include <gl/glaux.h>
#include <2dlib.h>

#include "main.h"
```

```
// GLOBAL VARIABLES
HWND hWnd_Application;
HINSTANCE hInst;

// WINDOWS PROCEDURE
LRESULT CALLBACK ApplicationProc(HWND hWnd, UINT uMsg, WPARAM wParam, LPARAM lParam)
{
    switch (uMsg)
    {
        case WM_CLOSE:
        {
            PostQuitMessage(0);
            return 0;
        }

        case WM_KEYDOWN:
        {
            keys[wParam] = TRUE;
            return 0;
        }

        case WM_KEYUP:
        {
            keys[wParam] = FALSE;
            return 0;
        }
    }

    // Pass All Unhandled Messages To DefWindowProc
    return DefWindowProc(hWnd,uMsg,wParam,lParam);
}

// WINDOWS MESSAGE LOOP AND APPLICATION ENTRY POINT
int WINAPI WinMain(HINSTANCE hThisInst, HINSTANCE hPrevInst, LPSTR lpszArgs, int
nWinMode)
{

    MSG msg;
    WNDCLASSEX wcl;

    // Create our Main Window
    wcl.cbSize = sizeof(WNDCLASSEX);

    wcl.hInstance = hThisInst;
    wcl.lpszClassName = "ArmyWar";
    wcl.lpfnWndProc = ApplicationProc;
    wcl.style = 0;
```

```
wcl.hIcon = LoadIcon(NULL, IDI_APPLICATION);
wcl.hIconSm = LoadIcon(NULL, IDI_WINLOGO);
wcl.hCursor = LoadCursor(NULL, IDC_ARROW);

wcl.lpszMenuName = NULL;
wcl.cbClsExtra = 0;
wcl.cbWndExtra = 0;

wcl.hbrBackground = (HBRUSH) GetStockObject(LTGRAY_BRUSH);

if(!RegisterClassEx(&wcl)) return 0;

hWnd_Application = CreateWindow(
    "ArmyWar",
    "ARMY WAR Online",
    WS_OVERLAPPEDWINDOW,
    CW_USEDEFAULT,
    CW_USEDEFAULT,
    CW_USEDEFAULT,
    CW_USEDEFAULT,
    HWND_DESKTOP,
    NULL,
    hThisInst,
    NULL
    );

ShowWindow(hWnd_Application, nWinMode);
UpdateWindow(hWnd_Application);

// Set Global Instance Variable
hInst = hThisInst;

// Start the Windows Message Loop
while(msg.message != WM_QUIT)
{
    if(PeekMessage(&msg, NULL, 0, 0, PM_REMOVE))
    {
        TranslateMessage(&msg);
        DispatchMessage(&msg);
    }
    else
    {
    }
}
return msg.wParam;
}
```

We are now able to execute the basic application, which will simply make a gray window appear on the screen. Figure 3 shows how this should look when we run the application.

Figure 3

Integrating the Login System (Part 1)

Now that we have a basic application we can work on, we want to build a login system on top of it. This will require the user to first login before accessing the functions contained within the application. We also need to add a feature to allow the player to create a user account if they do not already have one.

First, we need to add a resource script into our workspace so we can create dialogs to use in the application in the resource editor. To do this, select File, New... from the main menu in Visual Studio. Next, select the Resource Script from the dialog, and enter the filename as resource. When you press the OK button, notice the new Resource tab that has appeared between the ClassView and FileView tabs at the left side of the screen. This tab lists all the resources that you have included in the project.

Now that we have our resource script in our workspace, we need to add two dialogs into it: one for logging players in and one for creating new accounts.

Creating Our Dialogs

Let's first look at how we create the Login dialog. Select Insert from the main Visual Studio menu, followed by the Resource... option. A dialog will now be visible in the center of the screen that lists various resources that you can add into your workspace. Now click on the Dialog resource, and then click on the New button (on the Insert Resource dialog box). Once this is done, the following should be visible on the screen.

Figure 4

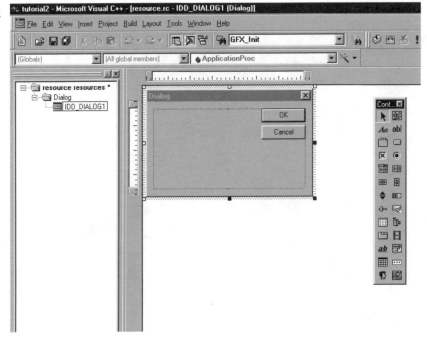

First, we want to rename the dialog in the left-hand section from IDD_DIALOG1 to IDD_LOGINDIALOG. To do this, simply right-click on IDD_DIALOG1 in the left-hand section, then left-click on Properties. Here you will see the name in an Edit box; change it here and then close the Properties dialog.

Next, we need to adjust the settings for our dialog. To do this, right-click anywhere on the dialog preview (in the right-hand window) and then left-click on Properties. The following dialog will now be visible on the screen.

Figure 5

The Dialog Properties box has the General tab currently selected. In this tab, we want to change the caption of the dialog from "Dialog" to "Login." This is the text that will appear in the title bar of the window.

Next, select the Styles tab so the following options are displayed on the dialog.

Figure 6

All we need to do here is make sure that the System menu check box is unchecked so that we do not have a Close button at the top right of our Login dialog.

Finally, select the More Styles tab so that the following options are visible.

Figure 7

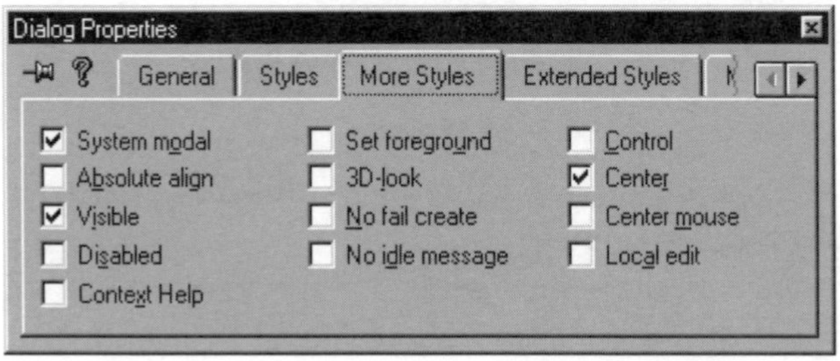

For the More Styles options, we want to check the System modal option so the dialog always stays on top, the Visible option so that we can see the dialog on the screen, and the Center option so the dialog is placed in the center of the screen.

You can now close the Dialog Properties dialog box.

Next, we need to add edit boxes and buttons so the user can enter their details into the Login dialog. Here is how our Login box should look after we add the buttons, edit boxes, and static text.

Figure 8

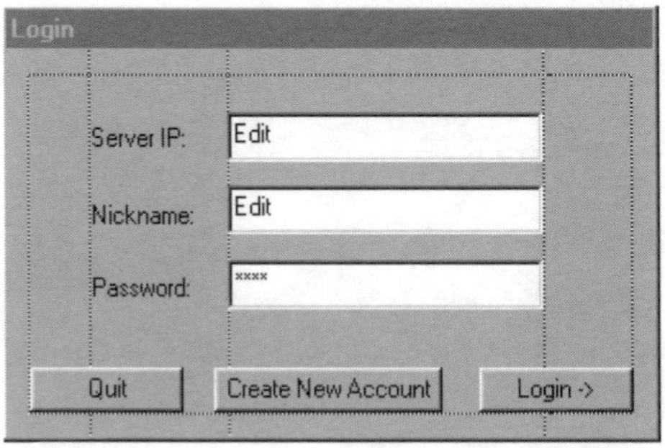

Notice here that we are not using the IP address common control. This is to ensure compatibility with the new versions of IP addresses, which may not be in the IPv4 format of xxx.xxx.xxx.xxx.

NOTE To get an edit box to hide password input (i.e., using * instead of the actual characters), right-click on the edit box, then click on the Properties option. Now select the Styles tab in the Properties dialog and check the Password option.

After we lay out our dialog, we need to set the names for the edit boxes and buttons so we can use them and also give them some meaning in our code. To change the name, simply right-click on the object (such as a button or edit box), then click on the Properties option. We will give the edit boxes the following names to identify them in order from top to bottom:

```
IDC_LOGIN_IPADDRESS
IDC_LOGIN_NICKNAME
IDC_LOGIN_PASSWORD
```

The buttons will have the following names from left to right:

```
IDC_LOGIN_QUIT
IDC_LOGIN_CREATEACCOUNT
IDC_DOLOGIN
```

That completes our Login dialog; we will now create our New Account dialog, and then implement them both in our code.

Insert this next dialog in the same way as the previous, selecting Insert, Resource… from the main Visual Studio menu. Also, all the options must be set the same as the Login dialog with the exception of the name, which for this dialog will be IDD_CREATEACCOUNT.

Next, we need to lay out the dialog to look like the following figure.

Figure 9

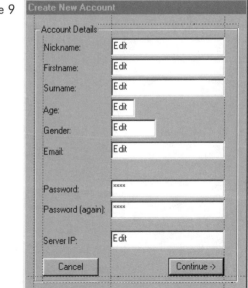

NOTE The Age box on this dialog should only be able to take numerical input. To do this, right-click on the Age edit box, and click on the Properties option. Next, click on the Styles tab of the Dialog Properties box and then check the Number option.

In this dialog, the edit boxes have the following names, from top to bottom:

```
IDC_CREATEACCOUNT_NICKNAME
IDC_CREATEACCOUNT_FIRSTNAME
IDC_CREATEACCOUNT_SURNAME
IDC_CREATEACCOUNT_AGE
IDC_CREATEACCOUNT_GENDER
IDC_CREATEACCOUNT_EMAIL
IDC_CREATEACCOUNT_PASSWORD1
IDC_CREATEACCOUNT_PASSWORD2
IDC_CREATEACCOUNT_IPADDRESS
```

The buttons have the following names, from left to right:

```
IDC_CREATEACCOUNT_CANCEL
IDC_CREATEACCOUNT_CONTINUE
```

Once this is done, we are ready to create the code that will bring these dialogs to life.

Coding the Login System

Now that we have our dialogs in place, we can implement our login code. First, we will add a new source file, login.cpp, into our workspace and also a header, login.h, so that we can keep our code reasonably modular. Once these files are in our workspace, we start by building up our login system in login.cpp.

First, we need to add the following includes to the top of the code:

```
#include <netlib.h>
#include <windows.h>
#include <gl/gl.h>
#include <gl/glu.h>
#include <gl/glaux.h>
#include <2dlib.h>

#include "resource.h"
#include "main.h"
#include "login.h"
```

Here we have the same code we added to the main.cpp source with the addition of resource.h, which contains the definitions for the resources we created in the resource editor, and login.h, which is the header specific to our new login.cpp source.

Next, we need to declare two local variables that will contain handles to our two dialogs, allowing us to interact with them after they have been created. We declare these variables with the following code:

```
// GLOBAL VARIABLES
HWND hWnd_LoginDialog = NULL;
HWND hWnd_CreateAccountDialog = NULL;
```

Note that we are also required to extern these variables in the login.h header file. This is done as follows:

```
// GLOBAL VARIABLES
extern HWND hWnd_LoginDialog;
extern HWND hWnd_CreateAccountDialog;
```

Next, we wish to create the two Windows procedures that our dialogs will use to process their messages. First, we will create the Windows procedure for the Login dialog. Here is the code segment we require to create this procedure:

```
// LOGINDIALOG PROCEDURE
LRESULT CALLBACK LoginDialogProc(HWND hWnd, UINT uMsg, WPARAM wParam, LPARAM lParam)
{
    switch (uMsg)
    {
        case WM_COMMAND:
        {
            switch(LOWORD(wParam))
            {
                case IDC_LOGIN_QUIT:
                    PostQuitMessage(0);
                    return 0;
                case IDC_LOGIN_CREATEACCOUNT:
                    if(!hWnd_CreateAccountDialog)
                        hWnd_CreateAccountDialog = CreateDialog(hInst,
                        MAKEINTRESOURCE(IDD_CREATEACCOUNT),hWnd,
                        (DLGPROC)CreateAccountDialogProc);
                    return 0;
                case IDC_DOLOGIN:
                    DoLogin();
                    return 0;
                default:
                    return 0;
            }

        }
        return 0;
    }
```

```
        case WM_CLOSE:
        {
            PostQuitMessage(0);
            return 0;
        }
    }

    // Pass All Unhandled Messages To DefWindowProc
    return 0;
}
```

The procedure for our Login dialog only processes two types of messages, the WM_CLOSE message and the WM_COMMAND message. The first is simply to allow the dialog to close correctly. The second is to handle button presses by the user and carry out commands based on which button was pressed. Let's look at this segment in more detail.

Within the WM_COMMAND case we have the following switch statement:

```
switch(LOWORD(wParam))
{
    case IDC_LOGIN_QUIT:
        PostQuitMessage(0);
        return 0;
    case IDC_LOGIN_CREATEACCOUNT:
        if(!hWnd_CreateAccountDialog)
        hWnd_CreateAccountDialog = CreateDialog(hInst,MAKEINTRESOURCE
        (IDD_CREATEACCOUNT),hWnd,(DLGPROC)CreateAccountDialogProc);
        return 0;
    case IDC_DOLOGIN:
        DoLogin();
        return 0;
    default:
        return 0;
}
```

This switch statement checks the Loword of the wParam of the command message to see if it matches any of the identification numbers of the buttons on the dialog. If it does, it follows the commands accordingly. Let's look at each Case individually:

```
case IDC_LOGIN_QUIT:
    PostQuitMessage(0);
    return 0;
```

The first Case responds if the Quit button is pressed. If it is pressed, the dialog posts a WM_QUIT message to the application, which, in turn, stops the execution of the application.

TUTORIAL 3

```
case IDC_LOGIN_CREATEACCOUNT:
        if(!hWnd_CreateAccountDialog)
        hWnd_CreateAccountDialog = CreateDialog(hInst,MAKEINTRESOURCE
        (IDD_CREATEACCOUNT),hWnd,(DLGPROC)CreateAccountDialogProc);
        return 0;
```

Next, we have the Create Account Case, which detects if the Create New Account button was pressed. If so, it first checks that a New Account dialog is not already open, then proceeds to create a New Account dialog based on the template we created in the resource editor previously. Notice here that when we create the dialog, we store the return value of the function in our global variable so we can manipulate the dialog from anywhere in the project.

```
case IDC_DOLOGIN:
    DoLogin();
    return 0;
```

Finally, we have the Case for the Login button being pressed. This calls a function that we will create later in this tutorial, which will attempt to log the player into the game.

Next, we will create the procedure for the Create Account dialog. Here is the code segment we use to create this procedure:

```
// CREATEACCOUNT PROCEDURE
LRESULT CALLBACK CreateAccountDialogProc(HWND hWnd, UINT uMsg, WPARAM wParam, LPARAM
lParam)
{
    switch (uMsg)
    {
        case WM_COMMAND:
        {
            switch(LOWORD(wParam))
            {
                case IDC_CREATEACCOUNT_CANCEL:
                    DestroyWindow(hWnd_CreateAccountDialog);
                    hWnd_CreateAccountDialog = NULL;
                    return 0;
                case IDC_CREATEACCOUNT_CONTINUE:
                    DoCreateAccount();
                    return 0;
                default:
                    return 0;

            }
            return 0;
        }
        case WM_CLOSE:
```

```
        {
//       PostQuitMessage(0);
            return 0;
        }
    }
        // Pass All Unhandled Messages To DefWindowProc
    return 0;
}
```

As you can see from the preceding code, it is very similar to the Login Dialog procedure. Let's look at the individual Case statements we require for this procedure's WM_COMMAND message.

```
case IDC_CREATEACCOUNT_CANCEL:
    DestroyWindow(hWnd_CreateAccountDialog);
    hWnd_CreateAccountDialog = NULL;
    return 0;
```

This Case is used to detect the Cancel button being pressed on the Create Account dialog. If the user presses this button, this statement will destroy the Create Account dialog and then set the global handle of the dialog to NULL (so that the Login Dialog will be able to re-create it if it is required again).

```
case IDC_CREATEACCOUNT_CONTINUE:
    DoCreateAccount();
    return 0;
```

The other Case is used when the user clicks the Continue button. When this occurs, this Case statement calls the DoCreateAccount function that we will create later in this tutorial. This function will attempt to process the information the user has entered and create an account on the MySQL server.

To do this, we need to send the information to a network application, which we are going to create later in this tutorial; we will simply leave this function empty for now. Note also that the DoLogin function works in the same way, so we will also leave this function blank.

```
// DOCREATEACCOUNT
int DoCreateAccount(void)
{

}

// DOLOGIN
int DoLogin(void)
{

}
```

Now we need to add the following four function prototypes to login.h, so that we can access them from other files in the project:

```
LRESULT CALLBACK LoginDialogProc(HWND hWnd, UINT uMsg, WPARAM wParam, LPARAM
lParam);
LRESULT CALLBACK CreateAccountDialogProc(HWND hWnd, UINT uMsg, WPARAM wParam,
LPARAM lParam);

int DoCreateAccount(void);
int DoLogin(void);
```

Next, we need to add the following include into main.cpp, after #include "main.h":

```
#include "login.h"
```

Finally, we need to add the following line of code just before we start the message loop in the WinMain function in main.cpp:

```
// Display the LoginDialog
    hWnd_LoginDialog = CreateDialog(hInst,MAKEINTRESOURCE(IDD_LOGINDIALOG),
    hWnd,(DLGPROC)LoginDialogProc);
```

This final line will cause the Login dialog to appear once the main application window has been created and is visible.

Now that we have our basic application and the foundation of our login system, we will take a look at how to create the server application before we finish off the client, as we need to create a common header file that will contain the message definitions that the client and server will use to pass messages to each other.

Creating the Login Server

Again, we need to create a new project in Visual Studio, but this time we need to add the following libraries, in the same way as we did for the client application:

```
netlib.lib mysql++.lib
```

The first library is the network library we created in the previous tutorial, and the second one is the MySQL C++ interface library. (See the end of Chapter 2 for more information on this library.)

Next, we need to create one blank source file and two header files for the project. First, create a new source file called server.cpp and a header file called server.h. These will contain the main server application. The other header we need to create is netcommon.h. This final header file will contain all the messages common to both the server and client applications, as both applications must use the same data structures to pass messages correctly between each other so it makes sense to use the same header.

First, we need to create a simple dialog that will represent our server in Windows. This is done in the same way as our previous dialogs and should look somewhat like the following figure.

Figure 10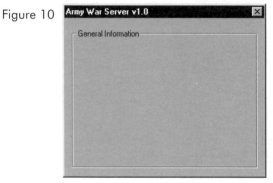

Note that if we compile the server under Linux, the dialog is neither relevant nor required. In this example, we have called the dialog IDD_SERVERDIALOG so we can reference it from our code.

Messages

Let's now look at how we code the server. First, we will declare all the messages we require to pass between the applications in our netcommon.h header file.

LobbyLogin Message

```
typedef struct
{
    int type;
    HOSTID toId;
    HOSTID fromId;
    char nickname[32];
    char password[32];
} TUT_MSG_LOBBYLOGIN_DATA;

#define TUT_MSG_LOBBYLOGIN 100
```

This first message will be used by the client to send the login details to the server. Note that the type, toId, and fromId variables are standard and are mainly used to keep track of what the message is, where it came from, and where it's going. Once the lobby login message has been sent, the server needs to tell the client the result of the attempted login, which leads us to the next message.

LobbyLoginFeedback Message

```
typedef struct
{
    int type;
    HOSTID toId;
    HOSTID fromId;
    char nickname[32];
    int result;
} TUT_MSG_LOBBYLOGIN_FEEDBACK_DATA;


#define TUT_MSG_LOBBYLOGIN_FEEDBACK 101
```

This message is used by the server to tell the client if the login was successful or not. We also need to define the results, which are as follows:

```
#define LOBBYLOGIN_RESULT_ACCEPTED          200
#define LOBBYLOGIN_RESULT_USERNAMEBAD       201
#define LOBBYLOGIN_RESULT_PASSWORDBAD       202
#define LOBBYLOGIN_RESULT_MYSQLERROR        203
```

These result definitions are sent back in the result variable. The client can use a Case statement to display useful output to the user, or log the player in if the server accepted the login details. We have similar messages for the new account signup.

LobbyCreateAccount Message

```
typedef struct
{
    int type;
    HOSTID toId;
    HOSTID fromId;
    char nickname[30];
    char firstname[50];
    char surname[50];
    int age;
    char gender[10];
    char password[50];
    char email[150];
} TUT_MSG_LOBBYCREATEACCOUNT_DATA;


#define TUT_MSG_LOBBYCREATEACCOUNT        102
```

When a user wishes to create an account on the client, the client must send the details to the server to allow the server to input the details into MySQL. This message simply holds all the required signup fields. The server must then send the result back to the client using the next message.

LobbyCreateAccountFeedback Message

```
typedef struct
{
    int type;
    HOSTID toId;
    HOSTID fromId;
    int result;
} TUT_MSG_LOBBYCREATEACCOUNT_FEEDBACK_DATA;


#define TUT_MSG_LOBBYCREATEACCOUNT_FEEDBACK 103
```

This final message simply sends an integer back from the server to the client to inform the client of whether the account signup was successful or not. As with the login feedback message, we need to define the different types of results there can be. These are as follows:

```
#define LOBBYCREATEACCOUNT_RESULT_ACCEPTED          300
#define LOBBYCREATEACCOUNT_RESULT_MYSQLERROR        301
```

The Header File

Now that we have our common messages defined, we can start creating our main server application.

First, let's create our server's header file, server.h. This will contain all our function prototypes and class information we require in the server application. The header file looks as follows:

```
/* Login Server */
#ifndef SERVER_H
#define SERVER_H

// Defines
#define KEEPALIVE_TIMEOUT       60

// Classes
class ArmyServerClass
{
    public:
        int Init(void);
        void Shutdown(void);
};

extern ArmyServerClass ArmyServer;

// Function Prototypes
void sendLobbyLoginMessage(NETMSG_GENERIC *Msg);
```

```
void Send(NETMSG_GENERIC *Msg);

#endif
```

As you can see there is not much to the header file. We have declared a simple
ArmyServerClass that contains an initialization and shutdown function. In addition, we have defined our keep alive timeout and prototyped our main functions
used in the server application.

The Main Server File

Now that we have our header, let's create our main server.cpp file. First, we need
to include the following files:

```
/* Login Server */
#ifndef _WINSOCKAPI_
#define _WINSOCKAPI_

#include <windows.h>
#include "resource.h"

#include <netLib.h>
#include <string.h>
#include <stdlib.h>
#include <stdio.h>
#include <mysql++>

#include "netcommon.h"
#include "server.h"
#include "assert.h"
```

Everything here is relatively straightforward. Note that we have included the
headers for both our network library netLib.h and the MySQL C++ interface
mysql++.

Once we have our headers included we can define our global variables. We only
require three globals: the first is a handle for our dialog window, the second is a
socket for our server, and the third is a global class for the server. These are
defined as follows:

```
HWND hWnd_netLib;
NET_Socket tutServer;
ArmyServerClass ArmyServer;
```

Next, we will create the initialization and shutdown functions for our ArmyServer
class. These functions will utilize the functions contained within the network
library we created in the previous tutorial. First, we start the initialization

function and attempt to start our network library. If this fails, we note this in the log file and exit the function. This is done in the following code segment:

```
int ArmyServerClass::Init(void)
{
    if(NET_Initialize() != 0)
    {
        LogString("Error initialising Communication Library!");
        return 1;
    }
```

Now that our library is ready, we can attempt to create a server on UDP Port 9009. Again, if the server creation fails, we note this in the log file. This is accomplished with the following code:

```
    if(tutServer.CreateServer(9009, NET_UDP) != 0)
    {
        LogString("Failed to Create the Server");
        return 1;
    }
```

Finally, we note in the log file that the server is now online and end our initialization function. This is done with the following segment of code:

```
    LogString("ONLINE");

    return 0;
}
```

Next, we will create the Shutdown function for our ArmyServer class. First, we note in the log file that we are shutting the server down, then we call the tutServer's Shutdown function, followed by the netLib shutdown function. Following is the complete code for the Shutdown function:

```
void ArmyServerClass::Shutdown(void)
{
    LogString("Shutting Down Server...");

    tutServer.Shutdown();
    NET_Shutdown();
}
```

Let's now look at the complete dialog procedure we require for the application, then we will look at what each part of it does:

```
LRESULT CALLBACK ServerDlgProc(HWND DialogWindow, UINT Message, WPARAM wParam,
LPARAM lParam)
{
    // Process Messages
```

```
switch(Message)
{

case WM_INITDIALOG:
    hWnd_netLib = DialogWindow;
    ArmyServer.Init();

    return(FALSE);

case WM_COMMAND:
    switch(wParam)
    {
    case IDCANCEL:
        ArmyServer.Shutdown();
        EndDialog(DialogWindow, FALSE);
        return FALSE;
    }
    break;


case USMSG_ACCEPT:
    tutServer.AcceptConnection();
    break;

default:
    break;

}

    return FALSE;
}
```

When the dialog is initialized, we assign the dialog handle to our application handle, then call the server initialization function from our ArmyServer class. This is done with this code segment, from the dialog procedure:

```
case WM_INITDIALOG:
    hWnd_netLib = DialogWindow;
    ArmyServer.Init();

    return(FALSE);
```

If the user exits the application, we call the ArmyServer class Shutdown function and then the Windows EndDialog function to close the dialog. This is done with the following code from the dialog procedure:

```
case WM_COMMAND:
    switch(wParam)
```

```
    {
    case IDCANCEL:
        ArmyServer.Shutdown();
        EndDialog(DialogWindow, FALSE);
        return FALSE;
    }
    break;
```

Finally, we need to be able to accept a connection from the client application. This is done with the final segment of the dialog procedure, which looks as follows:

```
case USMSG_ACCEPT:
    tutServer.AcceptConnection();
    break;
```

Now that we have our dialog procedure, we need our application entry point — the WinMain function. All we require this to do is create our dialog, so we can create it as follows:

```
int APIENTRY WinMain(HINSTANCE hInstance, HINSTANCE hPrevInstance, LPSTR lpCmdLine,
int nCmdShow)
{
    DialogBox((HINSTANCE) hInstance, MAKEINTRESOURCE(IDD_SERVERDIALOG),
        hWnd_netLib, (DLGPROC) ServerDlgProc);

    return 0;
}
```

Note here how we have used our dialog from the resource we created before, IDD_SERVERDIALOG, and assigned the procedure as the ServerDlgProc we created previously.

   Now we need to create a function to handle incoming login and create account attempts from the client application. We start the function as follows and create a switch statement to determine the type of message that has been retrieved:

```
void handleLobbyLoginMessages(NETMSG_GENERIC *Msg)
{
    // Here the generic message is used to get the type out of the message
    // structure. It is then used in the switch statement.
    switch(Msg->type)
    {
```

First, we will enable the server to handle a LobbyLogin message. We need to get the message data and store it in a local variable in the server. This is done with the following code segment. Also, note how we add the player attempting to login to the log file.

```
case TUT_MSG_LOBBYLOGIN:
    TUT_MSG_LOBBYLOGIN_DATA *LobbyLoginPtr;
```

```
        LobbyLoginPtr = (TUT_MSG_LOBBYLOGIN_DATA *) Msg;

        LogString("Got lobby login message (nick: %s)", LobbyLoginPtr->nickname);
```

Now we have all the login information stored in our local variable LobbyLoginPtr. This contains both the nickname and password the user entered into the client, as well as the host ID number of where the message came from. Now we need to set up the feedback message that the server will send back to the client (after we have checked the information in the MySQL database). This feedback message is set up as follows:

```
TUT_MSG_LOBBYLOGIN_FEEDBACK_DATA LobbyLoginFeedbackData;
        LobbyLoginFeedbackData.type = TUT_MSG_LOBBYLOGIN_FEEDBACK;
        LobbyLoginFeedbackData.toId = LobbyLoginPtr->fromId;
        LobbyLoginFeedbackData.fromId = tutServer.localId;
```

First, we create a local variable of the login feedback structure called LobbyLogin-FeedbackData. Then, we set the type of the message so that the client can determine which message it is receiving. Next, we set the toId variable of the feedback message to the fromId of the login message, which is contained within the LobbyLoginPtr variable. Finally, we set fromId of the feedback message to the server's local ID, which is stored in the tutServer class (part of netLib).

The final part to the feedback message is the result of the login attempt. To get the result, we must connect to the MySQL database and compare the password the user entered in the client to what is stored in the database.

When we attempt the connection, we use a Try/Catch statement, so we can easily recover from any errors that may occur. First, we open the Try statement and attempt a connection to the MySQL database on the same machine (which has an IP address of 127.0.0.1):

```
    try
    {
        // -> Create a connection to the database
        Connection con("onlinedata","127.0.0.1");
```

Notice here that we are trying to connect to the onlinedata database, which we created earlier in this tutorial. If for some reason we are not able to connect, the Try statement will fail and continue execution from the Catch statement, which we will add later.

After our connection to the database is established, we then need to create a query object, which is bound to our connection. We do this with the following code segment:

```
        // -> Create a query object that is bound to our connection
        Query query = con.query();
```

Now that we have our connection and a query bound to it, we need to set up our query so it will retrieve the correct password for the nickname we specify. We will also retrieve the user's id and firstname fields from the playerdata table in the database. We set up the query with the following code segment:

```
// -> Assign the query to that object
query << "SELECT id,firstname,password FROM playerdata
WHERE nickname = \"" << LobbyLoginPtr->nickname << "\"";
```

Notice here how we use the nickname from the LobbyLoginPtr variable, which is the nickname the user entered in the client application we retrieved from the message.

Since this time we are retrieving data from MySQL, we need to create a Result object to store the data that is sent back from MySQL once we execute the query. The following code segment executes the query and stores it in a Result object called res:

```
// -> Store the results from the query
Result res = query.store();
```

Now that we have our result stored in our Result object, we need to create an iterator and set it to the start of the results. Note that we also declare a Row object here, which will contain a single record of data at one time. All this is done with the following code:

```
Result::iterator i;
Row row;
i = res.begin();
```

Now that our iterator i is set to the start of the list of results, we need to first check that a result was obtained. If a result was not obtained, the most probable cause is that the nickname was not in the database. Following is our If statement to check that a result was present:

```
if(i!=res.end())
{
```

If a result was present, we then assign the current iterator to our Row object so we can access the information contained within the current record pointed to by the iterator.

Next, we make sure that the password we obtained from MySQL is the same as the password the user entered in the Login dialog. Following is the code segment that checks the password for equality:

```
if(!strcmp(password,row["password"]))
{
```

If the password was matched correctly, we then need to update the lastlogin date and the online status of the user in the database. Following is the code for the two queries we require to do this, respectively:

```
// -> Update the 'lastlogin' field to current date and time
query << "UPDATE playerdata SET lastlogin = NULL
WHERE id = " << row["id"];
query.execute();

// -> Set the player to 'online'
query << "UPDATE playerdata SET online = 1
WHERE id = " << row["id"];
query.execute();

// -> Player Login Successful!

LobbyLoginFeedbackData.result = LOBBYLOGIN_RESULT_ACCEPTED;
```

Notice in the preceding code that we utilize the user's ID number, which we obtained from the database at the same time as retrieving the password. In the first query, we simply update the user's lastlogin field with the NULL value so that the field is set to the current time and date. In the second instance, we set the user's online field to 1 to indicate that the player is now logged into the game. Also, note that we set the feedback message result to Accepted, so when we send it the client application will know that the login was accepted by the server.

We now require the Else part of the password matching If statement. This will handle what happens when the user's password does not match the nickname that was entered. All we need to do here is set the feedback message result to state that the password was not accepted. This is done with the following code segment:

```
    else
    {
        // -> Password did not match
        LobbyLoginFeedbackData.result = LOBBYLOGIN_
        RESULT_PASSWORDBAD;
    }
}
```

The final part to our Try statement is the case where a nickname was not found in the database. All we need to do here is simply set the feedback result to state that the server did not accept the nickname. This is done with the following code:

```
    else
    {
        // -> Nickname could not be found
        LobbyLoginFeedbackData.result = LOBBYLOGIN_RESULT_USERNAMEBAD;
```

```
                }
            }
```

Finally, we need to complete our Try/Catch statement by adding the Catch part. We will assume that any errors not handled internally in the Try statement will be classed as MySQL failures (such as the MySQL server not running). Therefore, all we require for our Catch statement is to set the feedback result to state that a database error has occurred. This is done with this next code segment:

```
catch (BadQuery er) // handle any connection errors
        {
                // -> mySQL Server not running?
                LobbyLoginFeedbackData.result = LOBBYLOGIN_RESULT_MYSQLERROR;
        }
```

Finally, we can send the feedback message back to the client as it will contain the appropriate result number. We do this using the sendLobbyLoginMessage procedure, which we will create later in this section. The code to send the feedback message is as follows:

```
                // Send the result back to the client
                sendLobbyLoginMessage((NETMSG_GENERIC *) &LobbyLoginFeedbackData);
                break;
```

The other message we need to be able to handle is the CreateAccount message. When the server receives this message, it needs to be able to insert the new account data into MySQL then send back the result to the client by means of a CreateAccountFeedback message.

First though, we need to copy the data from the incoming signup message into a local variable. This is done with the following code:

```
case TUT_MSG_LOBBYCREATEACCOUNT:

                TUT_MSG_LOBBYCREATEACCOUNT_DATA *LobbyCreateAccountPtr;
                LobbyCreateAccountPtr = (TUT_MSG_LOBBYCREATEACCOUNT_DATA *) Msg;
```

By doing this, we now have all the user's signup information stored in the LobbyCreateAccountPtr variable.

Next, we set up our CreateAccountFeedback message in the same way we did previously with our LoginFeedback message. This is done with the following code segment:

```
                TUT_MSG_LOBBYCREATEACCOUNT_FEEDBACK_DATA LobbyCreateAccountFeedbackData;
                LobbyCreateAccountFeedbackData.type = TUT_MSG_LOBBYCREATEACCOUNT_FEEDBACK;
                LobbyCreateAccountFeedbackData.toId = LobbyCreateAccountPtr->fromId;
                LobbyCreateAccountFeedbackData.fromId = tutServer.localId;
```

Again, notice how we first set the type of message to the CreateAccountFeedback message, then set toId to fromId of the CreateAccount message, which is stored in our local variable LobbyCreateAccountPtr.

When we attempt the connection to the database, we again use the Try/Catch statement, so we can easily recover from any errors that may occur. First, we open the Try statement and attempt a connection to our MySQL database on the local machine (127.0.0.1):

```
try
{
    // -> Create a connection to the database
    Connection con("onlinedata","127.0.0.1");
```

After our connection to the database is established, we then need to create a query object, which is bound to our connection. We do this with the following code segment:

```
// -> Create a query object that is bound to our connection
Query query = con.query();
```

Now that we have our query object, we can set up a single query that will add a new record of data into our playerdata table in our MySQL database. We use the following code to set the query to enter our data into the database:

```
// -> Add the players data
query << "INSERT INTO playerdata VALUES (NULL,\"" <<
LobbyCreateAccountPtr->nickname <<
        "\",\"" << LobbyCreateAccountPtr->firstname <<
        "\",\"" << LobbyCreateAccountPtr->surname <<
        "\"," << LobbyCreateAccountPtr->age <<
        ",\"" << LobbyCreateAccountPtr->gender <<
        "\",\"" << LobbyCreateAccountPtr->password <<
        "\",NULL,0,\"" << LobbyCreateAccountPtr->email <<
        "\")";
```

All we are doing in this code is substituting the actual data of an Insert query with the values that were sent from the client application. Remember that all the values are stored in the LobbyCreateAccountPtr variable, as we copied our message data into this variable.

After the query is set up, we can then execute it with the following simple code:

```
query.execute();
```

At this point, the user's account details are stored as a new record in the playerdata table. We can now set the result part of our feedback message to inform the client application that the account creation was successful. This is done with the following code:

```
// -> Send account created successfully message back to client...
LobbyCreateAccountFeedbackData.result = LOBBYCREATEACCOUNT
_RESULT_ACCEPTED;

}
```

Again, we need to create our Catch statement to catch any errors that occur within the Try statement. The most common reason for the Try statement failing is the database server not running, so we simply set the result to state that a database error has occurred. Here is the complete code segment for our Catch statement:

```
catch (BadQuery er) // handle any connection errors
{
    // -> Send a mySQL Error back to the client
    // (this should never happen)
    LobbyCreateAccountFeedbackData.result = LOBBYCREATEACCOUNT
    _RESULT_MYSQLERROR;
}
```

Finally, we can send the feedback message to the client. This is done in the same way as the LoginFeedback message, with the following code:

```
// Send the result back to the client
sendLobbyLoginMessage((NETMSG_GENERIC *) &LobbyCreateAccountFeedbackData);
```

Now we can complete our message handling function with the following code:

```
        break;
    default:
        break;
    }
}
```

Now we need to create a function that is controlled by our network library to check for incoming messages from the client application. This is simply a function that we will expand in later tutorials to handle more types of messages, such as lobby and game messages. Here is the code for our function to call our message handling functions:

```
void NET_HandleMessages(NETMSG_GENERIC *Msg)
{
    handleLobbyLoginMessages(Msg);
}
```

Notice how the function passes the message to the handleLobbyLoginMessages function for it to process the message. By doing it this way, we easily add different handling functions for different types of messages.

The final part of our server application is the function to handle sending messages. We start this function with the following code segment:

```
void sendLobbyLoginMessage(NETMSG_GENERIC *Msg)
{
    NETMSGDATA_DATASIZE DataMsg;
    memset(&DataMsg, 0, sizeof(NETMSGDATA_DATASIZE));
```

First, we create an empty Datasize message. The size part of this message is set to the size of the message we wish to send and sent to the client first so that the client knows the size of the real incoming message.

Next, we open a switch statement so we can handle more than one type of outgoing message. This is done with the following code:

```
    switch(Msg->type)
    {
```

The first message we will handle is the LoginFeedback message. First, we create a pointer of the message type and then assign the message pointer to our local pointer. This is done with the following code:

```
    case TUT_MSG_LOBBYLOGIN_FEEDBACK:
        TUT_MSG_LOBBYLOGIN_FEEDBACK_DATA *LobbyLoginFeedbackDataPtr;
        LobbyLoginFeedbackDataPtr = (TUT_MSG_LOBBYLOGIN_FEEDBACK_DATA *) Msg;
```

Next, we set our Datasize message to the size of our LoginFeedback message by using the sizeof function. This is done with the following code segment:

```
        DataMsg.type = NETMSG_DATASIZE;
        DataMsg.toId   = Msg->toId;
        DataMsg.fromId = Msg->fromId;
        DataMsg.size = sizeof(TUT_MSG_LOBBYLOGIN_FEEDBACK_DATA);
```

Now we send the Datasize message to the client with the following line of code:

```
        tutServer.Write(Msg->toId, (char *) &DataMsg,
        sizeof(NETMSGDATA_DATASIZE));
```

Once the Datasize message is sent, we can send our actual message with the following line of code:

```
        tutServer.Write(Msg->toId, (char *) LobbyLoginFeedbackDataPtr,
        sizeof(TUT_MSG_LOBBYLOGIN_FEEDBACK_DATA));
        break;
```

That is all we require to send our LoginFeedback message, so we can then close the Case statement and handle our other message, which is the CreateAccountFeedback message.

The CreateAccountFeedback message is handled in exactly the same way. First, the message is pointed to by a local pointer of the CreateAccountFeedback type. This is done with the following code:

```
case TUT_MSG_LOBBYCREATEACCOUNT_FEEDBACK:
    TUT_MSG_LOBBYCREATEACCOUNT_FEEDBACK_DATA *LobbyCreateAccount
    FeedbackDataPtr;
    LobbyCreateAccountFeedbackDataPtr = (TUT_MSG_LOBBYCREATEACCOUNT
    _FEEDBACK_DATA *) Msg;
```

Next, the Datasize message size variable is set to the actual size of our Create-AccountFeedback message. This is done in the same way as before with the following code:

```
DataMsg.type = NETMSG_DATASIZE;
DataMsg.toId  = Msg->toId;
DataMsg.fromId = Msg->fromId;
DataMsg.size = sizeof(TUT_MSG_LOBBYCREATEACCOUNT_FEEDBACK_DATA);
```

Once this is done, we can send the Datasize message with the following line of code:

```
tutServer.Write(Msg->toId, (char *) &DataMsg,
sizeof(NETMSGDATA_DATASIZE));
```

Then, finally, we can send our actual message and end our function:

```
tutServer.Write(Msg->toId, (char *) LobbyCreateAccountFeedbackDataPtr,
sizeof(TUT_MSG_LOBBYCREATEACCOUNT_FEEDBACK_DATA));
    break;

default:
    break;
    }
}
```

This completes the code for the server. Nothing interesting happens when you run it because we need to complete the client code so we can interact with it.

Server Application — Complete Code Listing

Here is the complete code listing for the server application. After the listing, we will complete the client application so we can create accounts and login using the server.

netcommon.h

```
#ifndef NETCOMMON_H
#define NETCOMMON_H
```

```
/*---------------------
   Lobby login messages
   ---------------------*/
typedef struct
{
    int type;
    HOSTID toId;
    HOSTID fromId;
    char nickname[32];
    char password[32];
} TUT_MSG_LOBBYLOGIN_DATA;

typedef struct
{
    int type;
    HOSTID toId;
    HOSTID fromId;
    char nickname[32];
    int result;
} TUT_MSG_LOBBYLOGIN_FEEDBACK_DATA;

typedef struct
{
    int type;
    HOSTID toId;
    HOSTID fromId;
    char nickname[30];
    char firstname[50];
    char surname[50];
    int age;
    char gender[10];
    char password[50];
    char email[150];
} TUT_MSG_LOBBYCREATEACCOUNT_DATA;

typedef struct
{
    int type;
    HOSTID toId;
    HOSTID fromId;
    int result;
} TUT_MSG_LOBBYCREATEACCOUNT_FEEDBACK_DATA;


/*----------------------------
   message number definitions
   ----------------------------*/
```

```
#define TUT_MSG_LOBBYLOGIN                       100     // login
#define TUT_MSG_LOBBYLOGIN_FEEDBACK              101     // login
#define TUT_MSG_LOBBYCREATEACCOUNT               102     // login
#define TUT_MSG_LOBBYCREATEACCOUNT_FEEDBACK      103     // login


#define LOBBYLOGIN_RESULT_ACCEPTED               200
#define LOBBYLOGIN_RESULT_USERNAMEBAD            201
#define LOBBYLOGIN_RESULT_PASSWORDBAD            202
#define LOBBYLOGIN_RESULT_MYSQLERROR             203


#define LOBBYCREATEACCOUNT_RESULT_ACCEPTED       300
#define LOBBYCREATEACCOUNT_RESULT_MYSQLERROR     301



#endif
```

server.h

```
/* Login Server */
#ifndef SERVER_H
#define SERVER_H

// Defines
#define KEEPALIVE_TIMEOUT       60

// Classes
class ArmyServerClass
{
    public:
        int Init(void);
        void Shutdown(void);
};

extern ArmyServerClass ArmyServer;

// Function Prototypes
void handleLobbyLoginMessages(NETMSG_GENERIC *Msg);
void sendLobbyLoginMessage(NETMSG_GENERIC *Msg);
void Send(NETMSG_GENERIC *Msg);

#endif
```

server.cpp

```
/* Login Server */
#ifndef _WINSOCKAPI_
#define _WINSOCKAPI_
```

```c
#include <windows.h>
#include "resource.h"

#include <netLib.h>
#include <string.h>
#include <stdlib.h>
#include <stdio.h>
#include <mysql++>

#include "netcommon.h"
#include "server.h"
#include "assert.h"

HWND hWnd_netLib;
NET_Socket tutServer;
ArmyServerClass ArmyServer;

int ArmyServerClass::Init(void)
{
    if(NET_Initialize() != 0)
    {
        LogString("Error initialising Communication Library!");
        return 1;
    }

    if(tutServer.CreateServer(9009, NET_UDP) != 0)
    {
        LogString("Failed to Create the Server");
        return 1;
    }

    LogString("ONLINE");

    return 0;
}

void ArmyServerClass::Shutdown(void)
{
    LogString("Shutting Down Server...");

    tutServer.Shutdown();
    NET_Shutdown();
}

LRESULT CALLBACK ServerDlgProc(HWND DialogWindow, UINT Message, WPARAM wParam,
LPARAM lParam)
{
```

```
    // Process Messages
    switch(Message)
    {
    case WM_INITDIALOG:
        hWnd_netLib = DialogWindow;
        ArmyServer.Init();

        return(FALSE);

    case WM_COMMAND:
        switch(wParam)
        {
        case IDCANCEL:
            ArmyServer.Shutdown();
            EndDialog(DialogWindow, FALSE);
            return FALSE;
        }
        break;

    case USMSG_ACCEPT:
        tutServer.AcceptConnection();
        break;

    default:
        break;
    }

    return FALSE;
}

int APIENTRY WinMain(HINSTANCE hInstance, HINSTANCE hPrevInstance, LPSTR lpCmdLine,
int nCmdShow)
{
    DialogBox((HINSTANCE) hInstance, MAKEINTRESOURCE(IDD_SERVERDIALOG),
        hWnd_netLib, (DLGPROC) ServerDlgProc);

    return 0;
}


void handleLobbyLoginMessages(NETMSG_GENERIC *Msg)
{
    // Here the generic message is used to get the type out of the message
    // structure. It is then used in the switch statement.
    switch(Msg->type)
    {
    case TUT_MSG_LOBBYLOGIN:
```

```
TUT_MSG_LOBBYLOGIN_DATA *LobbyLoginPtr;
LobbyLoginPtr = (TUT_MSG_LOBBYLOGIN_DATA *) Msg;

LogString("Got lobby login message (nick: %s)", LobbyLoginPtr->nickname);


TUT_MSG_LOBBYLOGIN_FEEDBACK_DATA LobbyLoginFeedbackData;
LobbyLoginFeedbackData.type          = TUT_MSG_LOBBYLOGIN_FEEDBACK;
LobbyLoginFeedbackData.toId          = LobbyLoginPtr->fromId;
LobbyLoginFeedbackData.fromId        = tutServer.localId;
strcpy(LobbyLoginFeedbackData.nickname,LobbyLoginPtr->nickname);

// mySQL Connection
try
{
    // -> Create a connection to the database
    Connection con("onlinedata", "127.0.0.1");

    // -> Create a query object that is bound to our connection
    Query query = con.query();

    // -> Assign the query to that object
    query << "SELECT id,firstname,password FROM playerdata
    WHERE nickname = \"" << LobbyLoginPtr->nickname << "\"";

    // -> Store the results from the query
    Result res = query.store();

    Result::iterator i;
    Row row;
    i = res.begin();

    if(i!=res.end())
    {
        row = *i;
        if(!strcmp(LobbyLoginPtr->password,row["password"]))
        {
            // -> Update the 'lastlogin' field to current date and time
            query << "UPDATE playerdata SET lastlogin = NULL
            WHERE id = " << row["id"];
            query.execute();

            // -> Set the player to 'online'
            query << "UPDATE playerdata SET online = 1
            WHERE id = " << row["id"];
            query.execute();
```

```
                            // -> Player Login Successful!
                            LobbyLoginFeedbackData.result = LOBBYLOGIN_RESULT_ACCEPTED;
                    }
                    else
                    {
                            // -> Password did not match
                            LobbyLoginFeedbackData.result = LOBBYLOGIN_RESULT
                            _PASSWORDBAD;
                    }
            }
            else
            {
                    // -> Nickname could not be found
                    LobbyLoginFeedbackData.result = LOBBYLOGIN_RESULT_USERNAMEBAD;
            }
    }
    catch (BadQuery er) // handle any connection errors
    {
            // -> mySQL Server not running?
            LobbyLoginFeedbackData.result = LOBBYLOGIN_RESULT_MYSQLERROR;
    }


    // Send the result back to the client
    sendLobbyLoginMessage((NETMSG_GENERIC *) &LobbyLoginFeedbackData);
    break;

case TUT_MSG_LOBBYCREATEACCOUNT:

    TUT_MSG_LOBBYCREATEACCOUNT_DATA *LobbyCreateAccountPtr;
    LobbyCreateAccountPtr = (TUT_MSG_LOBBYCREATEACCOUNT_DATA *) Msg;

    LogString("Got CreateAccount message");

    TUT_MSG_LOBBYCREATEACCOUNT_FEEDBACK_DATA LobbyCreateAccountFeedbackData;
    LobbyCreateAccountFeedbackData.type = TUT_MSG_LOBBYCREATEACCOUNT_FEEDBACK;
    LobbyCreateAccountFeedbackData.toId  = LobbyCreateAccountPtr->fromId;
    LobbyCreateAccountFeedbackData.fromId = tutServer.localId;

    // mySQL Connection
    try
    {
            // -> Create a connection to the database
            Connection con("onlinedata","127.0.0.1");

            // -> Create a query object that is bound to our connection
            Query query = con.query();
```

```
                    // -> Add the players data
                    query << "INSERT INTO playerdata VALUES (NULL,\"" <<
                    LobbyCreateAccountPtr->nickname <<
                        "\",\"" << LobbyCreateAccountPtr->firstname <<
                        "\",\"" << LobbyCreateAccountPtr->surname <<
                        "\"," << LobbyCreateAccountPtr->age <<
                        ",\"" << LobbyCreateAccountPtr->gender <<
                        "\",\"" << LobbyCreateAccountPtr->password <<
                        "\",NULL,0,\"" << LobbyCreateAccountPtr->email <<
                        "\")";
                    query.execute();

                    // -> Send account created successfully message back to client...
                    LobbyCreateAccountFeedbackData.result = LOBBYCREATEACCOUNT
                    _RESULT_ACCEPTED;

                }
                catch (BadQuery er) // handle any connection errors
                {
                    // -> Send a mySQL Error back to the client
                    // (this should never happen)
                    LobbyCreateAccountFeedbackData.result = LOBBYCREATEACCOUNT
                    _RESULT_MYSQLERROR;
                }


                // Send the result back to the client
                sendLobbyLoginMessage((NETMSG_GENERIC *) &LobbyCreateAccountFeedbackData);
                break;
            default:
                break;
        }
}


void NET_HandleMessages(NETMSG_GENERIC *Msg)
{
    handleLobbyLoginMessages(Msg);
}


void sendLobbyLoginMessage(NETMSG_GENERIC *Msg)
{
    NETMSGDATA_DATASIZE DataMsg;
    memset(&DataMsg, 0, sizeof(NETMSGDATA_DATASIZE));
```

```
        switch(Msg->type)
        {
        case TUT_MSG_LOBBYLOGIN_FEEDBACK:
            TUT_MSG_LOBBYLOGIN_FEEDBACK_DATA *LobbyLoginFeedbackDataPtr;
            LobbyLoginFeedbackDataPtr = (TUT_MSG_LOBBYLOGIN_FEEDBACK_DATA *) Msg;
            DataMsg.type = NETMSG_DATASIZE;
            DataMsg.toId   = Msg->toId;
            DataMsg.fromId = Msg->fromId;
            DataMsg.size = sizeof(TUT_MSG_LOBBYLOGIN_FEEDBACK_DATA);

            LogString("Lobby Login feedback to id %d (Msg->type: %d)",
            Msg->toId, Msg->type);

            tutServer.Write(Msg->toId, (char *) &DataMsg,
            sizeof(NETMSGDATA_DATASIZE));
            tutServer.Write(Msg->toId, (char *) LobbyLoginFeedbackDataPtr,
            sizeof(TUT_MSG_LOBBYLOGIN_FEEDBACK_DATA));
            break;

        case TUT_MSG_LOBBYCREATEACCOUNT_FEEDBACK:
            TUT_MSG_LOBBYCREATEACCOUNT_FEEDBACK_DATA
            *LobbyCreateAccountFeedbackDataPtr;
            LobbyCreateAccountFeedbackDataPtr =
            (TUT_MSG_LOBBYCREATEACCOUNT_FEEDBACK_DATA *) Msg;
            DataMsg.type = NETMSG_DATASIZE;
            DataMsg.toId   = Msg->toId;
            DataMsg.fromId = Msg->fromId;
            DataMsg.size = sizeof(TUT_MSG_LOBBYCREATEACCOUNT_FEEDBACK_DATA);

            LogString("Lobby CreateAccount feedback to id %d (Msg->type: %d)",
            Msg->toId, Msg->type);

            tutServer.Write(Msg->toId, (char *) &DataMsg,
            sizeof(NETMSGDATA_DATASIZE));
            tutServer.Write(Msg->toId, (char *) LobbyCreateAccountFeedbackDataPtr,
            sizeof(TUT_MSG_LOBBYCREATEACCOUNT_FEEDBACK_DATA));
            break;

        default:
            break;
        }
    }

#endif
```

TUTORIAL 3

Integrating the Login System (Part 2)

Now that we have the server application and our netcommon.h header file, we can complete the rest of the client application. First, we are going to add network.cpp and network.h to our client workspace.

Once our extra source files are in the project, we can then create our network code to send the login and account creation details to our login server. Then, finally, we can complete our DoLogin and DoCreateAccount functions in login.cpp.

Let's now look at the code we need in our network.h header file. First, we need two externs, which hold our serverSocket and also the IP address of the server application. These are declared as follows:

```
extern NET_Socket serverSocket;
extern char serverIP[64];
```

Then, the only other line of code we require in the header is the following prototype:

```
void sendLobbyLoginMessage(NETMSG_GENERIC *Msg);
```

This function is used in our network.cpp file to send our login and create account messages to the server.

Now that we have our header file, let's look at what we require in our main client network source file, network.cpp:

```
#include <netlib.h>
#include <windows.h>
#include <gl/gl.h>
#include <gl/glu.h>
#include <gl/glaux.h>
#include <2dlib.h>

#include "resource.h"
#include "main.h"
#include "login.h"
#include "network.h"

#include "..\tutLoginServer\netcommon.h"
```

We include all the standard header files we have included for the rest of the client application, with the addition of the netcommon.h header. When we include the netcommon.h header, we simply reference it directly from our server application; therefore, if we add more network message types we always have an up-to-date file for both of the applications.

Next, we declare our two required global variables, which are the serverSocket and the IPaddress of the server. These are declared as follows:

```
NET_Socket serverSocket;

char serverIP[64];
```

Now we can create a function to handle messages incoming from the server application. This will consist of feedback messages for both login and account creation. Just before we actually make this function, we need to add the following Case statement to the main application windows procedure:

```
case USMSG_CLOSECONNECTION:
{
        serverSocket.CloseConnection(wParam, lParam);
        return 0;

}
```

This extra Case will handle messages that will close active connections to the server (which we are going to use in this message handling function).

First, we need to start the function and switch the message type so we can handle the correct message coming into the function. This is done with the following code segment:

```
void handleLobbyLoginMessages(NETMSG_GENERIC *Msg)
{
        switch(Msg->type)
        {
```

The first message we are going to handle is the LoginFeedback message. So we create a Case in the switch statement for it and also assign the message data to a local pointer so we can easily reference the information in the message. This is done with the next code segment:

```
case TUT_MSG_LOBBYLOGIN_FEEDBACK:

                TUT_MSG_LOBBYLOGIN_FEEDBACK_DATA *LobbyLoginFeedbackPtr;
                LobbyLoginFeedbackPtr = (TUT_MSG_LOBBYLOGIN_FEEDBACK_DATA *) Msg;
```

Now that we have the message accessible from a local pointer, we need to switch the different result codes and react to them accordingly. Following is the switch we use for this:

```
                // Switch the result code
                switch(LobbyLoginFeedbackPtr->result)
                {
```

Notice how we simply access the Result variable from the pointer to the message LobbyLoginFeedbackPtr.

Let's look now at how we deal with each of the possibilities, the first being that the login details were accepted:

```
case LOBBYLOGIN_RESULT_ACCEPTED:

    MessageBox(NULL,"The login details were accepted","Message",MB_OK);

    // Complete Login Procedure (covered in the next tutorial)

    break;
```

As you can see, all we do is display a message box that informs the user that the login details were accepted. In the next tutorial, we will actually log the player into a game lobby and allow them to chat with other logged in players, then even later they will be able to create games and play online with other players.

Anyway, we also need to handle the Case where the username and/or password was not acceptable and also if some other database-related error occurred. This is done with the final three Cases that can be seen in the following code segment:

```
case LOBBYLOGIN_RESULT_PASSWORDBAD:
    SendMessage(hWnd_Application, USMSG_CLOSECONNECTION,
    NETID_SERVER, 1);
    MessageBox(NULL,"The password was not accepted","Message",MB_OK);
    ShowWindow(hWnd_LoginDialog,SW_SHOW);
    break;

case LOBBYLOGIN_RESULT_USERNAMEBAD:
    SendMessage(hWnd_Application, USMSG_CLOSECONNECTION,
    NETID_SERVER, 1);
    MessageBox(NULL,"The username was not accepted as
    valid","Message",MB_OK);
    ShowWindow(hWnd_LoginDialog,SW_SHOW);
    break;

case LOBBYLOGIN_RESULT_MYSQLERROR:
    SendMessage(hWnd_Application, USMSG_CLOSECONNECTION,
    NETID_SERVER, 1);
    MessageBox(NULL,"An unknown database error
    occurred","Message",MB_OK);
    ShowWindow(hWnd_LoginDialog,SW_SHOW);
    break;
}
break;
```

For each of the Cases, we send a Windows message to the main application Windows procedure to make it close the connection to the server, then we display to the user, by means of a message box, the error that occurred. Finally, in each Case, we make the login screen visible (as we hide it when a login is being attempted) with the ShowWindow function.

This completes the handling for the LoginFeedback message. The other message we must handle is the CreateAccountFeedback message. We do this in a very similar fashion, as it too uses result codes.

First, we create a Case for the CreateAccountFeedback message, then we again assign the message data to a local pointer for ease of access. This can be seen in the following code segment:

```
case TUT_MSG_LOBBYCREATEACCOUNT_FEEDBACK:

    TUT_MSG_LOBBYCREATEACCOUNT_FEEDBACK_DATA *LobbyCreateAccountFeedbackPtr;
    LobbyCreateAccountFeedbackPtr = (TUT_MSG_LOBBYCREATEACCOUNT_FEEDBACK_
    DATA *) Msg;
```

Once we have the message assigned to our local pointer, we can then switch the result code as we did previously with the LoginFeedback message. Here is the code for the start of the switch statement:

```
// Switch the result code
switch(LobbyCreateAccountFeedbackPtr->result)
{
```

We only have two types of results concerning the CreateAccountFeedback message; either it was successful or an unknown database error occurred.

First, we will deal the feedback message being successful. For this we use the following code segment:

```
case LOBBYCREATEACCOUNT_RESULT_ACCEPTED:
    SendMessage(hWnd_Application, USMSG_CLOSECONNECTION,
    NETID_SERVER, 1);
    MessageBox(hWnd_LoginDialog,"The new account details were
    accepted\nYou can now login with your new account
    details","Success!",MB_OK);
    break;
```

All we are doing here is closing the connection to the server (by sending a Windows message to the main application Windows procedure telling it to do this), then displaying a message box telling the user his information was accepted by the server.

We do exactly the same for the other result, except we change the information in the message box to state that an unknown database error occurred. This can be seen in the following code:

```
case LOBBYCREATEACCOUNT_RESULT_MYSQLERROR:
    SendMessage(hWnd_Application, USMSG_CLOSECONNECTION,
    NETID_SERVER, 1);
    MessageBox(NULL,"An unknown database error
    occurred","Message",MB_OK);
    break;
```

```
        }

        break;
    }
}
```

That concludes the message handling function. We must then include this handling function in the NET_HandleMessages function, so that it is used by our network library to handle incoming messages. This is done with the following function:

```
void NET_HandleMessages(NETMSG_GENERIC *Msg)
{
    handleLobbyLoginMessages(Msg);
}
```

Notice how this function simply passes the entire incoming message into our handleLobbyLoginMessages function to be processed. In later tutorials, we will be adding more handling functions in here to deal with other message types.

The final part of our network.cpp source file is the ability to send the required network messages, which in this case are the actual Login and Create Account messages (which the server receives and handles).

First, we start our send function and declare a local Datasize message using the following code segment:

```
void sendLobbyLoginMessage(NETMSG_GENERIC *Msg)
{
    NETMSGDATA_DATASIZE DataMsg;
    memset(&DataMsg, 0, sizeof(NETMSGDATA_DATASIZE));
```

Next, we start a switch statement, to decide which type of message we are trying to send. This is done with the following lines of code:

```
    switch(Msg->type)
    {
```

The first outgoing message we will deal with is the Login message. We need to first create a Case for this message, then assign the message data to a local pointer. This is done with the following code segment:

```
        case TUT_MSG_LOBBYLOGIN:
            TUT_MSG_LOBBYLOGIN_DATA *LobbyLoginDataPtr;
            LobbyLoginDataPtr = (TUT_MSG_LOBBYLOGIN_DATA *) Msg;
```

Next, we need to set up our Datasize message so that the server knows how large the message is going to be when we send it. This is done with the next code segment:

```
DataMsg.type = NETMSG_DATASIZE;
DataMsg.toId  = Msg->toId;
DataMsg.fromId = Msg->fromId;
DataMsg.size = sizeof(TUT_MSG_LOBBYLOGIN_DATA);
```

Notice again how we simply use the sizeof function to declare the size of the structure we are going to send, which in this case is the Tut_Msg_Lobby-Login_Data structure.

Once this is done, we can send our Datasize message to the server with the following line of code:

```
serverSocket.Write(Msg->toId, (char *) &DataMsg,
sizeof(NETMSGDATA_DATASIZE));
```

Then we can send our actual message and end the Case with the next two lines of code:

```
serverSocket.Write(Msg->toId, (char *) LobbyLoginDataPtr,
sizeof(TUT_MSG_LOBBYLOGIN_DATA));
break;
```

Sending the CreateAccount message is done in exactly the same way. First, we create the Case for it and assign the message to a local pointer. This is accomplished with the following code segment:

```
case TUT_MSG_LOBBYCREATEACCOUNT:
    TUT_MSG_LOBBYCREATEACCOUNT_DATA *LobbyCreateAccountDataPtr;
    LobbyCreateAccountDataPtr = (TUT_MSG_LOBBYCREATEACCOUNT_DATA *) Msg;
```

Then, again, we need to set up our Datasize message, this time using the size of the Tut_Msg_LobbyCreateAccount_Data structure. This is done with the following code:

```
DataMsg.type = NETMSG_DATASIZE;
DataMsg.toId  = Msg->toId;
DataMsg.fromId = Msg->fromId;
DataMsg.size = sizeof(TUT_MSG_LOBBYCREATEACCOUNT_DATA);
```

Now we can send the Datasize message with the next line of code:

```
serverSocket.Write(Msg->toId, (char *) &DataMsg,
sizeof(NETMSGDATA_DATASIZE));
```

Finally, we can send the actual CreateAccount message and finish our send message function. This is done with this final code segment for the network.cpp file:

```
serverSocket.Write(Msg->toId, (char *) LobbyCreateAccountDataPtr,
sizeof(TUT_MSG_LOBBYCREATEACCOUNT_DATA));
break;
    }
}
```

TUTORIAL 3

Now that we have our network section of the client complete, we can complete the final functions in our login.cpp file. Let's first look at the DoLogin function.

First, we start the function and create two local variables to store the user's username and password:

```
int DoLogin(void)
{
    char nickname[30];
    char password[50];
```

Next, we need to retrieve all the information from the edit boxes on the dialog, which consists of the IP address of the server, the username, and the password. This is done using the following code segment:

```
// -> First get the IP address of the server from the dialog
GetDlgItemText(hWnd_LoginDialog, IDC_LOGIN_IPADDRESS, serverIP, 16);

// -> Store the player data in local variables
GetDlgItemText(hWnd_LoginDialog, IDC_LOGIN_NICKNAME, nickname, 30);
GetDlgItemText(hWnd_LoginDialog, IDC_LOGIN_PASSWORD, password, 50);
```

To retrieve the information, we use a Win32 function, GetDlgItemText, which gets the text from the specified edit box and stores it in a char array.

Next, we will hide the window while the login is attempted. This is done with the Win32 function ShowWindow, which can be seen in the following line of code:

```
// -> Hide the Login Window
ShowWindow(hWnd_LoginDialog,SW_HIDE);
```

Now we need to establish a connection to the server. If the connection fails, we will display a message box to inform the user, then make the Login dialog visible again. This is accomplished in the following code segment:

```
// -> Connect to the server
if(serverSocket.ConnectToServer(serverIP, 9009, NET_UDP) == NET_INVALID_SOCKET)
{
    MessageBox(NULL, "Game Server Connection Error", "Fatal Error", MB_OK);
    ShowWindow(hWnd_LoginDialog,SW_SHOW);
    return 1;
}
```

Also notice here how we have used serverIP, which we obtained from the Login dialog. Now that we have a connection, we need to set up the Login message we wish to send to the server. We set up the message with the following code segment:

```
// -> Send Lobby Login Message
TUT_MSG_LOBBYLOGIN_DATA LobbyLoginData;
LobbyLoginData.type          = TUT_MSG_LOBBYLOGIN;
```

```
LobbyLoginData.toId              = NETID_SERVER;
LobbyLoginData.fromId            = serverSocket.localId;
strcpy(LobbyLoginData.nickname,nickname);
strcpy(LobbyLoginData.password,password);
```

First, we create a local variable called LobbyLoginData to hold the message (of the correct structure type which is Tut_Msg_LobbyLogin_Data). Then, we set the type of the message to Tut_Msg_LobbyLogin. This is so the server can correctly interpret the type of message it is receiving. Next, we set toId to NETId_Server, which is defined in our network library to represent the server. Then, we set fromId to the serverSocket.localId, which represents our client and is assigned when the connection is made. Note that fromId is used by the server to send the feedback message back to the client. Finally, we use the string copy function strcpy to copy the player's username and password into the message.

Now that we have our message set up correctly, we can send it and finish our DoLogin function with the following code segment:

```
sendLobbyLoginMessage((NETMSG_GENERIC *) &LobbyLoginData);

    return 0;
}
```

Note here how we are using the SendLobbyLoginMessage function we created in our network.cpp source file.

Now we can handle player login. We now finally need to finish our DoCreateAccount function.

First, we start the function and declare local variables to hold all the account information we need to send to the server. This is done with the following code segment:

```
int DoCreateAccount(void)
{
    char nickname[30];
    char firstname[50];
    char surname[50];
    int age;
    char gender[10];
    char password[50];
    char password2[50];
    char email[150];
```

Next, we get the IP address of the server from the Server IP edit box. This is done with the following code:

```
// -> First get the IP address of the server from the dialog
GetDlgItemText(hWnd_CreateAccountDialog, IDC_CREATEACCOUNT_IPADDRESS,
serverIP, 20);
```

Next, we can retrieve the rest of the account data in a similar fashion with the following code:

```
// -> Store the player data in local variables
GetDlgItemText(hWnd_CreateAccountDialog, IDC_CREATEACCOUNT_NICKNAME,
nickname, 30);
GetDlgItemText(hWnd_CreateAccountDialog, IDC_CREATEACCOUNT_FIRSTNAME,
firstname, 50);
GetDlgItemText(hWnd_CreateAccountDialog, IDC_CREATEACCOUNT_SURNAME,
surname, 50);
age = GetDlgItemInt(hWnd_CreateAccountDialog, IDC_CREATEACCOUNT_AGE,
NULL, FALSE);
GetDlgItemText(hWnd_CreateAccountDialog, IDC_CREATEACCOUNT_GENDER, gender, 10);
GetDlgItemText(hWnd_CreateAccountDialog, IDC_CREATEACCOUNT_PASSWORD1,
password, 50);
GetDlgItemText(hWnd_CreateAccountDialog, IDC_CREATEACCOUNT_PASSWORD2,
password2, 50);
GetDlgItemText(hWnd_CreateAccountDialog, IDC_CREATEACCOUNT_EMAIL, email, 150);
```

To save wasted messages and reduce the workload of the server, it makes sense to check the data before we send it. Therefore, we check that all the variables contain information with the following code segment:

```
// -> Check all the fields have been filled in
if(!strcmp(nickname,"") || !strcmp(firstname,"") || !strcmp(surname,"") ||
!strcmp(gender,"") || !strcmp(password,"") || !strcmp(email,"") || age < 1)
{
    MessageBox(hWnd_CreateAccountDialog, "Not all fields have been filled
    in!\n\nPlease check and try again...", "Information Error", MB_OK);
    return 0;
}
```

If a field does not contain any data, we inform the user by means of a message box and stop the function (i.e., we do not send the message to the server).

If all the fields were filled in, we can then continue and check that the two password fields match. This is done with the next code segment by utilizing the string compare function strcmp:

```
// -> Check the passwords match
if(strcmp(password,password2))
{
    MessageBox(hWnd_CreateAccountDialog,
        "The two passwords you entered do not match!\n\nPlease check and
        try again...", "Password Error", MB_OK);
    return 0;
}
```

If the password fields do not match, we again inform the user and do not send the message to the server.

If we have gotten to this stage, all the data is okay to send and we can establish a connection to the server with the following code:

```
// -> Connect to the server
if(serverSocket.ConnectToServer(serverIP, 9009, NET_UDP) == NET_INVALID_SOCKET)
{
    MessageBox(hWnd_CreateAccountDialog,
        "Game Server Connection Error", "Fatal Error", MB_OK);

    return 1;
}
```

Note that if the server connection could not be made, we display a server connection error message box to the user and stop the function. However, if we do manage to get a connection, we can then destroy the Create Account dialog with the following code:

```
DestroyWindow(hWnd_CreateAccountDialog);
hWnd_CreateAccountDialog = NULL;
```

Now we can set up the CreateAccount message that we need to send to the server. First, we create a local variable to store the message and set the type, toId, and fromId the same way we did for the Login message. This can be seen in the next code segment:

```
// -> Send the new account details to the server
TUT_MSG_LOBBYCREATEACCOUNT_DATA LobbyCreateAccountData;
LobbyCreateAccountData.type              = TUT_MSG_LOBBYCREATEACCOUNT;
LobbyCreateAccountData.toId              = NETID_SERVER;
LobbyCreateAccountData.fromId            = serverSocket.localId;
```

Next, we need to copy all the account information from the local variables into the message. This is accomplished with the following code:

```
strcpy(LobbyCreateAccountData.nickname,nickname);
strcpy(LobbyCreateAccountData.firstname,firstname);
strcpy(LobbyCreateAccountData.surname,surname);
LobbyCreateAccountData.age                = age;
strcpy(LobbyCreateAccountData.gender,gender);
strcpy(LobbyCreateAccountData.password,password);
strcpy(LobbyCreateAccountData.email,email);
```

Finally, we can send our CreateAccount message and end our function. This is done with this final code segment:

```
sendLobbyLoginMessage((NETMSG_GENERIC *) &LobbyCreateAccountData);
```

```
        return 1;
    }
```

This completes the client application.

Client Application — Complete Code Listing

This is the complete code listing for your reference. Note that the netcommon.h header file has been excluded here as there have been no changes to it since it was listed with the server application.

main.h

```
#define USMSG_CLOSECONNECTION WM_USER + 4

extern HWND hWnd_Application;
extern HINSTANCE hInst;

LRESULT CALLBACK ApplicationProc(HWND hWnd, UINT uMsg, WPARAM wParam, LPARAM
lParam);
```

main.cpp

```
#include <netLib.h>
#include <windows.h>
#include <gl/gl.h>
#include <gl/glu.h>
#include <gl/glaux.h>
#include <2dlib.h>

#include "resource.h"
#include "main.h"
#include "login.h"
#include "network.h"

#include "..\tutLoginServer\netcommon.h"

HWND hWnd_netLib;
HWND hWnd_Application;
HINSTANCE hInst;

// WINDOWS PROCEDURE
LRESULT CALLBACK ApplicationProc(HWND hWnd, UINT uMsg, WPARAM wParam, LPARAM lParam)
{
    switch (uMsg)
    {
        case WM_CLOSE:
        {
```

```
                    PostQuitMessage(0);
                    return 0;
            }

            case WM_KEYDOWN:
            {
                    keys[wParam] = TRUE;
                    return 0;
            }

            case WM_KEYUP:
            {
                    keys[wParam] = FALSE;
                    return 0;
            }

            case USMSG_CLOSECONNECTION:
            {
                    serverSocket.CloseConnection(wParam, lParam);
                    return 0;
            }
        }

    // Pass All Unhandled Messages To DefWindowProc
    return DefWindowProc(hWnd,uMsg,wParam,lParam);
}


// WINDOWS MESSAGE LOOP AND APPLICATION ENTRY POINT
int WINAPI WinMain(HINSTANCE hThisInst, HINSTANCE hPrevInst, LPSTR lpszArgs, int
nWinMode)
{

    MSG msg;
    WNDCLASSEX wcl;

    // Create our Main Window
    wcl.cbSize = sizeof(WNDCLASSEX);

    wcl.hInstance = hThisInst;
    wcl.lpszClassName = "ArmyWar";
    wcl.lpfnWndProc = ApplicationProc;
    wcl.style = 0;

    wcl.hIcon = LoadIcon(NULL, IDI_APPLICATION);
    wcl.hIconSm = LoadIcon(NULL, IDI_WINLOGO);
    wcl.hCursor = LoadCursor(NULL, IDC_ARROW);
```

```
wcl.lpszMenuName = NULL;
wcl.cbClsExtra = 0;
wcl.cbWndExtra = 0;

wcl.hbrBackground = (HBRUSH) GetStockObject(LTGRAY_BRUSH);

if(!RegisterClassEx(&wcl)) return 0;

hWnd_Application = CreateWindow(
    "ArmyWar",
    "ARMY WAR Online",
    WS_OVERLAPPEDWINDOW,
    CW_USEDEFAULT,
    CW_USEDEFAULT,
    640,
    480,
    HWND_DESKTOP,
    NULL,
    hThisInst,
    NULL
    );

// Set the Windows Handle for netLib
hWnd_netLib = hWnd_Application;

ShowWindow(hWnd_Application, nWinMode);
UpdateWindow(hWnd_Application);

// Set Global Instance Variable
hInst = hThisInst;

// Display the LoginDialog
hWnd_LoginDialog = CreateDialog(hInst,MAKEINTRESOURCE(IDD_LOGINDIALOG),
hWnd_Application,(DLGPROC)LoginDialogProc);

// Initialize the Network Library
if(NET_Initialize() != 0)
{
    MessageBox(NULL, "Error initialising Communication Library!",
        "Fatal Error", MB_OK);
    return 1;
}

// Start the Windows Message Loop
while(msg.message != WM_QUIT)
{
```

```
            if(PeekMessage(&msg, NULL, 0, 0, PM_REMOVE))
            {
                TranslateMessage(&msg);
                DispatchMessage(&msg);
            }
            else
            {
            }
    }
    return msg.wParam;
}
```

login.h

```
// GLOBAL VARIABLES
extern HWND hWnd_LoginDialog;
extern HWND hWnd_CreateAccountDialog;

LRESULT CALLBACK LoginDialogProc(HWND hWnd, UINT uMsg, WPARAM wParam, LPARAM
lParam);
LRESULT CALLBACK CreateAccountDialogProc(HWND hWnd, UINT uMsg, WPARAM wParam,
LPARAM lParam);

int DoCreateAccount(void);
int DoLogin(void);
```

login.cpp

```
#include <netlib.h>
#include <windows.h>
#include <gl/gl.h>
#include <gl/glu.h>
#include <gl/glaux.h>
#include <2dlib.h>

#include "resource.h"
#include "main.h"
#include "login.h"
#include "network.h"

#include "..\tutLoginServer\netcommon.h"


// GLOBAL VARIABLES
HWND hWnd_LoginDialog = NULL;
HWND hWnd_CreateAccountDialog = NULL;
```

```
// LOGINDIALOG PROCEDURE
LRESULT CALLBACK LoginDialogProc(HWND hWnd, UINT uMsg, WPARAM wParam, LPARAM lParam)
{
    switch (uMsg)
    {
        case WM_COMMAND:
        {
            switch(LOWORD(wParam))
            {
                case IDC_LOGIN_QUIT:
                    PostQuitMessage(0);
                    return 0;
                case IDC_LOGIN_CREATEACCOUNT:
                    if(!hWnd_CreateAccountDialog)
                        hWnd_CreateAccountDialog = CreateDialog(hInst,
                        MAKEINTRESOURCE(IDD_CREATEACCOUNT),hWnd_Application,
                        (DLGPROC)CreateAccountDialogProc);
                    return 0;
                case IDC_DOLOGIN:
                    DoLogin();
                    return 0;
                default:
                    return 0;

            }
            return 0;
        }
        case WM_CLOSE:
        {
            PostQuitMessage(0);
            return 0;
        }
    }

    // Pass All Unhandled Messages To DefWindowProc
    return 0;
}


// CREATEACCOUNT PROCEDURE
LRESULT CALLBACK CreateAccountDialogProc(HWND hWnd, UINT uMsg, WPARAM wParam,
LPARAM lParam)
{
    switch (uMsg)
    {
        case WM_COMMAND:
        {
```

```
            switch(LOWORD(wParam))
            {
                case IDC_CREATEACCOUNT_CANCEL:
                    DestroyWindow(hWnd_CreateAccountDialog);
                    hWnd_CreateAccountDialog = NULL;
                    return 0;
                case IDC_CREATEACCOUNT_CONTINUE:
                    DoCreateAccount();
                    return 0;
                default:
                    return 0;


            }
            return 0;
        }
        case WM_CLOSE:
        {
            return 0;
        }

        case WM_DESTROY:
            return 0;
    }

    // Pass All Unhandled Messages To DefWindowProc
    // return DefWindowProc(hWnd,uMsg,wParam,lParam);
    return 0;
}

// DOCREATEACCOUNT
int DoCreateAccount(void)
{
    char nickname[30];
    char firstname[50];
    char surname[50];
    int age;
    char gender[10];
    char password[50];
    char password2[50];
    char email[150];

    // -> First get the IP address of the server from the dialog
    GetDlgItemText(hWnd_CreateAccountDialog, IDC_CREATEACCOUNT_IPADDRESS,
    serverIP, 20);

    // -> Store the player data in local variables
```

```
GetDlgItemText(hWnd_CreateAccountDialog, IDC_CREATEACCOUNT_NICKNAME,
nickname, 30);
GetDlgItemText(hWnd_CreateAccountDialog, IDC_CREATEACCOUNT_FIRSTNAME,
firstname, 50);
GetDlgItemText(hWnd_CreateAccountDialog, IDC_CREATEACCOUNT_SURNAME,
surname, 50);
age = GetDlgItemInt(hWnd_CreateAccountDialog, IDC_CREATEACCOUNT_AGE, NULL,
FALSE);
GetDlgItemText(hWnd_CreateAccountDialog, IDC_CREATEACCOUNT_GENDER, gender, 10);
GetDlgItemText(hWnd_CreateAccountDialog, IDC_CREATEACCOUNT_PASSWORD1,
password, 50);
GetDlgItemText(hWnd_CreateAccountDialog, IDC_CREATEACCOUNT_PASSWORD2,
password2, 50);
GetDlgItemText(hWnd_CreateAccountDialog, IDC_CREATEACCOUNT_EMAIL, email, 150);

// -> Check all the fields have been filled in
if(!strcmp(nickname,"") || !strcmp(firstname,"") || !strcmp(surname,"") ||
!strcmp(gender,"") || !strcmp(password,"") || !strcmp(email,"") || age < 1)
{
    MessageBox(hWnd_CreateAccountDialog, "Not all fields have been filled
    in!\n\nPlease check and try again...", "Information Error", MB_OK);
    return 0;
}

// -> Check the passwords match
if(strcmp(password,password2))
{
    MessageBox(hWnd_CreateAccountDialog,
        "The two passwords you entered do not match!\n\nPlease check and
        try again...", "Password Error", MB_OK);
    return 0;
}

// -> Connect to the server
if(serverSocket.ConnectToServer(serverIP, 9009, NET_UDP) == NET_INVALID_SOCKET)
{
    MessageBox(hWnd_CreateAccountDialog,
        "Game Server Connection Error", "Fatal Error", MB_OK);

    return 1;
}

DestroyWindow(hWnd_CreateAccountDialog);
hWnd_CreateAccountDialog = NULL;

// -> Send the new account details to the server
TUT_MSG_LOBBYCREATEACCOUNT_DATA LobbyCreateAccountData;
```

```
        LobbyCreateAccountData.type              = TUT_MSG_LOBBYCREATEACCOUNT;
        LobbyCreateAccountData.toId              = NETID_SERVER;
        LobbyCreateAccountData.fromId            = serverSocket.localId;
        strcpy(LobbyCreateAccountData.nickname,nickname);
        strcpy(LobbyCreateAccountData.firstname,firstname);
        strcpy(LobbyCreateAccountData.surname,surname);
        LobbyCreateAccountData.age               = age;
        strcpy(LobbyCreateAccountData.gender,gender);
        strcpy(LobbyCreateAccountData.password,password);
        strcpy(LobbyCreateAccountData.email,email);

        sendLobbyLoginMessage((NETMSG_GENERIC *) &LobbyCreateAccountData);

        return 1;
}


// DOLOGIN
int DoLogin(void)
{
        char nickname[30];
        char password[50];

        // -> First get the IP address of the server from the dialog
        GetDlgItemText(hWnd_LoginDialog, IDC_LOGIN_IPADDRESS, serverIP, 16);

        // -> Store the player data in local variables
        GetDlgItemText(hWnd_LoginDialog, IDC_LOGIN_NICKNAME, nickname, 30);
        GetDlgItemText(hWnd_LoginDialog, IDC_LOGIN_PASSWORD, password, 50);

        // -> Hide the Login Window
        ShowWindow(hWnd_LoginDialog,SW_HIDE);

        // -> Connect to the server
        if(serverSocket.ConnectToServer(serverIP, 9009, NET_UDP) == NET_INVALID_SOCKET)
        {
                MessageBox(NULL, "Game Server Connection Error", "Fatal Error", MB_OK);
                ShowWindow(hWnd_LoginDialog,SW_SHOW);
                return 1;
        }

        // -> Send Lobby Login Message
        TUT_MSG_LOBBYLOGIN_DATA LobbyLoginData;
        LobbyLoginData.type              = TUT_MSG_LOBBYLOGIN;
        LobbyLoginData.toId              = NETID_SERVER;
        LobbyLoginData.fromId            = serverSocket.localId;
        strcpy(LobbyLoginData.nickname,nickname);
```

```
        strcpy(LobbyLoginData.password,password);

        sendLobbyLoginMessage((NETMSG_GENERIC *) &LobbyLoginData);

        return 0;
}
```

network.h

```
#ifndef __NETWORK_H
#define __NETWORK_H

extern NET_Socket serverSocket;
extern char serverIP[64];

void sendLobbyLoginMessage(NETMSG_GENERIC *Msg);

#endif
```

network.cpp

```
#include <netlib.h>
#include <windows.h>
#include <gl/gl.h>
#include <gl/glu.h>
#include <gl/glaux.h>
#include <2dlib.h>

#include "resource.h"
#include "main.h"
#include "login.h"
#include "network.h"

#include "..\tutLoginServer\netcommon.h"


NET_Socket serverSocket;

char serverIP[64];

void handleLobbyLoginMessages(NETMSG_GENERIC *Msg)
{
    switch(Msg->type)
    {
    case TUT_MSG_LOBBYLOGIN_FEEDBACK:

        TUT_MSG_LOBBYLOGIN_FEEDBACK_DATA *LobbyLoginFeedbackPtr;
        LobbyLoginFeedbackPtr = (TUT_MSG_LOBBYLOGIN_FEEDBACK_DATA *) Msg;
```

```
// Switch the result code
switch(LobbyLoginFeedbackPtr->result)
{
case LOBBYLOGIN_RESULT_ACCEPTED:

    MessageBox(NULL,"The login details were accepted","Message",MB_OK);

    // Complete Login Procedure (covered in the next tutorial)

    break;

case LOBBYLOGIN_RESULT_PASSWORDBAD:
    SendMessage(hWnd_Application, USMSG_CLOSECONNECTION,
    NETID_SERVER, 1);
    MessageBox(NULL,"The password was not accepted","Message",MB_OK);
    ShowWindow(hWnd_LoginDialog,SW_SHOW);
    break;

case LOBBYLOGIN_RESULT_USERNAMEBAD:
    SendMessage(hWnd_Application, USMSG_CLOSECONNECTION,
    NETID_SERVER, 1);
    MessageBox(NULL,"The username was not accepted as
    valid","Message",MB_OK);
    ShowWindow(hWnd_LoginDialog,SW_SHOW);
    break;

case LOBBYLOGIN_RESULT_MYSQLERROR:
    SendMessage(hWnd_Application, USMSG_CLOSECONNECTION,
    NETID_SERVER, 1);
    MessageBox(NULL,"An unknown database error
    occurred","Message",MB_OK);
    ShowWindow(hWnd_LoginDialog,SW_SHOW);
    break;
}
break;

case TUT_MSG_LOBBYCREATEACCOUNT_FEEDBACK:

    TUT_MSG_LOBBYCREATEACCOUNT_FEEDBACK_DATA *LobbyCreateAccountFeedbackPtr;
    LobbyCreateAccountFeedbackPtr = (TUT_MSG_LOBBYCREATEACCOUNT_
    FEEDBACK_DATA *) Msg;

    // Switch the result code
    switch(LobbyCreateAccountFeedbackPtr->result)
    {
    case LOBBYCREATEACCOUNT_RESULT_ACCEPTED:
```

```
            SendMessage(hWnd_Application, USMSG_CLOSECONNECTION,
            NETID_SERVER, 1);
            MessageBox(hWnd_LoginDialog,"The new account details were accepted
            \nYou can now login with your new account details","Success!",MB_OK);
            break;

        case LOBBYCREATEACCOUNT_RESULT_MYSQLERROR:
            SendMessage(hWnd_Application, USMSG_CLOSECONNECTION,
            NETID_SERVER, 1);
            MessageBox(NULL,"An unknown database error
            occurred","Message",MB_OK);
            break;

        }

        break;
    }
}


void NET_HandleMessages(NETMSG_GENERIC *Msg)
{
    handleLobbyLoginMessages(Msg);
}


void sendLobbyLoginMessage(NETMSG_GENERIC *Msg)
{
    NETMSGDATA_DATASIZE DataMsg;
    memset(&DataMsg, 0, sizeof(NETMSGDATA_DATASIZE));

    switch(Msg->type)
    {
    case TUT_MSG_LOBBYLOGIN:
        TUT_MSG_LOBBYLOGIN_DATA *LobbyLoginDataPtr;
        LobbyLoginDataPtr = (TUT_MSG_LOBBYLOGIN_DATA *) Msg;
        DataMsg.type      = NETMSG_DATASIZE;
        DataMsg.toId      = Msg->toId;
        DataMsg.fromId    = Msg->fromId;
        DataMsg.size      = sizeof(TUT_MSG_LOBBYLOGIN_DATA);

        LogString("Sending lobby login request to id %d (Msg->type: %d)",
        Msg->toId, Msg->type);

        serverSocket.Write(Msg->toId, (char *) &DataMsg,
        sizeof(NETMSGDATA_DATASIZE));
```

```
                    serverSocket.Write(Msg->toId, (char *) LobbyLoginDataPtr,
                    sizeof(TUT_MSG_LOBBYLOGIN_DATA));
                    break;

            case TUT_MSG_LOBBYCREATEACCOUNT:
                    TUT_MSG_LOBBYCREATEACCOUNT_DATA *LobbyCreateAccountDataPtr;
                    LobbyCreateAccountDataPtr = (TUT_MSG_LOBBYCREATEACCOUNT_DATA *) Msg;
                    DataMsg.type   = NETMSG_DATASIZE;
                    DataMsg.toId   = Msg->toId;
                    DataMsg.fromId = Msg->fromId;
                    DataMsg.size = sizeof(TUT_MSG_LOBBYCREATEACCOUNT_DATA);

                    LogString("Sending CreateAccount request to id %d (Msg->type: %d)",
                    Msg->toId, Msg->type);

                    serverSocket.Write(Msg->toId, (char *) &DataMsg,
                    sizeof(NETMSGDATA_DATASIZE));
                    serverSocket.Write(Msg->toId, (char *) LobbyCreateAccountDataPtr,
                    sizeof(TUT_MSG_LOBBYCREATEACCOUNT_DATA));
                    break;
            }
        }
```

Executing the Login System

Now that we have our login system coded, we can execute it. Remember that you must have the MySQL server running on the same computer as the server application, with the database we created earlier in the chapter set up correctly. One simple mistake in the database could cause failure when the server attempts to interact with it. Let's now execute the application and simulate a user performing the creation of a new account, followed by an attempt to login to the newly created account. Note that in the figures, we have excluded the background application window to increase the clarity of the images.

First, the user will be presented with the following login screen.

Figure 11

LIVERPOOL JOHN MOORES UNIVERSITY
LEARNING & INFORMATION SERVICES

From this dialog, the user will first click on the Create New Account button in order to create a new account to allow him or her to login to the game. When the user clicks the button the Create New Account dialog will appear.

Figure 12

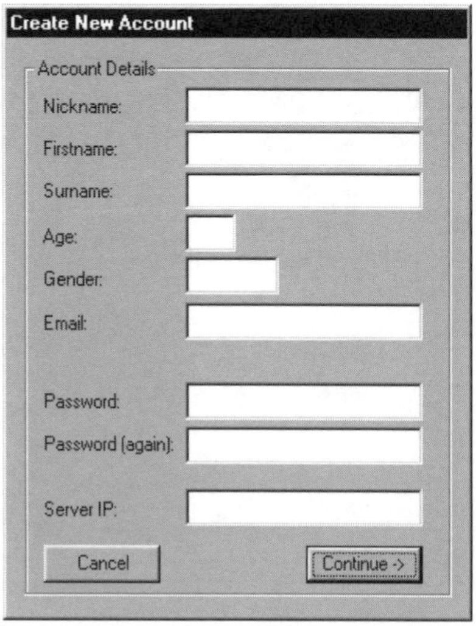

At this dialog, the user will enter his details correctly into the edit boxes and finally enter the server IP address as 127.0.0.1 (in this case we are running the server and the MySQL server on the same machine as the application). Here is how the dialog will look once the user has filled in his details. Note that the password fields both contain "qwerty."

Figure 13

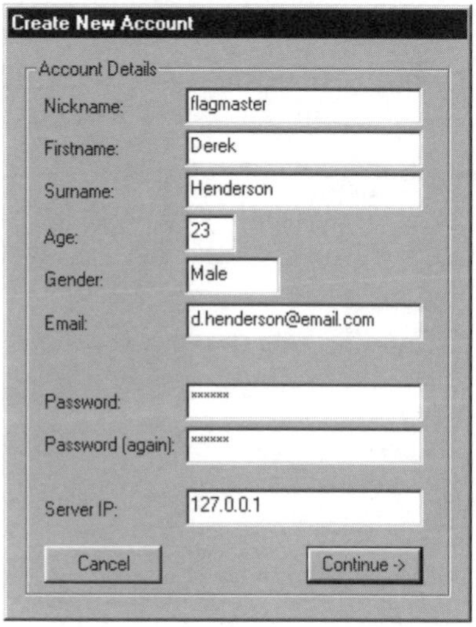

Once the user is satisfied with the details he has entered, he will proceed by clicking on the Continue button. If the MySQL server is running and the database is set up correctly, the data will be added to MySQL and the following message box will be displayed to the user.

Figure 14

The user will now acknowledge that his account has been created, click OK on the dialog, and fill his login details into the Login dialog, which will now be predominant on the screen. Here is how the Login dialog will look once the user has filled in the details.

Figure 15

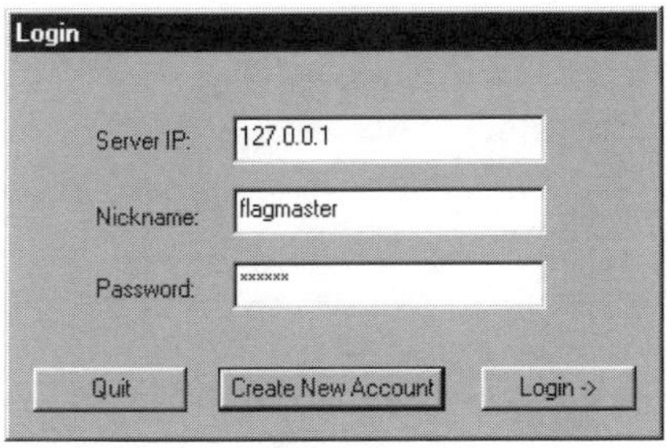

Note here that the user has entered "qwerty" in the password field. When the user now clicks the Login button, providing the server application and the MySQL server are running correctly, the following message box will appear.

Figure 16

Finally, if we look behind the scenes in the MySQL console, we can see the user's information in the playerdata table if we select the information from it using the following MySQL console command. Remember to first use the Use command to select the correct database:

```
mysql> SELECT * FROM playerdata;
```

When we execute this command from the console, we can see that the user's information was successfully entered into the database.

Figure 17

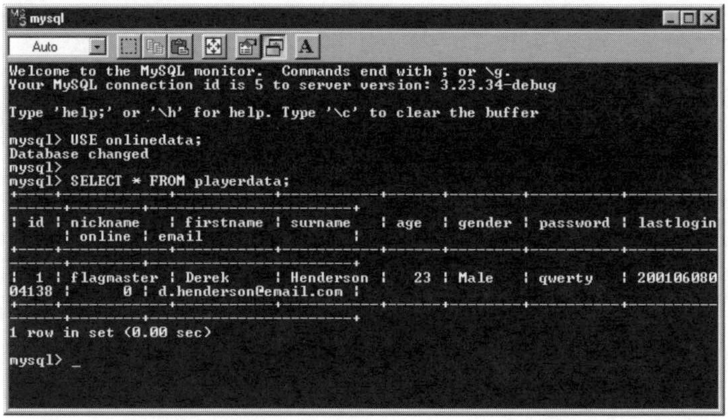

Summary

In this tutorial, we learned how to create the login system for the online game we are going to develop in the upcoming tutorials. This login system is a foundation and a lot can be built on top of it, such as the modification of user accounts. The same techniques utilized in the creation of this login system can easily be expanded upon to allow a much more advanced system to be developed.

Creating the Game Lobby

Introduction

In this tutorial we learn how to create the lobby for our game where the players can chat and create games to play. We will see how to use the network library to make the lobby work, but we will also learn how to create the Lobby dialog itself. The Lobby dialog is the screen where you see all the players, their chat messages, and the existing games. After this tutorial we can actually create and join the games in the lobby, but we cannot start the game yet. Starting and making the game work are explained in the next tutorial, Tutorial 5, "Creating Your Online Game."

Creating the Lobby Client Application

We will first create the client application for the lobby, which is an updated version of the login tutorial. This time when you login, the Lobby dialog is opened.

Creating the Dialogs

It is best to start off with creating the dialogs that we will use in the lobby. When we have the dialogs ready, we know what buttons there are and what dialog opens when you press the buttons and so on.

Lobby Dialog

The Lobby dialog is the main screen of the lobby. There you see all the players who have logged in, their chat messages, and the existing games. You can also see the buttons for creating a new game and joining an existing one. This dialog should also have a button for logging out from the server.

We create the Lobby dialog exactly the same way we created the earlier dialogs for login and signup. As we recall from the earlier tutorial, the dialogs are created from the Insert menu in Visual Studio. Select Resource…, click on Dialog to choose what to create, and then click the New button to create a new dialog. Now you see a new dialog (like the one when you created the login dialogs) in front of you, but it does not look at all like we want it to. So, let's modify the dialog.

First, we rename the dialog to IDD_LOBBYDIALOG. Click the right mouse button on the name of the new dialog in the list on the left side. Click on Properties and type the new name in. Now you can close the Properties window.

Figure 1

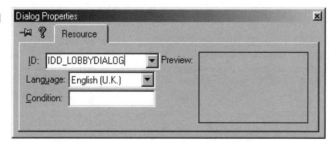

Once the name is set up properly, we can change the style of the dialog to correspond to what we want. Right-click anywhere and click on Properties in the pop-up menu (or double-click on the empty space in the dialog preview window) to open the Dialog Properties window.

The General tab does not have anything interesting for us in this case, so move on to the next tab — the Styles tab. In the Styles tab you see many check boxes and two combo boxes. Uncheck all the check boxes, choose Child as the dialog style from the upper combo box, and finally choose None for the border in the lower combo box. Now our dialog is a child window and has no border of its own. It also does not have a title bar showing its name. We do all this because this dialog is fitted into the game main window, and therefore, the Lobby dialog is not actually a window of its own.

Figure 2

The other tabs in the Dialog Properties window do not interest us, so it can be closed now.

Next, remove the OK and Cancel buttons that were added automatically into the dialog when it was created.

Figure 3

Now we have an empty dialog. Add buttons, edit boxes, and lists so that the complete Lobby dialog looks like the following figure.

Figure 4

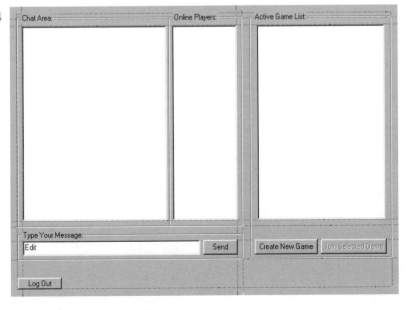

Now that the dialog is all laid out, we need to name the controls so that we can use them in the code as well. Of course, they already have names, but they are the default names based on the control type, so to make everything as clear as possible, we name the controls to correspond to their usage. Here is a list of the three list control names starting from left to right:

```
IDC_CHATLIST
IDC_PLAYERLIST
IDC_GAMELIST
```

We do not wish to sort any of the list items in any list in the lobby, so we disable the sorting option from each one. Double-click on the list (or right-click and choose Properties from the pop-up menu) to open the List Box Properties window. Uncheck the Sort check box on the Styles tab and close the Properties window. Repeat this for all the list boxes.

Figure 5

The Chat edit box and the Send button are named as follows:

```
IDC_CHATMESSAGE
IDC_SENDCHATMESSAGE
```

The Create New Game, Join Selected Game, and Log Out buttons are named as follows.

```
IDC_CREATEGAME
IDC_JOINGAME
IDC_LOGOUT
```

Note that the Join Selected Game button is disabled by default, because you can join a game only when you have selected one, and only when the selected game is not in progress. Disabling the button by default is done from the Push Button Properties window, which is opened by double-clicking on the button (or right-clicking on it and choosing Properties from the pop-up menu). Check the Disabled check box and close the Properties window.

Figure 6

The Lobby dialog is now complete. All we need to do now is create the other dialogs that open when you press the buttons in the Lobby dialog.

Create Game Dialog

We create the Create Game dialog the same way as the Lobby dialog. Let's start by naming the dialog IDD_CREATEGAME in the Dialog Properties window. Next, open the other Dialog Properties window by double-clicking on the empty space in the preview window.

Figure 7

On the Styles tab, set the dialog style to Popup and the border to Dialog Frame. Also make sure the Title bar check box is checked, and close the Properties window.

Lay out the dialog as shown in the following image.

Figure 8

Then, name the controls as shown in the following list, showing the Edit box name first, then the Cancel button, and lastly the OK button:

```
IDC_GAMENAME
IDC_CANCELCREATEGAME
IDC_DOCREATEGAME
```

When the user presses the OK button, one more dialog will open that shows the players who have joined that game and gives the game host the ability to start or cancel the game.

Create View Players Dialog

Again, we create the dialog as we have done before, and this time we name it IDD_CREATEVIEWPLAYERS. This dialog has the same properties as the Create Game dialog, so we will not go through them now.

Lay out the dialog as shown in the following image.

Figure 9

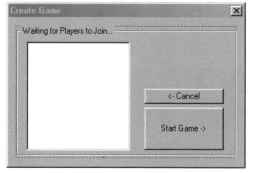

Then, name the controls as listed here. The first name in the list is for the player list box, the second for the Cancel button, and the last one for the Start Game button:

```
IDC_PLAYERSINGAME
IDC_CANCELGAME
IDC_STARTGAME
```

The Start Game button is the button used to start the actual game, but in this tutorial we stop in this dialog. Pressing the Start Game button using the source code within this tutorial does nothing. We still have the Join Game dialog to examine, though.

Join Game Dialog

Once more, we create the dialog as we have created all the other dialogs. This is the last dialog to create for this project. When it is created, name it IDD_JOIN-VIEWPLAYERS, as it is used only to show the players who have joined the game. We can also cancel the join if we do not wish to be part of the game after all.

Lay out the dialog as shown in the following figure.

Figure 10

Then name the two controls:

```
IDC_JOINPLAYERSINGAME
IDC_JOINCANCEL
```

Now all the dialogs are done, and we can move on to program the lobby system.

Game Code

Now that the lobby will be working for the first time in this game project, we need to add some variables to the game code that were not in the login tutorial. For some of these variables we need to allocate/free memory.

On the client side we need to change the following source files: init.cpp, main.cpp/main.h, and network.cpp/network.h. Plus, we add two new source files and their headers: chat.cpp/chat.h and lobby.cpp/lobby.h.

Main.cpp/Main.h

For the initialization part, we add the following variables into main.cpp:

```
Game_t *Game;
int Games;
int selectedGame;
int joinedGame = -1;
```

The Game structure holds information for each created game. The Games integer is the number of existing games, and selectedGame and joinedGame are indices corresponding to the selected game in the lobby list and the game joined by the local player (if not any, this variable is –1). We make the two latter ones external in main.h, as shown in the following piece of code:

```
extern int selectedGame;
extern int joinedGame;
```

Netcommon.h

The Game_t structure is defined in the netcommon.h header file. This header is included in both the server and the client application as it contains common variables and structures.

```
typedef struct
{
    char name[32];                      // Game name

    int player[NET_MAX_CONNECTIONS];    // Player list
    int players;                        // Amount of players

    bool inProgress;                    // Game in progress flag
} Game_t;

extern Game_t *Game;
extern int Games;
```

As we can see in the preceding piece of code, the Game_t structure stores the name of the game, the number of players, and the player index numbers. It also has a flag to tell if the game has been started (bool inProgress).

The Game structure and Games integer are made externals here, because they are used in both the server and the client application.

Init.cpp

In init.cpp we add two lines of code. These are for allocating and freeing the memory for the Game structure. This is shown in the following code. The Max_Games constant is defined in netcommon.h.

```
void InitializeGame(void)
{
    // Initialize Game structure and network
    Game = (Game_t *) calloc(MAX_GAMES, sizeof(Game_t));

    InitializeGameNetwork();
}

void UninitializeGame(void)
{
    // Un-initialize Game structure and network
    if(Game) free(Game);
```

```
        UninitializeGameNetwork();
    }
```

Chat System

The lobby has a very simple chat system. You can send messages to everyone who is in the lobby, but you cannot choose a particular recipient. Everyone will see all the messages. The chat can be used to arrange games or simply to chat about anything.

TutChatClass

On the server side, the chat system is handled by the network library. There is no extra code for this; the chat system just sends normal messages to all the clients within the network, and the clients handle the messages themselves. On the client side, there is a very simple C++ class for the chat system. The class is shown in the following code:

```
class TutChatClass
{
public:
    void SendMessage(char *text);
};


extern TutChatClass TutChat;
```

As you can see, there is only one function in the class and nothing else. Why put it in a class then? Why not just use one global function? To keep the chat system easily upgradeable. For example, we could store all the messages in a buffer so players will not lose any messages if they get disconnected, and so on. There is an unlimited amount of new features to put in. This tutorial, or any other tutorial in this book, does not add any new features, but you are encouraged to do so yourself.

SendMessage Function

The following code shows the SendMessage function in its entirety:

```
void TutChatClass::SendMessage(char *text)
{
    // Fill chat message data and send the message
    TUT_MSG_CHATMESSAGE_DATA ChatMessageData;

    ChatMessageData.type    = TUT_MSG_CHATMESSAGE;
    ChatMessageData.toId    = NETID_ALL;
    ChatMessageData.fromId  = serverSocket.localId;
```

```
strcpy(ChatMessageData.messageText, text);

LogString("Sending chat message: %s",
    ChatMessageData.messageText);

sendChatMessage((NETMSG_GENERIC *) &ChatMessageData);
}
```

The SendMessage function takes one parameter — a pointer to the message string itself:

```
void TutChatClass::SendMessage(char *text)
```

The only thing this function does is fill in the chat message data and send it to all the other clients connected to the server. Tut_Msg_ChatMessageData and Tut_Msg_ChatMessage are defined in netcommon.h.

```
// Fill chat message data and send the message
TUT_MSG_CHATMESSAGE_DATA ChatMessageData;

ChatMessageData.type    = TUT_MSG_CHATMESSAGE;
ChatMessageData.toId    = NETID_ALL;
ChatMessageData.fromId  = serverSocket.localId;
strcpy(ChatMessageData.messageText, text);

LogString("Sending chat message: %s",
    ChatMessageData.messageText);

sendChatMessage((NETMSG_GENERIC *) &ChatMessageData);
```

Here is the Tut_Msg_ChatMessageData structure. The data part of the message consists of only the 128-byte string that holds the text typed in the chat text box once it is sent.

```
typedef struct
{
    int type;
    HOSTID toId;
    HOSTID fromId;
    char messageText[128];
} TUT_MSG_CHATMESSAGE_DATA;
```

Handling Chat Messages

HandleChatMessages Function

This function handles the chat messages. If the message string is empty, the string is filled with the text "* MESSAGE WAS EMPTY *" to indicate that the message was not received correctly. Then the string is added to the chat text box.

```
void handleChatMessages(NETMSG_GENERIC *Msg)
{
    switch(Msg->type)
    {
    case TUT_MSG_CHATMESSAGE:
        // Chat message
        TUT_MSG_CHATMESSAGE_DATA *ChatMessagePtr;
        ChatMessagePtr = (TUT_MSG_CHATMESSAGE_DATA *) Msg;

        // Check if the message is empty
        if(strcmp(ChatMessagePtr->messageText, "") == 0)
        {
            strcpy(ChatMessagePtr->messageText,
                "* MESSAGE WAS EMPTY *");
        }

        // Add the string to the chat text box
        SendMessage(GetDlgItem(hWnd_LobbyDialog, IDC_CHATLIST),
            LB_ADDSTRING, 0,
            (LPARAM) ChatMessagePtr->messageText);

        break;
    }
}
```

Player Identification

Each player who logs in to the lobby has a lobby index number that is used to identify the player within the code. This is not the only index number the players have, though. Each player has a game index number, too, which is used to identify the player in a game that he or she has joined.

Logging In

To log in the player on the server, the LoginToServer function is called. It is called when the player nickname is successfully returned by the server in the handleLobbyLoginMessages function.

LoginToServer Function

This function is used to send the player login request to the server. The function is shown in the following code:

```
void LoginToServer(char *nickname)
{
    TUT_MSG_GAMELOGIN_DATA Msg;

    Msg.type        = TUT_MSG_GAMELOGIN;
    Msg.toId        = NETID_SERVER;
    Msg.fromId      = serverSocket.localId;
    strcpy(Msg.nickname, nickname);

    sendLoginMessage((NETMSG_GENERIC *) &Msg);
}
```

Game Lobby

Now we are ready to learn how to actually code the game lobby. As you should remember, there are four dialogs in the lobby system: the main Lobby dialog, the Create Game dialog, the Create View Players dialog, and the Join Game dialog. We need to be able to access these dialogs within the code, so we make window handles for them. The handles are shown in the following piece of code:

```
HWND hWnd_LobbyDialog;
HWND hWnd_CreateGameDialog;
HWND hWnd_JoinGameDialog;
HWND hWnd_CreateViewPlayersDialog;
```

Lobby Dialog

The Lobby dialog is created in main.cpp as shown in the following code. The dialog is not shown yet, though.

```
// Create the Lobby
hWnd_LobbyDialog =
    CreateDialog(hInst,MAKEINTRESOURCE(IDD_LOBBYDIALOG),
    hWnd_Application,(DLGPROC)LobbyDialogProc);
```

The Lobby dialog has its own procedure function, LobbyDialogProc, that is run constantly when the dialog exists. This function is normally used to check and handle the messages the window receives.

```
LRESULT CALLBACK LobbyDialogProc(HWND hWnd, UINT uMsg, WPARAM wParam, LPARAM lParam)
{
    char chatMessage[256];
    char temp[256];

    switch (uMsg)
    {
    case WM_COMMAND:
        switch(LOWORD(wParam))
        {
        case IDC_LOGOUT:
            // Logout from server
            LogoutFromServer();
            ShowWindow(hWnd_LobbyDialog,SW_HIDE);
            hWnd_LoginDialog =
                CreateDialog(hInst,
                MAKEINTRESOURCE(IDD_LOGINDIALOG),
                hWnd_Application,
                (DLGPROC)LoginDialogProc);
            break;

        case IDC_SENDCHATMESSAGE:
            // Send chat message by first retrieving it from
            // the text box, and then adding the player
            // nickname in the beginning
            GetWindowText(GetDlgItem(hWnd_LobbyDialog,
                IDC_CHATMESSAGE), temp, 255);

            sprintf(chatMessage, "%s: ",
                loggedPlayerLobby[localPlayerLobbyIndex].nickName);
            strcat(chatMessage, temp);

            TutChat.SendMessage(chatMessage);

            SetWindowText(GetDlgItem(hWnd_LobbyDialog,
                IDC_CHATMESSAGE), "");
            break;

        case IDC_CREATEGAME:
            // Create game
            CreateGame();
            break;
```

```
case IDC_JOINGAME:
    // Join game
    JoinGame();
    break;

default:
    // Check if a game is selected and activate /
    // deactivate the join button
    int count =
        SendMessage(GetDlgItem(hWnd_LobbyDialog,
        IDC_GAMELIST), LB_GETSELCOUNT, 0, 0);

    // If a game is selected, retrieve the game index
    // number and activate join button
    if(count)
    {
        int sel =
            SendMessage(GetDlgItem(hWnd_LobbyDialog,
            IDC_GAMELIST), LB_GETCURSEL, 0, 0);

        // If the selected game is not in progress,
        // activate join button
        if( (sel > -1) && (!Game[sel].inProgress) )
        {
            EnableWindow(GetDlgItem(hWnd_LobbyDialog,
                IDC_JOINGAME), TRUE);
        }
    }
    // If no game is selected, deactivate join button
    else
    {
        EnableWindow(GetDlgItem(hWnd_LobbyDialog,
            IDC_JOINGAME), FALSE);
    }

    // If no games exists, deactivate join button
    if(!Games)
    {
        EnableWindow(GetDlgItem(hWnd_LobbyDialog,
            IDC_JOINGAME), FALSE);
    }

    return 0;
}
return 0;
break;
```

```
        case WM_CLOSE:
            // Close window
            LogoutFromServer();
            PostQuitMessage(0);
            return 0;
            break;
    }

        // Pass All Unhandled Messages To DefWindowProc
        return DefWindowProc(hWnd,uMsg,wParam,lParam);
}
```

Here we first check if the message the window received is a window command message. If it is, we check which one it was by looking at the wParam variable.

```
switch (uMsg)
{
case WM_COMMAND:
    switch(LOWORD(wParam))
    {
        …
    }
}
```

Now we determine which button in the dialog was pressed by checking if the wParam variable contains any of the dialog button IDs. If the Logout button in the Lobby dialog was pressed, we start the logout process. First, the LogoutFrom-Server function is run. This function is explained later. Then the Lobby dialog is hidden and the Login dialog is re-created:

```
        case IDC_LOGOUT:
            // Logout from server
            LogoutFromServer();
            ShowWindow(hWnd_LobbyDialog,SW_HIDE);
            hWnd_LoginDialog =
                CreateDialog(hInst,
                MAKEINTRESOURCE(IDD_LOGINDIALOG),
                hWnd_Application,
                 (DLGPROC)LoginDialogProc);
            break;
```

If the Send Chat Message button was pressed, the chat message from the chat edit box is sent to all. The text string from the edit box is fetched with the Get-WindowText function. Then the username is added to the string and the whole string is sent. Finally, the edit box is reset.

```
    case IDC_SENDCHATMESSAGE:
        // Send chat message by first retrieving it from
```

```
// the text box, and then adding the player
// nickname in the beginning
GetWindowText(GetDlgItem(hWnd_LobbyDialog,
    IDC_CHATMESSAGE), temp, 255);

sprintf(chatMessage, "%s: ",
    loggedPlayerLobby[localPlayerLobbyIndex].nickName);
strcat(chatMessage, temp);

TutChat.SendMessage(chatMessage);

SetWindowText(GetDlgItem(hWnd_LobbyDialog,
    IDC_CHATMESSAGE), "");
break;
```

If the Create Game button was pressed, the CreateGame function is run. This function is explained later in this tutorial.

```
case IDC_CREATEGAME:
    // Create game
    CreateGame();
    break;
```

If the Join Selected Game button was pressed, the JoinGame function is run. This function is also explained later in the tutorial.

```
case IDC_JOINGAME:
    // Join game
    JoinGame();
    break;
```

If none of the buttons were pressed, we determine if the state of the join selected game should be changed. First, we retrieve the number of games selected in the game list. This is either one or zero. If a game is selected, its index number is retrieved and the state of the game is checked. If the game is not in progress, the Join Selected Game button is selectable. Otherwise, it is not.

```
default:
    // Check if a game is selected and activate / deactivate the
    // join button
    int count =
        SendMessage(GetDlgItem(hWnd_LobbyDialog,
        IDC_GAMELIST), LB_GETSELCOUNT, 0, 0);

    // If a game is selected, retrieve the game index number
    // and activate join button
    if(count)
    {
```

```
        int sel =
            SendMessage(GetDlgItem(hWnd_LobbyDialog,
            IDC_GAMELIST), LB_GETCURSEL, 0, 0);

        // If the selected game is not in progress,
        // activate join button
        if( (sel > -1) && (!Game[sel].inProgress) )
        {
            EnableWindow(GetDlgItem(hWnd_LobbyDialog,
                IDC_JOINGAME), TRUE);
        }
    }
    // If no game is selected, deactivate join button
    else
    {
        EnableWindow(GetDlgItem(hWnd_LobbyDialog,
            IDC_JOINGAME), FALSE);
    }

    // If no games exists, deactivate join button
    if(!Games)
    {
        EnableWindow(GetDlgItem(hWnd_LobbyDialog,
            IDC_JOINGAME), FALSE);
    }

    return 0;
```

Lastly, we check if the window is being closed. If yes, we logout from the server as we do when we press the Logout button:

```
case WM_CLOSE:
    // Close window
    LogoutFromServer();
    PostQuitMessage(0);
    return 0;
    break;
```

LogoutFromServer Function

The LogoutFromServer function is simply used to logout from the server:

```
void LogoutFromServer(void)
{
    LogString("Trying to log out from server (localId: %d)",
        serverSocket.localId);

    if(!serverSocket.localId)
```

```
            return;

    loggedPlayersLobby = 0;
    LogString("00 Local player logged out, resetting counter
            (logged players: %d)", loggedPlayersLobby);

    TUT_MSG_GAMELOGOUT_DATA Msg;

    Msg.type            = TUT_MSG_GAMELOGOUT;
    Msg.toId            = NETID_SERVER;
    Msg.fromId          = serverSocket.localId;
    Msg.playerIndex     = localPlayerLobbyIndex;

    sendLoginMessage((NETMSG_GENERIC *) &Msg);

    serverSocket.CloseConnection(NETID_SERVER, 1);
}
```

Before we try to send any data to the server, we should see if we have a local ID number. If we do, we have successfully connected to the server and we can exchange data with it. If we do not have the local ID number, it means that the connection does not exist, and we naturally cannot logout from the server, so the function returns immediately.

```
if(!serverSocket.localId)
    return;
```

We need to reset the lobby player counter here to keep the client up to date if it logs in again:

```
loggedPlayersLobby = 0;
```

Then, we send a notification to the server that we are logging out from it. The local player lobby index number must be provided within the message so the server knows what player to remove from the list. After that, the connection is closed.

```
TUT_MSG_GAMELOGOUT_DATA Msg;

Msg.type            = TUT_MSG_GAMELOGOUT;
Msg.toId            = NETID_SERVER;
Msg.fromId          = serverSocket.localId;
Msg.playerIndex     = localPlayerLobbyIndex;

sendLoginMessage((NETMSG_GENERIC *) &Msg);

serverSocket.CloseConnection(NETID_SERVER, 1);
```

Handling Remove Player Message

When a RemovePlayer message is sent to a client, it is handled in the handleLoginMessages function as shown here:

```
case TUT_MSG_GAMELOGIN_REMOVEPLAYER:
    // Remove player
    TUT_MSG_GAMELOGIN_REMOVEPLAYER_DATA *RemovePlayerPtr;
    RemovePlayerPtr =(TUT_MSG_GAMELOGIN_REMOVEPLAYER_DATA *) Msg;

    // Do not remove the local player (the local player is
    // gone already)
    if(RemovePlayerPtr->playerIndex == localPlayerLobbyIndex)
        break;

    // If the player index being removed is smaller than the
    // local player's lobby index, decrease the local lobby
    // index by one
    if(RemovePlayerPtr->playerIndex < localPlayerLobbyIndex)
        localPlayerLobbyIndex--;

    sprintf(text, "playerIndex: %d, localPlayerLobbyIndex: %d",
        RemovePlayerPtr->playerIndex,
        localPlayerLobbyIndex);

    // Remove player and refresh the player list
    removePlayer(RemovePlayerPtr->playerIndex);
    LobbyRefreshPlayerList();

    break;
```

First, we check that the RemovePlayer message is not about the local player. This case should never happen, but it is good to have it there to make sure. We decrease the local player lobby index if the one removed was smaller than the current local one. This is done because the player list on the server is updated also.

```
if(RemovePlayerPtr->playerIndex == localPlayerLobbyIndex)
    break;

if(RemovePlayerPtr->playerIndex < localPlayerLobbyIndex)
    localPlayerLobbyIndex--;
```

Finally, the player is removed from the client's player list and the list on the Lobby dialog is refreshed:

```
removePlayer(RemovePlayerPtr->playerIndex);
LobbyRefreshPlayerList();
```

RemovePlayer Function

This function removes the player from the client side. The function works the same way as on the server side; the player structure is updated by changing the remaining players' indexes by one if their index number is larger than the one removed.

```
void removePlayer(int playerIndex)
{
    int dis = 0;
    int discard = 0;

    discard = loggedPlayersLobby - playerIndex;

    loggedPlayersLobby--;
    LogString("-- Player logged out (remove)
        (logged players: %d)", loggedPlayersLobby);

    for(dis = 0; dis < discard; dis++)
    {
        memcpy(&loggedPlayerLobby[playerIndex+dis],
            &loggedPlayerLobby[playerIndex+dis+1],
            sizeof(playerServed_t));
    }
}
```

LobbyRefreshPlayerList Function

This function updates the list of players on the Lobby dialog. The list contents are first reset and then filled with the current players:

```
void LobbyRefreshPlayerList(void)
{
    // Reset player list
    SendMessage(GetDlgItem(hWnd_LobbyDialog, IDC_PLAYERLIST),
        LB_RESETCONTENT, 0, 0);

    // Fill player list
    for(int i = 0; i < loggedPlayersLobby; i++)
    {
        SendMessage(GetDlgItem(hWnd_LobbyDialog,
            IDC_PLAYERLIST), LB_ADDSTRING, 0,
            (LPARAM) loggedPlayerLobby[i].nickName);
    }
}
```

Creating a New Game

Creating a new game in the lobby is very simple. The player just has to press the New Game button and then enter a name for the new game. The game information is then sent to the server, and the server notifies the other clients about the new game.

CreateGame Function

The CreateGame function is run when the player presses the New Game button in the lobby. This function creates the New Game dialog and updates the selected game variable as shown in the following code:

```
void CreateGame(void)
{
    // Mark the amount of games as the selected game
    selectedGame = Games;

    // Create the create game dialog
    hWnd_CreateGameDialog = CreateDialog(hInst,
        MAKEINTRESOURCE(IDD_CREATEGAME),
        hWnd_Application, (DLGPROC) CreateGameDialogProc);

    ShowWindow(hWnd_CreateGameDialog, SW_SHOW);
}
```

CreateGameDialogProc Function

This function is the window procedure function for the Create Game dialog:

```
LRESULT CALLBACK CreateGameDialogProc(HWND hWnd, UINT uMsg, WPARAM wParam, LPARAM
lParam)
{
    char gamename[32];

    switch (uMsg)
    {
    case WM_COMMAND:
        switch(LOWORD(wParam))
        {
        case IDC_DOCREATEGAME:
            // Create the game. Retrieve the game name from
            // the text box.
            GetWindowText(GetDlgItem(hWnd_CreateGameDialog,
                IDC_GAMENAME), gamename, 32);
            DestroyWindow(hWnd_CreateGameDialog);
            DoCreateGame(gamename);
```

```
                break;

        case IDC_CANCELCREATEGAME:
            // Cancel game creation
            DestroyWindow(hWnd_CreateGameDialog);
            break;

        default:
            // Check if the game name has changed.
            if(SendMessage(GetDlgItem(hWnd_CreateGameDialog,
                IDC_GAMENAME), EM_GETMODIFY, 0, 0))
            {
                GetWindowText(GetDlgItem(
                    hWnd_CreateGameDialog, IDC_GAMENAME),
                    gamename, 32);

                // If the game name string is empty,
                // deactivate create game button
                if(strcmp(gamename, "") == 0)
                {
                    EnableWindow(GetDlgItem(
                        hWnd_CreateGameDialog,
                        IDC_DOCREATEGAME), FALSE);
                }
                else
                {
                    EnableWindow(GetDlgItem(
                        hWnd_CreateGameDialog,
                        IDC_DOCREATEGAME), TRUE);
                }
            }

            return 0;
        }
        return 0;
        break;
    }

    // Pass All Unhandled Messages To DefWindowProc
    return DefWindowProc(hWnd, uMsg, wParam, lParam);
}
```

When the player has given the game a name, the Create Game button is activated. When it is pressed, we get the game name from the edit box, destroy the Create Game dialog, and run the function to actually create the game.

```
case IDC_DOCREATEGAME:
    // Create the game. Retrieve the game name from the text box.
    GetWindowText(GetDlgItem(hWnd_CreateGameDialog,
        IDC_GAMENAME), gamename, 32);
        DestroyWindow(hWnd_CreateGameDialog);
        DoCreateGame(gamename);
        break;
```

We need to give the player the ability to cancel the game creation if the player
does not want to create the game after all. All we do here is destroy the Create
Game dialog, and we are back in the lobby:

```
case IDC_CANCELCREATEGAME:
    // Cancel game creation
    DestroyWindow(hWnd_CreateGameDialog);
    break;
```

The default action for this window procedure is that it checks if the game name in
the edit box is valid. It is valid when there is at least one letter in the edit box. If
the name is not valid, the Create Game button is not active.

```
default:
    // Check if the game name has changed.
    if(SendMessage(GetDlgItem(hWnd_CreateGameDialog,
        IDC_GAMENAME), EM_GETMODIFY, 0, 0))
    {
        GetWindowText(GetDlgItem(hWnd_CreateGameDialog,
            IDC_GAMENAME), gamename, 32);

        // If the game name string is empty,
        // deactivate create game button
        if(strcmp(gamename, "") == 0)
        {
            EnableWindow(GetDlgItem(hWnd_CreateGameDialog,
                IDC_DOCREATEGAME), FALSE);
        }
        else
        {
            EnableWindow(GetDlgItem(hWnd_CreateGameDialog,
                IDC_DOCREATEGAME), TRUE);
        }
    }
```

DoCreateGame Function

The DoCreateGame function is used to send the message to the server to create the game. The name of the game is sent within the message. That is the only unique variable, with the index number, to every game. When the message to create the game is sent, the local player must join it. To do that, we run the DoJoinGame function, which is explained later in the tutorial.

```
void DoCreateGame(char *name)
{
    // Destroy create game dialog
    DestroyWindow(hWnd_CreateGameDialog);

    // Send the message to notify of game creation
    TUT_MSG_GAME_DATA CreateGameData;

    CreateGameData.type      = TUT_MSG_CREATEGAME;
    CreateGameData.toId      = NETID_SERVER;
    CreateGameData.fromId    = serverSocket.localId;
    strcpy(CreateGameData.name, name);

    sendGameMessage((NETMSG_GENERIC *) &CreateGameData);

    // Join the game
    DoJoinGame(selectedGame);

    // Show the players joined the game
    CreateViewPlayers();
}
```

CreateViewPlayers Function

This function shows the dialog that shows the players who have joined the game:

```
void CreateViewPlayers(void)
{
    // Create view players dialog to show the players who have
    // joined the game
    hWnd_CreateViewPlayersDialog = CreateDialog(hInst,
        MAKEINTRESOURCE(IDD_CREATEVIEWPLAYERS),
        hWnd_Application,
          (DLGPROC) CreateViewPlayersDialogProc);

    ShowWindow(hWnd_CreateViewPlayersDialog, SW_SHOW);
}
```

CreateViewPlayersDialogProc Function

This is the function that handles the commands of the Create View Players dialog. Here we can start the game (in the final version) and cancel the game.

```
LRESULT CALLBACK CreateViewPlayersDialogProc(HWND hWnd, UINT uMsg, WPARAM wParam,
LPARAM lParam)
{
    switch (uMsg)
    {
    case WM_COMMAND:
        switch(LOWORD(wParam))
        {
        case IDC_STARTGAME:
            // Do nothing yet
            break;

        case IDC_CANCELGAME:
            // Cancel game by destroying the game
            DoDestroyGame(Game[selectedGame].name);
            DestroyWindow(hWnd_CreateViewPlayersDialog);
            break;

        default:
            return 0;
        }
        return 0;
        break;
    }

    // Pass All Unhandled Messages To DefWindowProc
    return DefWindowProc(hWnd, uMsg, wParam, lParam);
}
```

DoDestroyGame Function

This function sends a message to the server to destroy a game. The name of the game is used to destroy the correct game.

```
void DoDestroyGame(char *name)
{
    // No game joined, set the joinedGame index to -1
    joinedGame = -1;

    DestroyWindow(hWnd_CreateGameDialog);

    // Send the message to notify of game destruction
    TUT_MSG_GAME_DATA DestroyGameData;
```

```
DestroyGameData.type    = TUT_MSG_DESTROYGAME;
DestroyGameData.toId    = NETID_SERVER;
DestroyGameData.fromId  = serverSocket.localId;
strcpy(DestroyGameData.name, name);

sendGameMessage((NETMSG_GENERIC *) &DestroyGameData);
}
```

Joining a Game

Joining an existing game is even easier than creating a new one. All we need to do is select the game to join from the list and press the Join Selected Game button. If the game is not already in progress, we can join it.

JoinGame Function

This function is run when the player presses the Join Selected Game button in the lobby. First, it retrieves the game index (selectedGame) and then checks if the game is in progress already. If it is, the function returns because we cannot join games that are in progress. Otherwise, the player can join the game and we run the DoJoinGame function. Then, a dialog to show the joined players is opened.

```
void JoinGame(void)
{
    // Retrieve the selected game index number
    selectedGame = SendMessage(GetDlgItem(hWnd_LobbyDialog,
        IDC_GAMELIST), LB_GETCURSEL, 0, 0);

    // If game in progress, return
    if(Game[selectedGame].inProgress)
        return;

    // Join the selected game
    DoJoinGame(selectedGame);

    // Create the join game dialog
    hWnd_JoinGameDialog = CreateDialog(hInst,
        MAKEINTRESOURCE(IDD_JOINVIEWPLAYERS),
        hWnd_Application, (DLGPROC) JoinGameDialogProc);

    ShowWindow(hWnd_JoinGameDialog, SW_SHOW);
}
```

DoJoinGame Function

This function sends the message to the server to add the player to the selected game. The joinedgame variable is updated to correspond to the game the local player has joined. This function is run on both the host player (the player who creates the game) and the client players (players who join the existing game).

```
void DoJoinGame(int game)
{
    // Set the joined game index to the current game selection
    joinedGame = selectedGame;

    // Send the join game message
    TUT_MSG_PLAYER_DATA JoinGameData;

    JoinGameData.type        = TUT_MSG_JOINGAME;
    JoinGameData.toId        = NETID_SERVER;
    JoinGameData.fromId      = serverSocket.localId;
    JoinGameData.playerIndex = localPlayerLobbyIndex;
    JoinGameData.gameIndex   = game;

    sendGameMessage((NETMSG_GENERIC *) &JoinGameData);
}
```

JoinGameDialogProc Function

This is the Join Game dialog procedure function. The only thing we check here is if the Cancel button has been pressed. If it has, the player is logged out from the game.

```
LRESULT CALLBACK JoinGameDialogProc(HWND hWnd, UINT uMsg, WPARAM wParam, LPARAM
lParam)
{
    switch (uMsg)
    {
    case WM_COMMAND:
        switch(LOWORD(wParam))
        {
        case IDC_JOINCANCEL:
            // Cancel join by logging out of the game
            DoLogoffGame();
            DestroyWindow(hWnd_JoinGameDialog);
            break;

        default:
            return 0;
        }
```

TUTORIAL 4

```
        return 0;
        break;
}

// Pass All Unhandled Messages To DefWindowProc
return DefWindowProc(hWnd, uMsg, wParam, lParam);
}
```

DoLogoff Function

This function logs off the local player from a game:

```
void DoLogoffGame(void)
{
    // No game joined, set the joinedGame index to -1
    joinedGame = -1;

    // Send the log off message
    TUT_MSG_PLAYER_DATA LogoffGameData;

    LogoffGameData.type            = TUT_MSG_LOGOFFGAME;
    LogoffGameData.toId            = NETID_SERVER;
    LogoffGameData.fromId          = serverSocket.localId;
    LogoffGameData.playerIndex     = localPlayerLobbyIndex;
    LogoffGameData.gameIndex       = selectedGame;

    sendGameMessage((NETMSG_GENERIC *) &LogoffGameData);
}
```

Updating the Lobby Lists

The lobby lists must be updated from time to time. There is no point in updating them if they have not changed, so the following functions are run when the server informs the client of changes.

LobbyRefreshJoinedPlayerList Function

This function updates the list of joined players on both the host and client dialogs:

```
void LobbyRefreshJoinedPlayersList(void)
{
    // Reset players in game lists
    SendMessage(GetDlgItem(hWnd_CreateViewPlayersDialog,
        IDC_PLAYERSINGAME), LB_RESETCONTENT, 0, 0);

    SendMessage(GetDlgItem(hWnd_JoinGameDialog,
        IDC_JOINPLAYERSINGAME), LB_RESETCONTENT, 0, 0);
```

```
    // Fill players in game lists
    for(int i = 0; i < Game[selectedGame].players; i++)
    {
        SendMessage(GetDlgItem(hWnd_CreateViewPlayersDialog,
            IDC_PLAYERSINGAME), LB_ADDSTRING, 0, (LPARAM)
            loggedPlayerLobby[Game[selectedGame].player[i]].nickName);

        SendMessage(GetDlgItem(hWnd_JoinGameDialog,
            IDC_JOINPLAYERSINGAME), LB_ADDSTRING, 0, (LPARAM)
            loggedPlayerLobby[Game[selectedGame].player[i]].nickName);
    }
}
```

LobbyRefreshGameList Function

This function updates the game list on the Lobby dialog. If a game is in progress, the string "(in progress)" is added following the game name. Otherwise, just the game name is displayed.

```
void LobbyRefreshGameList(void)
{
    char temp[128];

    // Reset game list
    SendMessage(GetDlgItem(hWnd_LobbyDialog, IDC_GAMELIST),
        LB_RESETCONTENT, 0, 0);

    // Fill game list
    for(int i = 0; i < Games; i++)
    {
        strcpy(temp, Game[i].name);

        // If game in progress, add the text to indicate this
        if(Game[i].inProgress)
        {
            strcat(temp, " (in progress)");
        }

        SendMessage(GetDlgItem(hWnd_LobbyDialog, IDC_GAMELIST),
            LB_ADDSTRING, 0, (LPARAM) temp);
    }
}
```

Creating the Lobby Server Application

The server side of the network application works similarly with the existing games. It also updates the game list when a new game is created or an existing one is destroyed. But what is more important is that it informs the clients of these changes.

PlayerServed_t Structure

The playerServed_t structure stores information about the players who have logged in on the server. The username, player ID number, and host ID number are unique for all the players. The two arrays: playerSync and gameSync, are used to keep the player in synchronization with the other players and the existing games.

```
typedef struct
{
    char userName[32];
    long playerId;            // global index
    HOSTID hostId;

    bool playerSync[NET_MAX_CONNECTIONS];
    bool gameSync[NET_MAX_CONNECTIONS];
} playerServed_t;
```

ArmyServerClass Init Function

The Init function of the ArmyServer class is used to initialize everything. It is run when the program is started. We add the Game structure and the Games integer to the server as well. We allocate the memory for it in the Init function of the ArmyServer class as shown here:

```
int ArmyServerClass::Init(void)
{
    if(NET_Initialize() != 0)
    {
        LogString("Error initialising Communication Library!");
        return 1;
    }

    if(tutServer.CreateServer(9009, NET_UDP) != 0)
    {
        LogString("Failed to Create the Server");
        return 1;
    }
```

```
    LoggedInPlayer = (playerServed_t *)
        calloc(NET_MAX_CONNECTIONS, sizeof(playerServed_t));
    playersLoggedIn = 0;

    Game = (Game_t *) calloc(MAX_GAMES, sizeof(Game_t));
    Games = 0;

    LogString("ONLINE");

    return 0;
}
```

Here we allocate memory for the LoggedInPlayer and Game structures. This is new compared to the function in the login tutorial. The LoggedInPlayer structure stores information about all the players who are logged in, and the Game structure contains information about the existing games:

```
LoggedInPlayer = (playerServed_t *)
    calloc(NET_MAX_CONNECTIONS, sizeof(playerServed_t));
playersLoggedIn = 0;

Game = (Game_t *) calloc(MAX_GAMES, sizeof(Game_t));
Games = 0;
```

ArmyServerClass Shutdown Function

The Shutdown function of the ArmyServer class is used to shut everything down and free allocated memory:

```
void ArmyServerClass::Shutdown(void)
{
    LogString("Shutting Down Server...");

    if(LoggedInPlayer)      free(LoggedInPlayer);
    if(Game)                free(Game);

    tutServer.Shutdown();
    NET_Shutdown();
}
```

The only thing that is new in this function compared to the one in the login tutorial is that we now deallocate the memory that we have allocated:

```
if(LoggedInPlayer)      free(LoggedInPlayer);
if(Game)                free(Game);
```

Handling Login Messages

When a player logs in on the game server, it sends a Tut_Msg_GameLogin message to the server. This message is handled by the server in the handle-LoginMessages function. The following code shows what happens when the game login message is received:

```
case TUT_MSG_GAMELOGIN:
    TUT_MSG_GAMELOGIN_DATA *LoginPtr;
    LoginPtr = (TUT_MSG_GAMELOGIN_DATA *) Msg;

    LogString("Got login message (nick: %s)",
        LoginPtr->nickname);

    // Update server's data of players
    ArmyServer.LoggedInPlayer[ArmyServer.playersLoggedIn].hostId=
        LoginPtr->fromId;

    strcpy(ArmyServer.LoggedInPlayer[ArmyServer.playersLoggedIn].
        userName, LoginPtr->nickname);
    ArmyServer.playersLoggedIn++;

    LogString("++ Players logged in: %d",
        ArmyServer.playersLoggedIn);

    TUT_MSG_GAMELOGIN_FEEDBACK_DATA GameLoginFeedbackData;

    // Send the player feedback of the login
    GameLoginFeedbackData.type = TUT_MSG_GAMELOGIN_FEEDBACK;
    GameLoginFeedbackData.toId = LoginPtr->fromId;
    GameLoginFeedbackData.fromId = tutServer.localId;
    GameLoginFeedbackData.playerIndex =
        ArmyServer.playersLoggedIn - 1;

    LogString("Sending login feedback");

    sendLoginMessage((NETMSG_GENERIC *) &GameLoginFeedbackData);

    handlePlayerSync();
    handleGameSync();

    break;
```

At first, the new player data is stored in the LoggedInPlayer structure. The index number for the new player is the current number of players before we increase it. So, when the very first player logs in, he or she will get the index number 0. Then the number of players is increased and the next player will get index number 1, and so on.

```
// Update server's data of players
ArmyServer.LoggedInPlayer[ArmyServer.playersLoggedIn].hostId=
    LoginPtr->fromId;

strcpy(ArmyServer.LoggedInPlayer[ArmyServer.playersLoggedIn].
    userName, LoginPtr->nickname);
ArmyServer.playersLoggedIn++;
```

After the player list is updated, we send login feedback to the new player. The data part of the feedback message contains the player's index value. This is the index value for the player in the lobby. There is also another index number for each player for each game they join (game index number), but this number is not handled here.

```
TUT_MSG_GAMELOGIN_FEEDBACK_DATA GameLoginFeedbackData;

// Send the player feedback of the login
GameLoginFeedbackData.type = TUT_MSG_GAMELOGIN_FEEDBACK;
GameLoginFeedbackData.toId = LoginPtr->fromId;
GameLoginFeedbackData.fromId = tutServer.localId;
GameLoginFeedbackData.playerIndex = ArmyServer.playersLoggedIn-1;

LogString("Sending login feedback");

sendLoginMessage((NETMSG_GENERIC *) &GameLoginFeedbackData);
```

Finally, the player's synchronization with the other players and existing games are handled. The HandlePlayerSync and HandleGameSync functions are explained later in this tutorial.

```
handlePlayerSync();
handleGameSync();
```

Handling Logout Messages

The logout message is handled on the server in the handleLogoutMessages function as shown in the following code:

```
case TUT_MSG_GAMELOGOUT:
    TUT_MSG_GAMELOGOUT_DATA *LogoutPtr;
    TUT_MSG_GAMELOGIN_REMOVEPLAYER_DATA GameLoginRemovePlayerPtr;

    LogoutPtr = (TUT_MSG_GAMELOGOUT_DATA *) Msg;

    LogString("Got logout message (from host: %d)",
```

```
        LogoutPtr->fromId);

    ArmyServer.LogoutPlayer(LogoutPtr->playerIndex);

    // Send notification to all that a player logged out
    GameLoginRemovePlayerPtr.type =
        TUT_MSG_GAMELOGIN_REMOVEPLAYER;
    GameLoginRemovePlayerPtr.toId = NETID_ALL;
    GameLoginRemovePlayerPtr.fromId = tutServer.localId;
    GameLoginRemovePlayerPtr.playerIndex =
        LogoutPtr->playerIndex;

    sendLoginMessage((NETMSG_GENERIC *)
        &GameLoginRemovePlayerPtr);
    break;
```

First, the player is removed from the server's list of logged in players by using the LogoutPlayer function. Then a notification of this is sent to all the clients.

LogoutPlayer Function

This function removes the player from the server's list of logged in players:

```
void ArmyServerClass::LogoutPlayer(int playerIndex)
{
    int dis = 0;
    int discard = 0;

    LogString("Logging out player %d", playerIndex);

    // Loop through all possible logged players
    for(int i = 0; i < NET_MAX_CONNECTIONS; i++)
    {
        // Set the logging out player's sync flags down,
        // and set the other players' sync flag of the
        // logging out player down
        LoggedInPlayer[playerIndex].playerSync[i] = 0;
        LoggedInPlayer[i].playerSync[playerIndex] = 0;

        // Loop through all possible games
        for(int j = 0; j < MAX_GAMES; j++)
        {
            // Set the logging out player's game sync
            // flags down
            LoggedInPlayer[playerIndex].gameSync[j] = 0;
        }
    }
```

```
// Figure out how many LoggedInPlayer members to move
discard = playersLoggedIn - playerIndex;

playersLoggedIn--;

LogString("-- Players logged in %d", playersLoggedIn);

// Move all the required LoggedInPlayer
// members one position forward
for(dis = 0; dis < discard; dis++)
{
    memcpy(&LoggedInPlayer[playerIndex+dis],
        &LoggedInPlayer[playerIndex+dis+1],
        sizeof(playerServed_t));
}

// Move all the required player sync flags
// one position forward
for(i = 0; i < playersLoggedIn; i++)
{
    for(dis = 0; dis < discard; dis++)
    {
        LoggedInPlayer[i].playerSync[playerIndex+dis] =
            LoggedInPlayer[i].playerSync[playerIndex+dis+1];
    }
}

// Synchronize players again
handlePlayerSync();
handleGameSync();
}
```

First of all, the player's synchronization flags are updated. The player who is logging out will be out of sync with everybody and all the games. Also, the rest of the players will be set out of sync with the player who is logging out.

```
// Loop through all possible logged players
for(int i = 0; i < NET_MAX_CONNECTIONS; i++)
{
    // Set the logging out player's sync flags down,
    // and set the other players' sync flag of the
    // logging out player down
    LoggedInPlayer[playerIndex].playerSync[i] = 0;
    LoggedInPlayer[i].playerSync[playerIndex] = 0;

    // Loop through all possible games
    for(int j = 0; j < MAX_GAMES; j++)
```

```
        {
            // Set the logging out player's game sync flags down
            LoggedInPlayer[playerIndex].gameSync[j] = 0;
        }
    }
```

Then, the player data is removed by moving the other players' data one position backward in the list. The number of players is decreased.

```
// Figure out how many LoggedInPlayer members to move
discard = playersLoggedIn - playerIndex;

playersLoggedIn--;

LogString("-- Players logged in %d", playersLoggedIn);

// Move all the required LoggedInPlayer
// members one position forward
for(dis = 0; dis < discard; dis++)
{
    memcpy(&LoggedInPlayer[playerIndex+dis],
        &LoggedInPlayer[playerIndex+dis+1],
        sizeof(playerServed_t));
}
```

Then the player sync flags are updated once more, because the player indexes changed. Finally, the HandlePlayerSync and HandleGameSync functions are run to update the clients' player and game data:

```
// Move all the required player sync flags
// one position forward
for(i = 0; i < playersLoggedIn; i++)
{
    for(dis = 0; dis < discard; dis++)
    {
        LoggedInPlayer[i].playerSync[playerIndex+dis] =
            LoggedInPlayer[i].playerSync[playerIndex+dis+1];
    }
}

// Synchronize players again
handlePlayerSync();
handleGameSync();
```

HandlePlayerSync Function

This function checks if a player is synchronized with the rest of the players. This means that the function checks if the player knows about the other players. If not, a message is sent to the player to introduce the unknown player.

```
void handlePlayerSync(void)
{
    TUT_MSG_GAMELOGIN_ADDPLAYER_DATA GameLoginAddPlayerData;

    LogString("handlePlayerSync() run (logged in: %d)",
        ArmyServer.playersLoggedIn);

    // Loop through all logged players
    for(int i = 0; i < ArmyServer.playersLoggedIn; i++)
    {
        // Loop through all logged players again
        for(int j = 0; j < ArmyServer.playersLoggedIn; j++)
        {
            // Check if the player is not in sync with
            // the other player
            if( (!ArmyServer.LoggedInPlayer[i].playerSync[j]) )
            {
                // i = player not in sync
                // j = player to check the sync with

                // Send add player message to the player
                // not in sync
                GameLoginAddPlayerData.type =
                    TUT_MSG_GAMELOGIN_ADDPLAYER;
                GameLoginAddPlayerData.toId =
                    ArmyServer.LoggedInPlayer[i].hostId;
                GameLoginAddPlayerData.fromId =
                    tutServer.localId;
                GameLoginAddPlayerData.index = j;
                strcpy(GameLoginAddPlayerData.nickname,
                    ArmyServer.LoggedInPlayer[j].userName);

                LogString("Sending add player (%d)
                    message to %d", j, i);

                sendLoginMessage((NETMSG_GENERIC *)
                    &GameLoginAddPlayerData);

                // Mark the player to be in sync with
                // the other player
                ArmyServer.LoggedInPlayer[i].playerSync[j]=1;
```

```
                }
            }
        }
    }
```

First, we loop through all the players, so that every player also loops through the other players. In this double loop we check the synchronization flag. If it is not set, a message is sent to the player who is not in sync with the one being compared:

```
// Loop through all logged players
for(int i = 0; i < ArmyServer.playersLoggedIn; i++)
{
    // Loop through all logged players again
    for(int j = 0; j < ArmyServer.playersLoggedIn; j++)
    {
        // Check if the player is not in sync with the
        // other player
        if( (!ArmyServer.LoggedInPlayer[i].playerSync[j]) )
        {
            ...
        }
    }
}
```

The message data is filled here so that the data is sent to the player in the first loop and the player who is being added is in the second loop. Then the synchronization flag is set up to notify that the player with index i is synced with player number j (but not necessarily vice versa):

```
// i = player not in sync
// j = player to check the sync with

// Send add player message to the player not in sync
GameLoginAddPlayerData.type = TUT_MSG_GAMELOGIN_ADDPLAYER;
GameLoginAddPlayerData.toId = ArmyServer.LoggedInPlayer[i].hostId;
GameLoginAddPlayerData.fromId = tutServer.localId;
GameLoginAddPlayerData.index = j;
strcpy(GameLoginAddPlayerData.nickname,
    ArmyServer.LoggedInPlayer[j].userName);

LogString("Sending add player (%d) message to %d", j, i);

sendLoginMessage((NETMSG_GENERIC *) &GameLoginAddPlayerData);

// Mark the player to be in sync with the other player
ArmyServer.LoggedInPlayer[i].playerSync[j] = 1;
```

HandleGameSync Function

This function works similarly to handlePlayerSync, but this time we are checking the synchronization with the existing games:

```
void handleGameSync(void)
{
    TUT_MSG_ADDGAME_DATA AddGameData;
    TUT_MSG_PLAYER_DATA AddPlayerPtr;

    LogString("handleGameSync() run (games: %d)", Games);

    // Loop through all logged players
    for(int i = 0; i < ArmyServer.playersLoggedIn; i++)
    {
        // Loop through all games
        for(int game = 0; game < Games; game++)
        {
            // Check if the player is not in sync with the game
            if(!ArmyServer.LoggedInPlayer[i].gameSync[game])
            {
                // i = player not in sync
                // game = game index

                // Send add game message to the player
                AddGameData.type = TUT_MSG_ADDGAME;
                AddGameData.toId =
                    ArmyServer.LoggedInPlayer[i].hostId;
                AddGameData.fromId = tutServer.localId;
                AddGameData.inProgress =
                    Game[game].inProgress;
                strcpy(AddGameData.name, Game[game].name);

                LogString("Sending add game
                    (%d) message to player %d", game, i);

                sendGameMessage((NETMSG_GENERIC *)
                    &AddGameData);

                // Send add player messages to add the
                // players to the game
                for(int p = 0; p < Game[game].players; p++)
                {
                    AddPlayerPtr.type = TUT_MSG_ADDPLAYER;
                    AddPlayerPtr.toId =
                        ArmyServer.LoggedInPlayer[i].hostId;
                    AddPlayerPtr.fromId = tutServer.localId;
```

```
                                AddPlayerPtr.playerIndex =
                                    Game[game].player[p];
                                AddPlayerPtr.gameIndex = game;

                                LogString("Sending (game) add
                                    player (%d) message to player %d",
                                    Game[game].player[p], i);

                                sendGameMessage((NETMSG_GENERIC *)
                                    &AddPlayerPtr);
                        }

                        // Mark the player to be in sync with the game
                        ArmyServer.LoggedInPlayer[i].gameSync[game]=1;
                    }
                }
            }
        }
```

First, we loop through the players and the existing games to check if the player is synchronized with the game:

```
// Loop through all logged players
for(int i = 0; i < ArmyServer.playersLoggedIn; i++)
{
    // Loop through all games
    for(int game = 0; game < Games; game++)
    {
        // Check if the player is not in sync with the game
        if(!ArmyServer.LoggedInPlayer[i].gameSync[game])
        {
            ...
        }
    }
}
```

If the player is not synced with the game, a message is sent to the player to add the game to the games list:

```
// i = player not in sync
// game = game index

// Send add game message to the player
AddGameData.type = TUT_MSG_ADDGAME;
AddGameData.toId = ArmyServer.LoggedInPlayer[i].hostId;
AddGameData.fromId = tutServer.localId;
AddGameData.inProgress = Game[game].inProgress;
strcpy(AddGameData.name, Game[game].name);
```

```
LogString("Sending add game (%d) message to player %d", game, i);

sendGameMessage((NETMSG_GENERIC *) &AddGameData);
```

If the player is not in sync with the game, it means that the player also does not know about the players who have joined the existing games. So this information is sent next. Then the game sync flag is set up:

```
// Send add player messages to add the players to the game
for(int p = 0; p < Game[game].players; p++)
{
    AddPlayerPtr.type = TUT_MSG_ADDPLAYER;
    AddPlayerPtr.toId = ArmyServer.LoggedInPlayer[i].hostId;
    AddPlayerPtr.fromId = tutServer.localId;
    AddPlayerPtr.playerIndex = Game[game].player[p];
    AddPlayerPtr.gameIndex = game;

    LogString("Sending (game) add
        player (%d) message to player %d",
        Game[game].player[p], i);

    sendGameMessage((NETMSG_GENERIC *) &AddPlayerPtr);
}

// Mark the player to be in sync with the game
ArmyServer.LoggedInPlayer[i].gameSync[game] = 1;
```

Creating a Game

When a client creates a game, it sends a Tut_Msg_CreateGame message to the server. This message, as well as the other game related messages, is handled in the handleGameMessages function.

```
case TUT_MSG_CREATEGAME:
    TUT_MSG_GAME_DATA *CreateGamePtr;
    CreateGamePtr = (TUT_MSG_GAME_DATA *) Msg;

    AddGame(CreateGamePtr->name);

    LogString("++ Game %s added", CreateGamePtr->name);

    break;
```

AddGame Function

The AddGame function adds a game on the server game list, and then sends a notification to the clients about this, so they can do the same. All the players who are logged in at the moment are synced with the game, so their game sync flag for the new game is set up:

```
void AddGame(char *name)
{
    // Set the game name and player amount to initial state
    strcpy(Game[Games].name, name);
    Game[Games].players = 0;

    // Set the game sync flag up for each currently logged player
    for(int i = 0; i < ArmyServer.playersLoggedIn; i++)
    {
        ArmyServer.LoggedInPlayer[i].gameSync[Games] = 1;
    }

    Games++;

    // Send the add game message
    TUT_MSG_ADDGAME_DATA AddGamePtr;

    AddGamePtr.type       = TUT_MSG_ADDGAME;
    AddGamePtr.toId       = NETID_ALL;
    AddGamePtr.fromId     = tutServer.localId;
    AddGamePtr.inProgress = Game[Games - 1].inProgress;
    strcpy(AddGamePtr.name, name);

    sendGameMessage((NETMSG_GENERIC *) &AddGamePtr);
}
```

DestroyGame Function

When a client destroys a game, the message is handled as follows:

```
case TUT_MSG_DESTROYGAME:
    TUT_MSG_GAME_DATA *DestroyGamePtr;
    DestroyGamePtr = (TUT_MSG_GAME_DATA *) Msg;

    RemoveGame(DestroyGamePtr->name);

    break;
```

RemoveGame Function

This function removes a game from the server's game list and sends a message to the clients to inform them about this. The clients will remove the game as well.

```
void RemoveGame(char *name)
{
    int i = 0; // Game index
    int dis = 0;
    int discard = 0;

    // Get the game index number by comparing the game names
    for(i = 0; i < Games; i++)
    {
        if(strcmp(Game[i].name, name) == 0)
        {
            break;
        }
    }

    // Set all the players' game sync with this game down
    for(int j = 0; j < ArmyServer.playersLoggedIn; j++)
    {
        ArmyServer.LoggedInPlayer[j].gameSync[i] = 0;
    }

    Game[i].players = 0;

    // Figure out how many games to move
    discard = Games - i;
    Games--;

    // Move the required games one position forward
    for(dis = 0; dis < discard; dis++)
    {
        memcpy(&Game[i+dis], &Game[i+dis+1], sizeof(Game_t));
    }

    // Send remove game message
    TUT_MSG_GAME_DATA RemoveGamePtr;

    RemoveGamePtr.type      = TUT_MSG_REMOVEGAME;
    RemoveGamePtr.toId      = NETID_ALL;
    RemoveGamePtr.fromId    = tutServer.localId;
    strcpy(RemoveGamePtr.name, name);
```

```
        sendGameMessage((NETMSG_GENERIC *) &RemoveGamePtr);
    }
```

Joining a Game

The JoinGame message is handled as follows on the server:

```
case TUT_MSG_JOINGAME:
    TUT_MSG_PLAYER_DATA *JoinGamePtr;
    JoinGamePtr = (TUT_MSG_PLAYER_DATA *) Msg;

    JoinGame(JoinGamePtr->playerIndex, JoinGamePtr->gameIndex);

    break;
```

JoinGame Function

This function adds a player to a game and increases the number of players. A notification is then sent to every client.

```
void JoinGame(int playerIndex, int gameIndex)
{
    // Add the player to the game
    Game[gameIndex].player[Game[gameIndex].players] = playerIndex;
    Game[gameIndex].players++;

    // Send add player message
    TUT_MSG_PLAYER_DATA AddPlayerPtr;

    AddPlayerPtr.type          = TUT_MSG_ADDPLAYER;
    AddPlayerPtr.toId          = NETID_ALL;
    AddPlayerPtr.fromId        = tutServer.localId;
    AddPlayerPtr.playerIndex   = playerIndex;
    AddPlayerPtr.gameIndex     = gameIndex;

    sendGameMessage((NETMSG_GENERIC *) &AddPlayerPtr);
}
```

LogOff Game

Game logoff messages are handled as shown in the following code:

```
case TUT_MSG_LOGOFFGAME:
    TUT_MSG_PLAYER_DATA *LogoffGamePtr;
    LogoffGamePtr = (TUT_MSG_PLAYER_DATA *) Msg;

    LogoffGame(LogoffGamePtr->playerIndex,
```

```
                    LogoffGamePtr->gameIndex);

        break;
```

LogOffGame Function

This function logs off the player from a game. The player is removed from the game's list of players, and a message is sent to the clients to tell them about this.

```
void LogoffGame(int playerIndex, int gameIndex)
{
    int dis = 0;
    int discard = 0;

    // Figure out how many players to move
    discard = Game[gameIndex].players - playerIndex;
    Game[gameIndex].players--;

    // Move the required players one position forward
    for(dis = 0; dis < discard; dis++)
    {
        Game[gameIndex].player[playerIndex+dis] =
        Game[gameIndex].player[playerIndex+dis+1];
    }

    // Send remove player message
    TUT_MSG_PLAYER_DATA RemovePlayerPtr;

    RemovePlayerPtr.type          = TUT_MSG_REMOVEPLAYER;
    RemovePlayerPtr.toId          = NETID_ALL;
    RemovePlayerPtr.fromId        = tutServer.localId;
    RemovePlayerPtr.playerIndex   = playerIndex;
    RemovePlayerPtr.gameIndex     = gameIndex;

    sendGameMessage((NETMSG_GENERIC *) &RemovePlayerPtr);
}
```

Handling Game Messages on the Server

Here is the server-side handleGameMessages function in its entirety:

```
void handleGameMessages(NETMSG_GENERIC *Msg)
{
    switch(Msg->type)
    {
    case TUT_MSG_CREATEGAME:
        // Create game
```

```
            TUT_MSG_GAME_DATA *CreateGamePtr;
            CreateGamePtr = (TUT_MSG_GAME_DATA *) Msg;

            AddGame(CreateGamePtr->name);

            LogString("++ Game %s added", CreateGamePtr->name);

            break;

        case TUT_MSG_DESTROYGAME:
            // Destroy game
            TUT_MSG_GAME_DATA *DestroyGamePtr;
            DestroyGamePtr = (TUT_MSG_GAME_DATA *) Msg;

            RemoveGame(DestroyGamePtr->name);

            break;

        case TUT_MSG_JOINGAME:
            // Join game
            TUT_MSG_PLAYER_DATA *JoinGamePtr;
            JoinGamePtr = (TUT_MSG_PLAYER_DATA *) Msg;

            JoinGame(JoinGamePtr->playerIndex,
                JoinGamePtr->gameIndex);

            break;

        case TUT_MSG_LOGOFFGAME:
            // Logoff game
            TUT_MSG_PLAYER_DATA *LogoffGamePtr;
            LogoffGamePtr = (TUT_MSG_PLAYER_DATA *) Msg;

            LogoffGame(LogoffGamePtr->playerIndex,
                LogoffGamePtr->gameIndex);

            break;
    }
}
```

Handling Game Messages on the Client

The game message handling on the clients is done similarly to the server. When a new game is created, it is created exactly the same way as on the server, etc. This, and the rest of the game messages, are handled in the handleGameMessages function (client version), as shown here:

```
void handleGameMessages(NETMSG_GENERIC *Msg)
{
    int i = 0;
    int dis = 0;
    int discard = 0;

    switch(Msg->type)
    {
    case TUT_MSG_ADDGAME:
        // Add game
        TUT_MSG_ADDGAME_DATA *AddGamePtr;
        AddGamePtr = (TUT_MSG_ADDGAME_DATA *) Msg;

        // Get the game data from the message and
        // increase game amount
        strcpy(Game[Games].name, AddGamePtr->name);
        Game[Games].inProgress = AddGamePtr->inProgress;
        Game[Games].players = 0;
        Games++;

        LogString("++ Game %s added", AddGamePtr->name);

        // Refresh game list
        LobbyRefreshGameList();

        break;

    case TUT_MSG_REMOVEGAME:
        // Remove game
        TUT_MSG_GAME_DATA *RemoveGamePtr;
        RemoveGamePtr = (TUT_MSG_GAME_DATA *) Msg;

        // Get the game index by comparing the game
        // names to the name in the message
        for(i = 0; i < Games; i++)
        {
            if(strcmp(Game[i].name, RemoveGamePtr->name) == 0)
            {
                break;
            }
        }

        // Figure out how many games to move in the structure
        discard = Games - i;

        Games--;
        LogString("-- Game %s removed", RemoveGamePtr->name);
```

```
        // Move all required games one position forward
        for(dis = 0; dis < discard; dis++)
        {
            memcpy(&Game[i+dis], &Game[i+dis+1],
                sizeof(Game_t));
        }

        // If the local selected game is the game
        // that is being removed, close the join game
        // dialog to make sure it is not open
        if(selectedGame == i)
        {
            DestroyWindow(hWnd_JoinGameDialog);
        }

        // Refresh game list
        LobbyRefreshGameList();

        break;

case TUT_MSG_ADDPLAYER:
        // Add player to game
        TUT_MSG_PLAYER_DATA *AddPlayerPtr;
        AddPlayerPtr = (TUT_MSG_PLAYER_DATA *) Msg;

        // Copy player data from the message to the game
        Game[AddPlayerPtr->gameIndex].player[Game[AddPlayerPtr->
            gameIndex].players] =
            AddPlayerPtr->playerIndex;
        Game[AddPlayerPtr->gameIndex].players++;

        LogString("++ Player %d added to game %d",
            AddPlayerPtr->playerIndex,
            AddPlayerPtr->gameIndex);

        // Refresh joined players list
        LobbyRefreshJoinedPlayersList();

        break;

case TUT_MSG_REMOVEPLAYER:
        // Remove player from game
        TUT_MSG_PLAYER_DATA *RemovePlayerPtr;
        RemovePlayerPtr = (TUT_MSG_PLAYER_DATA *) Msg;

        // Figure out how many players to move in the structure
```

```
        discard = Game[RemovePlayerPtr->gameIndex].players -
            RemovePlayerPtr->playerIndex;

    Game[RemovePlayerPtr->gameIndex].players--;

    // Move all required players one position forward
    for(dis = 0; dis < discard; dis++)
    {
        Game[RemovePlayerPtr->gameIndex].player[RemovePlayerPtr->
            playerIndex+dis] =
        Game[RemovePlayerPtr->gameIndex].player[RemovePlayerPtr->
            playerIndex+dis+1];
    }

    LogString("-- Player %d removed from game %d",
        RemovePlayerPtr->playerIndex,
        RemovePlayerPtr->gameIndex);

    // Refresh joined players list
    LobbyRefreshJoinedPlayersList();

    break;
    }
}
```

Handling the Game Host

Notice that the game data is not added to the Game structure on the local host when you create the game. All the clients add the data when they receive a notification from the server to do so — even the host. We could make the Game data be added in locally immediately when the game is created, but then we would need to make our server send the data to only the non-host clients. That requires extra work and makes the code more complex. Plus the advantage of not sending the data to one client is not that big.

The clients' interaction with the server makes the lobby have a life of its own, because all the players' actions in it change it. We can now create games and join them, but we still are not able to start the game. Here we have a screen shot of the working lobby.

Figure 11

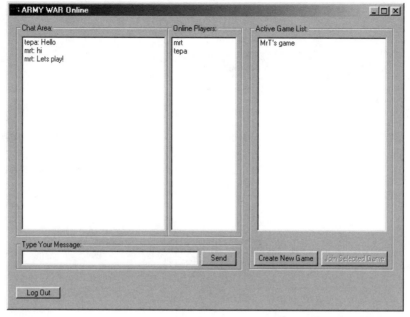

Summary

In this tutorial we learned how to create the lobby for our online game. We learned what type of information should be displayed in the lobby and how to lay out the dialogs for that. We learned how to create a simple chat system that can be used to arrange the games or just chat casually. We also learned how to code the lobby system and how to make the clients interact with the server within the lobby. Now that the lobby works, we can create and join games. That means we can now create the actual game engine and see how to make the players move.

Tutorial 5

Creating Your Online Game

Introduction

This is the last tutorial in our project of creating our very own online game. In this tutorial we learn how to make our game handle the player input and show the result on the local and remote clients. So basically we will learn how we should send the player movement and other command data to the other clients. The server will route all the commands to all the clients, and we can then see the movement of the players and the flag on our screens.

The main idea is to send as little data as possible, and let the clients handle the data individually as much as possible so the server does not take part in the data handling. Its job is just to route the messages to the correct destination. We will learn how to do this in this tutorial.

There is one new source file and its header added to the game project in this final version: engine.cpp/engine.h. This is where all the game engine code is.

Creating a Game

Starting a Game

We learned how to create a game in the lobby tutorial, but we left the Start Game button code out then. Now we add the code to start the game in the Create View Players dialog procedure function. When the Start Game button is pressed, the following code is run:

```
case IDC_STARTGAME:
    StartGame();
    DestroyWindow(hWnd_CreateViewPlayersDialog);
    break;
```

StartGame Function

This function sends a message to the server telling it that the game is starting. The player list dialog is destroyed, and the host client starts to wait for the message to start the game engine. That message is sent to all the players who have joined the game that is starting.

```
void StartGame(void)
{
    // Destroy dialog showing the players joined the game
    DestroyWindow(hWnd_CreateViewPlayersDialog);

    // Send start game message
    TUT_MSG_STARTGAME_DATA StartGameData;

    StartGameData.type        = TUT_MSG_STARTGAME;
    StartGameData.toId        = NETID_SERVER;
    StartGameData.fromId      = serverSocket.localId;
    StartGameData.gameIndex   = selectedGame;

    sendGameMessage((NETMSG_GENERIC *) &StartGameData);
}
```

Receiving the Start Game Message

Each player who has joined the game that is about to start gets a message from the server to start the game. Even the host player will receive this message. The game engine is not started on the host machine before this message has been received. The following code is run when the message arrives. This code is located in the handleGameMessages function.

```
case TUT_MSG_STARTGAME:
    // Start game
    TUT_MSG_STARTGAME_DATA *StartGamePtr;
    StartGamePtr = (TUT_MSG_STARTGAME_DATA *) Msg;

    LogString("Got a start game message");

    // Set the game in progress flag up
    Game[StartGamePtr->gameIndex].inProgress = TRUE;

    // If the local joined game equals with
    // the game that is starting, start the engine
    if(joinedGame == StartGamePtr->gameIndex)
    {
        LogString("!Game starting!");
        SendMessage(hWnd_Application, USMSG_STARTGAME, 0, 0);
    }

    break;
```

When the start game message is received, the game is marked to be in progress. That makes the game unjoinable. This is not always the case in some network games. Some games allow you to join the game even when the game is already running. It is only a design issue; this method does not require much extra work.

```
// Set the game in progress flag up
Game[StartGamePtr->gameIndex].inProgress = TRUE;
```

Then we check if the local player has joined the game that is starting. This check must be done, because all the players get notification of starting games, even if some of these players have not joined the game. A message is sent to the main application window to start the game so the network thread loop can return.

```
// If the local joined game equals with
// the game that is starting, start the engine
if(joinedGame == StartGamePtr->gameIndex)
{
    LogString("!Game starting!");
    SendMessage(hWnd_Application, USMSG_STARTGAME, 0, 0);
}
```

Handling Main Application Window Messages

We must start the game from the main application window so we can let the network thread loop return to process other messages. Similarly, the game is shut down and the connections are closed the same way. We also handle the keyboard input in the same procedure function.

ApplicationProc Function

```c
LRESULT CALLBACK ApplicationProc(HWND hWnd, UINT uMsg, WPARAM wParam, LPARAM lParam)
{
    switch (uMsg)
    {
        case WM_CLOSE:
        {
            PostQuitMessage(0);
            return 0;

        }
        case WM_KEYDOWN:
        {
            keys[wParam] = TRUE;
            return 0;
        }

        case WM_KEYUP:
        {
            keys[wParam] = FALSE;
            return 0;
        }

        case WM_SIZE:
        {
            GFX_Resize(LOWORD(lParam),HIWORD(lParam));
            return 0;
        }

        case USMSG_STARTGAME:
            DoStartGame();
            break;

        case USMSG_SHUTDOWNGAME:
            ENGINE_Shutdown();
            break;

        case USMSG_CLOSECONNECTION:
```

```
                serverSocket.CloseConnection(wParam, lParam);
                break;
        }

        // Pass All Unhandled Messages To DefWindowProc
        return DefWindowProc(hWnd,uMsg,wParam,lParam);
}
```

The keyboard input of the game is handled as shown in the following code. When a key is pressed down, it is marked to be TRUE in the keys array. When the keys are up, they have the value FALSE.

```
case WM_KEYDOWN:
{
    keys[wParam] = TRUE;
    return 0;
}

case WM_KEYUP:
{
    keys[wParam] = FALSE;
    return 0;
}
```

If the game window is resized, the engine handles it in the following code:

```
case WM_SIZE:
{
    GFX_Resize(LOWORD(lParam),HIWORD(lParam));
    return 0;
}
```

The window messages are handled as shown in the following piece of code:

```
case USMSG_STARTGAME:
    DoStartGame();
    break;

case USMSG_SHUTDOWNGAME:
    ENGINE_Shutdown();
    break;

case USMSG_CLOSECONNECTION:
    serverSocket.CloseConnection(wParam, lParam);
    break;
```

Updating the Game Screen

The game screen is updated by the ENGINE_Render function. It is run in the application main loop whenever there is nothing else happening. This is shown in the following code:

```
// Start the Windows Message Loop
while(msg.message != WM_QUIT)
{
    if(PeekMessage(&msg, NULL, 0, 0, PM_REMOVE))
    {
        TranslateMessage(&msg);
        DispatchMessage(&msg);
    }
    else
    {
        ENGINE_Render();
    }
}
```

DoStartGame Function

This function starts the game engine on the local host. Before that, the Join Game dialog is closed (if it is open), the game list is refreshed, and the local player game index number is retrieved from the game's player list. This index (localPlayer-GameIndex) number is the number that is used to identify each player in a game.

```
void DoStartGame(void)
{
    // Destroy join game dialog
    DestroyWindow(hWnd_JoinGameDialog);

    // Refresh the game list to show the 'in progress' flag
    LobbyRefreshGameList();

    // Get the local player game index
    for(int i = 0; i < Game[selectedGame].players; i++)
    {
        if(Game[selectedGame].player[i] ==
            localPlayerLobbyIndex)
        {
            localPlayerGameIndex = i;
            break;
        }
    }

    // Initialize game engine
```

```
        ENGINE_Init();
}
```

Game Engine

The game engine is stored in engine.cpp/engine.h. Naturally, it uses the network library to make the players move on all the clients. The game engine uses our 2D library to make the players and other graphics appear on the screen.

Here is what the game looks like when it is done.

Figure 1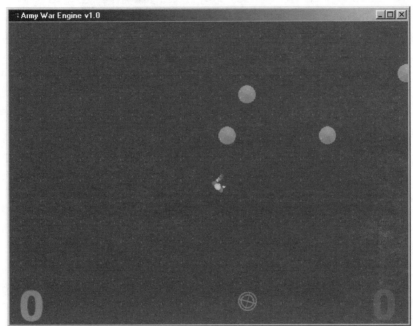

Player Synchronization

It is very important to synchronize the player movement data somehow. Imagine a situation where one player has a high-speed Internet connection, and another player has a very slow connection. When these two players move their players at the same time, the player with the high-speed connection gets the notification of the movement to the server and to the other clients faster. The synchronization is done so that each client keeps track of the local player movement and then sends the exact position of the player from time to time. This means that a player's position shown on the remote hosts' screen may not be really true. When the exact position is sent, the real position is updated on the remote hosts. This must be done again and again, because the player positions start to get out of sync as soon as the players move again.

Local Player Movement Variables

There are some movement variables for each local player that are updated constantly by the engine. They are shown here:

```
int local_x;          // Reference coordinate
int local_y;          // Reference coordinate
```

The reference coordinates are used only for reference when the player's position is sent to the network. These reference coordinates are not used in drawing the player character. The reference coordinate is always up to date and accurate, but because the network always has a small delay, we cannot keep track of accurate coordinates that way. That is why this kind of reference coordinate exists.

```
bool southeast;       // Direction flag
bool southwest;       // Direction flag
bool northeast;       // Direction flag
bool northwest;       // Direction flag
bool south;           // Direction flag
bool north;           // Direction flag
bool east;            // Direction flag
bool west;            // Direction flag
bool stopped;         // Direction flag
```

These direction flags are simply used to mark the current direction of the local player.

> **NOTE**   There are more advanced ways of synchronizing players than the one introduced here. One way is to use specific time periods to tell when something should happen. For example, one second could be divided into five segments. Each client starts to count these segments at the same time. Actual commands are received on segment one, acknowledged on segment two, and issued on segment three. The loop goes on like this all the time, and all the clients issue the commands at the same time.

Data Structures

We store the player and bullet data in the game in separate structures. Let's take a closer look at how this is done.

Player Data

The player data of each game is stored in the following structure. It consists of the player game index number, x and y coordinates, delta-x and delta-y movement values, starting coordinates, direction in degrees, team, and finally fire delay.

```
// Player Data
struct player_t
{
    int playerIndex;
    int x,y;
    int dx,dy;
    int start_x,start_y; // for re-spawning
    int dir;
    int team;
    int fire_delay;
};
```

Bullet Data

The bullet data is stored in the structure shown here. It consists of the coordinates, direction, life time, and team variables.

```
// Bullet Data
struct bullet_t
{
    int x,y;
    int dir;
    int life_remaining;
    int team;
};
```

Creating the Game World

The functions in this section are responsible for creating the game world.

ENGINE_Init Function

The ENGINE_Init function is run once on every client when a game starts. It initializes the engine by setting up the graphics system, generating the map, and delivering it to all the clients. Also, all the players are created and located correctly by this function. The players are divided into two teams: red and blue.

```
void ENGINE_Init(void)
{
    // Init the Graphics Engine
    GFX_Init("Army War Engine v1.0", 640, 480, 16, 0,
        ApplicationProc);

    // Load Required Graphics
    GFX_LoadBitmap(&grass,      "gfx\\grass.bmp");
    GFX_LoadBitmap(&redman,     "gfx\\redman.bmp");
    GFX_LoadBitmap(&blueman,    "gfx\\blueman.bmp");
```

```
GFX_LoadBitmap(&tree,       "gfx\\tree.bmp");
GFX_LoadBitmap(&redtarget,  "gfx\\redtarget.bmp");
GFX_LoadBitmap(&bluetarget, "gfx\\bluetarget.bmp");
GFX_LoadBitmap(&flag,       "gfx\\flag.bmp");

GFX_LoadBitmap(&rednumbers[0], "gfx\\red0.bmp");
GFX_LoadBitmap(&rednumbers[1], "gfx\\red1.bmp");
GFX_LoadBitmap(&rednumbers[2], "gfx\\red2.bmp");
GFX_LoadBitmap(&rednumbers[3], "gfx\\red3.bmp");
GFX_LoadBitmap(&rednumbers[4], "gfx\\red4.bmp");
GFX_LoadBitmap(&rednumbers[5], "gfx\\red5.bmp");
GFX_LoadBitmap(&rednumbers[6], "gfx\\red6.bmp");
GFX_LoadBitmap(&rednumbers[7], "gfx\\red7.bmp");
GFX_LoadBitmap(&rednumbers[8], "gfx\\red8.bmp");
GFX_LoadBitmap(&rednumbers[9], "gfx\\red9.bmp");

GFX_LoadBitmap(&bluenumbers[0], "gfx\\blue0.bmp");
GFX_LoadBitmap(&bluenumbers[1], "gfx\\blue1.bmp");
GFX_LoadBitmap(&bluenumbers[2], "gfx\\blue2.bmp");
GFX_LoadBitmap(&bluenumbers[3], "gfx\\blue3.bmp");
GFX_LoadBitmap(&bluenumbers[4], "gfx\\blue4.bmp");
GFX_LoadBitmap(&bluenumbers[5], "gfx\\blue5.bmp");
GFX_LoadBitmap(&bluenumbers[6], "gfx\\blue6.bmp");
GFX_LoadBitmap(&bluenumbers[7], "gfx\\blue7.bmp");
GFX_LoadBitmap(&bluenumbers[8], "gfx\\blue8.bmp");
GFX_LoadBitmap(&bluenumbers[9], "gfx\\blue9.bmp");

// Create the map...
if(localPlayerGameIndex == 0)
{
    ENGINE_GenerateRandomMap();

    // Send map details to other players...
    TUT_MSG_MAPINFO_DATA MapMsg;

    MapMsg.type       = TUT_MSG_MAPINFO;
    MapMsg.toId       = NETID_ALL;
    MapMsg.fromId     = serverSocket.localId;
    memcpy(MapMsg.map, mapdata, sizeof(mapdata));

    sendGameMessage((NETMSG_GENERIC *) &MapMsg);
}

// Create the players...

// Set currently assigned players to 0
ingame_players = 0;
```

```
// Divide the players between the two teams
int i; // loop variable

    // Add blue players
    place_pos_x = 46;
    half_players = Game[selectedGame].players / 2;
    for(i=0;i<half_players;i++)
    {
        ENGINE_AddPlayer(BLUE_TEAM);
    }

    // Add red players
    place_pos_x = 46;
    half_players = Game[selectedGame].players -
        half_players;
    for(i=0;i<half_players;i++)
    {
        ENGINE_AddPlayer(RED_TEAM);
    }

local_x = players[localPlayerGameIndex].start_x;
local_y = players[localPlayerGameIndex].start_y;

southeast = 0;
southwest = 0;
northeast = 0;
northwest = 0;
south = 0;
north = 0;
east = 0;
west = 0;
stopped = 0;

// Set the scroll positions
scroll_x = 40*32;
if(players[localPlayerGameIndex].team == RED_TEAM)
{
    scroll_y = 90*32;
}
else
{
    scroll_y = 0;
}

// Set the flag position
flag_x = 49*32;
```

```
        flag_y = 49*32;
        player_with_flag_id = -1;

        // Reset Score Counters
        red_score = 0;
        blue_score = 0;

        // Set the engine as ready
        engine_inited = 1;
    }
```

First, we initialize the graphics system. The 2D library sets the window to draw the game into, and the game graphics are loaded into the variables that are declared in the beginning of engine.cpp.

```
// Init the Graphics Engine
GFX_Init("Army War Engine v1.0", 640, 480, 16, 0,
    ApplicationProc);

// Load Required Graphics
GFX_LoadBitmap(&grass,      "gfx\\grass.bmp");
GFX_LoadBitmap(&redman,     "gfx\\redman.bmp");
GFX_LoadBitmap(&blueman,    "gfx\\blueman.bmp");
GFX_LoadBitmap(&tree,       "gfx\\tree.bmp");
GFX_LoadBitmap(&redtarget,  "gfx\\redtarget.bmp");
GFX_LoadBitmap(&bluetarget, "gfx\\bluetarget.bmp");
GFX_LoadBitmap(&flag,       "gfx\\flag.bmp");

GFX_LoadBitmap(&rednumbers[0], "gfx\\red0.bmp");
GFX_LoadBitmap(&rednumbers[1], "gfx\\red1.bmp");
GFX_LoadBitmap(&rednumbers[2], "gfx\\red2.bmp");
GFX_LoadBitmap(&rednumbers[3], "gfx\\red3.bmp");
GFX_LoadBitmap(&rednumbers[4], "gfx\\red4.bmp");
GFX_LoadBitmap(&rednumbers[5], "gfx\\red5.bmp");
GFX_LoadBitmap(&rednumbers[6], "gfx\\red6.bmp");
GFX_LoadBitmap(&rednumbers[7], "gfx\\red7.bmp");
GFX_LoadBitmap(&rednumbers[8], "gfx\\red8.bmp");
GFX_LoadBitmap(&rednumbers[9], "gfx\\red9.bmp");

GFX_LoadBitmap(&bluenumbers[0], "gfx\\blue0.bmp");
GFX_LoadBitmap(&bluenumbers[1], "gfx\\blue1.bmp");
GFX_LoadBitmap(&bluenumbers[2], "gfx\\blue2.bmp");
GFX_LoadBitmap(&bluenumbers[3], "gfx\\blue3.bmp");
GFX_LoadBitmap(&bluenumbers[4], "gfx\\blue4.bmp");
GFX_LoadBitmap(&bluenumbers[5], "gfx\\blue5.bmp");
GFX_LoadBitmap(&bluenumbers[6], "gfx\\blue6.bmp");
GFX_LoadBitmap(&bluenumbers[7], "gfx\\blue7.bmp");
```

```
GFX_LoadBitmap(&bluenumbers[8], "gfx\\blue8.bmp");
GFX_LoadBitmap(&bluenumbers[9], "gfx\\blue9.bmp");
```

The map is generated only on the game host. The map data is then sent to all the rest of the players. Because there is no delay in initializing the game even if all the players are not ready, some players may get the map data after the game engine is already running. The trees will then appear from thin air, but this is not a big deal.

```
// Create the map...
if(localPlayerGameIndex == 0)
{
    ENGINE_GenerateRandomMap();

    // Send map details to other players...
    TUT_MSG_MAPINFO_DATA MapMsg;

    MapMsg.type         = TUT_MSG_MAPINFO;
    MapMsg.toId         = NETID_ALL;
    MapMsg.fromId       = serverSocket.localId;
    memcpy(MapMsg.map, mapdata, sizeof(mapdata));

    sendGameMessage((NETMSG_GENERIC *) &MapMsg);
}
```

The players are added next. The number of players is divided into two and the players are then divided into two teams. The local player's movement information is also set to the initial state here.

```
// Create the players...

// Set currently assigned players to 0
ingame_players = 0;

// Divide the players between the two teams
int i; // loop variable

    // Add blue players
    place_pos_x = 46;
    half_players = Game[selectedGame].players / 2;
    for(i=0;i<half_players;i++)
    {
        ENGINE_AddPlayer(BLUE_TEAM);
    }

    // Add red players
    place_pos_x = 46;
    half_players = Game[selectedGame].players - half_players;
    for(i=0;i<half_players;i++)
```

```
        {
              ENGINE_AddPlayer(RED_TEAM);
        }

local_x = players[localPlayerGameIndex].start_x;
local_y = players[localPlayerGameIndex].start_y;

southeast = 0;
southwest = 0;
northeast = 0;
northwest = 0;
south = 0;
north = 0;
east = 0;
west = 0;
stopped = 0;
```

ENGINE_GenerateRandomMap Function

This function generates the map, as the function name says, randomly. Each time you start a game, the map is generated this way, so you will never see two maps alike.

First, all the map data is reset to zero, so there are no trees yet. Then we use the Rand function to randomize the map for us.

```
void ENGINE_GenerateRandomMap(void)
{
    // Make all land passable
    for(int i=0;i<100;i++)
    {
        for(int j=0;j<100;j++)
        {
            mapdata[i][j] = 0;
        }
    }

    // Place some random trees
    // (avoiding the players start locations)
    for(i=0;i<300;i++)
    {
        mapdata[rand()%100][(rand()%80)+10] = 1;
    }
}
```

ENGINE_AddPlayer Function

This function adds a player to a team. Depending on which team the player is added to, the starting point changes. If there is more than one player on a team, the players will be placed in a row, so they do not overlap each other. The maximum number of players in a game is 16.

```c
void ENGINE_AddPlayer(int team)
{
    if(ingame_players < 16)
    {
        players[ingame_players].dx = 0;
        players[ingame_players].dy = 0;

        players[ingame_players].x = place_pos_x*32;

        if(team == BLUE_TEAM)
        {
            players[ingame_players].y = 4*32;
            players[ingame_players].dir = SOUTH;
        }
        else
        {
            players[ingame_players].y = 96*32;
            players[ingame_players].dir = NORTH;
        }

        players[ingame_players].start_x =
                players[ingame_players].x;
        players[ingame_players].start_y =
                players[ingame_players].y;
        players[ingame_players].team = team;

        ingame_players++;
        place_pos_x++;
    }
}
```

ENGINE_Shutdown Function

The engine is shut down using the following function. All the keys used in this game are set in the "up" position, because the application procedure may not update them correctly while shutting down the graphics system.

```c
void ENGINE_Shutdown(void)
{
    if(engine_inited)
```

```
        {
            // Make sure all the keys are up
            keys[VK_UP]        = FALSE;
            keys[VK_DOWN]      = FALSE;
            keys[VK_RIGHT]     = FALSE;
            keys[VK_LEFT]      = FALSE;
            keys[VK_SPACE]     = FALSE;
            keys[VkKeyScan('q')] = FALSE;

            // Shutdown graphics engine
            GFX_Shutdown();
            engine_inited = 0;
        }
    }
```

Updating the Game World

As we already know, the game world is drawn and updated by the ENGINE_Render function that is run in the game's main loop.

ENGINE_Render Function

All the drawing is done inside the GFX section, beginning with the call to GFX_Begin and ending with the call to GFX_End. The logic of the game is then run, starting by processing the keyboard input and moving on to moving the players and collision checking.

```
void ENGINE_Render(void)
{
    if(engine_inited == 1)
    {
        GFX_Begin();
        {
            ENGINE_DrawMap();
        }
        GFX_End();

        ENGINE_ProcessInput();
        ENGINE_UpdatePlayers();
        ENGINE_UpdateBullets();
        ENGINE_CheckBulletCollisions();
        ENGINE_CheckFlagCollisions();
    }
}
```

ENGINE_DrawMap Function

This function draws the map by drawing the grass tiles, trees, players and their bases, and the flag.

```
void ENGINE_DrawMap(void)
{
    // Work out how many tiles have been scrolled
    tile_scroll_x = scroll_x/32;
    tile_scroll_y = scroll_y/32;

    for(int i=(tile_scroll_x)-2;i<(tile_scroll_x)+21;i++)
    {
        for(int j=(tile_scroll_y)+15;j>(tile_scroll_y)-2;j--)
        {
            GFX_Blit(&grass, (32*i)-(scroll_x),
                (32*j)-(scroll_y), 32, 32, 0);

            // Draw a tree if required
            if(mapdata[i][j] == 1)
            {
                GFX_Blit(&tree, (32*i)-(scroll_x),
                    (32*j)-(scroll_y), 32, 32, 0);
            }

            // Draw the static targets
            if(i==49 && j==3)
            {
                // draw the blue target
                GFX_Blit(&bluetarget, (32*i)-(scroll_x),
                    (32*j)-(scroll_y),
                    32, 32, target_rotation);
            }
            if(i==49 && j==97)
            {
                // draw the red target
                GFX_Blit(&redtarget, (32*i)-(scroll_x),
                    (32*j)-(scroll_y),
                    32, 32, target_rotation);
            }
        }
    }

    // Render the flag
    GFX_Blit(&flag, (flag_x)-(scroll_x),
        (flag_y)-(scroll_y), 32, 32, 0);
```

```
// Render the players
for(i=0;i<ingame_players;i++)
{
    if(players[i].team == RED_TEAM)
    {
        GFX_Blit(&redman, (players[i].x)-(scroll_x),
                (players[i].y)-(scroll_y),
                32, 32, (float) players[i].dir);
    }
    if(players[i].team == BLUE_TEAM)
    {
        GFX_Blit(&blueman, (players[i].x)-(scroll_x),
                (players[i].y)-(scroll_y),
                32, 32, (float) players[i].dir);
    }
}

// Render Bullets
for(i=0;i<MAX_BULLETS;i++)
{
    if(bullets[i].life_remaining > 0)
    {
        if(bullets[i].team == RED_TEAM)
        {
            GFX_RectFill((bullets[i].x-2)-(scroll_x),
                (bullets[i].y-2)-(scroll_y),
                (bullets[i].x+2)-(scroll_x),
                (bullets[i].y+2)-(scroll_y), 200, 0, 0);
        }
        if(bullets[i].team == BLUE_TEAM)
        {
            GFX_RectFill((bullets[i].x-2)-(scroll_x),
                (bullets[i].y-2)-(scroll_y),
                (bullets[i].x+2)-(scroll_x),
                (bullets[i].y+2)-(scroll_y), 0, 0, 200);
        }
    }
}

// Finally, Render the Team Scores
GFX_Blit(&rednumbers[red_score], 5, 410, 64, 64, 0);
GFX_Blit(&bluenumbers[blue_score], 570, 410, 64, 64, 0);

// Rotate the target
if(target_rotation < 360)
    target_rotation += 1;
else
```

```
        target_rotation -= target_rotation;
}
```

ENGINE_ProcessInput Function

This function processes the keyboard input. It is the function that makes the
player characters move on every client, by sending the movement and shooting
notifications to everyone. What is to be noted is that even the local player's movement is not handled before it is received from the server. The reason for this is
player synchronization. The players may seem to move differently on different
machines, so we need to make sure the local player is moving in sync with the
others.

```
void ENGINE_ProcessInput(void)
{
    TUT_MSG_PLAYERDIRECTION_DATA Msg;
    Msg.type            = TUT_MSG_PLAYERDIRECTION;
    Msg.toId            = NETID_ALL;
    Msg.fromId          = serverSocket.localId;
    Msg.playerIndex     = localPlayerGameIndex;

    TUT_MSG_PLAYERADDBULLET_DATA BulMsg;
    BulMsg.type         = TUT_MSG_PLAYERADDBULLET;
    BulMsg.toId         = NETID_ALL;
    BulMsg.fromId       = serverSocket.localId;
    BulMsg.playerIndex  = localPlayerGameIndex;

    if(keys[VkKeyScan('q')])
    {
        LogString("Q pressed");

        // Host
        if(localPlayerGameIndex == 0)
        {
            DoDestroyGame(Game[selectedGame].name);
        }
        else
        {
            DoLogoffGame();
        }

        ENGINE_Shutdown();

        return;
    }

    // Fire Button
```

```
if(keys[VK_SPACE] &&
    players[localPlayerGameIndex].fire_delay == 0)
{

    players[localPlayerGameIndex].fire_delay = 20;

    sendPlayerMessage((NETMSG_GENERIC *) &BulMsg);
}

// SOUTHEAST
if(keys[VK_DOWN] && keys[VK_RIGHT])
{
    if(!southeast)
    {
        Msg.x       = local_x;
        Msg.y       = local_y;
        Msg.north   = 0;
        Msg.south   = 1;
        Msg.east    = 1;
        Msg.west    = 0;

        sendPlayerMessage((NETMSG_GENERIC *) &Msg);

        stopped = 0;
        southeast = 1;
        southwest = 0;
        northeast = 0;
        northwest = 0;
        south = 0;
        north = 0;
        east = 0;
        west = 0;
    }

    local_x += 2;
    local_y += 2;
}
// SOUTHWEST
else if(keys[VK_DOWN] && keys[VK_LEFT])
{
    if(!southwest)
    {
        Msg.x       = local_x;
        Msg.y       = local_y;
        Msg.north   = 0;
        Msg.south   = 1;
        Msg.east    = 0;
        Msg.west    = 1;
```

```
            sendPlayerMessage((NETMSG_GENERIC *) &Msg);

            stopped   = 0;
            southeast = 0;
            southwest = 1;
            northeast = 0;
            northwest = 0;
            south     = 0;
            north     = 0;
            east      = 0;
            west      = 0;
        }

        local_x -= 2;
        local_y += 2;
    }
    // NORTHEAST
    else if(keys[VK_UP] && keys[VK_RIGHT])
    {
        if(!northeast)
        {
            Msg.x       = local_x;
            Msg.y       = local_y;
            Msg.north   = 1;
            Msg.south   = 0;
            Msg.east    = 1;
            Msg.west    = 0;

            sendPlayerMessage((NETMSG_GENERIC *) &Msg);

            stopped   = 0;
            southeast = 0;
            southwest = 0;
            northeast = 1;
            northwest = 0;
            south     = 0;
            north     = 0;
            east      = 0;
            west      = 0;
        }

        local_x += 2;
        local_y -= 2;
    }
    // NORTHWEST
    else if(keys[VK_UP] && keys[VK_LEFT])
```

```
    {
        if(!northwest)
        {
            Msg.x          = local_x;
            Msg.y          = local_y;
            Msg.north      = 1;
            Msg.south      = 0;
            Msg.east       = 0;
            Msg.west       = 1;

            sendPlayerMessage((NETMSG_GENERIC *) &Msg);

            stopped = 0;
            southeast = 0;
            southwest = 0;
            northeast = 0;
            northwest = 1;
            south = 0;
            north = 0;
            east = 0;
            west = 0;
        }

        local_x -= 2;
        local_y -= 2;
    }
    // SOUTH
    else if(keys[VK_DOWN])
    {
        if(!south)
        {
            Msg.x          = local_x;
            Msg.y          = local_y;
            Msg.north      = 0;
            Msg.south      = 1;
            Msg.east       = 0;
            Msg.west       = 0;

            sendPlayerMessage((NETMSG_GENERIC *) &Msg);

            stopped = 0;
            southeast = 0;
            southwest = 0;
            northeast = 0;
            northwest = 0;
            south = 1;
            north = 0;
```

```
                east = 0;
                west = 0;
        }

        local_y += 2;
}
// NORTH
else if(keys[VK_UP])
{
        if(!north)
        {
                Msg.x          = local_x;
                Msg.y          = local_y;
                Msg.north      = 1;
                Msg.south      = 0;
                Msg.east       = 0;
                Msg.west       = 0;

                sendPlayerMessage((NETMSG_GENERIC *) &Msg);

                stopped = 0;
                southeast = 0;
                southwest = 0;
                northeast = 0;
                northwest = 0;
                south = 0;
                north = 1;
                east = 0;
                west = 0;
        }

        local_y -= 2;
}
// EAST
else if(keys[VK_RIGHT])
{
        if(!east)
        {
                Msg.x          = local_x;
                Msg.y          = local_y;
                Msg.north      = 0;
                Msg.south      = 0;
                Msg.east       = 1;
                Msg.west       = 0;

                sendPlayerMessage((NETMSG_GENERIC *) &Msg);
```

```
            stopped = 0;
            southeast = 0;
            southwest = 0;
            northeast = 0;
            northwest = 0;
            south = 0;
            north = 0;
            east = 1;
            west = 0;
        }

        local_x += 2;

        return;
    }
    // WEST
    else if(keys[VK_LEFT])
    {
        if(!west)
        {
            Msg.x        = local_x;
            Msg.y        = local_y;
            Msg.north    = 0;
            Msg.south    = 0;
            Msg.east     = 0;
            Msg.west     = 1;

            sendPlayerMessage((NETMSG_GENERIC *) &Msg);

            stopped = 0;
            southeast = 0;
            southwest = 0;
            northeast = 0;
            northwest = 0;
            south = 0;
            north = 0;
            east = 0;
            west = 1;
        }

        local_x -= 2;
    }
    // STOPPED
    else
    {
        if(!stopped)
        {
```

```
        Msg.x        = local_x;
        Msg.y        = local_y;
        Msg.north    = 0;
        Msg.south    = 0;
        Msg.east     = 0;
        Msg.west     = 0;

        sendPlayerMessage((NETMSG_GENERIC *) &Msg);

        stopped = 1;
        southeast = 0;
        southwest = 0;
        northeast = 0;
        northwest = 0;
        south = 0;
        north = 0;
        east = 0;
        west = 0;
    }
  }
```

When a player presses an arrow key to move the player, the direction of movement is determined. Then the flag of that direction is set up and a movement
message is sent to everyone. Now if the player keeps the key pressed down, only
the local player's reference coordinates are updated. No message is sent before
the direction changes, or the player stops. So each client will receive notification
of only the keyboard's state changes. When a key is pressed, a message is sent.
When no keys are pressed, a message is sent. In between there are no messages
sent anywhere. Because of possible network lag, we cannot rely on just the speed
value, so we send the position of the local player each time too.

ENGINE_UpdatePlayers Function

This function updates the players' coordinates based on the direction data we
receive from each player. This function also checks for collisions with any trees. If
we hit a tree, the reference coordinate of the local player is updated here to stop
the player. The screen scrolls with the player, and that is updated in this function
also.

```
void ENGINE_UpdatePlayers(void)
{
    // Loop through all the players
    for(int i = 0; i < ingame_players; i++)
    {
        if(players[i].dir == SOUTHEAST)
        {
```

```
                    // Check collision with a tree
                    if(mapdata[(players[i].x+32+2)/32]
                        [(players[i].y+2+32)/32])
                    {
                        if(i == localPlayerGameIndex)
                        {
                            local_x = players[i].x;
                            local_y = players[i].y;
                        }
                        continue;
                    }
                }


                if(players[i].dir == SOUTHWEST)
                {
                    // Check collision with a tree
                    if(mapdata[(players[i].x-2)/32]
                        [(players[i].y+2+32)/32])
                    {
                        if(i == localPlayerGameIndex)
                        {
                            local_x = players[i].x;
                            local_y = players[i].y;
                        }
                        continue;
                    }
                }


                if(players[i].dir == NORTHEAST)
                {
                    // Check collision with a tree
                    if(mapdata[(players[i].x+32+2)/32]
                        [(players[i].y-2)/32])
                    {
                        if(i == localPlayerGameIndex)
                        {
                            local_x = players[i].x;
                            local_y = players[i].y;
                        }
                        continue;
                    }
                }


                if(players[i].dir == NORTHWEST)
                {
                    // Check collision with a tree
                    if(mapdata[(players[i].x-2)/32]
```

```
                    [(players[i].y-2)/32])
        {
                if(i == localPlayerGameIndex)
                {
                    local_x = players[i].x;
                    local_y = players[i].y;
                }
                continue;
        }
}

if(players[i].dir == SOUTH)
{
    // Check collision with a tree
    if(mapdata[(players[i].x+16)/32]
            [(players[i].y+2+32)/32])
    {
            if(i == localPlayerGameIndex)
            {
                    local_y = players[i].y;
            }
            continue;
    }
}

if(players[i].dir == NORTH)
{
    // Check collision with a tree
    if(mapdata[(players[i].x+16)/32]
            [(players[i].y-2)/32])
    {
            if(i == localPlayerGameIndex)
            {
                    local_y = players[i].y;
            }
            continue;
    }
}

if(players[i].dir == EAST)
{
    // Check collision with a tree
    if(mapdata[(players[i].x+32+2)/32]
            [(players[i].y+16)/32])
    {
            if(i == localPlayerGameIndex)
            {
```

```
                               local_x = players[i].x;
                        }
                    continue;
                }
            }

        if(players[i].dir == WEST)
        {
            // Check collision with a tree
            if(mapdata[(players[i].x-2)/32]
                [(players[i].y+16)/32])
            {
                if(i == localPlayerGameIndex)
                {
                    local_x = players[i].x;
                }
                continue;
            }
        }

    // Move players
    players[i].x += players[i].dx;
    players[i].y += players[i].dy;
}

// Scroll the map to follow the local player
if((players[localPlayerGameIndex].x-scroll_x) > 340)
{
    if(scroll_x <= 3200-(19*32)-2)
        scroll_x+=2;
}
if((players[localPlayerGameIndex].x-scroll_x) < 300)
{
    if(scroll_x>=2)
        scroll_x-=2;
}
if((players[localPlayerGameIndex].y-scroll_y) > 260)
{
    if(scroll_y <= 3200-(15*32)-2)
        scroll_y+=2;
}
if((players[localPlayerGameIndex].y-scroll_y) < 220)
{
    if(scroll_y>=2)
        scroll_y-=2;
}
```

```
        // Fire Delay
        if(players[localPlayerGameIndex].fire_delay > 0)
            players[localPlayerGameIndex].fire_delay--;
}
```

ENGINE_UpdateBullets Function

The bullets are updated in this function. Each client updates the bullets itself, because they act exactly the same way every time.

```
void ENGINE_UpdateBullets(void)
{
    for(int i=0;i<MAX_BULLETS;i++)
    {
        if(bullets[i].life_remaining > 0)
        {
            switch(bullets[i].dir)
            {
            case NORTH:
                bullets[i].y-=4;
                break;
            case NORTHEAST:
                bullets[i].x+=4;
                bullets[i].y-=4;
                break;
            case EAST:
                bullets[i].x+=4;
                break;
            case SOUTHEAST:
                bullets[i].x+=4;
                bullets[i].y+=4;
                break;
            case SOUTH:
                bullets[i].y+=4;
                break;
            case SOUTHWEST:
                bullets[i].x-=4;
                bullets[i].y+=4;
                break;
            case WEST:
                bullets[i].x-=4;
                break;
            case NORTHWEST:
                bullets[i].x-=4;
                bullets[i].y-=4;
                break;
            }
```

```
                bullets[i].life_remaining--;
            }
        }
    }
```

ENGINE_CheckBulletCollisions Function

The bullet collision detecting is done in this function. This function is also run individually by every client. If a bullet hits an opposing team member, the player gets killed and is transferred back to the starting point.

```
void ENGINE_CheckBulletCollisions(void)
{
    for(int i=0;i<MAX_BULLETS;i++)
    {
        if(bullets[i].life_remaining > 0)
        {
            // Check if the bullet is in
            // contact with an opposing team member.
            for(int j=0;j<ingame_players;j++)
            {
                if(players[j].team != bullets[i].team &&
                    bullets[i].x > players[j].x &&
                    bullets[i].x < players[j].x+32
                    && bullets[i].y > players[j].y &&
                    bullets[i].y < players[j].y+32)
                {
                    // Kill + Respawn the player
                    players[j].x = players[j].start_x;
                    players[j].y = players[j].start_y;

                    if(localPlayerGameIndex == j)
                    {
                        local_x = players[j].x;
                        local_y = players[j].y;

                        scroll_x = local_x - 320;
                        scroll_y = local_y - 240;
                    }

                    // Check if the player was
                    // holding the flag
                    if(j == player_with_flag_id)
                    {
                        // Respawn the flag
                        player_with_flag_id = -1;
                        flag_x = 49*32;
```

```
                            flag_y = 49*32;
                    }

                    break;
                }
            }
        }
    }
}
```

ENGINE_CheckFlagCollisions Function

This function actually does more than its name tells us. It does check the flag collisions, by first checking if a player picked it up and then checking if the flag is taken to the team's base. After that it checks the team scores, and if a team has 10 points, the game ends. So this function also checks if the victory requirements have been reached.

```
void ENGINE_CheckFlagCollisions(void)
{
    if(player_with_flag_id != -1)
    {
        // Move the flag with the player
        flag_x = players[player_with_flag_id].x;
        flag_y = players[player_with_flag_id].y;

        // Check if the player is at home base
        if(players[player_with_flag_id].team == BLUE_TEAM)
        {
            if(players[player_with_flag_id].x+16 > (49*32) &&
                players[player_with_flag_id].x+16 < (50*32) &&
                players[player_with_flag_id].y+16 > (3*32) &&
                players[player_with_flag_id].y+16 < (4*32))
            {
                flag_x = 49*32;
                flag_y = 49*32;
                player_with_flag_id = -1;
                blue_score++;
            }
        }
        if(players[player_with_flag_id].team == RED_TEAM)
        {
            if(players[player_with_flag_id].x+16 > (49*32) &&
                players[player_with_flag_id].x+16 < (50*32) &&
                players[player_with_flag_id].y+16 > (97*32) &&
                players[player_with_flag_id].y+16 < (98*32))
            {
```

```
                    flag_x = 49*32;
                    flag_y = 49*32;
                    player_with_flag_id = -1;
                    red_score++;
                }
            }
        }
        else
        {
            // Check if anyone is in contact with the flag
            for(int j=0;j<ingame_players;j++)
            {
                if(players[j].x+16>flag_x &&
                    players[j].x+16<flag_x+32 &&
                    players[j].y+16>flag_y &&
                    players[j].y+16<flag_y+32)
                {
                    player_with_flag_id = j;

                    break;
                }
            }
        }

        // Check team scores
        if(red_score > 1)
        {
            if(localPlayerGameIndex == 0)
            {
                DoDestroyGame(Game[selectedGame].name);
            }

            final_winning_team = RED_TEAM;
            ENGINE_Shutdown();

            if(players[localPlayerGameIndex].team == RED_TEAM)
            {
                MessageBox(NULL, "Your team (RED) won!",
                    "Victory", MB_OK);
            }
            else
            {
                MessageBox(NULL, "The other team (RED) won",
                    "Failure", MB_OK);
            }
        }
        if(blue_score > 1)
```

```
        {
            if(localPlayerGameIndex == 0)
            {
                DoDestroyGame(Game[selectedGame].name);
            }

            final_winning_team = BLUE_TEAM;
            ENGINE_Shutdown();

            if(players[localPlayerGameIndex].team == BLUE_TEAM)
            {
                MessageBox(NULL, "Your team (BLUE) won!",
                    "Victory", MB_OK);
            }
            else
            {
                MessageBox(NULL, "The other team (BLUE) won",
                    "Failure", MB_OK);
            }
        }
    }
}
```

Handling Player Messages

The player messages are handled in the handlePlayerMessages function as shown
here:

```
void handlePlayerMessages(NETMSG_GENERIC *Msg)
{
    switch(Msg->type)
    {
    case TUT_MSG_PLAYERDIRECTION:
        // Player direction
        TUT_MSG_PLAYERDIRECTION_DATA *DirectionPtr;
        DirectionPtr = (TUT_MSG_PLAYERDIRECTION_DATA *) Msg;

        // Copy the player coordinates
        players[DirectionPtr->playerIndex].x = DirectionPtr->x;
        players[DirectionPtr->playerIndex].y = DirectionPtr->y;

        // Stopped
        if( (!DirectionPtr->south) && (!DirectionPtr->north) &&
            (!DirectionPtr->west) && (!DirectionPtr->east))
        {
            players[DirectionPtr->playerIndex].dx = 0;
            players[DirectionPtr->playerIndex].dy = 0;
        }
```

```
// Southeast
if( (DirectionPtr->south) && (DirectionPtr->east) )
{
    players[DirectionPtr->playerIndex].dir = SOUTHEAST;
    players[DirectionPtr->playerIndex].dx = 2;
    players[DirectionPtr->playerIndex].dy = 2;
    break;
}
// Southwest
if( (DirectionPtr->south) && (DirectionPtr->west) )
{
    players[DirectionPtr->playerIndex].dir = SOUTHWEST;
    players[DirectionPtr->playerIndex].dx = -2;
    players[DirectionPtr->playerIndex].dy = 2;
    break;
}
// Northeast
if( (DirectionPtr->north) && (DirectionPtr->east) )
{
    players[DirectionPtr->playerIndex].dir = NORTHEAST;
    players[DirectionPtr->playerIndex].dx = 2;
    players[DirectionPtr->playerIndex].dy = -2;
    break;
}
// Northwest
if( (DirectionPtr->north) && (DirectionPtr->west) )
{
    players[DirectionPtr->playerIndex].dir = NORTHWEST;
    players[DirectionPtr->playerIndex].dx = -2;
    players[DirectionPtr->playerIndex].dy = -2;
    break;
}
// South
if(DirectionPtr->south)
{
    players[DirectionPtr->playerIndex].dir = SOUTH;
    players[DirectionPtr->playerIndex].dx = 0;
    players[DirectionPtr->playerIndex].dy = 2;
    break;
}
// North
if(DirectionPtr->north)
{
    players[DirectionPtr->playerIndex].dir = NORTH;
    players[DirectionPtr->playerIndex].dx = 0;
    players[DirectionPtr->playerIndex].dy = -2;
```

```
            break;
        }
        // West
        if(DirectionPtr->west)
        {
            players[DirectionPtr->playerIndex].dir = WEST;
            players[DirectionPtr->playerIndex].dx = -2;
            players[DirectionPtr->playerIndex].dy = 0;
            break;
        }
        // East
        if(DirectionPtr->east)
        {
            players[DirectionPtr->playerIndex].dir = EAST;
            players[DirectionPtr->playerIndex].dx = 2;
            players[DirectionPtr->playerIndex].dy = 0;
            break;
        }

        break;

    case TUT_MSG_PLAYERADDBULLET:
        // Add bullet
        TUT_MSG_PLAYERADDBULLET_DATA *AddBulletPtr;
        AddBulletPtr = (TUT_MSG_PLAYERADDBULLET_DATA *) Msg;

        // Add a bullet in the game world
        ENGINE_AddBullet(players[AddBulletPtr->playerIndex].x +
            16, players[AddBulletPtr->playerIndex].y + 16,
            players[AddBulletPtr->playerIndex].dir,
            players[AddBulletPtr->playerIndex].team);

        break;
    }
}
```

ENGINE_AddBullet Function

This function adds a bullet in the game world. This function is used locally on each client.

```
void ENGINE_AddBullet(int x,int y,int dir,int team)
{
    // find an empty slot in the array
    int empty_id = -1;
    for(int i=0;i<MAX_BULLETS;i++)
    {
```

```
            if(bullets[i].life_remaining <= 0)
            {
                empty_id = i;
                break;
            }
        }

        // If a slot has been found
        if(empty_id != -1)
        {
            // Add the bullet...
            bullets[empty_id].x              = x;
            bullets[empty_id].y              = y;
            bullets[empty_id].dir            = dir;
            bullets[empty_id].life_remaining = 30;
            bullets[empty_id].team           = team;
        }
    }
```

Game Server

The only change on the server side, compared to the server in the lobby tutorial, is that it now handles the game start message. This message is handled in the handleGameMessages function. The game's in progress flag is set up, and the notification is sent to all the clients.

```
case TUT_MSG_STARTGAME:
    TUT_MSG_STARTGAME_DATA *StartGamePtr;
    StartGamePtr = (TUT_MSG_STARTGAME_DATA *) Msg;

    Game[StartGamePtr->gameIndex].inProgress = TRUE;

    TUT_MSG_STARTGAME_DATA StartGame;

    StartGame.type          = TUT_MSG_STARTGAME;
    StartGame.toId          = NETID_ALL;
    StartGame.fromId        = tutServer.localId;
    StartGame.gameIndex     = StartGamePtr->gameIndex;

    sendGameMessage((NETMSG_GENERIC *) &StartGame);

    break;
```

Running the Server on Unix

Obviously, we need to separate Unix and Windows application entry functions. On Windows, that is the WinMain function; on Unix it is the Main function.

Main Function

This function is the entry point for the Unix version of the server. At first it initializes the server as daemon. Then we make the server ignore the SIGPIPE signal so the program does not terminate if the pipe gets broken. This does not affect the application functionality. A more detailed explanation of this is beyond the scope of this book.

```c
int main(void)
{
    printf("Welcome to Army War Server v1.0\n");
    printf("-----------------------------\n");
    printf("Running daemon...\n\n");

    // Initialize daemon
    daemon_init();

    // Ignore the SIGPIPE signal, so the program does not
    // terminate if the pipe gets broken
    signal(SIGPIPE, SIG_IGN);

    // Initialize server
    if(ArmyServer.Init() != 0)
    {
        exit(0);
    }

    // Keep server alive as long as we are online
    while(tutServer.Online)
    {
    }
}
```

Daemon_init Function

To run the server as daemon (on the background) on Unix, we need to initialize the daemon system using the following function. First we use the Unix Fork function to create a new process. Once that is done, we exit the main process. We are now in the new process. Then we use the Unix Setsid function to become process group and session leader. Finally, we close the in, out, and error descriptors we got from the main process. The process now runs as a daemon.

```
static int daemon_init(void)
{
    pid_t pid;

    // Fork a new process
    if((pid = fork()) < 0)
    {
        return -1;
    }
    // If the process ID is positive non-zero,
    // exit the main process
    else if(pid != 0)
    {
        exit(0);
    }

    // Become process group and session leader
    setsid();

    // Close file descriptors (in, out, error)
    close(1);
    close(2);
    close(3);

    return 0;
}
```

Summary

In this last tutorial we learned how to create the game using our 2D library and how to make the networking part work. We learned how the player commands should be sent to ensure the best possible performance in the network. We now know that the best method is to let the clients do all the movement updating and object creation, and let the server route the commands only to those who need to know about them.

This concludes our online game project. We have now created a fully playable online game! The methods used in this game project are usable in larger projects as well, but feel free to think of new ones. Any method that gives the server more free processing time is a good method. So keep on designing and good luck!

Appendix A

Byte Ordering Functions

htons Function (Unix, Win32)

```
uint16_t htons(uint16_t host16bitvalue);
```

Host to network short. Converts host byte order to network byte order and returns it in short format.

htonl Function (Unix, Win32)

```
uint32_t htonl(uint32_t host32bitvalue);
```

Host to network long. Converts host byte order to network byte order and returns it in long format.

ntohs Function (Unix, Win32)

```
uint16_t htons(uint16_t net16bitvalue);
```

Network to host short. Converts network byte order to host byte order and returns it in short format.

ntohl Function (Unix, Win32)

```
uint32_t htonl(uint32_t net32bitvalue);
```

Network to host long. Converts network byte order to host byte order and returns it in long format.

Appendix B

NetLib.h

The NetLib.h header file is used to see the functionality of the NetLib library. It makes it easy to see what functions are available in the network library so it is a useful reference to have.

```
#ifndef __NETLIB_H
#define __NETLIB_H

#ifdef WIN32
    #pragma comment (lib,"ws2_32.lib")
    #pragma message ("Auto linking WinSock2 library")

    #include <winsock2.h>
#else
    #include <netinet/in.h>
#endif

#include <stdio.h>
#include <stddef.h>

// Define SOCKET data type for UNIX (defined in WinSock for Win32)
// And socklen_t for Win32
#ifdef WIN32
    typedef int socklen_t;
#else
    typedef int SOCKET;
```

```
    #ifndef TRUE
    #define TRUE 1
    #endif
    #ifndef FALSE
    #define FALSE 0
    #endif
#endif

// Define id types
typedef int HOSTID;

// User messages
#ifdef WIN32
    #define USMSG_ACCEPT          WM_USER + 1
#endif

#define NET_BUFFSIZE              10240
#define NET_MESSAGE_BUFFER        128
#define NET_IOTIMEOUT             100      // ms

// return values
#define NET_ERROR                 -1
#define NET_OK                    0

// host ids
#define NETID_UNKNOWN             -2
#define NETID_ALL                 -1
#define NETID_SERVER              0

// netLib system message types. All system messages must be negative.
#define NETMSG_DATASIZE           -1
#define NETMSG_GIVEID             -2
#define NETMSG_KNOCK              -3
#define NETMSG_CLOSE_CONNECTION   -4

// netLib system message structures
typedef struct
{
    int type;          // Message type
    HOSTID toId;       // Destination host id
    HOSTID fromId;     // Source host id
} NETMSG_GENERIC;

// confirmation
typedef struct
{
    int conf;
```

```
} NETMSG_CONF;

// used to send incoming data buffer's size
typedef struct
{
    int type;
    HOSTID toId;
    HOSTID fromId;
    int size;
} NETMSGDATA_DATASIZE;

// Definitions
#define NET_MAX_CONNECTIONS         20
#define NET_DEFAULT_PORT            9009

// Connection protocols
#define NET_TCP                     0
#define NET_UDP                     1

// Error codes
#ifdef WIN32
    #define NET_INVALID_SOCKET      INVALID_SOCKET
#else
    #define NET_INVALID_SOCKET      -1
#endif

#define NET_INVALID_PROTOCOL        -2

// Message buffer class
class MessageBuffer_t
{
public:
    int id;                         // destination host id
    char buf[NET_BUFFSIZE];         // the message data itself
    size_t count;                   // length of the data
    SOCKET socket;                  // socket
    struct sockaddr_in sockAddr;    // socket address
    socklen_t sockLen;              // socket address length
    bool processing;                // buffer being processed flag
};

// Remote host class
class RemoteHost_t
{
public:
    SOCKET socket;                  // socket
    sockaddr_in inetSockAddr;       // socket address
```

```
#ifdef WIN32
    int addrLen;                        // socket address length
#else
    socklen_t addrLen;                  // socket address length
#endif

    bool online;                        // host online flag
    bool thread;                        // thread running flag
    bool NonBlocking;                   // non-blocking flag

    int messageCounter;                 // message buffer counter
    int bufsize;                        // the length of the next message

    int lastMessageTime;                // seconds from last message

    int InMessages;                     // Input buffer messages
    MessageBuffer_t *InMessageBuffer;

#ifdef WIN32
    HANDLE SocketInputEvent;
#endif

    void RecordMessage(void);
};

class NET_Socket
{
private:
    int GiveLocalIdTCP(void);
    void FindNextFreeHostIndex(void);

    // Server creation helper functions
    int CreateUnixTCPServer(SOCKET listenSock);
    int CreateWinTCPServer(SOCKET listenSock);
    int CreateUnixUDPServer(SOCKET sock);
    int CreateWinUDPServer(SOCKET sock);
    int CreateTCPServer(SOCKET sock);
    int CreateUDPServer(SOCKET sock);
    int CreateUnixServer(int port, int Protocol);
    int CreateWinServer(int port, int Protocol);

#ifdef WIN32
    int WinHandleEvents(int id, LPWSANETWORKEVENTS NetworkEvents);
#endif

    HOSTID NextFreeHostIndex;
```

```
public:
    NET_Socket();
    ~NET_Socket();

    // Uninitialization functions
    void CloseConnection(int id, int active);
    void Shutdown(void);

    // Miscellanous functions
    int SetNonBlocking(int id, u_long setBlocking);
    int GiveLocalIdUDP(sockaddr_in clientAddr);
    void AcceptConnection(void);
    int CreateServer(int port, int Protocol);
    int ConnectToServer(char *ipAddressString, int port, int Protocol);

    // Data reading / writing functions
    int ReadToBuffer(HOSTID id, size_t count, bool NonBlocking);

    int Read(int id, char *buf, size_t count);
    int Write(int id, char *buf, size_t count);
    void WriteAll(char *buf, size_t count);

    int ReadFrom(SOCKET sock, char *buf, size_t count,
            struct sockaddr *sockAddr, socklen_t *sockLen, bool NonBlocking);

    int WriteTo(SOCKET sock, char *buf, size_t count,
            struct sockaddr *sockAddr, socklen_t sockLen);

    HOSTID GetNextFreeHostIndex(void) { return NextFreeHostIndex; }

    // Message processing functions
    void ProcessMessageBuffer(int id);
    void ProcessMessages(int id);

    int HandleSocketInputEvent(int id);
    int HandleSocketOutputEvent(int id);
#ifdef WIN32
    HANDLE SocketOutputEvent;
#endif

    // Miscellanous variables
    SOCKET listenSocket;                    // Listening socket

    int localId;                            // Local host id
    bool Online;                            // Local online flag
```

```
        int RemoteHosts;                        // Amount of remote hosts
        RemoteHost_t *RemoteHost;

        int Port; // Port in use
};

// Thread parameter structure
typedef struct
{
        int id;                                 // host id
        NET_Socket *netParamSocket;             // NET_Socket pointer
} threadParam_t;


// Platform dependent function prototypes
#ifdef WIN32
        void NET_WinIOThreadFunc(void *ParamPtr);
        void NET_WinUDPServerIOThreadFunc(void *ParamPtr);
#else
        void *NET_UnixIOThreadFunc(void *ParamPtr);
        void *NET_UnixUDPServerIOThreadFunc(void *ParamPtr);
#endif

// Common function prototypes
void StartLog(void);
void LogString(char *string, ...);
int NET_Initialize(void);
int NET_InitializeWinSock(void);
void NET_Shutdown(void);


// External functions and variables
#ifdef WIN32
        extern HWND hWnd_netLib;
#endif

extern void NET_HandleMessages(NETMSG_GENERIC *Msg);

#endif
```

Index

* indicates reference contains code listing.

Looking for more?

Check out Wordware's market-leading Game Developer's Library featuring the following new releases and upcoming titles.

Hot off the Press:

Modeling a
Character in
3DS Max

1-55622-815-5
$44.95
7½ x 9¼
544 pp.

Game Design
Theory &
Practice

1-55622-735-3
$49.95
7½ x 9¼
608 pp.

Advanced 3-D
Game
Programming
with DirectX 8.0

1-55622-513-X
$59.95
7½ x 9¼
592 pp.

Coming Soon:

3-D Game Math Primer
1-55622-911-9 • $49.95

Java2 Game Development
1-55622-905-4 • $59.95

1-55622-854-6 • $39.95
7½ x 9¼ • 400 pp.

1-55622-850-3 • $59.95
7½ x 9¼ • 500 pp.

Backlist Bestsellers:

Linux 3D
Graphics
Programming

1-55622-723-X
$59.95
7½ x 9¼
624 pp.

Advanced Linux
3D Graphics
Programming

1-55622-853-8
$59.95
7½ x 9¼
640 pp.

Designing
Arcade
Computer Game
Graphics

1-55622-755-8
$49.95
7½ x 9¼
544 pp.

For more information, visit us online at www.wordware.com.

Gamedev.net

The most comprehensive game development resource

○ The latest news in game development
○ The most active forums and chatrooms anywhere, with insights and tips from experienced game developers
○ Links to thousands of additional game development resources
○ Thorough book and product reviews
○ Over 1000 game development articles!
    Game design
    Graphics
    DirectX
    OpenGL
    AI
    Art
    Music
    Physics
    Source Code
    Sound
    Assembly
    And More!

Gamedev.net

OpenGL is a registered trademark of Silicon Graphics, Inc.
Microsoft, DirectX are registered trademarks of Microsoft Corp. in the United States and/or other countries.

About the CD

The companion CD-ROM contains all the source code from the book as well as many useful tools and applications discussed in the book.

The CD will autorun when you insert it in your CD drive. Click the Continue button on the page that appears to view the contents. (If the CD does not autorun, simply use Windows Explorer to browse the CD.)

The directories and their contents are:

- Software—mySQL for Linux and Windows, DBI modules for Perl, and WinZip 8.0 SHAREWARE EVALUATION version (not the registered version)
- Source Code—source code from the book
- Libraries—openGL 1.2 SDK, 2DLIB, and mySQL++

Also included is a partial version of NVIDIA SDK version 5.0. For more information, see NVSDK.htm in the nvidia SDK directory. Note that this directory must be accessed using Windows Explorer.

Warning: Opening the CD package makes this book nonreturnable.

CD/Source Code Usage License Agreement

Please read the following CD/Source Code usage license agreement before opening the CD and using the contents therein:

1. By opening the accompanying software package, you are indicating that you have read and agree to be bound by all terms and conditions of this CD/Source Code usage license agreement.

2. The compilation of code and utilities contained on the CD and in the book are copyrighted and protected by both U.S. copyright law and international copyright treaties, and is owned by Wordware Publishing, Inc. Individual source code, example programs, help files, freeware, shareware, utilities, and evaluation packages, including their copyrights, are owned by the respective authors.

3. No part of the enclosed CD or this book, including all source code, help files, shareware, freeware, utilities, example programs, or evaluation programs, may be made available on a public forum (such as a World Wide Web page, FTP site, bulletin board, or Internet news group) without the express written permission of Wordware Publishing, Inc. or the author of the respective source code, help files, shareware, freeware, utilities, example programs, or evaluation programs.

4. You may not decompile, reverse engineer, disassemble, create a derivative work, or otherwise use the enclosed programs, help files, freeware, shareware, utilities, or evaluation programs except as stated in this agreement.

5. The software, contained on the CD and/or as source code in this book, is sold without warranty of any kind. Wordware Publishing, Inc. and the authors specifically disclaim all other warranties, express or implied, including but not limited to implied warranties of merchantability and fitness for a particular purpose with respect to defects in the disk, the program, source code, sample files, help files, freeware, shareware, utilities, and evaluation programs contained therein, and/or the techniques described in the book and implemented in the example programs. In no event shall Wordware Publishing, Inc., its dealers, its distributors, or the authors be liable or held responsible for any loss of profit or any other alleged or actual private or commercial damage, including but not limited to special, incidental, consequential, or other damages.

6. One (1) copy of the CD or any source code therein may be created for backup purposes. The CD and all accompanying source code, sample files, help files, freeware, shareware, utilities, and evaluation programs may be copied to your hard drive. With the exception of freeware and shareware programs, at no time can any part of the contents of this CD reside on more than one computer at one time. The contents of the CD can be copied to another computer, as long as the contents of the CD contained on the original computer are deleted.

7. You may not include any part of the CD contents, including all source code, example programs, shareware, freeware, help files, utilities, or evaluation programs in any compilation of source code, utilities, help files, example programs, freeware, shareware, or evaluation programs on any media, including but not limited to CD, disk, or Internet distribution, without the express written permission of Wordware Publishing, Inc. or the owner of the individual source code, utilities, help files, example programs, freeware, shareware, or evaluation programs.

8. You may use the source code, techniques, and example programs in your own commercial or private applications unless otherwise noted by additional usage agreements as found on the CD.

Warning: Opening the CD package makes this book nonreturnable.